NEW DIRECTIONS IN ECONOMETRIC PRACTICE

To Krystyna, Sonia, Anna and Michał

New Directions in Econometric Practice

General to Specific Modelling, Cointegration and Vector Autoregression

SECOND EDITION

Wojciech W. Charemza and Derek F. Deadman

Edward Elgar
Cheltenham, UK • Northampton, MA, USA

Published by
Edward Elgar Publishing Limited
Glensanda House
Montpellier Parade
Cheltenham
Glos GL50 1UA
UK

Edward Elgar Publishing, Inc.
William Pratt House
9 Dewey Court
Northampton
Massachusetts 01060
USA

First published 1992 (1 85278 461 X)
Reprinted 1993 (twice)
Paperback edition 1993 (1 85278 846 1)
Second cased edition 1997
Second paperback edition 1997
Reprinted 2003

This book has been printed on demand to keep the title in print.

A catalogue record for this book is available from the British Library

Library of Congress Cataloguing in Publication Data
Charemza, Wojciech
    New direction in econometric practice: general to specific
modelling, cointegration and vector autoregression / Wojciech W.
Charemza and Derek F. Deadman. – 2nd ed.
    Includes bibliographical references and index.
    1.Econometric models. 2. Autoregression (Statistics) 3. Vector
analysis. 4. Cointegration. I. Deadman, Derek. II. Title.
HB139.C435 1997
330'.01'5195–dc21   96–52264
                                                                 CIP

ISBN 978 1 85898 600 5 (2nd cased edition)
      978 1 85898 603 6 (2nd paperback edition)

Contents

Foreword by Richard E. Quandt

The present volume represents an innovative approach to teaching econometrics. Most of the existing texts share two basic characteristics: (a) they concentrate on expositing econometric theory and techniques and (b) they cover 'standard' econometric techniques, such as (generalized) regression models, simultaneous equations models, limited dependent variable models, etc. The authors of the present text take a different approach, which practical researchers will find most welcome and which will answer the oft-heard question by students, 'Yes, yes, it's nice to know all these techniques, but if I do some research, how do I know what to do next?'

The volume exposits in detail the process by which empirical research is done. After a brief critique of the Cowles Foundation approach, it starts out with a most welcome chapter on data mining, a subject that is woefully neglected not only in the teaching of econometrics, but, one suspects, often in the practice of it. It then turns to the methodology introduced in the important 1978 paper of Davidson, Hendry, Srba and Yeo. It is a particularly interesting unifying theme of the book that the various techniques that are discussed chapter-by-chapter are nearly always illustrated with reference to the consumption model in that pioneering paper. The volume is thus one in which important techniques and methods are introduced and in which these methods are invariably applied to a concrete case that accompanies the reader from beginning to end.

An excellent discussion of error correction models is followed by a chapter that espouses the general philosophy of going from a general model to a more specific one and does this in the context of autoregressive-distributed lag models. Cointegration, vector autoregressions and Granger causality follow in neat order. The last two chapters deal with the various exogeneity concepts on the one hand and with nonnested models and encompassing on the other. The authors succeed entirely in reaching a happy balance between 'proving things' (although no arduous proofs of any kind are ever presented), providing rationales or explanations, and illustrating the material by working out the appropriate technique or procedure in the context of the consumption function model.

Many of these concepts that are systematically covered here are either completely omitted in standard textbooks or are given only the scantiest mention. It is a *tour de force* to write a book that makes all these concepts completely accessible to students on an intermediate level, i.e. those that have had no more than one course in statistics. It is safe to predict that teachers and students alike will relish the clarity, as well as the concrete orientation of this excellent volume.

Princeton University   RICHARD E. QUANDT

Preface to Second Edition

The intention of offering non-specialist econometricians an intuitive understanding of recent developments in the modelling of economic time series remains the same as the first edition. To this end, we have attempted to react positively to some constructive suggestions made by reviewers of the earlier edition, and to build upon that edition by including a substantial amount of new material. We have taken the opportunity to clarify explanations and develop points throughout the text. The statistical tables included in the first edition for the Dickey-Fuller statistics have been recomputed for a greater number of sample sizes and are derived from a substantially greater number of replications. New tables are included for Dickey-Hasza-Fuller and *HEGY* seasonal integration tests, and for the Perron 'additive outlier' integration test. A data appendix is now added to aid those students who wish to follow up our worked examples for themselves. Most of the computations reported in the book have been redone using the latest version of *PC-GIVE*. Also references have been substantially updated and the number of exercises for discussion doubled.

The new material is primarily concentrated in the chapters on cointegration (Chapter 5) and vector autoregression (Chapter 6). Specifically, new simulation results are included in Chapter 5 to illustrate the differences between stochastic trends with and without drift, and between stochastic and deterministic seasonality. Simulation is also used to illustrate the distributions of Dickey-Fuller statistics. An extended analysis is given of the *HEGY* approach to seasonal integration testing which has become increasingly popular of late in applied work. We have extended the discussion on testing for the order of integration of a variable by including a description of the Dickey-Pantula approach, by an examination of whether or not a constant and trend should be included in test equations, and by a consideration of testing in the presence of structural breaks. A simulation exercise illustrates the difference between series for which linear combinations are and are not stationary as an introduction to the analysis of cointegrated series.

Chapter 6 now additionally contains the impulse response analysis of a vector autoregressive model. Within the *VAR* framework, we also present an extended discussion and an intuitive account of the Johansen approach to cointegration analysis and especially that of the Granger Representation Theorem. Although the computations of this approach are now routinely calculated by several econometric packages, a simple account of the basic principles is rarely presented to students.

We would like to thank Simon Arnold and Ziggy MacDonald for their help and comments. We are also indebted to Mike Pokorny who has generously allowed us to reproduce data from his book *'An Introduction to Econometrics'* for this new edition.

Preface

This book has its origins in a series of undergraduate lectures entitled 'The theory and applications of economic modelling' given over several years by both authors at the University of Leicester. Our experience is that nowadays, when there are so many excellent econometric textbooks and computing packages available, diligent students do not normally encounter particular difficulties in absorbing the principles of econometric theory, or in carrying out the estimation of models. Combining these elements with relevant economic theory to produce a convincing piece of empirical econometric modelling is another matter. Whilst it seems natural and superficially appealing to students to run countless regressions and attempt to choose that which appears to be the 'best' model, this approach has been widely criticized as failing to provide credible results. Unfortunately, descriptions of alternative systematic (and methodologically superior) practices of deriving sound econometric models tend to be available only in abstract and difficult academic articles

In this book we have attempted to remedy this problem by explaining the basic concepts and computations of contemporary econometric methodologies at a level accessible to non-specialists. The methodologies described include general-to-specific modelling, cointegration and vector autoregressive (VAR) modelling. These are all relevant for time series rather than cross-section econometrics.

The book is intended to be suitable for final year undergraduates, economic practitioners and postgraduates who wish to apply modern econometric techniques as part of essentially non-econometric theses. More advanced readers will need to supplement this book by following up the further reading which is given in each chapter.

It is assumed that the reader has followed an introductory course in mathematical statistics and multiple regression analysis (including basic tests on the General Linear Model), and also has some knowledge of elementary macroeconomics. For Chapters 6 and 7, an understanding of linear simultaneous equation models would be useful, although a short introduction to this is given.

In order to illustrate the approaches to modelling discussed in this book, we have used a single example throughout. The model of Davidson, Hendry, Srba and Yeo of UK aggregate consumption expenditure, published in 1978, which was a major influence on recent developments in applied econometric analysis, is re-examined in the light of these new developments. Whilst it is possible to study particular chapters in isolation, since the basic example is that of the model above, it is advisable that the reader at least glances through Chapter 3 where this model is discussed.

Most chapters are accompanied by a stylized output generated from the use of the computer package *PC-GIVE*. When the book was started, this package provided the most convenient tool for calculating the modern diagnostic tests and procedures necessary to implement the new methodologies (for example, a series of Lagrange Multiplier tests or the Johansen cointegration procedure). Such has been the increase in interest in these new techniques that currently several other packages exist which will perform nearly all of the computations discussed in this book. Examples of such packages are *TSP* version 4.2, *REG-X*, and the 1991 versions of *MICROFIT* and *RATS*.

A special debt is owed by the authors to Richard Quandt who has provided a continuous stream of encouragement and suggestions, and who has generously consented to write a foreword to the book. We were also most fortunate and grateful for comments received from David Hendry which have materially improved the text in many places. In addition we wish to acknowledge the help we have had from both students and colleagues at Leicester, particularly from Francis Green, Peter Jackson, George Norman and Sailesh Tanna who have read the entire text, and Ali Al-Nowaihi and Catherine Price who have commented on various chapters. We also wish to thank Maria Blangiewicz of Gdańsk University who helped greatly in the computation of the tables which appear in the Appendix. Both authors wish to blame the other for any remaining errors.

Chapter 1

Traditional Methodology in Retrospect

1.1 Introduction

It has become common for economists to express or discuss a theory in terms of an equation or a set of equations. Even elementary economics textbooks present postulated relationships between economic variables in an algebraic form, and make inferences by mathematical manipulations. It is then quite natural to attempt to give quantitative measures to these relationships. The most widely used tool of economists to determine empirical forms of theoretical constructs is that of *econometrics*.

The likely originator of the term 'econometrics' defined it as '...the unification of economic theory, statistics, and mathematics...' (Frisch (1936, p.95)). Much of the early empirical work in economics (that is, prior to 1940) was concerned with the measurement of demand elasticities, and the representation of the business cycle. To a great extent, this reflected the activity of economists in developing theory in these areas, and the particular availability of reasonably long runs of statistical data on agricultural commodities, foreign trade and various industries. The later development of national income accounting in conjunction with Keynesian economic theory created new opportunities for the econometric analysis of macroeconomic series, including complete models of economies. These estimated macroeconomic models could be used for economic policy purposes, such as forecasting or simulation.

Reflecting these possibilities, the *objectives* of econometrics have been described by Christ (1966, p.4) as:

> the production of quantitative economic statements that either explain the behaviour of variables we have already seen, or forecast (i.e. predict) behaviour that we have not yet seen, or both.

Irrespective of which of these objectives is being considered, it is clear that in order to undertake econometric analysis one must have:

1. Economic theory,
2. Statistical data,
3. A method that allows for the expression of the economic theory using the statistical data (in practice, a theory of estimation stemming from econometric theory),

4. A 'know-how', which tells us how to apply the estimation theory to the statistical data, and how to decide whether this application has been successful.

The problem is illustrated by the following example of a Keynesian consumption function. The theory which is further developed in Chapter 3 says that:

a) Real consumption at time t, denoted by C_t, is a 'fairly stable' function of real income (Y_t) in the same period,

Consumption
$$C_t = f(Y_t) \quad \text{Income}$$

b) $MPC = dC_t / dY_t < 1$,

   where MPC is the marginal propensity to consume.

c) $MPC < APC$ where $APC = C_t / Y_t$,

   and APC denotes the average propensity to consume.

d) As real income rises the APC falls.

This is the *economic theory*, that is point (1) above. Statistical data representing the theoretical constructs can be found in, say, a statistical yearbook to meet point (2). The *theory of estimation* gives rise to a selection of estimation methods (ordinary least squares for example) relevant for point (3). But what about 'know how'?

   One can formulate a practically infinite number of models consistent with this simple form of the Keynesian theory that could be estimated from suitable data, such as:

$$C_t = \alpha_0 + \alpha_1 Y_t + \text{error term} ,$$

$$C_t = \alpha_0 + \alpha_1 Y_t + \alpha_2 Y_{t-1} + \text{error term} ,$$

$$C_t = \alpha_0 + \alpha_1 Y_t + \alpha_2 C_{t-1} + \alpha_3 Z_t + \text{error term} ,$$

where, for example, Z_t could be an interest rate, a measure of wealth, or some consumption rationing measure, and the 'error term' stands for the combined influence of other variables omitted from the equations, none of which are individually important enough to be explicitly included. The problem of 'know how' is to apply an estimation method which combines the statistical data, the economic theory and the statistical theory in such a way as to lead to the 'best' model from the point of view of fulfilling the objectives of econometrics, either in *explaining* consumption, or in *forecasting* it, or both.

Christ (1966, pp. 4-6) discusses six properties that would be considered desirable in an estimated model: relevance, simplicity, theoretical plausibility, explanatory ability, accuracy of coefficients and forecasting ability. A 'good' model will display all of these properties to some degree. However, the existence of a potentially large number of theoretically plausible models which also satisfy some or all of the criteria makes the model choice problem a nontrivial one in practice. 'Know hows' relate to methods of defining 'good' models, and to finding them.

The 'know hows' of econometrics are the subject of this book. We call a 'know how' a *methodology*. A formal definition of methodology is given by Durbin (1988) as the:

> Study or knowledge of the methods or practices used in a scientific or other intellectual discipline, either (a) that part of training which deals explicitly with the "how to's" of a field, e.g. statistical methods and how to apply them; or (b) conscious awareness on the part of a practitioner of the often unconsciously implemented "How to's". The latter sense is particularly important when something has gone wrong and a new beginning or new direction is needed to solve a problem.

However, a more light-hearted view of methodology is that of Leamer (1983a, p.40):

> Methodology, like sex, is better demonstrated than discussed, though often better anticipated than experienced.

In this book, we will discuss and demonstrate some modern methodological approaches to econometric model building. Of course, we hope the experience of reading the book proves rewarding.

1.2 Principles of Traditional Methodology

Morgan (1990, p.11) in her detailed history of econometrics argues that, by the 1940s, theory and practice had developed into a programme which can be recognized as modern econometrics. This programme is widely associated with the Cowles Commission for Research in Economics. The Cowles Commission was founded in Chicago in 1932 by the American businessman Alfred Cowles, originally to undertake work on the determination of stock market prices. In fact, its primary research area became that of econometrics, and to this end it grouped together several of the leading mathematical statisticians and econometricians in the United States at that time (for instance Haavelmo, Hurwicz, Klein, Koopmans and Wald). Simultaneously in Europe, Frisch (who also acted as a research consultant for the Cowles Commission) and Tinbergen were pursuing their work on time series analysis and macrodynamic modelling, though often in disagreement with each other and with those on the Cowles Commission staff. A crucial development and an important link between all these researchers was provided by Haavelmo (a former research assistant to Frisch) whose 1944 paper 'The Probability

Approach in Econometrics' formed the basis upon which the Cowles Commission developed the macrodynamic modelling of Tinbergen.

The Haavelmo paper moved the emphasis of econometrics from the measurement of parameters (for example demand elasticities) and the problems of the quality of statistical data, to the testing of theories. The methodology reflecting this new emphasis which is now identified with the Cowles Commission emerged via a series of theoretical monographs published by the Commission, and within empirical work carried out by researchers in the 1940s attempting to implement some of the Commission's ideas. No specific 'know how' was formally presented. Instead, a consensus of opinion grew up as to the assumptions which were appropriate for the building and testing of econometric models. In most cases, these assumptions were 'hidden' rather than explicit, and must be inferred from the published work of that time.

To make these inferences, therefore, we will consider one of the earliest of all econometric textbooks (Tinbergen (1951)). This text surveys a wide range of empirical studies from this crucial period, and also presents what have now become accepted as the central assumptions of the Cowles Commission methodology.

A typical Cowles Commission time series model can be described in the following form: W, Z exogenous

$$Y_t = \alpha X_t + \theta W_t + error1 \ , \quad Y, X \quad endogenous \tag{1.1}$$

which can be accompanied by another equation or equations, say:

$$X_t = \beta Y_t + \gamma Z_t + error2 \ . \tag{1.2}$$

We will not discuss any assumptions concerning the errors of these equations. This is essentially a problem for estimation theory.

Tinbergen (1951, p.207) tells us that:

> the first thing to be done in any particular application is to give a correct economic analysis of the relation to be investigated ... Two things should be carefully kept in mind: first, the necessity to know exactly what relation one really is interested in and second to know what factors enter into this relation.

In modern parlance, we would say that:
1. *Zero restrictions* on the parameters in equations (1.1) and (1.2) above are known. The parameter on the variable Z_t in equation (1.1) is equal to zero, as is the parameter on W_t in equation (1.2). That is, the theory says that Z_t does not appear in equation (1.1), and W_t does not appear in equation (1.2).

Tinbergen (pp. 19-20) asks: 'What should be the mathematical form of the relation? ... A very general mathematical theorem is of advantage in all these cases: namely, that within a small range of variation, nearly every function can be approximated by a *linear* one.' In relation to the parameters of these functions, Tinbergen (p.205) states:

> It is often maintained that the method of multiple correlation is too rigid since it assumes the regression coefficients to be constant. It is very easy, however, to replace those coefficients by functions of other variables which means that they will be variable ... On the other hand it may be observed that experience supplies us with cases of a remarkable constancy of regression coefficients.

We can summarize these ideas as:

2. The relations are *invariant in time*. The parameters of the two-equation model above, namely α, β, θ and γ are taken as unchanging for different values of t. Thus, the model repeats itself for each t. It is conditional only on the values of the variables, and not on time.

Also, the previous statement by Tinbergen implies:

3. The parameters are *structurally invariant*, that is they are invariant with respect to changes in the variables of the model. Movements in parameters are permitted to be (at least in part) systematically related to movements in variables which do not appear in the model being investigated, but not to movements of those appearing in the model.

In relation to the variables in a model, Tinbergen says (p.14):

> The problem usually is to explain the changes in the magnitude of a phenomenon, X, from the changes in the size of other phenomena, Y, Z, and so on, which we may call the causes of X.

When more than one relation exists between the variables to be studied (as in the two-equation model above), Tinbergen (p.201) tells us:

> it is very useful to make a distinction between the simultaneous variables which have to be explained by the set of equations and the so-called "predetermined" variables which may also be found in the equations. Predetermined variables may be either data or lagged values of the simultaneous variables.

Hence, it was assumed that:

4. It is known *a priori* which variable is a *cause*, and which is a *result* of the relation (the *causal ordering* is known). It is known, therefore, which variables in the model are *endogenous* (values determined within the model) and which are *exogenous* (values determined outside the model). Thus, in the two equation model above, it would be natural to specify X_t and Y_t as endogenous, and W_t and Z_t as exogenous.

Perhaps the most interesting comments made by Tinbergen from the point of view of this book are those relating to the testing of theories in economics. Let x be the variable to be explained, and x' the predicted value of x from the regression equation. Then Tinbergen states (p.195) that:

> as to the testing of the theory, two extreme cases may present themselves:

(1) if x and x' are badly correlated, the theory is erroneous or at least incomplete;

(2) if the correlation between x and x' is complete, the theory does not contradict the facts.

Tinbergen (pp. 84-85) thus explains that:

> The statistician, when testing a relation set up by economic theory, may draw unconditional and conditional conclusions. The unconditional conclusions, however, are only negative. These conclusions may play a role when the theory is checked. If, namely, the correlation coefficient turns out to be too low (in comparison to the standard set before), the conclusion must be that the relation is incompatible with the facts. In other words, the theory is incorrect, or at least incomplete. The positive conclusions which can be drawn do not appear when the theoretical relation is checked: it cannot be proved that a theory is correct. The correlation may be high: other theories, however, may also lead to a high correlation ... If we want to draw positive conclusions, additional information is necessary ...

Tinbergen concentrates on three additional conditions which he suggests must be present before positive statements or inferences can be made from an estimated regression having a high multiple correlation coefficient (or equivalently, high coefficient of determination). These conditions essentially imply that the estimated relationship is properly specified. Specifically, the first condition is that there should be no significant determining factors omitted from the regression. This reflected the belief at that time that, in practice, errors of omission (specification errors) were more important than errors of measurement (Tinbergen (1951, p.200)). Secondly, any statements made are conditional upon the lag lengths on variables being correct. These lag lengths need not be specified in advance, but can be determined by trial and error to maximize the correlation between the variable to be explained and its predicted values (Tinbergen (1951, p.86)). Finally, and most important to Tinbergen (p.86), estimated regression coefficients should have the signs expected for them from the economic theory being modelled.

Thus, positive conclusions made from an estimated model were *conditional* on the assumed relationship being correct in its choice of variables and length of lags and so on. The additional conditions over and above a high correlation for a model needed to be satisfied before inferences could be made from that estimated model.

In retrospect, given these guidelines, it is not surprising that empirical investigations placed great weight on a combination of the goodness of fit of their models and the consistency of the signs of estimated parameters with the given theory. The theory could be rejected if the data seemed inconsistent with it, as evidenced, for example, by a low multiple correlation coefficient. However, more than one theory could be supported by the data, and any conclusions were conditional upon the relationship being correct. In other words:

5. The model *cannot be verified directly against 'rival' models*. It can be tested with the use of 'classical' (Neyman-Pearson type) tests against 'nature'. Usually this meant the use of R^2 (the coefficient of determination), Student-t ratios and F tests (see Chapter 2). Tintner (1952, p.187), writing at about the same time, makes this same point explicitly when discussing time series models. He states: 'There is as yet no valid procedure for the choice between various theories and hypotheses.'

With these guidelines for model building and testing established, econometrics entered its mature period. The 1950s and 1960s represented the high-water mark for the profession, with a massive expansion of both theory and empirical studies. The Cowles Commission emphasis on simultaneous equation models was reflected in an increase in both the number and size of estimated macroeconometric models. The pioneering structural multi-equation model is usually recognized as the 24 equation model of the Dutch economy constructed in 1936 by Tinbergen (an English version of this work was published in Tinbergen (1959)). Another widely discussed early model (termed Klein's Model I) was the six equation model describing the inter-war economy of the USA published by Klein (1950). The tendency was to build larger and larger models. Whilst the Klein and Goldberger (1955) model consisted of 20 equations, the 1965 version of the Brookings model had 160 equations (see Duesenberry *et al.* (1965)), and the Brookings MARK II model about 200 equations (see McCarthy (1972)). Wynn and Holden (1974, pp. 120-172) provide a comparative review of seven models published between 1950 and 1965, and Nerlove (1965) gives a tabular survey of econometric models covering the same period.

For their pioneering work in econometrics, Tinbergen and Frisch were jointly awarded the first Nobel prize in Economics, and the same award went to Klein and Haavelmo, two more members of the Cowles Commission, some years later. A great spirit of optimism and confidence in the future of econometrics existed. Econometric theory as enshrined in standard econometric texts presented a vision of a central core of accepted analysis which was being continuously refined and developed. The assumptions of the Cowles Commission approach outlined above were rarely questioned. Econometrics was viewed as a set of techniques necessary to handle the relaxation of the assumptions of the General Linear Model required because of the special problems faced by economists. Typically a 'true' model was introduced which would exhibit some particular problem (for example, heteroscedastic or serially correlated errors) and the properties of the ordinary least squares estimator for this model were investigated. A 'better' estimator would then be proposed.

1.3 The Failure of Traditional Econometrics

The growing scepticism towards the value of traditional econometric analysis which followed the 'golden age' of econometrics of the 1950s and 1960s may be illustrated by the following two remarks:

> On pessimistic days I doubt that economists have learned anything from the mountains of computer print-outs that fill their offices. On especially pessimistic days, I doubt that they ever will. (Leamer (1983b, p.325)),

and:

> Even within the academic profession, one is sensing a doubt as to whether the generation of more numbers for their own sake is fruitful. The ad hoc approach of many practising econometricians to the problem of hypothesis testing and inference is illustrated by the popular image of much econometrics as a high R^2 in search of a theory. Garbage in - garbage out is how many describe their own activity. (Desai (1976, p.vii))

These views of the value of applied econometric research became increasingly held from the mid 1970s onwards. As noted above, the two preceding decades had been full of optimism for econometrics. Unfortunately the real practical problems of model specification and selection had been rarely addressed, and a gap developed between what theorists were developing 'on the top floor' and what applied econometricians were actually doing with data 'in the basement'.

Not knowing what was an appropriate methodological approach to the building of econometric models in practice, applied workers developed their own. Computing advances removed one major obstacle to routine calculation, which led to the Cowles Commission methodology being systematically abused in ways detailed in Chapter 2 below. Such was the scale of this abuse that eventually in applied research much econometric work became ultimately unconvincing (see Leamer (1983a, p.37)). By the middle of the 1970s, this disquiet on the progress of applied research was becoming evident, as indicated by Desai's remark above. (See also the further reading at the end of this chapter.)

Moreover, the forecasting performance of several large scale macroeconometric models was found to be poor. Simple mechanistic time series methods provided severe competition to forecasts made using large and expensive models, which supposedly incorporated the knowledge of the working of the economic system built up on the back of extensive econometric research over many years. For instance, Cooper (1972) compared one-step-ahead forecasts made with the use of seven structural econometric models of the USA economy with a naive forecast obtained from an autoregressive model. In most cases the naive forecasts were superior to those from the econometric models. Although later studies on the comparison of time series and econometric forecasts have been more favourable to those of econometrics (see Granger and Newbold (1986, pp. 287-292) for a survey), a belief grew up that the simpler and cheaper time series methods could be at least as accurate as those from large scale econometric models.

From the earlier position of self-confidence, self doubt became widespread within the profession. Economists who were willing to say something about applied econometrics were divided into three groups:

1. Those who dismissed econometrics as alchemy;

2. Those who still believed in the traditional approach, pointing at wrong specification and imperfect estimation methods as the principal cause of the crisis in applied econometrics;

3. Those who postulated revisions of the five Cowles Commission assumptions above.

This book will concentrate on the third group who have reacted positively to the deficiencies that they perceived in traditional methodology. A number of alternative methodological approaches have been proposed, and while econometricians do not claim to have all the answers to the problems of model building, there is a new vitality and spirit of enquiry in applied research.

To return to the opening remark of this section, Leamer also states 'But there are optimistic days as well' (Leamer (1983b, p.325)). The remainder of this book will concern itself with an examination of some of the new methodological approaches which have given rise to this optimism, and provide guidelines for the practical analysis of time series data which avoid some of the weaknesses of traditional methodology.

1.4 Suggestions for Further Reading

An examination of the work of the Cowles Commission (renamed the Cowles Foundation for Economic Research in 1955) is to be found in Epstein (1987). Morgan (1990, Chapter 8) contains a detailed discussion of Haavelmo's 1944 paper, and its importance to econometric methodology. Aldrich (1989) also considers this paper, particularly with reference to questions of the structural invariance of models. Discussions of the difficulties in using traditional methodology are to be found in Hendry (1980) and Sims (1980). An interesting overview of the history and methodology of econometrics has been given by Spanos (1986, Chapter 1). Monographs covering these issues are Hendry and Morgan (1995) and Morgan (1990). Klein (1971b) gives an optimistic view of the results of three decades of econometrics and of its future (see also Bodkin *et. al* (1991), where more historical details can be found). Worswick (1972) argued that much less had been learnt from this work than was generally thought. Further, often contradictory comparisons of the predictive performances and policy analyses of structural econometric models can be found in Naylor, Seales and Wichern (1972), McNees (1979), Christ (1975) and Malinvaud (1981). The performance of econometric models in the 1980s are discussed, *inter alia*, in Wallis (1989) for the UK, and in Adams and Klein (1991) for the USA. A thorough theoretical approach to issues of econometric methodology together with a new classification is given by Dharmapala and McAleer (1996).

Chapter 2

Data Mining

2.1 Model Selection through 'Data Mining'

'Data mining' in its various forms reflects the general problem of not being in a position to conduct controlled experiments. This may lead to procedures which use a fixed data sample in some sequential manner to arrive at the final model specification. Suppose that we define a 'good' model as a specification which exhibits a high coefficient of determination, 'significant' Student-t ratios and possibly a Durbin-Watson statistic close to 2. A tempting and quite common practice is the taking of the widest possible set of variables (called here the 'candidates') which might eventually enter the model, running numerous regressions using as the regressors subsets of the entire set of the 'candidates', and then selecting the 'best' regression, that is that with the highest coefficient of determination or with the highest Student-t ratios.

Imagine that the aim is to model the consumption function. The investigator might prepare a set of potential regressors such as lagged consumption, total personal disposable income, expected income (measured, for instance, as the one-step-ahead prediction of income), income adjusted for the stock of liquid assets, total wealth of the last period and total wealth averaged over the last two periods. These variables can in turn be deflated by at least two different price indices: the retail price index and the cost-of-living index. This gives rise to a set of 12 potential explanatory variables and enables the formulation of some sensible looking consumption functions defined for a particular choice of deflator, such as:

1. consumption explained by its own lagged value and current unadjusted income;
2. consumption explained by current and expected income;
3. consumption explained by its own lagged value and current adjusted income;
4. consumption explained by current unadjusted income and lagged wealth.

By changing the deflator, another four equations can be formulated. Why not estimate them all and choose the one that has good Student-t ratios and a high R^2 ? If, on these criteria, the 'best' is equation 4 and the 'worst' is equation 2, we may even conclude that the analysis shows the significant impact of current income on consumption and that expected income does not influence current consumption. Would such a conclusion be justified?

Approaches such as these, termed 'data mining', gave rise to published models in the 1960s and early 1970s consisting usually of a lot of equations with convincing statistics and impressive 'goodness-of-fit' measures. Typically, an equation of such a model is presented in the form:

$$y_t = \underset{(5.21)}{2.134} + \underset{(3.02)}{0.345 \cdot} x_t + \textit{residual error}$$

$$R^2 = 0.956 \ , \ DW = 2.10 \ ,$$

with Student-t values in parentheses below the parameter estimates and with R^2 and DW standing respectively for the coefficient of determination and the Durbin-Watson statistic. It turns out, as we shall show in the remaining sections of this chapter, that neither R^2 nor t-values are very useful as powerful selection criteria precisely because their values can be influenced by, and to some extent are under the control of the experimenter. Exclusive reliance on R^2 and t-statistics as model choice criteria can easily lead to the selection of poor models.

2.2 The R^2 and Student-t Statistic Criteria

(a) The R^2 criterion
First let us regard the coefficient of determination as merely a non-stochastic descriptive measure of a model, namely the square of the correlation coefficient between the dependent variable of an equation and its least squares prediction. It is usually defined for an equation with an intercept and estimated by the ordinary least squares (*OLS*) method as:

$$R^2 = 1 - \frac{\sum \hat{u}_t^2}{\sum (y_t - \bar{y})^2} \ , \ \text{or} \ \ R^2 = 1 - \frac{S_u^2}{S_y^2} \cdot \frac{T-k}{T} \ ,$$

where the $\hat{u}_t$ are *OLS* residuals, y_t denotes observations on the dependent variable with a mean $\bar{y}$ and variance S_y^2 ($t=1, 2, \dots ,T$) and S_u^2 is an unbiased estimate of the error term variance, that is:

$$S_u^2 = \frac{1}{T-k} \cdot \sum \hat{u}_t^2 \ ,$$

where Σ stands for a summation over the entire sample (from $t=1$ to $t=T$ and k is the number of regressors. Suppose now that we wish to add a new regressor, say z_t, to the already existing set of regressors, $x_{1t}, x_{2t}, \dots, x_{kt}$. As its name implies, the *OLS* method produces estimates of parameters that minimize the sum of the squares of the residuals in the fitted model. If the residual sum of squares in the regression of y_t on $x_{1t}, x_{2t}, \dots, x_{kt}$ is $\sum \hat{u}_t^2$, the residual sum of squares in the regression of y_t on all the x_ts and the new variable z_t, say $\sum \hat{e}_t^2$, cannot be greater than $\sum \hat{u}_t^2$ even if z_t is not significantly correlated with y_t. Consequently, adding a new explanatory variable is always 'good' if one wishes to improve goodness of fit. This problem is partially overcome by using the 'adjusted' R^2 value, which takes into account the number of explanatory variables, that is by computing the adjusted coefficient of determination:

$$\bar{R}^2 = 1 - \frac{T-1}{T-m} \cdot (1-R^2) , \qquad \textit{Adjusted } R^2$$

where m is the number of explanatory variables.

The use of either R^2 or $\bar{R}^2$ as a decision variable to choose between models is a dangerous procedure. It has been shown (for example Theil (1971, pp. 543-545), or Johnston (1984, pp. 504-505)) that, *on average*, the $\bar{R}^2$ associated with a 'true' model will exceed that from an incorrectly specified model. But this result holds only 'on average'; it does *not* imply that a 'false' model cannot have an $\bar{R}^2$ greater than that of a 'true' model, and the mechanical choosing of models on the basis of their $\bar{R}^2$ is likely to result in the choice of such 'false' models. Clearly, also, the criterion of maximizing $\bar{R}^2$ is of no use when none of the models considered is a 'true' or 'good' model. Dhrymes (1970b, pp. 177-185) proved that in adding a variable to a model, the $\bar{R}^2$ for this new model will increase if the Student-t value associated with this new variable exceeds unity, which is well below the values normally required for statistical significance at conventional levels of significance.

The R^2 criterion is also not useful for making a selection from regressions having different dependent variables (forms of a model). To see why this is so, consider the *OLS* estimation of the regressions:

$$y_t = \beta_0 + \beta_1 x_{1t} + \beta_2 x_{2t} + error , \tag{2.1}$$

and:

$$y_t - x_{1t} = \theta_0 + \theta_1 x_{1t} + \theta_2 x_{2t} + error . \tag{2.2}$$

OLS will force the estimates of the intercepts to be equal, the coefficients on x_{2t} to be equal and the estimates of β_1 and θ_1 to obey the restriction $\theta_1 = \beta_1 - 1$. The residuals will be identical, and thus the residual sums of squares from equations (2.1) and (2.2) will be the same. However, as the left-hand side (dependent) variables in the two equations are different, the total sum of squares to be explained and hence the R^2 values in the two models will differ. We may conclude that if the model is merely re-written so that there is a change in the variation of the 'dependent variable', there will be an alteration in the associated coefficient of determination.

When it comes to testing whether the explanatory variables are singly or jointly significant, one always faces the problem reflected in the *Leamer critique* of structural models. This relates to the 'fragility' of statistical inferences made using the non-experimental data typically available to econometricians (see Leamer (1983a)). Suppose that we wish to test whether the reduction in the residual sum of squares obtained by adding a new variable, say x_{k+1}, to the model is significant. The null hypothesis H_0 is then:

$$H_0 : \beta_{k+1} = 0 \quad ,$$

and the appropriate test statistic may be expressed in terms of R^2 as:

$$F = \frac{R^2 - R_0^2}{(1 - R^2)} \cdot (T - k - 1) \sim F(1, T - k - 1) \quad .$$

Here R_0^2 is the coefficient of determination obtained for the restricted model, that is from the estimated model with only k explanatory variables, and R^2 is computed for the model estimated with the full set of $k + 1$ explanatory variables. However, as the sample size T increases, the value of F will tend to increase. Simultaneously, with the increase in the number of degrees of freedom, the critical values for the F test decrease. Consequently, it is easy to finish up with a 'significant' F statistic even for a meaningless increase in R^2. More generally, Leamer (1983a, p.39) states that:

> Diagnostic tests such as goodness-of-fit tests, without explicit alternative hypotheses, are useless since, if the sample size is large enough, any maintained hypothesis will be rejected ... Such tests therefore degenerate into elaborate rituals for measuring the effective sample size.

Although the test above has been written in terms of R^2, that is in terms of the coefficient of determination, it is not a test of the significance of R^2. In the General Linear Model where the explanatory variables are taken as non-stochastic, R^2 is purely a descriptive statistic, as has been stressed by Koerts and Abrahamse (1969). There are severe problems in attempting to use R^2 for statistical inference in the General Linear Model, and in particular as a test statistic in the determination of the correct specification of an economic model. To be used as a test statistic, it would be necessary to be able to determine the sampling distribution or distribution function of R^2. Koerts and Abrahamse (1969, Chapter 8) show that the distribution function of R^2 depends on both the unknown error variance and the particular values taken by the explanatory variables in the model (to which the distribution function of R^2 is particularly sensitive). Hence, values of R^2 belonging to different models (for example with different explanatory variables) cannot be compared in any straightforward way as they may have quite different distribution functions. In particular, this result gives no support to the practice of choosing a final specification on the grounds of the highest coefficient of determination.

(b) The Student-t criterion

A potential misuse of the Student-t statistic criterion is illustrated below by a simple example. Suppose that we have a set of four potential explanatory variables and the problem is to model aggregate consumption:

C_t - aggregate consumption,

Y_t - national income,

M_t - a measure of the stock of money,

P_t - consumers' price index,

PD_t - retail price index.

Suppose that we adopt a level of significance of $\alpha = 0.05$, and the number of observations is 25. Four *OLS* regressions have been run, giving the following t-values:

Regression 1: C on	Y	and		P
	(1.3)			(2.0)
Regression 2: C on	M	and		P
	(1.1)			(1.5)
Regression 3: C on	Y	and		PD
	(1.7)			(2.0)
Regression 4: C on	M	and		PD
	(2.2)			(2.3)

The Student-t ratios for the coefficients on particular variables are given in brackets and the tabulated critical value of the Student-t test is 2.06. Commonly, regression 4 seems to be preferred, because the t-statistics are the highest. Do the t-statistics mean that the parameters in this regression are statistically significant at the 0.05 level of significance? The answer is: we don't know whether they are significant or not, because the regression result was selected out of four outcomes *conditionally* on the other three results.

Why is this important? Consider the following example. Imagine that there is a 'dependent' variable y_t and 100 'explanatory' variables $x_{1t}, x_{2t}, ..., x_{100t}$. Assume that the distributions of all these variables are identical and independent. Hence, the explanatory variables are uncorrelated with y_t. Suppose that we have 100 vectors of realizations on these variables (one vector for each variable) and we fit an *OLS* regression of y_t on x_{1t}, then of y_t on x_{2t} and so on. At a significance level of 0.05 we can expect that about five out of these 100 regressions will be 'significant', that is they will have Student-t values lying in the rejection region. If we select these five models and ignore the rest, we will have five 'good' models, despite the fact that the explanatory variables are uncorrelated with y_t.

Consider a further example. Suppose that we wish to fit the 'best' (in terms of the highest Student-t ratio) regression model explaining aggregate consumption expenditure in the United Kingdom for the period 1957-1975. Using quarterly data, we have 76 observations available (this same set of data will be discussed and used extensively in the numerical examples in later chapters). The general form of the model is the following:

$$CONS_t = \alpha_0 y_t + \alpha_1 Q1_t + \alpha_2 Q2_t + \alpha_3 Q3_t + \alpha_4 Q4_t + \varepsilon_t \ ,$$

where $CONS_t$ denotes aggregate consumption expenditure, y_t is an explanatory variable, ε_t is an error term and $Q1_t, Q2_t, Q3_t$ and $Q4_t$ are seasonal dummy variables (that is, $Q1_t$ is equal to one for the first quarter of each year and zero otherwise, and so on). How do you react to the information that the Student-t value for the parameter α_0 on the variable y_t is 2.48? It definitely looks impressive, being in the critical region of the Student-t test and, according to the traditional interpretation, indicates a significant positive influence on consumption by y_t. But perhaps it would be useful to know what the variable y_t stands for? Well, it is nothing but a series of 76 random numbers generated from the standard normal distribution with zero mean and variance of one. Obviously, it would be rather heroic to argue that random numbers generated by a computer have anything in common with aggregate consumption in the UK. But why did we have such a 'significant' t-value? Quite simply, this is *the highest Student-t value selected out of 100 trials*. One hundred series of 76 normal random numbers were generated and $CONS_t$ was regressed on each of these series. Most of the regression results were, as expected, nonsensical (for instance, for the very first regression the t-value was, quite justifiably, equal to -0.11), but among them there were a few which looked quite sensible. If the best of them were selected, there is 'statistical evidence' for the claim that aggregate consumption in the UK is determined by random numbers!

For the case of orthogonal 'explanatory' variables it is straightforward to evaluate probabilities that regressors not correlated with the dependent variable appear to be significant, that is belong to the conventionally evaluated critical region (see Lovell (1983)). To show this, let us assume that an investigator believes that a dependent variable, y_t, is determined by at most two explanatory variables, but has a list of ten equally plausible explanatory variables to choose from. These 'candidate' variables are denoted as $x_{1t}, x_{2t}, ..., x_{10t}$. In fact and, of course, unknown to the investigator, none of the ten variables is related to y_t. If *a priori* theory could direct or restrict the set of potential explanatory variables to only two of them, say x_{1t} and x_{2t}, then only a single regression of the form:

$$y_t = \beta_0 + \beta_1 x_{1t} + \beta_2 x_{2t} + u_t \quad ,$$

would be run. In such a case, the probability of rejecting the null hypothesis that $\beta_1 = \beta_2 = 0$, that is the probability of a Type I error (rejecting the true null hypothesis), is at whatever nominal level of significance the test is conducted. In the text below we denote the nominal (or claimed) level of significance that is conventionally adopted in order to read from tables of critical values of the Student-t distribution for $T-k-1$ degrees of freedom by α while the true probability of the Type I error, the true significance level, is denoted by α^*. Evidently, if we select two explanatory variables out of two candidates, then $\alpha^* = \alpha$.

Suppose, however, that data mining was performed so that the model adopted is the result of selection following exploratory regression analysis. To simplify matters, it is assumed that there is no multicollinearity among the potential regressors so that all the x_{it} variables are orthogonal to each other, and the variance of the error term is known. With orthogonal regressors, the coefficient obtained on x_{it} will be the same whether or not other x_{it} variables appear in an equation fitted by *OLS*. Thus, in order to select the two variables to enter the regression, ten simple regressions can be run and the two explanatory variables with the highest associated Student-t statistic for their estimated coefficients selected. The problem is to determine the actual Type I error involved in this procedure; that is, the probability that the t-statistic in the final selected form will appear to be significant at the nominal significance level.

If the nominal significance level is taken to be 0.05 then, under the given assumptions, when the ten regressions are run the probabilities of obtaining $X=0$, 1, 2,..., 10 nominally significant t-values are given by the binomial distribution:

$$P(X = x) = \frac{10!}{x!(10-x)!} p^x (1-p)^{10-x} \quad ,$$

where x is the number of 'successes' (significant t-values) in these ten independent trials and p is the probability of a success in any trial.

With $p = 0.05$, then:

$$P(X = 0) = 0.5987$$
$$P(X = 1) = 0.3151$$
$$P(X = 2) = 0.0746$$
$$P(X = 3) = 0.0105$$

$$\cdot \qquad \cdot$$
$$\cdot \qquad \cdot$$

$$P(X = 10) = \text{approximately zero} \, .$$

Thus, in running ten regressions the probability that none will display a significant coefficient is only 0.5987 even when, in fact, no explanatory variable is related to y_t.

The true significance level involved (α^*) in presenting the final selected equation can now be determined. If the two variables with the highest Student-t statistics are selected, then the probability that neither coefficient is found to be statistically significant is:

P(first not signif.)· P(second not signif. | first not signif.) ,

but as these are independent events, this probability is equal to:

$$(1-\alpha^*)\cdot(1-\alpha^*) = (1-\alpha^*)^2 \ .$$

The value of α^* may then be found by equating this probability to the probability given above that no coefficients turn out to be significant when all ten regressions are run, so that:

$$(1-\alpha^*)^2 = P(X = 0) = 0.5987 \ ,$$

which gives $\alpha^* = 0.226$. This is considerably above the nominal level of 0.05, at which the coefficients would normally be tested. Thus the nominal significance level understates the probability of incorrectly rejecting the null hypothesis that the regression coefficients are zero when the regressors have been selected on the basis of their Student-t statistics. The difference between the true and nominal level of significance is the essence of 'Lovell bias', which refers to the alteration that needs to be made to the nominal significance level where regressors are selected from a set of 'candidates'. More generally, Lovell's 'rule of thumb' for computing the true significance level α^* when selecting k regressors out of c 'candidates' at a nominal significance level α is:

$$\alpha^* = 1-(1-\alpha)^{c/k} \ ,$$

which can be approximated as:

$$\tilde{\alpha}^* \approx \frac{c}{k}\cdot\alpha \ .$$

Again, if $c = k$, then $\alpha^* = \alpha$. That is, the true and nominal significance levels are equal if no data mining is performed

In practice the effect of data mining might be not as devastating as shown by the scale of 'Lovell bias'. The potential explanatory variables are often not orthogonal. For example, the various measures of income in the consumption function are likely to be correlated with each other. This would lead to a reduction in 'Lovell bias'. Unfortunately, the need to estimate the error variance is likely to work in the opposite direction. Lovell (1983) concludes that the 'rule of thumb' above still provides a rough and ready guide to the exaggerated claims of significance that are likely to arise from data mining in these more realistic cases.

2.3 Pretesting and Model Selection

One particular form of sequential model formulation that has been investigated in some detail is termed 'pretesting' and, like typical data mining, relates to model choice following preliminary testing for significance.

Consider the following (true) regression equation (given in deviations from means, so that the intercept term disappears):

$$y_t = \beta_1 x_{1t} + \beta_2 x_{2t} + error \quad .$$

There are at least three straightforward estimates of the parameter β_1:

1. The multiple regression estimate, say $\hat{\beta}_1$, which is generally unbiased with the sample variance $\sigma^2 / \sum x_{1t}^2 (1 - r^2)$, where r is the linear correlation coefficient of x_{1t} and x_{2t}, and σ^2 is the variance of the error term.

2. The simple regression estimate, say $\hat{b}_1$, obtained when y_t is regressed on x_{1t} alone, which will generally be biased (unless $\beta_2 = 0$ or x_{1t} and x_{2t} are orthogonal), with a sample variance (generally smaller than that in 1), equal to $\sigma^2 / \sum x_{1t}^2$.

3. The 'pretest' estimator, say $\hat{\beta}_1^*$, such as:

$$\hat{\beta}_1^* = \begin{cases} \hat{b}_1 & if \ |t| \le t_\alpha \\ \hat{\beta}_1 & if \ |t| > t_\alpha \end{cases},$$

where t is the calculated Student-t ratio associated with the multiple regression estimate of β_2, which is compared with the tabulated value t_α at the α level of significance. It is assumed that no data mining has preceded the choice of the two regressors, so that α is also the true significance level.

Thus, the pretest estimator in this simple case is the result of a choice between the simple and multiple regression estimate of the coefficient on x_{1t} based on a Student-t test of the significance of the other regression coefficient, β_2. Its statistical properties are complicated. Bancroft (1944) has shown, however, that the pretest estimator is generally biased. If bias were the only criterion, then $\hat{\beta}_1^*$ would be taken to be the multiple regression estimate, $\hat{\beta}_1$. However, the restriction on the model when x_{2t} is omitted may give rise to a more efficient estimator of β_1 and hence one may be prepared to incur some bias in order to achieve greater efficiency. Wallace and Ashar

(1972) have considered the three estimators above explicitly on the grounds of a mean square error (*MSE*) criterion (that is sampling variance + (bias)^2; see for example Pindyck and Rubinfeld (1991, p.29)), which allows for a comparison to be made between biased and unbiased estimators with different variances.

For the case above, it is easy to show that the mean square errors of the simple and multiple regression estimates of β_1 are:

$$MSE(\hat{b}_1) = \frac{\sigma^2}{\sum x_{1t}^2} + \beta_2^2 r^2 \frac{\sum x_{2t}^2}{\sum x_{1t}^2} \quad ,$$

$$MSE(\hat{\beta}_1) = \frac{\sigma^2}{\sum x_{1t}^2 (1 - r^2)} \quad .$$

Then:

$$MSE(\hat{b}_1) \le MSE(\hat{\beta}_1) \text{ if } \frac{\beta_2^2}{\text{var}(\hat{\beta}_2)} \le 1 \quad ,$$

where $\text{var}(\hat{\beta}_2)$ is the true (not estimated) sampling variance of the *OLS* estimator of β_2. This ratio bears a superficial resemblance to the (squared) Student-t statistic that would be used to test the statistical significance of β_2. Unfortunately, there is no implied relationship between the finding of a statistically significant coefficient for β_2 using $t = 1$ as the critical value for the Student-t test, and for $MSE(\hat{\beta}_1)$ to be lower than $MSE(\hat{b}_1)$.

For a given value of $\text{var}(\hat{\beta}_2)$ there is a range of values of β_2 for which the mean square error of the simple regression estimator exceeds that of the multiple regression estimator, and another range where the opposite is true. From the point of view of sequential model building, however, it would be attractive if it could be shown that the pretest estimator $\hat{\beta}_1^*$ had a lower *MSE* than that for either $\hat{b}_1$ or $\hat{\beta}_1$ over the whole range of possible β_2 values. The form and derivation of the *MSE* for the pretest estimator is complicated (see Judge *et al.* (1985, Section 3.1.3) for a general analysis) and is not given here. One of the most interesting findings of Wallace and Ashar, however, was that for a given sample variance of $\hat{\beta}_2$ there is no range of values of β_2 for which the mean square error of the pretest estimator is lower than the mean square errors of both $\hat{\beta}_1$ and $\hat{b}_1$. The implication of this is that leaving the specification of the model to be determined solely by the data will be less successful than a specification based on a strong (and correct) prior belief either that x_{2t} should be included or excluded. The general form of the mean square error function for $\hat{\beta}_1^*$ (that is for the pretest estimator) depends on the level of significance α adopted for the Student-t test on β_2. Weak prior beliefs about the importance of x_{2t} in the regression can be reflected through the choice of a larger value for α. Wallace and Ashar (1972) conclude: 'If we are not sure *a priori* whether a particular variable(s) belongs in a model, pretesting in the sense discussed here or in more elaborate step-wise regression selector programs will, on average, yield estimators that are sure to be worse than least squares estimators derived from an accurate prior specification.'

2.4 Data Mining and the Failure of Traditional Econometrics

We can draw together the implications of data mining for econometric model building by considering the following rather extreme case which may, however, contain elements familiar to any instructor of econometrics. Suppose that a student asks for your comments on the quality of an estimated regression which includes all the standard diagnostic statistics such as Student-t values, a Durbin-Watson statistic and a coefficient of determination. Would it be relevant to ask for details as to how this model was obtained? Would it alter your opinion as to the credibility of the model if the student said that the functional form tested was derived on the basis of careful economic reasoning and was the only regression fitted, as compared with the knowledge that this regression was the outcome of an extensive and unstructured search involving the fitting of many equations? Is the meaning of the test statistics affected by the process by which the model was developed from a fixed data sample?

It is the implication of this chapter that the credibility that can be ascribed to any reported econometric estimate is most assuredly related to the process by which it was generated. Realistically, it is natural that econometricians will wish to use a fixed data sample in some sequential way. The pure case of the reasoned economic argument leading to a well-defined model which is estimated and tested just the once from the available data sample conflicts with common sense. Surely the sample evidence contained within estimated models should be useful in the improvement of our understanding of the process which has generated the observed data? That is, in practice, some amount of data mining is inevitable.

However, Section 1.3 noted the disquiet that emerged regarding traditional econometric methodology, undermining the credibility that could be attached to its results. This chapter has indicated that it was not the Cowles Commission framework as such that was the problem (although, as we will see, certain assumptions of this approach are open to discussion). More generally, it was the abuse of the methodological principles implied by the Cowles Commission, and in particular the widespread growth of data mining in its various forms, that are recognized as the central weakness of the prevailing methodology as actually practised. Applied econometrics had singularly failed to provide models that produced satisfactory out-of-sample predictions, or resolved competing economic theories. The important question then is not whether data mining will be involved in the modelling of economic relationships, but how this should be done. It is the contention of the remaining chapters of this book that it is possible to conduct a structured and purposeful approach to econometric model building that avoids the worst aspects of data mining. Because of this, the models that result will simply be that much more convincing.

2.5 Suggestions for Further Reading

The original Lovell (1983) paper was followed by some additional contributions and extensions by Denton (1985), Caudill (1988), McAleer and Veall (1995) and, in an original context of investment portfolio management, by Markovitz and Xu (1994). A thorough, formal treatment of this problem is given by Chatfield (1995). In econometric textbooks, the problems posed by data mining are discussed briefly by Johnston (1984, pp. 501-504), Maddala (1988, pp. 420-421) and Kmenta (1986, pp. 598-600), and more fully by Goldberger (1991, Chapter 24) and Hendry (1995, Chapter 15). An important discussion of the place of data mining in the wider context of econometric methodology has been given by Granger (1990, pp. 8-11). The problem of data mining is related to the more general area of *specification searches* which has an extensive literature of its own (see for example Leamer (1978) or Maddala (1981)). An argument against the Leamer critique of the spurious significance tests in large samples is given in Phillips (1988a) in an article which forms part of a symposium on econometric methodology. A useful review of the early pretest literature is given by Wallace (1977) and a discussion of the Wallace and Ashar example is included in Kennedy (1990). A humorous account of data mining is given by Karni and Shapiro (1980). It is also important to notice that the expression 'data mining' has recently been used in a different context, as a description of some computing-intensive methods of network analysis.

Chapter 3

Origins of a Modern Methodology: the *DHSY* Consumption Function

3.1 Introduction

It is widely acknowledged that the work of Davidson, Hendry, Srba and Yeo (1978) (*DHSY* hereafter) on modelling aggregate consumption in the UK has had an important influence on the way many econometricians now use time series data to model economic relationships. Some of the strands of their analysis have since received considerable attention which in turn has led to the development of new econometric approaches and ideas. These new developments include general to specific modelling (see Chapter 4), cointegration analysis (see Chapter 5) and encompassing (see Chapter 8).

It will be useful, therefore, to reconsider the original *DHSY* analysis, albeit in a simplified and modified form, in order to outline some of the methodological questions posed by this paper. This chapter will also give an introduction to the theory of consumption modelling, and will explain the notation and meaning of the computer output produced by a modern econometric software package.

3.2 Economic Background

Since econometric modelling deals with the interaction of economic theory and empirical analysis, it will be useful to discuss some economic theory relevant to the formulation of models of aggregate consumption expenditure. Two of the main economic theories of the consumption function are the Absolute Income Hypothesis (Keynes (1936)), and the Permanent Income Hypothesis (Friedman (1957)). Hereafter, these theories will be denoted simply as *AIH* and *PIH*.

Keynes's 'fundamental psychological law' stated that 'men are disposed, as a rule and on the average, to increase their consumption as their income increases, but not by as much as the increase in their income' (Keynes (1936, p.96)). In the terminology that has become standard, the *marginal propensity to consume* is less than unity. Keynes also expected that the proportion of income saved would increase as incomes increased, so that the *average propensity to consume* would decline. Income and consumption were expressed in real terms. As is common with most macroeconomic theory, the theory was presented in terms of individual behaviour, but used to describe aggregate behaviour, despite the well-known aggregation problem (for example see Allen (1966, pp. 694-701)). Much attention was given to the differences between short run and long run behaviour of aggregate consumption (a distinction which as will be seen is reflected in the way *DHSY* ultimately formulated their model). The marginal propensity to consume was thought to be sensitive to the money value of wealth, and its short run value was expected to be less than its long run value.

The simplest formulation of a model which captures at least some of these ideas and which could be estimated from time series data is:

AIH

$$CONS_t = \alpha + \beta \cdot INC_t + \varepsilon_t \ , \qquad \qquad (3.1)$$

Inc = current real income

where consumption $(CONS_t)$ and income (INC_t) are measured in real *per capita* form, and ε_t is an error term. Here it is assumed that the intercept α is positive and, according to the *AIH*, the marginal propensity to consume (MPC) or β, is greater than zero but less than one.

As the average propensity to consume (APC) is the ratio of consumption to income, then:

$$APC = \frac{CONS_t}{INC_t} = \frac{\alpha}{INC_t} + \beta \ .$$

Hence, as income rises, the APC falls. In the long run as income rises, $APC = MPC$, but for the short run (for example for cyclical data), $MPC < APC$.

The 'stylized history of the early econometrics of the consumption function' has been examined by Thomas (1989) and Spanos (1989). This history is that, initially, short time series were used to estimate equation (3.1) above, with results which at first appeared consistent with the Keynesian postulates. Subsequently, however, long data series became available for the United States which indicated no reduction in the APC over time, and which was therefore inconsistent with this simple formulation. Moreover, the short run function appeared to have an intercept which increased over time, whilst budget (cross section) studies suggested that the average propensity to consume moved cyclically. 'New' theories of aggregate consumption behaviour were put forward to explain these apparent anomalies. Although Thomas and Spanos argue that this is a distortion of the way in which events actually proceeded, by the late 1950s there existed a substantial body of theoretical and empirical work on aggregate consumption behaviour alternative to the Absolute Income Hypothesis (see Farrell (1959) or Ferber (1962)).

Of these 'new' theories, perhaps the most enduring has been that of the Permanent Income Hypothesis. As the name suggests, individuals or consuming units are seen as making consumption decisions on the basis of expected, normal or permanent income, rather than on measured current real income as in the *AIH*. Permanent income is defined as the maximum amount a consuming unit thinks it could consume while maintaining its wealth position intact. Consumption is defined in a physical rather than a monetary sense, in that expenditure on durable goods in any period is treated as saving (apart from any depreciation of the asset in that period). The difference between measured and permanent (or planned) income is termed transitory income and the difference between measured and permanent consumption is termed transitory consumption. Two of the central assumptions of the *PIH* are that:

1. permanent consumption $(CONS_t^p)$ is proportional to permanent income, (INC_t^p),

    or: $CONS_t^p = \alpha_1 \cdot INC_t^p$, $\qquad\qquad$ (3.2)

and:

2. transitory consumption and transitory income are uncorrelated (that is 'windfall gains' are saved or spent on durable goods, rather than spent on nondurables).

This theory gives rise to several implications which can be tested (particularly with the use of cross section data) without the need to measure permanent income or consumption. Direct estimation of equation (3.2) above requires measures of both these concepts.

Actual consumption expenditure on non-durables $(CONS_t)$ is usually taken to stand for permanent consumption, both on the grounds that the consumer unit has some direct control over actual consumption expenditure, and because any discrepancy between the two (transitory consumption) will appear in the error term of the equation and not pose any particular econometric problems. Thus, equation (3.2) above could now be written as:

$$CONS_t = \alpha_1 \cdot INC_t^p + \varepsilon_t \ , \qquad\qquad (3.3)$$

where ε_t is an error term.

Measurement of permanent income can be approached through the use of the adaptive expectations hypothesis, where permanent income (INC_t^p) alters between periods in proportion to the difference between actual income (INC_t) in a period, and permanent income in the previous period. Thus:

$$INC_t^p - INC_{t-1}^p = (1-\lambda)(INC_t - INC_{t-1}^p) \ , \qquad\qquad (3.4)$$

$$0 < \lambda < 1 \ .$$

With these assumptions about the measurement of permanent consumption and income, equation (3.2) above may now be written in a form suitable for estimation by using the so-called Koyck transformation (for example see Kmenta (1986, pp. 528-529) or Johnston (1984, pp. 346-348)). That is, substitute INC_t^p in (3.3) by $INC_{t-1}^p + (1-\lambda)(INC_t - INC_{t-1}^p)$ from (3.4), giving:

$$CONS_t = \alpha_1[INC_{t-1}^p + (1-\lambda)INC_t - (1-\lambda)INC_{t-1}^p] + \varepsilon_t$$

$$= \alpha_1\lambda INC_{t-1}^p + \alpha_1(1-\lambda)INC_t + \varepsilon_t \quad . \tag{3.5}$$

Lagging equation (3.3), and multiplying it by λ gives:

$$\lambda CONS_{t-1} = \lambda\alpha_1 INC_{t-1}^p + \lambda\varepsilon_{t-1} \quad ,$$

and subtracting this from (3.5) yields:

$$CONS_t - \lambda CONS_{t-1} = \alpha_1(1-\lambda)INC_t + (\varepsilon_t - \lambda\varepsilon_{t-1}) \quad .$$

This may be written as:

PIH

$$CONS_t = \beta_1 CONS_{t-1} + \beta_2 INC_t + v_t \quad , \tag{3.6}$$

where: MPC

$$\beta_1 = \lambda, \quad \beta_2 = \alpha_1(1-\lambda), \text{ and } v_t = \varepsilon_t - \lambda\varepsilon_{t-1} \quad .$$

The coefficient β_2 in equation (3.6) is the short run marginal propensity to consume. In the long run, if the economy reaches a static equilibrium, consumption and income will be constant from period to period. Long run parameters may then be derived from (3.6) by solving this equation for long run consumption, $CONS^*$, assuming that $CONS^* = CONS_t = CONS_{t-1}$, so that:

$$CONS^* = \frac{\beta_2}{1-\beta_1} \cdot INC_t + \frac{1}{1-\beta_1} \cdot v_t \quad ,$$

where the long run average and marginal propensities to consume are $\dfrac{\beta_2}{1-\beta_1}$

and the long run income elasticity of consumption is unity.

If a consumption function is estimated using measured consumption and measured income in the form:

$$CONS_t = \delta_0 + \delta_1 \cdot INC_t + \varepsilon_t \quad ,$$

then the *PIH* would predict (among other things) that:

1. the marginal propensity to consume (δ_1) will be less than the average propensity to consume;

2. the income elasticity of consumption would tend to rise the longer the time series over which the function is fitted; and

3. the marginal propensity to consume estimated from real *per capita* data would be less than that for undeflated data.

Another rationale for an econometric equation in the form of (3.6) is that of *habit persistence*. A consumer is viewed as having a desired level of consumption, $CONS_t^d$, which is related to current income. When current income alters, inertial factors prevent an immediate movement to the new desired consumption level. Instead, a partial movement is made, so that:

$$CONS_t^d = \alpha + \beta \cdot INC_t \quad,$$

with:

$$CONS_t - CONS_{t-1} = (1-\gamma)(CONS_t^d - CONS_{t-1}) + \varepsilon_t \quad,$$

$$0 < \gamma < 1 \quad.$$

This leads to an estimating form:

$$CONS_t = (1-\gamma) \cdot \alpha + \gamma \cdot CONS_{t-1} + (1-\gamma) \cdot \beta \cdot INC_t + \varepsilon_t \quad,$$

which is similar to equation (3.6), though it has an intercept term. Other aggregate consumption theories also lead to estimating forms similar to equation (3.6).

3.3 Models of Absolute and Permanent Income

Most of the empirical results in this book have been obtained through the use of the latest version of the package *PC-GIVE*, namely *PC-GIVE 8.1 Professional*. *PC-GIVE 8.1 Professional* is a computer package for econometric data analysis and estimation which may be run on *IBM* and *IBM*-compatible personal computers. *GIVE* stands for Generalised Instrumental Variables Estimators. It is an interactive menu-driven package originally constructed to reflect aspects of the econometric methodology presented in the Davidson *et al.* (1978) paper, and hence is especially relevant for the analysis of time series data. Some features of *PC-GIVE* are described in Hendry (1989). Such has been the growth of interest in the methodological developments in econometric modelling since *DHSY*, that several other packages are available which will perform nearly all the computations in this book. These include the latest versions of *TSP*, *REG-X*, *MICROFIT* and *RATS*.

PC-GIVE provides a wide and rich set of descriptive and diagnostic statistics. We will concentrate, however, on only a small part of this potential output, namely the basic statistics available following the estimation of a single equation by ordinary least squares. To illustrate and explain these statistics, consider the estimation of the models for the Absolute and Permanent Income Hypotheses introduced in Section 3.2 above.

To facilitate direct comparison with the *DHSY* model, the data chosen are UK quarterly seasonally unadjusted non-durable consumption expenditure and personal disposable income from the first quarter of 1957 (denoted by 1957(1)), to the fourth quarter of 1975 (1975(4)), in millions of pounds at 1970 prices. The data is listed in the Data Appendix. The data were taken from Pokorny (1987, p.408), which may differ slightly from the unpublished data used in the Davidson *et al.* (1978) paper (see Pokorny (1987, note 9, p.399)). This and the fact that we are using a different computing package than that available in 1978 accounts for the small differences between the original *DHSY* results and those reported below where direct comparison is possible.

As lagged values of these variables will be required, five observations at the start of the sample are used to create these variables. An important test of any model is how well it predicts out-of-sample periods, so the last 20 observations (1971(1) to 1975(4)) are reserved for this evaluation. Hence, the estimation period (hereafter termed the sample period) becomes 1958(2) to 1970(4), a sample of 51 observations. Figure 3.1 displays the scatter diagram of consumption and income for this sample period. This figure shows an evident correlation between the two variables. Nevertheless, the dispersion of points seems to increase with the values of consumption and income, which suggests that the appropriate form of the consumption function may not be a simple linear relationship between consumption and income.

Fig. 3.1: Correlation between consumption and income

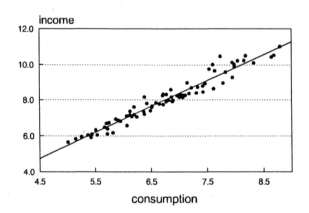

For further analysis it will be useful to have some specific notation for in-sample and out-of-sample (forecast or post sample) periods.

We will denote the time series as:

$t = 1, 2, ..., T, T + 1, ..., T^*$, where $T = 51$ and $T^* = 71$, so that:

$t = 1, 2, ..., T$ is the sample period, and

$t = T + 1, ..., T^*$ is the forecast or post sample period.

Consider the estimation of equation (3.1) above, the simplest formulation of the consumption function presented. The computer output for this estimation is presented in Section 3.7 under MODEL 3.1. The parameter estimates for the intercept (*Constant*) and income variable (*INC*) are given in the column headed '*Coefficient*'. The other statistics reported are as follows.

(1)   *RSS* : the residual (error) sum of squares of the fitted model.

(2) σ : the estimated standard error of the residuals, calculated as:

$$\sigma = \left(\frac{RSS}{T-k} \right)^{1/2}$$

where k is the number of independent variables in the model, including the intercept. (Here, $k=2$, and $=51$.)

(3)   *Std.Error*: These are the estimated standard errors of the coefficients, obtained as the square roots of the diagonal elements of the variance-covariance matrix of the *OLS* estimators (for example, see Johnston (1984, p.173)).

(4)   *HCSE*: Heteroscedastic Consistent Standard Errors. These are consistent estimates of the standard errors of the regression coefficients if the errors in the model are heteroscedastic. If these values and those for the standard errors in (3) above differ markedly, heteroscedasticity may be inferred. In such a case, the *HCSE* measure may be preferred. The formulae for their computation are given in White (1980).

(5)   *t-value*: The ratio of the estimated parameter value to its estimated standard error used to test the null hypothesis that the parameter is equal to zero. Under the null hypothesis and additional assumptions about normality for the error term, the ratio has the Student-t distribution with $T-k$ degrees of freedom.

(6) R^2 : Coefficient of determination as defined and discussed in Chapter 2.

(7) F : Statistic used for testing the null hypothesis that all the parameters in the model (apart from the intercept) are jointly equal to zero. It is defined as:

$$F = \frac{ESS / (k-1)}{RSS / (T-k)} = \frac{R^2 / (k-1)}{(1-R^2) / (T-k)} ,$$

where *ESS* is the explained sum of squares of the model. Under the null hypothesis, the ratio has the F-distribution with $k-1$ and $T-k$ degrees of freedom (see Johnston (1984, p.186)). In this case, as there is only one parameter to be tested, the F value is equal to the square of the t-value on this parameter, as may be confirmed. The number in square brackets following the F-value in the computer output is the probability of obtaining that value under the null hypothesis from a central F-distribution with the degrees of freedom shown (the probability value).

(8)   *DW* : Durbin-Watson statistic. This is used to test for autocorrelated errors in the model, and particularly for first order autocorrelation. It is calculated from the residuals of the fitted model. Formally, tests are conducted using the appropriate statistical tables, which are widely available (for example in Johnston (1984, pp. 554-557)). These tables are applicable to models containing an intercept term. Loosely, the hypothesis of no first order autocorrelation in the errors will not be rejected if the *DW* value is close to 2 (Johnston (1984, p.314)). The test may be misleading if a lagged dependent variable is present among the regressors, as in this case the calculated Durbin-Watson value is biased upwards towards 2 (see Durbin (1970)). Different tables (Farebrother (1980)) should be used when there is no intercept in the regression.

(9)   *Forecast Chi^2*: test for the constancy of the parameters of the model (including the error variance) in the post sample period compared with its values for the sample period. It is defined as:

$$Forecast\ Chi^2 = \frac{\sum_{t=T+1}^{T^*} e_{ft}^2}{\sigma^2} = \frac{(T^* - T) \cdot MSE_f}{\sigma^2} \quad ,$$

where $MSE_f = \dfrac{\sum e_{ft}^2}{T^* - T}$ and e_{ft} is the forecast error made for period t

$(t = T + 1, ..., T^*)$ using the post sample data on the independent variables with the vector of estimated model parameters obtained from the sample data. It should be recalled that in the discussion on the choice of sample period, 20 observations were reserved for the evaluation of the model in out-of-sample periods. Under the null hypothesis that all parameter values are unchanged between the sample and post sample periods, this statistic is (asymptotically) distributed as χ^2 with $(T^* - T)$ degrees of freedom. The test has weak power (that is, the probability that the test will correctly reject a false null hypothesis is low), and should be used as a signal rather than a thorough test. In the computer output, values of *Forecast Chi^2* statistics marked with a * or ** relate to values which are significant at the 5% and 1% significance levels respectively.

Significance means parameters are not constant

(10) *Chow*: A model specification test on the constancy of the model's parameters over the entire sample and post sample (forecast) periods. Formally, it is calculated as:

$$Chow = \frac{(RSS^* - RSS)/(T^* - T)}{RSS/(T - k)} \quad ,$$

where RSS^* is the residual sum of squares from the model estimated using both sample and post sample data. The null hypothesis is the same as that for the *Forecast Chi²* test in (9) above. Under the null hypothesis, the *Chow* test has (asymptotically) the F distribution with T^*-T and $T-k$ degrees of freedom. Rejection of the null implies rejection of the model estimated over sample and forecast periods. For a more detailed discussion of this test see Harvey (1990, pp. 183-184). As with the *Forecast Chi²* test, statistics marked with a * or ** relate to values which are significant at the 5% and 1% significance levels respectively.

Two other features of the computer output which will be used in the discussion of various estimated models are as follows:

(11) *Standard Errors of Forecast*: A graph of actual and forecast values for the post sample data, along with error bars of (±) two standard errors of forecast (see Johnston (1984, pp. 42-45)) is produced (see for example Figure 3.2). The error bands provide 95% confidence intervals for the forecast, or a range within which actual values would be expected to lie if the model was performing in the post sample period as it had in the sample period.

(12) *Lagged Variables*: In Section 3.7, and in subsequent chapters, lagged variables will be denoted in the computer output in the column headed 'Variable', by the name of the variable followed by the length of lag. Thus, for example, consumption lagged one period is CONS_1 (MODEL 3.2) and the difference between the logarithms of consumption and income, both lagged four periods, is lc_li_4 (MODEL 3.7).

With these diagnostic statistics, we can return to MODEL 3.1 in Section 3.7, in order to comment on the adequacy of equation (3.1) to represent aggregate consumption over the sample and post sample periods. The fit of the model is satisfactory. Both coefficients are statistically significant, a comment that can be made given the acceptable value of the Durbin-Watson statistic. The conventional and heteroscedastic consistent standard errors of the estimated coefficients are not dissimilar so that heteroscedasticity in the errors is not indicated. At the mean values of consumption and income, the *APC* is 0.858. The *MPC* of 0.728 is less than the *APC*. However, the post sample performance of this simple model is far from satisfactory. Figure 3.2 indicates that the forecast values are generally above the realized values, and in some cases the realized values lie outside the confidence limits for the forecast. Both the *Forecast Chi^2* and the *Chow* test reject the null hypothesis of no change in the model's parameters between the sample and post sample periods.

Fig. 3.2: Prediction from MODEL 3.1

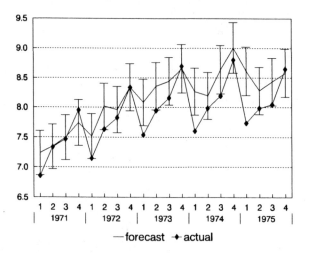

Estimation of a simple form of the Permanent Income Hypothesis (equation (3.6), but including an intercept) is no more satisfactory. The computer output for MODEL 3.2 indicates not only the failure of this model to satisfy the forecast tests, but also includes a negative coefficient on the lagged consumption variable, which is inconsistent with the *PIH*.

One reason for the observed weakness of the models estimated to represent the Absolute and Permanent Income Hypotheses might be the lack of attention paid to the time series properties of the data. The graph of the consumption and income data for both sample and post sample periods given in Figure 3.3 shows the marked trends and seasonal patterns exhibited by both series. This suggests that the estimation of the model might be improved if one took account of these features of the data series.

It would be possible to repeat the estimation of the two models above using detrended and deseasonalized data, but this approach is generally not recommended. If series have been seasonally adjusted by different methods, the economic relationship between the series may be distorted (see Wallis (1974)). This can be important as it is not always clear how official statistics have been seasonally adjusted. An alternative way forward is to follow Hendry (1974) and use a combination of trend and seasonal dummy variables to model these effects. It is shown later in the text that using trend and seasonal dummy variables is not the only alternative to using detrended and seasonally adjusted data. Technically (see Chapter 5) the use of such dummy variables corresponds to the assumption that the model is subject to a 'deterministic trend' and 'deterministic seasonality'.

Fig. 3.3: Time series of consumption and income

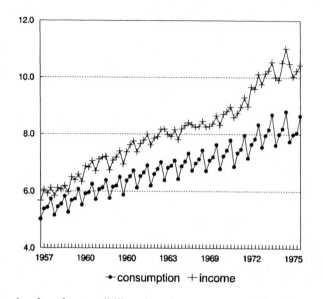

→ consumption + income

There is also the possibility that there were special effects or events within the sample period which may have distorted the series. Advance warning of possible purchase tax increases in a forthcoming budget may have caused consumers to switch expenditure from the second quarter to the first quarter of 1968. A similar reaction may have occurred between the first two quarters of 1973 relating to the introduction of Value Added Tax. It therefore seems reasonable to include a special dummy variable to allow for the presence of such effects in the periods identified above.

In order to model these trend, seasonal and special effects, define new variables as follows:

$$Seasonal_t = \begin{cases} 1 & \text{in first quarter} \\ 0 & \text{otherwise} \end{cases},$$

$$Seasonal\_1_t = \begin{cases} 1 & \text{in second quarter} \\ 0 & \text{otherwise} \end{cases},$$

$$Seasonal\_2_t = \begin{cases} 1 & \text{in third quarter} \\ 0 & \text{otherwise} \end{cases},$$

$$T = t = 1, 2, 3, ..., 51 ,$$

$$DT_t = Seasonal_t \cdot T, \quad DT1_t = Seasonal\_1_t \cdot T, \quad DT2_t = Seasonal\_2_t \cdot T,$$

$$DO_t = \begin{cases} 1 & \text{for 1968(1) and 1973(1)} \\ -1 & \text{for 1968(2) and 1973(2)} \\ 0 & \text{otherwise} \end{cases},$$

The variables $Seasonal_t$, $Seasonal\_1_t$ and $Seasonal\_2_t$ are seasonal dummy variables. $Seasonal_t$ is automatically created by *PC-GIVE* to take the value of unity in the first period of a year. There is no $Seasonal\_3_t$ variable as the estimated model will include an intercept term and the joint presence of all four dummy variables and an intercept term would make the model estimation procedure break down (see Johnston (1984, p.226)). The variable T is a time trend. The variables DT_t, $DT1_t$ and $DT2_t$ allow for multiplicative seasonality, where the absolute value of the seasonal effect changes over time. Thus the consecutive values of $DT1_t$ will be 1, 0, 0, 0, 5, 0, 0, 0, 9, 0, 0, 0, etc. (recall that the sample period starts at a second quarter of a year so that $T = 1$ refers to a second quarter observation). DO_t relates to the special effects that might have caused expenditure switching prior to budget announcements.

The equation to be estimated is now:

Model 3.3

$$CONS_t = \beta_0 + \beta_1 INC_t + \beta_2 Seasonal_t + \beta_3 Seasonal\_1_t + \beta_4 Seasonal\_2_t$$
$$+ \beta_5 T + \beta_6 DT_t + \beta_7 DT1_t + \beta_8 DT2_t + \beta_9 DO_t + \varepsilon_t \quad .$$

The results of estimating this equation are reported in Section 3.7 under MODEL 3.3. The majority of the variables which have now been added to the earlier model of the Absolute Income Hypothesis are statistically significant at conventional levels of significance. The computer output for this extended model also shows, however, that it fails the *Forecast Chi²* and *Chow* tests. In addition, Figure 3.4 shows that some realizations lie outside the confidence intervals for the forecasts.

When the new variables are added to the model for Permanent Income (equation (3.6) with an intercept term), the estimated model (MODEL 3.4 in Section 3.7) now has the expected sign for the coefficient on lagged consumption compared with the earlier result in MODEL 3.2. However, MODEL 3.4 fails the forecast tests and, as Figure 3.5 shows, produces confidence intervals for forecasts that do not include the realized values, particularly towards the end of the post sample period.

The implied long run marginal propensity to consume from MODEL 3.4 is $\dfrac{0.225}{1 - 0.273}$ or 0.310 which is very low compared with what would be expected under either the Absolute or Permanent Income Hypotheses. Similarly, the long run income elasticity of consumption calculated at the mean values of consumption and income is only 0.36 (see Pokorny (1987), p.384), well below the value of unity for the theory the model purports to represent.

Fig. 3.4: Prediction from MODEL 3.3

Fig. 3.5: Prediction from MODEL 3.4

3.4 The *DHSY* Model

It is not our intention to provide a detailed account of the *DHSY* paper. A good discussion on these lines is to be found in Pokorny (1987, pp. 380-397). Rather, we will concentrate on those points in the *DHSY* analysis which represented substantial methodological departures from what was generally practised in applied econometrics at that time.

The model that will be considered initially and which will eventually lead to a developed *DHSY* model is:

$$\Delta_4 cons_t = \beta_1 \Delta_4 inc_t + \beta_2 \Delta\Delta_4 inc_t + \beta_3 \Delta_4 DO_t + \varepsilon_t \ , \tag{3.7}$$

where $cons_t$ and inc_t are the natural logarithms of the consumption and income variables defined in Section 3.3, DO_t is the 'special effects' variable also defined there, ε_t is an error term, and the symbols Δ and Δ_4 denote difference operators such that:

$$\Delta x_t = x_t - x_{t-1} \ ,$$

and:

$$\Delta_4 x_t = x_t - x_{t-4} \ .$$

A justification for the use of logarithms and differences will be discussed below.

At first glance, this equation would seem to have very little similarity to either MODEL 3.3 or 3.4 which were the estimated forms of the representations of the Absolute and Permanent Income Hypotheses. However, it was not the intention of *DHSY* to provide a new theory of aggregate consumption, but rather to model this variable within the framework of generally accepted theory. We will see shortly that equation (3.7) does in fact have an interpretation consistent with the Permanent Income Hypothesis.

The use of logarithms in this model rather than the raw data in levels can be justified on grounds of both statistical and economic theory. Figure 3.3 seems to show that the dispersion of the consumption series increases with the level of the series. This may also be true for the income series. MODEL 3.4 allowed for a changing seasonal pattern by use of the variables DT_t, $DT1_t$ and $DT2_t$. However, if the standard deviation of a series is proportional to its level, then data expressed in terms of logarithms will exhibit approximately constant variance (see Cryer (1986, pp. 94-95)). Chapter 5 will indicate why it is useful to work with data which exhibits a constant variance. In the *DHSY* model, however, such a data transformation is not only a technical matter. As will become evident shortly, the economic model developed by *DHSY* naturally leads to the use of variables in logarithmic form.

The model presented above and estimated as MODEL 3.4 used a time trend variable to model the upward tendency of the data in levels. If logarithms are now used instead of levels, the series will display a linear trend if the raw data display exponential growth. The marked seasonal pattern of the data was modelled in MODEL 3.4 by seasonal dummy variables. The use of time trends and seasonal dummies is not only expensive in terms of degrees of freedom but, as we indicated above, may also be considered to be rather *ad hoc* in nature. Investigators often prefer to try to model trend and seasonal effects simultaneously within an estimated model, rather than introduce special variables in an attempt to eliminate their effect (for example, see Granger and Newbold (1986, p.37)).

In particular, it is common to handle trend and seasonal effects by *differencing* the data. Consider the following artificial example displayed below in which x_t and z_t are linear and quadratic trends respectively. If we take the series as representing three years of quarterly data, new series with additive seasonal effects can be constructed by simply adding seasonal effects of (say) -1, -1, -2 and $+4$ to each appropriate quarterly value. This yields the series f_t (linear trend with additive seasonality) and g_t (quadratic trend with additive seasonality).

x_t	f_t	z_t	g_t	v_t	l_t	Δl_t
1	0	1	0	-	-	-
2	1	4	3	-	-	-
3	1	9	7	-	-	-
4	8	16	20	-	-	-
5	4	25	24	4	24	-
6	5	36	35	4	32	8
7	5	49	47	4	40	8
8	12	64	68	4	48	8
9	8	81	80	4	56	8
10	9	100	99	4	64	8
11	9	121	119	4	72	8
12	16	144	148	4	80	8

The variables v_t and l_t represent the effect of *seasonal differencing*. Thus;

$$v_t = f_t - f_{t-4} = \Delta_4 f_t \quad,$$

and:

$$l_t = g_t - g_{t-4} = \Delta_4 g_t \quad.$$

A *seasonal difference* is simply the difference between an observation and its value for the corresponding season one year before. If the variables are measured in logarithms, then the seasonal differences can be shown to be measures of the growth rates of the variables (see Cryer (1986, p.95)). One should note, however, that seasonal dummy variables and seasonal differences do not account for precisely the same phenomenon. The difference between deterministic and stochastic seasonality will be discussed in Chapter 5.

It can be seen immediately from the figures above that seasonal differencing converts a linear trend with an additive seasonal effect (f_t) to a constant (that is to a variable with no trend or seasonal pattern). Seasonal differencing of the quadratic trend with additive seasonality (g_t) however, results in a series (l_t) which still contains a trend but with no seasonal pattern. The final column of figures shows that this trend can be modelled by taking the *first differences* of the seasonally differenced series. That is, Δl_t is defined as:

$$\Delta l_t = l_t - l_{t-1} = (g_t - g_{t-4}) - (g_{t-1} - g_{t-5}) \ ,$$

and this series contains neither trend nor seasonal effects.

From inspection of Figure 3.3 it seems that both consumption and income may be subject to linear trends. Formal tests for this conjecture will be given in Chapter 5. Both variables also display a marked seasonal pattern. From the remarks and example above, it would seem reasonable to re-estimate the models of the Absolute and Permanent Income Hypotheses using logarithms and seasonal differencing of the variables rather than time trends and seasonal dummies. For example, reconsider MODEL 3.3 in Section 3.7 where now the consumption and income variables are measured in natural logarithms and the trend and seasonal dummy variables are omitted:

$$cons_t = \alpha_1 + \alpha_2 inc_t + \alpha_3 DO_t + \varepsilon_t \ . \tag{3.8}$$

Lagging equation (3.8) by four periods and subtracting the result from equation (3.8) yields:

$$\Delta_4 cons_t = \alpha_2 \Delta_4 inc_t + \alpha_3 \Delta_4 DO_t + \Delta_4 \varepsilon_t \ . \tag{3.9}$$

This is not quite the same as the initial model presented at the start of this section. This was:

Model 3.5

$$\Delta_4 cons_t = \beta_1 \Delta_4 inc_t + \beta_2 \Delta\Delta_4 inc_t + \beta_3 \Delta_4 DO_t + \varepsilon_t \ , \tag{3.7}$$

where:

$$\Delta\Delta_4 inc_t = (inc_t - inc_{t-4}) - (inc_{t-1} - inc_{t-5}) \ .$$

Compared with equation (3.9), this equation has an extra term $\Delta\Delta_4 inc_t$. From our discussion above, the term $\Delta\Delta_4 inc_t$ could be an appropriate form for the income variable if income displayed nonlinear growth. Whether on this interpretation it would also be sensible to include the term Δinc_t in the equation is something the reader might like to think about after considering Chapter 5 on *cointegration*.

However, the term $\Delta\Delta_4 inc_t$ may be given an economic rather than a statistical interpretation. Equation (3.7) implies that consumption this quarter is the same as in the corresponding quarter one year before, modified by β_1 times the change in income over this same period. Under the Permanent Income Hypothesis, for β_1 to be positive it must be that some of this increase in income is treated as an increase in permanent income. Suppose that this change in income is larger than the change in income on an annual basis experienced in the previous quarter, that is, suppose $\Delta\Delta_4 inc_t$ is positive. Then if the consumer considers this extra rise to be transitory income, the consumer will reduce consumption from the level implied by treating the whole of the income increase as permanent. The converse argument would hold where $\Delta\Delta_4 inc_t$ was negative. Thus, on the grounds of economic theory, β_2 may be expected to be negative.

The results of estimating equation (3.7) are given in Section 3.7 under MODEL 3.5. On statistical grounds, this represents an improvement over both MODELS 3.3 and 3.4 in explaining aggregate consumption. The coefficients on the income variables are statistically significant and carry their expected signs under the Permanent Income Hypothesis. The parameter constancy tests do not signal the problems that were encountered earlier. Figure 3.6 displays the confidence intervals for the forecasts which invariably include the realized values. The seasonal differencing introduced to model the seasonal pattern of the data is at least as successful as the use of seasonal dummy variables. The main statistical qualification to the foregoing is the rather low value for the Durbin-Watson statistic. This implies that caution should be exercised on any statements about statistical significance, and could indicate that some important variables may have been omitted from the analysis.

Equation (3.7) is a restricted or *specific* case of a more *general* model. Equation (3.7) can be written as:

$$cons_t = cons_{t-4} + (\beta_1 + \beta_2)inc_t - (\beta_1 + \beta_2)inc_{t-4} - \beta_2 inc_{t-1} + \beta_2 inc_{t-5}$$
$$+ \beta_3 DO_t - \beta_3 DO_{t-4} + \varepsilon_t \quad .$$

This a restricted form of the general equation: *Model 3.6*

$$cons_t = \theta_1 cons_{t-4} + \theta_2 inc_t + \theta_3 inc_{t-4} + \theta_4 inc_{t-1} + \theta_5 inc_{t-5}$$
$$+ \theta_6 DO_t + \theta_7 DO_{t-4} + \varepsilon_t \quad , \tag{3.10}$$

with restrictions:

$$\theta_1 = 1 \ , \quad \theta_2 = -\theta_3 \ , \quad \theta_4 = -\theta_5 \ \text{ and } \ \theta_6 = -\theta_7 \ .$$

Fig. 3.6: Prediction from MODEL 3.5

—forecast →actual

MODEL 3.6 in Section 3.7 gives the results of fitting the unrestricted equation (3.10). The coefficient on lagged consumption is close to unity. The signs on income and income lagged four periods are approximately equal but opposite in sign, as are the coefficients on income lagged one and five periods, and the special events variable lagged one and four periods. Generally, we may conclude that the unrestricted and restricted estimates are quite close, so that on the grounds of statistical efficiency, equation (3.7) which is the restricted form of equation (3.10) would be preferred. Formal tests for restrictions on models such as these will be presented in Chapter 4.

Apart from the questionable value for the Durbin-Watson statistic noted above, there is a major reason to feel unhappy with equation (3.7). This equation can be rejected on the grounds of economic theory rather than statistical diagnostic testing.

The economic theories considered in Section 3.2 were 'steady state' or long run theories. That is, they related economic variables in situations where any adjustments of the consumer units to positions of disequilibrium were assumed to have been completed. Economic models should have sensible interpretations for both situations of *static equilibrium*, where the variables are assumed to be unchanging between periods, and for *stable equilibrium*, where all variables are changing at some constant rate.

It can be seen immediately that equation (3.7) has no static equilibrium solution. In the long run, the special effects variable DO_t may be ignored. For static equilibrium, $cons_t = cons_{t-4}$ and $inc_t = inc_{t-4}$, so that $\Delta_4 cons_t = \Delta_4 inc_t = \Delta\Delta_4 inc_t = 0$. In this situation, equation (3.7) reduces to the uninformative result:

$$0 = \beta_1 \cdot 0 + \beta_2 \cdot 0 \ ,$$

which is not a long run relationship between consumption and income.

In order to consider whether equation (3.7) has a stable equilibrium solution, assume that both consumption and income are growing at a constant rate of $100 \cdot g\%$ per annum. Provided g is not bigger than about 0.2, the seasonal differences $\Delta_4 cons_t$ and $\Delta_4 inc_t$ will closely approximate g (see Cryer (1986, p.95)). Thus we may take $\Delta_4 cons_t = \Delta_4 inc_t = g$ so that consequently, $\Delta\Delta_4 inc_t = 0$. The 'long run' version of MODEL 3.5 may be written as:

$$\Delta_4 cons_t = 0.674 \cdot \Delta_4 inc_t \ ,$$

which implies a long run income elasticity of only 0.674, which is well below the unitary value called for by the economic theories considered earlier. It is not possible to solve MODEL 3.5 for a stable equilibrium solution as substituting g into the equation above gives:

$$g = 0.674 \cdot g \ .$$

The conclusion is that the model represented by equation (3.7) and estimated as MODEL 3.5 is useful in reflecting short run behaviour only. This model fails to generate plausible long run properties of the relationship between consumption and income.

DHSY considered that what was needed was a model which would generate a long run unitary income elasticity of consumption. As the economic theories considered earlier suggested a long run proportionality between consumption and income, the long run solution should be of the form:

$$CONS_t = K \cdot INC_t \ ,$$

where K is a constant for any given growth rate, so that the long run ratio of consumption to income (the APC) is also constant.

Equation (3.7) explained the current level of consumption expenditure in terms of adjustments made to consumption for the corresponding quarter one year before. Suppose that one year ago the consumer did not experience an APC of K. That is, suppose:

$$\frac{CONS_{t-4}}{INC_{t-4}} \neq K \quad \text{or} \quad (cons_{t-4} - inc_{t-4}) \neq ln\, K \quad .$$

If this ratio was greater than K, then in order to try to get back to a long run equilibrium path, the consumer in period t will reduce its consumption relative to $CONS_{t-4}$ and *vice versa* for a ratio smaller than K. Hence, it is worthwhile considering adding a term $(cons_{t-4} - inc_{t-4})$ to equation (3.7), yielding:

$$\Delta_4 cons_t = \beta_1 \Delta_4 inc_t + \beta_2 \Delta\Delta_4 inc_t + \beta_3 \Delta_4 DO_t$$
$$+ \beta_4 (cons_{t-4} - inc_{t-4}) + \varepsilon_t \qquad (3.11)$$

error correction

where β_4 is expected to be negative.

Through this new term, the consumer is seen as attempting to correct a short run disequilibrium position. Accordingly, equation (3.11) is said to contain an *error correction mechanism*, represented by the term $(cons_{t-4} - inc_{t-4})$.

Equation (3.11) represents a marked theoretical improvement over the models considered earlier in that it has both static and stable equilibrium solutions.

For static equilibrium, the equation solves as:

$$\beta_4 (cons_{t-4} - inc_{t-4}) = 0 \quad ,$$

and as in general, $\beta_4 \neq 0$, then:

$$cons_t = inc_t \quad ,$$

which implies a long run unitary income elasticity of consumption.

For stable equilibrium, where consumption and income are growing at a constant rate g, the model solves as:

$$g = \beta_1 g + \beta_4 (cons_{t-4} - inc_{t-4}) \quad , \quad \text{or:}$$

$$cons_{t-4} = inc_{t-4} + \frac{g \cdot (1 - \beta_1)}{\beta_4} \quad .$$

The long run consumption function can then be written as:

$$CONS_t = \psi \cdot INC_t \quad , \qquad (3.12)$$

where $\psi = \exp\left\{ \frac{g \cdot (1 - \beta_1)}{\beta_4} \right\} \quad .$

Equation (3.12) exhibits a unitary elasticity as required. As $\beta_4 < 0$, the long run *APC* in equation (3.12) is inversely related to the rate of growth, g, a finding consistent with inter-country evidence (Davidson *et al.* (1978, p.681)).

The results of fitting equation (3.11) are given under MODEL 3.7 in Section 3.7. All coefficients are statistically significant and carry their expected signs under the theory outlined above. However, the model fails the tests of parameter constancy at the 1% level of significance, and some realizations lie outside the confidence intervals for forecasts, especially towards the end of the forecast period as can be seen in Figure 3.7. As the Durbin-Watson statistic lies in the indeterminate range (5% level), all statements regarding statistical significance must be treated with caution.

Fig. 3.7: Prediction from MODEL 3.7

Compared with the sample period, the post sample period experienced much higher rates of inflation. *DHSY* considered that the continuing relatively poor performance of their model in the forecast or post sample period might have been due to the omission of inflation effects. As the model is estimated using variables measured in real terms, what is envisaged are possible effects of price changes not seen as being immediately reflected in money income changes. Such effects could work either to increase or reduce real consumption from what it otherwise would have been.

There could be a 'money illusion' effect (Branson and Klevorick (1969)) if consumers do not notice the increase in prices, but interpret a rise in money income as an increase in real income. This would imply a positive coefficient on a price change variable introduced into equation (3.11).

Alternatively, Deaton (1977) has argued that inflation is often unanticipated, with consumers interpreting the price rises of goods they typically purchase as relative price increases rather than as a general rise in the aggregate price level. This may be the case particularly when inflation is accelerating. The response of consumers to unanticipated inflation viewed in this way would be to reduce their real consumption, leading to what Deaton has termed 'involuntary saving through unanticipated inflation'.

To allow for these potential inflation effects, and to be consistent with the terms already in equation (3.11), Davidson *et al.* (1978) estimated an equation of the form:

$$\Delta_4 cons_t = \beta_1 \Delta_4 inc_t + \beta_2 \Delta\Delta_4 inc_t + \beta_3 \Delta_4 DO_t$$
$$+ \beta_4 (cons_{t-4} - inc_{t-4}) + \beta_5 inf_t + \beta_6 \Delta inf_t + \varepsilon_t \quad , \quad (3.13)$$

where the rate of inflation is approximated by $inf_t = \Delta_4 p_t$, and where p_t is the natural logarithm of the implicit price deflator used to construct the series on $CONS_t$. This is the final form of the *DHSY* model for aggregate consumption expenditure that we shall consider. Under the Deaton hypothesis, if inflation is unanticipated β_5 will be negative, and if inflation is both accelerating and unanticipated, then β_6 will also be negative.

MODEL 3.8 in Section 3.7 reports the estimation of equation (3.13) for the sample period. The Durbin-Watson statistic has increased in value compared with MODEL 3.7, and is now above the upper bound value for the test. Both parameter constancy tests now imply that the null hypothesis of no parameter value changes between the sample and post sample periods cannot be rejected. Figure 3.8 shows that there is good agreement between model forecasts and realizations, with the realizations falling within the 95% confidence limits for the forecasts. With a constant rate of growth of real income and a constant rate of inflation, the model has a stable equilibrium solution of the required form.

3.5 Methodological Aspects of *DHSY* Modelling

One of the implications of data mining was that an investigator would almost certainly end up with a model that, superficially at least, seemed consistent with the theory postulated and which received support from the data. The corollary is that for any widely researched area, the potential exists for the coexistence of many such alternative models. This is clearly unfortunate. Though not linking the large number of alternative empirical models of aggregate consumption expenditure specifically to data mining, *DHSY* did regard the existence of a 'plethora of substantially different quarterly equations' (Davidson *et al.* (1978, p.661)) estimated from essentially the same data sets and reflecting similar theories as representing a serious weakness of traditional methodology.

Fig. 3.8: Prediction from MODEL 3.8

— forecast ✦ consumption

They suggested that a minimal requirement of any new model should be that it could explain why previous researchers got their results, as well as providing some explanation of something that previous models did not. New models should be interpretable within an explicit (economic) theoretical framework, and be consistent with the properties of the observed data. The major innovation here is the requirement to be able to explain, or incorporate, previous research findings. This is not a trivial task. In the *DHSY* study, this problem was approached by first standardizing three rival models so that they reflected common data sets, methods of seasonal adjustment and other data transformations, and functional forms. Second, a general model was constructed which contained the three alternative models as special cases. Technically, the three models were *nested* within a general model, so that each individual model was a specific or special case of this general model. Statistical tests were then used to determine whether the constraints on the general model necessary to give rise to a specific model were supported by the data. The initial *DHSY* model considered above (equation (3.7)) was the result of just this procedure. The idea that one should start with a general model and progressively simplify it by means of significance tests is also central to the *DHSY* approach to building a particular model, as well as the model choice or selection problem outlined above.

When one model can explain or account for the behaviour or performance of another rival model, the former model is said to *encompass* the latter. Clearly, a general model should encompass a restricted or nested form of the model. However, if the restrictions cannot be rejected, the 'parsimonious' or restricted model would be preferred because data limitations favour the estimation of the simplest acceptable model. The encompassing principle is not limited to the case of nested models. Procedures exist which allow separate rival models to be compared where neither model can be obtained as a special case of the other. Chapter 8 will explore the encompassing principle in more detail, and consider some tests proposed for non-nested models.

Economic theorists have tended to concentrate on developing theories that explain static or long run relationships between economic variables. In Section 3.4 above, for example, it was considered important that from the point of view of established theory, an estimated consumption function should exhibit a long run unitary income elasticity of consumption. *Cointegration* analysis is concerned with the development of tests relevant for investigating long run relationships, and will be discussed in detail in Chapter 5.

Theorists are normally silent on the short run dynamics of their models, such as the lag lengths appropriate for each of the variables. An approach to modelling short run dynamics was proposed in Davidson *et al.* (1978, p.680) and has been developed by Hendry (1979). An 'overparametized' model is defined which contains more lags than are expected to be necessary. The model is then reduced in scale by a sequence of statistical tests. One advantage of this approach is that the significance level for the sequence of tests is known (see Section 4.5 below). This is in contrast with approaches which start with 'simple' models that are successively made more complicated by the addition of new variables or longer lag lengths on existing variables in response to various diagnostic tests. In the Davidson *et al.* (1978) paper, these short run dynamics were modelled through an error correction mechanism, which allowed consumption to return to its long run growth path following a disturbance which took it from this path.

Starting with a general model and subjecting it to a sequence of tests of restrictions to determine if there is an acceptable specific model is termed *general to specific* modelling. A simple example was given in Section 3.4 where restricted and unrestricted versions of equation (3.10) were compared. Further applications of this principle to the *DHSY* model will be considered in Chapter 4.

It would be wrong to see the *DHSY* model as representing a complete break from the Cowles Commission methodology considered in Chapter 1. There we listed and explained five assumptions of this methodology, namely

1. *A priori* restrictions;
2. Time invariance of parameters;
3. Parameter invariance with respect to changes in variables;
4. Known causal ordering;
5. No verification against rival models.

Only in respect of the fifth of these assumptions did Davidson *et al.* (1978) attempt to move away from the Cowles Commission framework. The paper contained several ideas which have subsequently been developed and represented an example of what 'best practice' econometrics could achieve within the confines of traditional methodology. The *DHSY* model is not entirely free from data mining, as the inflation effects were added to correct for an observed weakness of that model. Some data mining is inevitable in any applied study. However, in this case, the development of the model was the outcome of a systematic and directed testing of a sequence of models constrained throughout by the requirements of what was considered to be a relevant economic theory. In so far as this approach was decidedly uncommon, the results carried conviction.

3.6 Testing for Parameter Constancy

Two important assumptions of the Cowles Commission methodology were that the parameters in any model formulated to describe an economic relationship should be constant over time and should be invariant to alterations in the distribution of the variables that make up the model. Chapter 7 will introduce the concept of *structural invariance* which is concerned with the second of these questions.

With respect to the time constancy of parameters, we have already introduced the *Forecast Chi*^{2} and *Chow* tests to compare the performance of a model between the sample and post sample (or forecast) periods. Whilst these are useful guides to parameter constancy, it would also be advantageous to consider the stability of the parameters in the sample period, and to be able to identify specific points within the sample and/or post sample periods where a structural break in the model may have occurred. Three diagnostic tools relevant for such inquiries are the plots of *recursive least squares coefficients, one-step residuals* and *scaled recursive Chow test statistics*.

(a) Recursive Least Squares Coefficients

As interest is on the behaviour of the parameters of the model over time, an obvious starting point would be to plot each estimated coefficient against time. That is, starting from the small sub sample of $t = 1, 2, ..., n$, where $n \geq k$, estimate the k parameters of the model by ordinary least squares. Then extend the sample period by one observation to $t = 1, 2, ..., n+1$, and re-estimate the model. Continue this procedure until the estimation period is the complete sample $t = 1, 2, ..., T$. For each regression, the values of the coefficients may be plotted against the latest time period in the sample used for the estimation of that regression.

Formally, let X_t represent the $t \times k$ matrix of observations on the k independent variables, and x_t be the tth row of X_t (that is, the observations on the independent variables at time t). Let y_t^* be the $t \times 1$ vector of observations and y_t be the observation at time t, on the dependent variable. Then the *OLS* estimator of the $k \times 1$ vector of parameters, β_t, in the relation:

$$y_t = x'_t \cdot \beta_t + u_t \quad , \quad t \geq n \quad ,$$

is: $\hat{\beta}_t = (X'_t \cdot X_t)^{-1} \cdot X'_t \cdot y^*_t$.

This vector of estimated coefficients is calculated sequentially for $t = n$, then $t = n + 1$, up to $t = T$, by rolling forward the data admitted to the sample one period at a time. Updating (or *recursive*) formulae exist which allow for the re-estimation of $\hat{\beta}_t$ when a new period is added to the sample without the need to recompute the inverse of $(X'_t \cdot X_t)$ each time. Hence, these least squares estimates are called *recursive least squares* coefficients.

As an illustration, consider the recursive least squares estimation of the coefficients of the concluding *DHSY* model (equation (3.13)) considered in Section 3.5, using the same sample period, 1958(2) to 1970(4). For computational reasons, the variable DO_t will be omitted from the analysis. (Students should try to work out why this is necessary.)

Time paths of the coefficients in the model are presented in Figures 3.9 to 3.13. The initial instability of the parameter estimates for all the variables simply reflects the small number of observations used to estimate them at the start of the recursions.

As can be seen, the coefficients on $\Delta_4 inc_t$, $(cons_{t-4} - inc_{t-4})$ and inf_t remain relatively stable over the sample period. The coefficients for both $\Delta\Delta_4 inc_t$ and Δinf_t are less stable, however, taking positive values around 1963/64 before becoming negative. MODEL 3.9 in Section 3.7 gives the *OLS* estimates for the last recursion, using the full sample data. MODEL 3.9 is thus the same as MODEL 3.8 but with the variable DO_t omitted. There is little difference between the parameter estimates of these two equations. For future reference, MODEL 3.10 gives the results when the entire sample and post sample data are used.

(b) One-Step Residuals
At each recursion, an *OLS* residual for the last period in the sample, $\tilde{v}_t$, can be obtained as:

$$\tilde{v}_t = y_t - x'_t \cdot \hat{\beta}_t \quad .$$

From the set of such residuals available at time t, the standard error of the regression, $\hat{\sigma}_t = \left[\dfrac{\sum \tilde{v}_t^2}{t - k} \right]^{1/2}$, may be calculated.

RLS Coefficients: MODEL 3.8

Fig. 3.9: *d4li*

Fig. 3.10: *dd4li*   **Fig. 3.11:** *lc_li_4*

Fig. 3.12: *inf*   **Fig. 3.13:** *dinf*

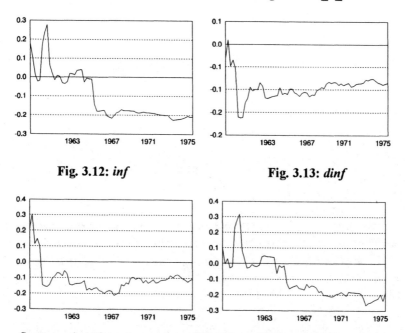

Suppose that there is a structural break somewhere within the sample period. Then the coefficients of the model should be relatively stable for successive recursions until that point is reached. Similarly, the residual calculated for the last period in each sample used in a recursion should be of the same order of magnitude as those that preceded it. Once the break point is reached, however, the residual calculated for this period is likely to appear abnormal compared with the other residuals, as the model will provide a poor fit for the break period.

Thus another guide to parameter constancy in a model is provided by plotting the residual for the last period in the sample used for the recursion against time. This residual is termed a *one-step residual*. The plot also includes error bands of $\pm 2 \cdot \hat{\sigma}_t$ around zero. Values of one-step residuals which lie outside these bands are suggestive of either 'outlier' (or exceptional) values for y_t or of some alteration in the structural parameters of the model.

Figure 3.14 shows the plot of the one-step residuals for MODEL 3.9. It can be seen, for example, that there may have been a structural break in the model in the first quarter of 1965 as for this period, the recursive one-step residual lies outside the error band. There are similar breaks in the first quarters of 1966 and 1971.

Fig. 3.14: One-step residuals: MODEL 3.9

(c) Scaled Recursive Chow Test
A test for the statistical significance of a possible break is provided by a *recursive Chow test*. If the residual sum of squares for the model fitted by *OLS* up to and including period $t-1$ is *RSS*, and if the corresponding residual sum of squares for the model fitted up to and including period t is RSS^*, then the Chow test statistic is calculated as:

$$Chow_t = \frac{(RSS^* - RSS)}{RSS / (t-k)} \ .$$

Under the null hypothesis that there has been no structural change in the model between periods $t-1$ and t, this statistic has the F distribution with 1 and $t-k$ degrees of freedom. This statistic can be calculated for each recursion and plotted against time. As the statistic and the critical values of F are functions of t, it is useful to divide the *Chow* value by its 5% critical value from the tables of F to yield a *scaled recursive Chow test* for each recursion. Hence, the statistic plotted in Figure 3.15 is:

$$\frac{Chow_t}{F_{0.05}(1, \ t-k)} \ ,$$

which under the null hypothesis should be less than unity. Values of this statistic greater than unity imply that the null of no structural change between periods $t-1$ and t would be rejected at the 5% level of significance.

Figure 3.15 indicates that the earlier suggestion of a structural break in the model in the first quarter of 1965 is supported by a statistically significant scaled *Chow* test value. There are also significant values for the first quarters of 1966 and 1971 which clearly correspond to the substantial negative values of the one-step residuals for these periods shown in Figure 3.14.

Fig 3.15: Scaled recursive Chow test MODEL 3.9

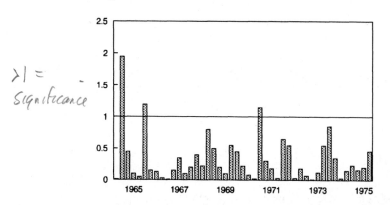

Many books and articles use a further set of residuals to test for parameter constancy. It is important not to confuse the tests above with those based on what are called recursive residuals. From any recursion, one could calculate a *one-step-ahead prediction error* (or *innovation*) for period t as:

$$v_t = y_t - x_t' \cdot \hat{\beta}_{t-1} \ ,$$

by using the parameter vector estimated from the data up to and including $t-1$. These residuals can be shown to be unbiased and uncorrelated, but heteroscedastic. When each residual is divided by a term proportional to the square root of its variance, the result is termed a *standardized innovation* or *recursive residual*.

3.7 Stylized Computer Output (*PC-GIVE*)

Simple form of Absolute Income Hypothesis
MODEL 3.1: Modelling CONS by OLS (equation (3.1) in text)
The present sample is: 1958 (2) to 1975 (4) less 20 forecasts
The forecast period is: 1971 (1) to 1975 (4)

$$Cons = \alpha + \beta Inc + \varepsilon$$

Variable	Coefficient	Std.Error	t-value	HCSE
Constant	981.08	243.12	4.035	249.81
INC	0.7284	0.0320	22.78	0.0339

$R^2 = 0.9137465$ F(1, 49) = 519.09 [0.0000] σ = 180.86 DW = 2.24
RSS = 1602807.863 for 2 variables and 51 observations

Tests of parameter constancy over: 1971 (1) to 1975 (4)
Forecast Chi^2 (20) = 84.551 [0.0000] **
Chow F(20, 49) = 2.4583 [0.0054] **

Simple form of Permanent Income Hypothesis
MODEL 3.2: Modelling CONS by OLS (equation (3.6) in text with an intercept)
The present sample is: 1958 (2) to 1975 (4) less 20 forecasts
The forecast period is: 1971 (1) to 1975 (4)

$$Cons_t = \beta_1 Cons_{t-1} + \beta_2 Inc_t + \varepsilon$$

Variable	Coefficient	Std.Error	t-value	HCSE
Constant	1277.9	257.30	4.966	289.88
CONS_1	-0.2073	0.0803	-2.581	0.0680
INC	0.8656	0.0612	14.15	0.0481

problematic

$R^2 = 0.9242611$ F(2, 48) = 292.88 [0.0000] σ = 171.235 DW = 1.84
RSS = 1407420.329 for 3 variables and 51 observations

Tests of parameter constancy over: 1971 (1) to 1975 (4)
Forecast Chi^2 (20) = 93.696 [0.0000] **
Chow F(20, 48) = 2.2328 [0.0118] *

Absolute Income Hypothesis with trend and dummies
MODEL 3.3: Modelling CONS by OLS

equation p.34

the present sample is: 1958 (2) to 1975 (4) less 20 forecasts
the forecast period is: 1971 (1) to 1975 (4)

Variable	Coefficient	Std.Error	t-value	HCSE
Constant	3748.8	222.29	16.864	260.42
INC	0.3008	0.0362	8.299	0.0422
Seasonal	-397.98	43.210	-9.210	41.117
Seasonal_1	-211.11	36.700	-5.752	39.396
Seasonal_2	-184.54	36.242	-5.092	31.039
Trend	23.417	2.0495	11.426	2.3114
DT	-5.8448	1.1828	-4.941	1.0186
DT1	-2.2435	1.1094	-2.022	1.3196
DT2	-0.8448	1.0914	-0.774	0.9347
DO *spec. effect*	48.087	32.654	1.473	26.180

$R^2 = 0.9961798$ F(9, 41) = 1187.9 [0.0000] σ = 41.6106 DW = 1.81
RSS = 70989.10186 for 10 variables and 51 observations

Tests of parameter constancy over: 1971 (1) to 1975 (4)

Forecast Chi^2(20)= 121.9 [0.0000] **
Chow F(20, 41) = 3.5938 [0.0003] **

Permanent Income Hypothesis with trend and dummies
MODEL 3.4: Modelling CONS by OLS
The present sample is: 1958 (2) to 1975 (4)
The forecast period is: 1971 (1) to 1975 (4)

Variable	Coefficient	Std.Error	t-value	HCSE
Constant	2755.2	506.38	5.441	544.57
CONS_1	0.2727	0.1261	2.163	0.1362
INC	0.2253	0.0493	4.572	0.0518
Seasonal	-486.70	58.280	-8.351	62.883
Seasonal_1	-118.95	55.061	-2.16	62.547
Seasonal_2	-190.26	36.739	-5.179	35.244
Trend	17.024	3.5485	4.797	3.9378
DT	-6.0410	1.1367	-5.314	1.1273
DT1	-1.6199	1.1012	-1.471	1.3214
DT2	-0.2894	1.0766	-0.269	1.0960
DO	75.543	33.760	2.238	20.425

$R^2 = 0.99658$ F(10, 40) = 1165.5 [0.0000] σ = 39.8616 DW = 2.09
RSS = 63557.79132 for 11 variables and 51 observations

Tests of parameter constancy over : 1971 (1) to 1975 (4)

Forecast Chi^2(20) = 125.03[0.0000] **
Chow F(20, 40) = 3.2765[0.0007] **

(**WARNING**: Please note that the explanatory variables in MODEL 3.4 display quite a high degree of multicollinearity, and that some versions of *PC-GIVE* will not compute these results. The results in the table above were computed from *PC-GIVE* version 8.0. Difficulties may be experienced with version 8.1)

P 38
P (3.7)

Introducing logarithms and differences
MODEL 3.5: Modelling d4lc by OLS (equation (3.7) in text)
The present sample is: 1958 (2) to 1975 (4) less 20 forecasts
The forecast period is: 1971 (1) to 1975 (4)

Variable	Coefficient	Std.Error	t-value	HCSE
d4li	0.674000	0.0339624	19.845	0.0308935
d4DO	0.007691	0.0047491	1.619	0.0038933
dd4li	-0.265817	0.0593472	-4.479	0.0660308

$R^2 = 0.8933373$ $\sigma = 0.008868546$ DW = 1.03
* R^2 does NOT allow for the mean *
RSS = 0.0037752535916 for 3 variables and 51 observations

Tests of parameter constancy over: 1971 (1) to 1975 (4)

Forecast $\text{Chi}^2(20)=$ 22.11 [0.3346]
Chow F(20, 48) = 1.0099 [0.4690]

P-39
P (3.10)

Unrestricted version of MODEL 3.5
MODEL 3.6 Modelling lc by OLS (equation (3.10) in text)
The present sample is: 1958 (2) to 1975 (4) less 20 forecasts
The forecast period is: 1971 (1) to 1975 (4)

Variable	Coefficient	Std.Error	t-value	HCSE
lc_4	0.999125	0.0323817	30.86	0.0295100
li	0.302992	0.0541476	5.596	0.0607858
li_1	0.148182	0.0492374	3.010	0.0456960
li_4	-0.280538	0.0531150	-5.282	0.0631281
li_5	-0.168649	0.0486789	-3.465	0.0419204
DO	0.009426	0.0050360	1.872	0.0022949
DO_4	-0.007708	0.0046553	-1.656	0.0018907

$R^2 = 0.9999995$ $\sigma = 0.006468832$ DW = 1.68
* R^2 does NOT allow for the mean *
RSS = 0.0018412149296 for 7 variables and 51 observations

Tests of parameter constancy over: 1971(1) to 1975(4)

Forecast $\text{Chi}^2 (20) = 59.725[0.0000]$ **
Chow F(20, 44) = 2.2392[0.0130] *

Error-correction model
MODEL 3.7: Modelling d4lc by OLS (equation (3.11) in text)
The present sample is: 1958 (2) to 1975 (4) less 20 forecasts
The forecast period is: 1971 (1) to 1975 (4)

P 42 (3.11)

Variable	Coefficient	Std.Error	t-value	HCSE
d4li	0.507478	0.0367877	13.795	0.0386359
dd4li	-0.174524	0.0466681	-3.740	0.0401210
lc_li_4	-0.056120	0.0089799	-6.250	0.0087067
d4DO	0.008267	0.0035480	2.330	0.0018165

$R^2 = 0.941746$ $\sigma = 0.006623395$ DW = 1.58
* R^2 does NOT allow for the mean *
RSS = 0.0020618599435 for 4 variables and 51 observations

Tests of parameter constancy over: 1971 (1) to 1975 (4)

Forecast $Chi^2(20)$= 76.126 [0.0000] **
Chow F(20, 47) = 2.7862 [0.0020] **

Error-correction and inflation
p44 (3.13)

MODEL 3.8: Modelling d4lc by OLS (equation (3.13) in text)
The present sample is: 1958 (2) to 1975 (4) less 20 forecasts
The forecast period is: 1971 (1) to 1975 (4)

Variable	Coefficient	Std.Error	t-value	HCSE
d4li	0.496387	0.0401386	12.367	0.0343748
dd4li	-0.214160	0.0510585	-4.194	0.0374750
lc_li_4	-0.084311	0.0230297	-3.661	0.0197156
d4DO	0.007561	0.0033316	2.269	0.0014472
inf	-0.101365	0.0728136	-1.392	0.0675699
dinf	-0.193429	0.1149830	-1.682	0.1040440

$R^2 = 0.9510961$ $\sigma = 0.006202008$ DW = 1.74
* R^2 does NOT allow for the mean *
RSS = 0.00173092063 for 6 variables and 51 observations
Tests of parameter constancy over: 1971 (1) to 1975 (4)

Forecast $Chi^2(20)$= 23.174 [0.2803]
Chow F(20, 45) = 1.0789 [0.4020]

Testing for parameter constancy: recursive least squares
MODEL 3.9: Modelling d4lc by RLS, variable DO omitted
The present sample is: 1958 (2) to 1975 (4) less 20 forecasts
The forecast period is: 1971 (1) to 1975 (4)

Variable	Coefficient	Std.Error	t-value	HCSE
d4li	0.499163	0.0418907	11.916	0.0382439
dd4li	-0.186471	0.0517676	-3.602	0.0448798
lc_li_4	-0.084580	0.0240458	-3.517	0.0223405

inf	-0.104316	0.0760153	-1.372	0.0724393
dinf	-0.208234	0.1198650	-1.737	0.1125600

$R^2 = 0.9454991$ $\sigma = 0.006475747$ DW = 1.96
* R^2 does NOT allow for the mean *
RSS = 0.0019290236086 for 5 variables and 51 observations

Tests of parameter constancy over: 1971 (1) to 1975 (4)

Forecast $Chi^2(20)$= 23.767 [0.2527]
Chow F(20, 46) = 1.1451 [0.3417]

As MODEL 3.9, but estimated for the entire sample: 1958:2 - 1975: 4
MODEL 3.10: Modelling d4lc by RLS
The present sample is: 1958 (2) to 1975 (4)

Variable	Coefficient	Std.Error	t-value	HCSE
d4li	0.494884	0.0313028	15.810	0.2777270
dd4li	-0.210731	0.0417670	-5.045	0.0340274
lc_li_4	-0.087091	0.0130465	-6.675	0.0122981
inf	-0.112609	0.0243328	-4.628	0.0220772
dinf	-0.235723	0.0932488	-2.528	0.1034480

$R^2 = 0.9455928$ $\sigma = 0.00661662$ DW = 2.22
* R^2 does NOT allow for the mean *
RSS = 0.0028894571761 for 5 variables and 71 observations

3.8 Suggestions for Further Reading

The economic theory which underlies the Absolute and Permanent Income Hypotheses is discussed in various macroeconomic textbooks (for example Levačić and Rebmann (1982) or Gapinski (1982). More advanced theoretical and empirical analysis on the Permanent Income Hypothesis is given in Hall (1978), Flavin (1981), Christious, Eichenbaum and Marshall (1991), and Campbell and Mankiw (1990, 1991).

The literature on the *DHSY* model and its predecessors and followers is quite voluminous. The *DHSY* model itself represented the development of an earlier model of aggregate demand by Hendry (1974). Among later works, that of Hendry and von Ungern-Sternberg (1980) which developed the *DHSY* model with a redefined income variable should be mentioned. Patterson (1986) has presented an analogue to the *DHSY* model based on annual rather than quarterly data, and investigated its structural stability through tests based on recursive residuals. Hendry, Muellbauer and Murphy (1990) have reconsidered the *DHSY* model from the perspective of ten years advancement in econometrics. Hendry (1993) gives numerous examples of further developments of consumption function modelling.

Recursive least squares estimation and inference into stability testing, developed originally by Brown, Durbin and Evans (1975), is now included in most contemporary econometric textbooks. Particularly popular are the CUSUM and CUSUMSQ tests (for example see Johnston (1984, pp. 384-392), or Harvey (1990, pp. 153-154)). An example of the use of these tests is Deadman and Ghatak (1981). A generalization of the CUSUM test to include models containing lagged dependent variables has been given by Kramer, Ploberger and Alt (1988). These tests can be regarded as analogous to the scaled recursive Chow test presented in this chapter. Pesaran, Smith and Yeo (1985) give a review of various tests of structural stability. Examples of the use of recursive estimation analysis are Charemza and Ghatak (1990), and especially Hendry and Ericsson (1991).

Chapter 4

General to Specific Modelling

4.1 Autoregressive Distributed Lag Modelling

One of the main methodological innovations of the Davidson *et al.* (1978) approach to modelling consumption (see Chapter 3) was that a 'good' empirical econometric model could be developed by starting from a relatively large, general model and by gradually reducing its size and transforming the variables through the testing of various linear and nonlinear restrictions. Let us reconsider equations (3.7) and (3.10) from Chapter 3. We said that equation (3.10) was a *general* one, without any restrictions on parameters and (3.7) was a *specific* one. That is, equation (3.7) could be derived from equation (3.10) by imposing various restrictions on the parameters in equation (3.10). After estimation, we compared the results for (3.10) (MODEL 3.6 in Section 3.7) with that for (3.7) (MODEL 3.5) and concluded that because the unrestricted estimates seemed quite close to those implied by the restrictions, the specific model was a valid one, in that it did not contradict the general model.

In this chapter we present a detailed discussion of *general to specific* modelling. By general to specific modelling we mean the formulation of a fairly unrestricted dynamic model, herewith called a general model, which is subsequently tested, transformed and reduced in size by performing a number of tests for restrictions. A general model in a convenient notation is presented and sets of restrictions on this model which would eventually lead to economically interpretable models are discussed. We also describe how the validity of the restrictions imposed may be tested statistically, as the procedure applied in Chapter 3 (namely judging intuitively whether the restricted and unrestricted coefficients are 'close' or 'remote' from each other) is not statistically rigorous.

The general model is usually described in an *autoregressive distributed lag (ADL)* form. This means that a dependent variable y_t is expressed as a function of its own lagged values, and the current and lagged values of all explanatory variables. A straightforward notation for an *ADL* model uses the *lag operator* L^r, defined for a variable x_t as:

$$L^r x_t = x_{t-r} \ .$$

It is also convenient to use *scalar polynomials* in L:

$$\alpha(L) = \sum_{i=m}^{n} \alpha_i L^i \quad,$$

so that:

$$\alpha(L)x_t = \sum_{i=m}^{n} \alpha_i L^i x_t = \alpha_m x_{t-m} + \alpha_{m+1} x_{t-m-1} + \ldots + \alpha_n x_{t-n} \quad.$$

That is, $\alpha(L)x_t$ is a weighted sum of lagged values of a variable x_t up to the level of n. Normally m is zero or one but it may be negative if the notation is to be used for a model which includes leads as well as lags.

The simple first order autoregressive model:

$$y_t = \alpha y_{t-1} + \varepsilon_t \quad,$$

can be rewritten using the lag operator as:

$$(1 - \alpha L)y_t = \varepsilon_t \quad.$$

Also consider a finite distributed lag model:

$$y_t = \beta_0 x_t + \beta_1 x_{t-1} + \beta_2 x_{t-2} + \ldots + \beta_n x_{t-n} + \varepsilon_t \quad.$$

In the notation using the lag operator, this becomes:

$$y_t = b(L)x_t + \varepsilon_t \quad, \quad m = 0 \quad.$$

If lagged values of y_t are added to this distributed lag model, the result is called an *autoregressive distributed lag model*, and is denoted as:

$$y_t = a_1 y_{t-1} + a_2 y_{t-2} + \ldots + a_k y_{t-k} + \beta_0 x_t + \beta_1 x_{t-1} + \beta_2 x_{t-2} + \ldots + \beta_n x_{t-n} + \varepsilon_t \quad,$$

or, in the more concise notation using the polynomial lag operator:

$$a(L)y_t = b(L)x_t + \varepsilon_t \quad,$$

where:

$$a(L) = \sum_{i=0}^{k} a_i L^i \quad, \quad a_0 = 1 \quad, \quad a_i = -a_i \quad, \quad i = 1, 2, \ldots, k.$$

In order for the variable y_t to meet what are called 'stationarity conditions' (see Chapter 5 below), it is required that the roots of the lag polynomial $a(L)$ 'lie outside the unit circle'. That is, they are larger than one in absolute value (see Granger and Newbold (1986, pp. 6-10)).

For simplicity, it is often assumed that a general *ADL* model contains no leads (that is $m \geq 0$) and that the number of lags for all the variables is identical, so that in the equation above, $k = n$. For such a case the notation

ADL(k) denotes an autoregressive distributed lag model containing lags for all the variables up to the level of k. For an *ADL* model with unequal number of lags for each variable, the commonly used notation is $ADL(k_1, k_2,..., k_m)$; for example, an *ADL* model with three variables in which there are five lags imposed on the first two variables and two lags on the third would be written as *ADL*(5, 5, 2).

The lag polynomial notation may be generalized to include models with more than one explanatory variable, for instance where there are N right-hand side variables $x_{1t}, x_{2t},..., x_{Nt}$. One of these variables may be the intercept if required. The *ADL* model for this case may be denoted:

$$a(L)y_t = \sum_{i=1}^{N} b_i(L)x_{it} + \varepsilon_t \quad .$$

Consider a simple *ADL*(1) model with one explanatory variable:

$$y_t = \alpha_1 y_{t-1} + \beta_0 x_t + \beta_1 x_{t-1} + \varepsilon_t \quad . \tag{4.1}$$

This is in the form of:

$$a(L)y_t = b(L)x_t + \varepsilon_t \quad , \tag{4.2}$$

where:

$$a(L) = \sum_{i=0}^{1} a_i L^i \quad , \quad a_0 = 1 \quad , \quad a_1 = -\alpha_1 \quad , \quad b(L) = \sum_{i=0}^{1} \beta_i L^i \quad .$$

There are at least ten economically sensible specific models that can be derived from the general model (4.1) by the imposition of restrictions on the parameters α_1, β_0 and β_1. (For a more detailed discussion and generalization of this example see Hendry and Richard (1983) or Hendry, Pagan and Sargan (1984, pp. 1040- 1049).)

Eight out of the ten of these possible restrictions on (4.1) are straightforward:

1. $\alpha_1 = \beta_1 = 0$ static regression,
2. $\beta_0 = \beta_1 = 0$ first-order autoregressive process,
3. $\alpha_1 = \beta_0 = 0$ leading indicator equation,
4. $\alpha_1 = 1$, $\beta_0 = -\beta_1$ equation in first differences,
5. $\alpha_1 = 0$ first-order finite distributed lag equation,
6. $\beta_1 = 0$ partial adjustment equation,
7. $\beta_0 = 0$ 'dead-start' model, with lagged information only,
8. $\beta_1 = -\alpha_1$ proportional response model: the explanatory variables are x_t and $(y_{t-1} - x_{t-1})$.

Case 9 is algebraically more difficult to work out. We would like to derive an equation in first differences with an error-correction mechanism. In order to do so, subtract y_{t-1} from both sides of (4.1), and add and subtract $\beta_0 \cdot x_{t-1}$ to the right-hand side of (4.1). After some simplification this gives:

$$\Delta y_t = (\alpha_1 - 1)y_{t-1} + \beta_0 \Delta x_t + (\beta_0 + \beta_1)x_{t-1} + \varepsilon_t \ .$$

This equation contains an error-correction mechanism of the type $y_{t-1} - x_{t-1}$ (see Chapter 3) if the following restriction is fulfilled:

9. $\alpha_1 - 1 = -(\beta_0 + \beta_1)$.

The final restriction on the parameters of (4.1) which will be considered involves the concept of *common factors*. To introduce this concept, let λ_i be a root of a polynomial $a(L) = 0$. That is, it is a solution of the equation:

$$a(L) = \sum_{i=0}^{n} a_i L^i = 0 \ .$$

In addition, let δ_i be a root of a polynomial $b(L) = 0$, or:

$$b(L) = \sum_{i=0}^{s} b_i L^i = 0 \ .$$

If some λ_is coincide with δ_is, we say that the polynomials have *common factors*. In the context of *ADL* modelling one is often interested in a special case, where the *ADL* model:

$$a(L)y_t = b(L)x_t + \varepsilon_t \ ,$$

can be written down with the use of polynomial lag operators containing one common root:

$$a(L) = (1 - \rho L)a^*(L) \quad , \quad b(L) = (1 - \rho L)b^*(L) \quad ,$$

giving a model with first order autocorrelated disturbances:

$$a^*(L)y_t = b^*(L)x_t + u_t \ ,$$

where:

$$u_t = \rho u_{t-1} + \varepsilon_t \quad , \quad \text{or } u_t = (1 - \rho L)^{-1}\varepsilon_t \ .$$

The relevance of the common factor restriction can be illustrated by a simple static regression equation with first order autocorrelated disturbances:

$$y_t = \beta_0 x_t + u_t \ ,$$

where:

$$u_t = \rho u_{t-1} + \varepsilon_t \quad , \quad |\rho| < 1 \quad ,$$

which can also be rewritten as:

$$y_t = \beta_0 x_t + \rho y_{t-1} - \rho \cdot \beta_0 x_{t-1} + \varepsilon_t \quad ,$$

or as:

$$(1 - \rho L) \cdot y_t = \beta_0 (1 - \rho L) \cdot x_t + \varepsilon_t \quad ,$$

which is an *ADL*(1) model with a common factor.

This last equation is in fact a version of (4.1) with the nonlinear restriction:

10. $\beta_1 = -\alpha_1 \cdot \beta_0$, since ρ replaces α_1 .

Restriction 10 is usually called a *common factor* or *COMFAC* restriction. The importance of this result will be developed in Section 4.4 of this chapter. However, it is worth noting here that if restriction 10 is valid, then rather than estimate equation (4.1) with a nonlinear restriction, a simpler procedure would be to estimate the simple static regression model allowing for first order autocorrelated errors. If the restriction is rejected, then evidence of autocorrelation in the simple static equation reflects 'misspecified dynamics' in that the variables x_{t-1} and y_{t-1} have been erroneously omitted from this equation.

The examples above illustrate that there is a practically infinite number of specific models which are economically sensible which can be derived from a general autoregressive distributed lag model. The *ADL*(1) model alone covers at least ten important specific models, including one with serially correlated errors. This finding suggests a systematic way of developing a specific model which avoids the worst features of data mining. We should start from a sufficiently general *ADL* model and then gradually reduce its size by examining restrictions imposed on parameters.

4.2 Testing Restrictions

An important implication of Section 4.1 is that we must have a tool which can be used for testing whether or not the restrictions of interest which lead to a specific model are valid, or equivalently, whether or not the restrictions contradict the general model. Thus we want a statistical test of the null hypothesis that the restrictions imposed on the general model are true, or more precisely, that these restrictions cannot be rejected at a given level of significance. In some cases there is little problem. For instance, in equation (4.1) the test of any of the restrictions 5, 6 or 7 that $\alpha_1 = 0$, $\beta_1 = 0$ or $\beta_0 = 0$ can simply be performed with the use of the Student-*t* test. If the Student-*t* ratio indicates that the tested coefficient in the estimated general model is significantly different from zero, the restriction is not valid and the model cannot be simplified by dropping the corresponding variable. Also, joint tests for linear restrictions such as restrictions 1 to 4 in (4.1) can be performed with the use of the F test for linear restrictions, described in virtually all textbooks of econometric theory (for example Harvey (1990, p.64), Johnston (1984, pp. 182-189) or Kmenta (1986, pp. 416-422)). For m linear restrictions in a linear regression model with normal disturbances, T observations and k estimated parameters in the general (unrestricted) model, the well-known F test for the validity of these restrictions is:

$$F = \frac{(SSE_0 - SSE)/m}{SSE/(T-k)} \ ,$$

where SSE_0 stands for the residual sum of squares of the restricted model and SSE for the residual sum of squares of the unrestricted model. Under the null hypothesis that the linear restrictions imposed are true, the statistic has an F distribution with $(m, \ T-k)$ degrees of freedom (see Section 3.3).

However, the above test is not general enough to cover more complex restrictions which are likely to be imposed in the process of general to specific modelling. For instance, the *COMFAC* restriction 10, discussed in Section 4.1, is nonlinear and therefore cannot be tested with the use of the F statistic above.

Several tests have been suggested for testing both linear and nonlinear restrictions in a general econometric model. The most well known are the Likelihood Ratio, Wald and Lagrange Multiplier (score) tests. An intuitive account of the nature of these tests following Buse (1982) is given below.

Consider a simple null hypothesis relating to a single parameter θ of the form $\theta = \theta_0$. The alternative hypothesis is $\theta \neq \theta_0$. The maximum likelihood estimate of θ is the value which maximizes the likelihood function, given the set of sample data (for instance, see Freund and Walpole (1987, pp. 350-354)). That is, it is the value of θ which maximizes the probability of obtaining the observed data. We may call this value the unrestricted (or unconstrained) estimate of θ, and denote it as $\hat{\theta}$. Unless the unconstrained estimate is equal to θ_0, the value taken by the likelihood function using θ_0 as the value of the parameter will be lower than that using the unconstrained estimate. If $logL(\hat{\theta})$ and $logL(\theta_0)$ denote the values of the (natural) logarithms of the likelihood functions for $\hat{\theta}$ and θ_0 respectively, then the Likelihood Ratio (*LR*) statistic may be defined as:

$$LR = 2 \cdot (logL(\hat{\theta}) - logL(\theta_0)) \ .$$

This statistic has an asymptotic χ^2 distribution with one degree of freedom. 'Large' values of *LR* thus indicate substantial differences between the 'most likely' value for θ suggested by the sample data, and the value suggested by the null hypothesis, which is the rationale for rejecting the null hypothesis in such cases. For any specific difference between θ_0 and $\hat{\theta}$ the value of the *LR* statistic will depend on the degree of curvature of the loglikelihood function, and *vice versa*. This curvature may be measured by the absolute value of the change in the slope of the loglikelihood function, or $d^2 logL(\theta)/d\theta^2$.

The Wald (*W*) test weights the (squared) distance between θ_0 and $\hat{\theta}$ by the expected curvature of the loglikelihood function, or:

$$W = (\theta_0 - \hat{\theta})^2 \cdot I(\hat{\theta}) \ ,$$

where $I(\hat{\theta}) = -E(d^2 \log L(\theta)/d\theta^2)$ evaluated at $\theta = \hat{\theta}$. $I(\theta)$ is called the information matrix. *W* is asymptotically distributed as χ^2 with one degree of freedom, and as with the *LR* test, 'large' values of the test statistic will lead to rejection of the null hypothesis.

The Lagrange multiplier (*LM*) test also involves the curvature of the loglikelihood function, but in this case it is for the constrained rather than the unconstrained model. By definition, the slope of the loglikelihood function is zero at its maximum value. If θ_0 is 'close' to $\hat{\theta}$, then the slope at this point should be about zero. The *LM* test weights the (squared) slope of the loglikelihood function evaluated at $\theta = \theta_0$, denoted by $S(\theta_0)$ by the inverse of the curvature at this point. Since the greater is the curvature of the loglikelihood function at θ_0 the closer θ_0 will be to $\hat{\theta}$, the inverse of this curvature is taken so that values of the test statistic will be small when θ_0 is close to $\hat{\theta}$. Thus the *LM* statistic in this case is defined as:

$$LM = (S(\theta_0))^2 \cdot I(\theta_0)^{-1} \ ,$$

where as before, the expected value of the curvature is used, but where it is now evaluated at θ_0 rather than at $\hat{\theta}$. As with the Likelihood Ratio and Wald test statistics for this case, this statistic has an asymptotic χ^2 distribution with one degree of freedom. 'Large' values of *LM* leading to rejection of the null hypothesis will be obtained when the slope of the loglikelihood function at θ_0 differs markedly from zero.

The differences between the Likelihood Ratio, Wald and Lagrange Multiplier tests are illustrated in Figure 4.1 (adapted from Buse (1982)).

Fig. 4.1: Likelihood Ratio, Wald and Lagrange Multiplier tests

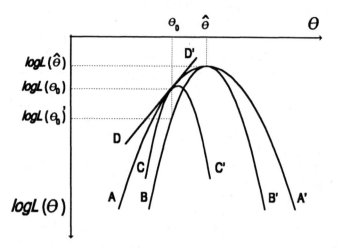

The curve AA′ represents a loglikelihood function for a parameter θ denoted as $logL(\theta)$. Its unconstrained maximum value $(logL(\hat{\theta}))$ is at $\theta = \hat{\theta}$, while its value at the constrained parameter value θ_0 is $logL(\theta_0)$. Hence, according to the Likelihood Ratio formula, the distance between $logL(\hat{\theta})$ and $logL(\theta_0)$ is $LR/2$. If, however, the loglikelihood function has a different curvature, say BB′, the value of the loglikelihood function at the constrained parameter value is $logL(\theta_0)'$ and then the value of the Likelihood Ratio test differs from that for AA′, despite the fact that the distance between $\hat{\theta}$ and θ_0 is unchanged. The Wald statistic may not depend so strongly upon the change in the curvature, since the curvature itself (or, strictly speaking, its estimate) is used for weighting the squared differences between the constrained and unconstrained parameter values. For the Lagrange Multiplier test, the unconstrained loglikelihood function is not estimated. What is estimated instead is the constrained loglikelihood function CC′ (that is the function when the restrictions implied by the null hypothesis are imposed). The extent of the difference from zero of the slope of the constrained function CC′ at θ_0 (weighted by the curvature) forms the basis of the test. This slope is depicted in Figure 4.1 by the line DD′.

All three of these tests have natural generalizations to vectors of parameters rather than the single parameter case that has been considered here. Whilst all three statistics have the same asymptotic distribution, the following relationship between the sample values may be shown to hold for linear models (for example see Maddala (1988, pp. 84-86) or Berndt and Savin (1977)):

$W \geq LR \geq LM$.

Thus, in practice, it is possible (say) to reject a null hypothesis by the W test but fail to reject this same hypothesis by the other two tests.

One feature of the tests is the different information they require. The Likelihood Ratio test requires computations involving both restricted and unrestricted parameters. The Wald test only requires computations based on the unrestricted estimates, and the Lagrange Multiplier test only computations based on the restricted estimates. As the estimation of models subject to restrictions may be difficult in practice, the Wald test may be a particularly attractive option in some circumstances.

Let us consider the application of both Lagrange Multiplier and Wald tests to the testing of restrictions in an *ADL* model. (An example of a Likelihood Ratio test is given in Chapter 6 below.) We will firstly describe the Lagrange Multiplier (*LM*) test.

In order to test a set of (possibly nonlinear) restrictions, start from the ordinary least squares estimation of the *restricted model* (STEP 1). If the total number of parameters in the unrestricted model is k and there are m restrictions imposed, the number of parameters estimated in STEP 1 is $k - m$. For the estimated restricted model compute residuals, say ε_{0t} (STEP 2). Next, regress ε_{0t} on all the variables which appear in the *unrestricted*, that is general, model (STEP 3). At STEP 3 the total number of estimated parameters is k. For this regression, where ε_{0t} acts as the dependent variable, compute the coefficient of determination denoted as R_0^2 (STEP 4). From R_0^2 the *LM* statistic is computed as:

$$LM = T \cdot R_0^2 \ .$$
(4.3)

Given some general assumptions, under the null hypothesis (that is under the hypothesis that the tested restrictions are valid) *LM* has an asymptotic χ^2 distribution with m degrees of freedom. Although the *LM* statistic in (4.3) has been used extensively in econometric inference, it has been shown (see Kiviet (1986)) that it rejects true null hypotheses too often, and that the Lagrange Multiplier statistic in its F distribution form (denoted herewith by *LMF*) has better statistical properties. This is also a straightforward function of the coefficient of determination R_0^2, namely:

$$LMF = \frac{T - k}{m} \cdot \frac{R_0^2}{1 - R_0^2} \ ,$$
(4.4)

where T is the sample size and k is the number of coefficients in the unrestricted model. The *LMF* statistic under the null hypothesis has an asymptotic F distribution with $(m, T-k)$ degrees of freedom.

The second test outlined here for verifying hypotheses relating to linear and nonlinear restrictions is the Wald test. As was noted earlier, one major advantage of this test compared with the *LMF* test is that it only requires the estimation of the unrestricted model, which is particularly useful if the restricted model is difficult to estimate.

The general form of the Wald test is relatively simple for the testing of linear restrictions, but considerably more complicated for the testing of multiple nonlinear restrictions (see Harvey (1990, pp. 166-168)). However, for the case of a single nonlinear restriction, the Wald test may be computed as follows:

$$W = \frac{\left[f(\hat{\beta})\right]^2}{g(\hat{\beta}) \cdot V(\hat{\beta}) \cdot g(\hat{\beta})'} \quad ,$$

where:

$f(\hat{\beta}) = 0$ is the restriction written in terms of the unrestricted estimates,

$g(\hat{\beta})'$ is the transpose of the $1 \times k$ vector of partial derivatives of the restriction evaluated at the k unrestricted parameter estimates; and

$V(\hat{\beta})$ is the estimated variance-covariance matrix of the unrestricted parameter estimates (for example, see Johnston (1984, p.173 and pp. 180-181)).

As an example, consider the form of the Wald test for restriction 10 in Section 4.1 above. The unrestricted model was:

$$y_t = \alpha_1 y_{t-1} + \beta_0 x_t + \beta_1 x_{t-1} + \varepsilon_t \quad ,$$

and the nonlinear restriction to be tested was:

$$\beta_1 + \alpha_1 \beta_0 = 0 \quad .$$

If the unrestricted estimates of the parameters are denoted as $\hat{\alpha}_1$, $\hat{\beta}_0$ and $\hat{\beta}_1$, then in the notation above:

$$f(\hat{\beta}) = \hat{\beta}_1 + \hat{\alpha}_1 \hat{\beta}_0 \quad ,$$

and

$$g(\hat{\beta}) = \left[\frac{\partial f(\hat{\beta})}{\partial \hat{\alpha}_1}, \quad \frac{\partial f(\hat{\beta})}{\partial \hat{\beta}_0}, \quad \frac{\partial f(\hat{\beta})}{\partial \hat{\beta}_1} \right] \quad = \quad (\hat{\beta}_0 \quad \hat{\alpha}_1 \quad 1) \quad .$$

The Wald statistic for this case is then:

$$W = \frac{(\hat{\beta}_1 + \hat{\alpha}_1 \cdot \hat{\beta}_0)^2}{\begin{bmatrix} \hat{\beta}_0 & \hat{\alpha}_1 & 1 \end{bmatrix} \begin{bmatrix} V(\hat{\beta}) \end{bmatrix} \begin{bmatrix} \hat{\beta}_0 \\ \hat{\alpha}_1 \\ 1 \end{bmatrix}} \quad .$$

Under the null hypothesis that the restriction is valid, W is asymptotically distributed as χ^2 with one degree of freedom.

One drawback of the Wald test is that it may be sensitive to the particular way in which the nonlinear restriction is expressed, in that its calculated value may be different for algebraically equivalent ways of expressing the restriction. Thus if the nonlinear restriction in the example above was rewritten as:

$$1 + \frac{\alpha_1 \beta_0}{\beta_1} = 0 \quad ,$$

the numerical value of the Wald test statistic in finite samples may differ from that calculated using the original formulation of the nonlinear restriction.

To summarize, general to specific modelling consists of:
1. Formulating and estimating a general unrestricted *ADL* model, and,
2. Successive testing for particular restrictions, perhaps by the use of Lagrange Multiplier or Wald tests.

4.3. Modelling the UK Consumption Function

In this section we return to the example of modelling quarterly UK aggregate consumption for the period 1957-1975. We will determine whether or not a consumption function analogous to that of the *DHSY* model can be derived and empirically supported from a general autoregressive distributed lag model. The transformations required are algebraically more involved than those given in Section 4.1, partly because we are now dealing with a model based on quarterly data.

We start with a general *ADL* model. In the final version of the original *DHSY* model the maximum lag length for $cons_t$ was equal to four, the maximum lag length for inc_t was five, and the maximum lag length for the inflation variable (inf_t) was one (see (3.13)). The fifth lag for inc_t is not immediately obvious in (3.13) but note that:

$$\Delta\Delta_4 inc_t = \Delta(inc_t - inc_{t-4}) = (inc_t - inc_{t-4}) - (inc_{t-1} - inc_{t-5}) \quad .$$

It seems reasonable to start from a general *ADL* model with five lags for *cons$_t$* and for *inc$_t$* and one lag for inflation, that is an *ADL*(5, 5, 1) model. In the notation using the lag operator the general model becomes:

$$a(L)cons_t = b(L)inc_t + c(L)inf_t + \varepsilon_t \quad , \tag{4.5}$$

where:

$$a(L) = 1 - \alpha_1 L - \alpha_2 L^2 - \alpha_3 L^3 - \alpha_4 L^4 - \alpha_5 L^5 \quad ,$$

$$b(L) = \beta_0 + \beta_1 L + \beta_2 L^2 + \beta_3 L^3 + \beta_4 L^4 + \beta_5 L^5 \quad ,$$

$$c(L) = \gamma_0 + \gamma_1 L \quad .$$

Altogether, there are 13 parameters to estimate in this general model. To increase the efficiency of the estimators we increase the sample period by including the 20 post sample observations (see Section 3.2), which gives a total number of 71 observations.

The estimates of this 13 parameter general equation are given under MODEL 4.1 in Section 4.6. As before, bear in mind the differences between the text and the computer output notation. The logarithm of *per capita* personal consumption, or *cons$_t$*, is denoted in the computer output as 'lc', the logarithm of total *per capita* disposable personal income, *inc$_t$* by 'li' and the inflation variable ($\Delta_4 p_t$) by 'inf'. Cursory inspection of MODEL 4.1 does not reveal anything exciting. The model seems to fit the data well, with the coefficient of determination virtually equal to one. This is hardly surprising for a model with 13 explanatory variables. Nevertheless there are a lot of seemingly 'insignificant' variables.

The static long run equation is computed from the estimates in MODEL 4.1 by equating each variable at all of its lags, that is:

$$cons^* = cons_t = cons_{t-1} = \ldots = cons_{t-5} \quad ,$$

$$inc^* = inc_t = inc_{t-1} = \ldots = inc_{t-5} \quad ,$$

$$inf^* = inf_t = inf_{t-1} \quad ,$$

and solving the equation for *cons**. This gives:

$$cons^* = \beta^* inc^* + \gamma^* inf^* \quad ,$$

where:

$$\beta^* = \frac{\sum_{j=0}^{5}\beta_j}{1-\sum_{j=1}^{5}\alpha_j} \quad , \quad \gamma^* = \frac{\sum_{j=0}^{1}\gamma_j}{1-\sum_{j=1}^{5}\alpha_j} \quad .$$

The computed long run coefficients β^* and γ^* are given in the long run equation below MODEL 4.1. We will not discuss here how the asymptotic standard errors of the estimated β^* and γ^* coefficients reported in brackets below the estimates have been computed (for the full formulae see Hendry (1989, pp. 51-53)). Note that the estimated standard error for β^* equal to 0.0108, is relatively low in comparison with the corresponding parameter (1.005), and the result is consistent with a long run unitary income elasticity of consumption.

However, the joint tests on the significance of each set of variables shows that none of the explanatory variables in (4.5), namely $cons_t$ lagged from one to five, inc_t lagged from zero to five and inf_t lagged from zero to one, can be entirely eliminated. The F statistics reported below the static long run solution for MODEL 4.1 for the particular sets of explanatory variables treated as omitted variables are significant so that none of these variables can be entirely excluded from the model on purely statistical grounds. The 5% critical value of the F distribution with (2, 60) degrees of freedom is 3.15, while the lowest computed F value is 11.446. The degrees of freedom in the numerator (five for $cons_t$, six for inc_t, and two for inf_t) are the number of restrictions imposed on the general model. The degrees of freedom in the denominator (58) is the difference between the sample size of 71 less the 13 estimated parameters. These F statistics are the Lagrange Multiplier LMF statistics described in Section 4.2. For instance, the value 14.142 for inc_t has been obtained in an equivalent way to the following. First, MODEL 4.1 was re-estimated with all six of the inc_t variables excluded. This is equivalent to estimating the ADL model with the set of restrictions, $\beta_0 = \beta_1 = \beta_2 = \beta_3 = \beta_4 = \beta_5 = 0$. Next, the residuals of this restricted model were regressed on the entire set of 13 explanatory variables, including all the inc_t variables. For this regression, the coefficient of determination was computed. This coefficient of determination, say R_0^2, was used in turn to compute the Lagrange Multiplier statistic according to the formula (4.4):

$$LMF = \frac{71-13}{6} \cdot \frac{R_0^2}{1-R_0^2} = 14.142 \quad .$$

Analogously, the Lagrange Multiplier tests for the joint significance of each lag (that is jointly $cons_{t-1}$, inc_{t-1}, inf_{t-1}, and then $cons_{t-2}$ and inc_{t-2}, etc.) have been calculated. The insignificant values for lags two and three indicates that the two and three period lags on the variables do not contribute significantly to the model. In other words, an hypothesis that the coefficients of $cons_{t-2}$ and inc_{t-2}, or that $cons_{t-3}$ and inc_{t-3} are jointly zeros, cannot be rejected.

The *first stage of model reduction* may now be performed by eliminating all the explanatory variables lagged by two and three periods. This reduces the total number of the parameters to be estimated to nine.

The results of estimating this reduced model are shown as MODEL 4.2 in Section 4.6. The PROGRESS to DATE results compare the residual sum of squares and the estimated standard error of the residuals of both models. The differences are evidently not great. This intuitive finding is confirmed by the Lagrange Multiplier test for testing the four restrictions which, if valid, transform the general equation (4.5) into the more specific form:

$$cons_t = \alpha_1 cons_{t-1} + \alpha_4 cons_{t-4} + \alpha_5 cons_{t-5} + \beta_0 inc_t + \beta_1 inc_{t-1}$$
$$+ \beta_4 inc_{t-4} + \beta_5 inc_{t-5} + \gamma_0 inf_t + \gamma_1 inf_{t-1} + \varepsilon_t \quad , \tag{4.6}$$

by imposing the restrictions: $\alpha_2 = \alpha_3 = \beta_2 = \beta_3 = 0$ on the general equation. The *LMF* statistic for testing the reduction from equation (4.5) to equation (4.6) is equal to 0.697, which is clearly not significant. Therefore the four explanatory variables lagged by two and three periods can be safely eliminated from the model..

The next step in the process of sequential reduction is to attempt to move to the original *DHSY* function. In fact, a slightly simplified form of the *DHSY* model is derived which omits the variable DO_t (compare with equation (3.13)), that is:

$$\Delta_4 cons_t = \theta_1 \Delta_4 inc_t + \theta_2 (cons_{t-4} - inc_{t-4}) + \theta_3 \Delta\Delta_4 inc_t$$
$$+ \theta_4 inf_t + \theta_5 \Delta inf_t + error_t \quad . \tag{4.7}$$

(The notation of the parameters of the *DHSY* model has been changed in comparison with that used in Chapter 3, in that the coefficients are now denoted by θ s rather than by β s.) It is difficult immediately to spot the required restrictions on (4.6) which will give rise to (4.7). They become more evident if equation (4.6) is transformed by adding and subtracting four period lags of the variables $cons_t$ and inc_t multiplied by coefficients of the non-lagged variables, and $\gamma_1 inf_t$ to the right-hand side of equation (4.6). That is, add and subtract $cons_{t-4}$, $\beta_0 inc_{t-4}$, and $\gamma_1 inf_t$ to the right-hand side of (4.6). After a little manipulation, the following may be derived:

$$\Delta_4 cons_t = \alpha_1 cons_{t-1} + (\alpha_4 - 1)cons_{t-4} + \alpha_5 cons_{t-5} + \beta_0 \Delta_4 inc_t$$
$$+ (\beta_0 + \beta_4)inc_{t-4} + \beta_1 inc_{t-1} + \beta_5 inc_{t-5} \tag{4.8}$$
$$+ (\gamma_0 + \gamma_1)inf_t - \gamma_1 \Delta inf_t + \varepsilon_t \quad .$$

If the following four restrictions are imposed on (4.8):

1. $\alpha_1 = 0$,
2. $\alpha_4 - 1 = -(\beta_0 + \beta_4)$,
3. $\alpha_5 = 0$,
4. $\beta_1 = -\beta_5$,

then model (4.8) becomes:

$$\Delta_4 cons_t = \beta_0 \Delta_4 inc_t + (\gamma_0 + \gamma_1)inf_t + (\alpha_4 - 1)(cons_{t-4} - inc_{t-4})$$
$$+ \beta_1 \Delta_4 inc_{t-1} - \gamma_1 \Delta inf_t + \varepsilon_t. \tag{4.9}$$

At first sight, the model in (4.9) does not look like the *DHSY* model, but in fact equation (4.9) *is* numerically equivalent to equation (4.7). That is, its parameters are deterministic linear functions of those of the *DHSY* model. To see this add and subtract $\beta_1 \Delta_4 inc_t$ to and from the right-hand side of (4.9), and rearrange terms to give:

$$\Delta_4 cons_t = (\beta_0 + \beta_1)\Delta_4 inc_t - \beta_1(\Delta_4 inc_t - \Delta_4 inc_{t-1})$$
$$+ (\alpha_4 - 1)(cons_{t-4} - inc_{t-4}) + (\gamma_0 + \gamma_1)inf_t \tag{4.10}$$
$$- \gamma_1 \Delta inf_t + \varepsilon_t \quad .$$

Now, it is easy to see that (4.10) is identical to the *DHSY* model (4.7) where:

$$\theta_1 = \beta_0 + \beta_1 \ , \quad \theta_2 = \alpha_4 - 1 \ , \quad \theta_3 = -\beta_1 \ ,$$
$$\theta_4 = \gamma_0 + \gamma_1 \ , \quad \theta_5 = -\gamma_1 \ , \quad error_t = \varepsilon_t \quad .$$

To confirm the equivalence of models (4.7) and (4.9), one could estimate them both and compare the results (see MODEL 4.3 and MODEL 4.4 in Section 4.6). The notation for the variables in the computer output is identical to that used in Chapter 3 (that is 'lc_li_4' stands for $(cons_{t-4} - inc_{t-4})$, 'dd4li' for $\Delta \Delta_4 inc_t$, etc.) The estimates of equations (4.7) and (4.9) are identical, with the exception of the 'composite' coefficient on $\Delta_4 inc_t$. The original *DHSY* coefficient of $\Delta_4 inc_t$, namely 0.494884 in MODEL 4.3 is the sum of the coefficients of $\Delta_4 inc_t$ and $\Delta_4 inc_{t-1}$ in MODEL 4.4, that is 0.284153 and 0.210731.

Model reduction has proceeded by a sequence of steps. Firstly, equation (4.5) (the general *ADL* model with 13 parameters to estimate) was reduced to equation (4.6) (the general *ADL* model with four zero-type restrictions on the coefficients of the variables lagged by two and three periods), resulting in a model with nine parameters to estimate. Secondly, equation (4.6) was in its turn reduced to the *DHSY* model in the form of equation (4.9), with five parameters. The PROGRESS to DATE printout under MODEL 4.4 in Section 4.6 shows an increase in the residual sum of squares while moving from equation (4.6) to equation (4.9) (*RSS* rises from 0.0025 to 0.0029). The significance of this rise may be tested by the Lagrange Multiplier test for the validity of the restrictions imposed on the general model. If equation (4.9) is tested as the restricted form of equation (4.5), that is with all the 4+4=8 restrictions imposed, the *LMF* statistic is 1.3989 and is not significant (the degrees of freedom for this *F* distribution are (8, 59). Consequently, we cannot reject the hypothesis that the *DHSY* model is a specific form of the general autoregressive distributed lag model. Similarly, if we test equation (4.9) as a restricted form of equation (4.6) (the more specific *ADL* model, with lags of order two and three removed), with four restrictions imposed, the *LMF* statistic is 2.1417. The 5% critical value for an $F(4, 63)$ distribution is (by interpolation) 2.52. Hence, at the 5% level of significance we cannot reject the hypothesis that the *DHSY* model is a restricted form of (4.6), that is of an *ADL* model which contains lags of order one, four and five. In the terminology that will be developed in Chapter 8, we may say that equation (4.9) is *nested* within equations (4.5) and (4.6).

Of course, being acceptable as a specific form of a general *ADL* model is not in itself sufficient for an estimated equation to be taken as a satisfactory description of the process being investigated. Further requirements on the equation have been suggested by Hendry and Richard (1982, 1983) as criteria for model acceptance. Three of these, namely consistency with an economic theory, parameter constancy, and randomness of model residuals, we have encountered already. Others, such as properties of *weakly exogenous regressors* and *encompassing* will be discussed in Chapters 7 and 8 below.

4.4 *COMFAC* Analysis

The presence of autocorrelated errors as evidenced by (say) a significant Durbin-Watson test statistic may be the result of some misspecification of the model, for example that some important variables have been omitted from the regression (see Maddala (1988, pp. 208-209)). The common factor (*COMFAC*) approach introduced in Section 4.1 showed, however, that the existence of autocorrelation in a static model did not necessarily imply that something was wrong with the model. It might merely be an indication of the fact that the valid model is in fact an autoregressive distributed lag model with some common factor restrictions present. In this case, such autocorrelation can be regarded as a 'simplification, not a nuisance' (Hendry and Mizon (1978)) in that it allows the use of a simpler model which follows from the imposition of restrictions on the general model.

Consider the estimation of a static consumption function with the same variables as those in the *DHSY* model. The static equation is:

$$cons_t = \varphi_1 inc_t + \varphi_2 inf_t + u_t \;\;, \tag{4.11}$$

and its estimates are given as MODEL 4.5 in Section 4.6. Our primary interest is now in the autocorrelation diagnostics of this model. The Durbin-Watson statistic of 1.53 is on the verge of being significant at the 5% level of significance. (The appropriate tables in this case are those of Farebrother (1980) as there is no intercept in the regression.) The estimated first order autocorrelation coefficient is equal to 0.457. However, it is also worth testing for autocorrelation of a higher order, especially as the model is estimated using seasonally unadjusted quarterly data with no seasonal dummies. Indeed, in this case, there appears to be quite large error autocorrelation coefficients at lags four and five as well as at the first lag. For testing the joint presence of autocorrelation of orders 1, 2, 3, 4 and 5, the familiar Lagrange Multiplier approach has been applied once again. This consists simply of computing the ordinary least squares residuals of (4.11), denoted by $\hat{u}_t$, and testing whether in the equation:

$$cons_t = \varphi_1 inc_t + \varphi_2 inf_t + \rho_1 \hat{u}_{t-1} + \rho_2 \hat{u}_{t-2} + \rho_3 \hat{u}_{t-3} + \rho_4 \hat{u}_{t-4} + \rho_5 \hat{u}_{t-5} + \varepsilon_t \;\;,$$

the hypothesis that $\rho_1 = \rho_2 = \rho_3 = \rho_4 = \rho_5 = 0$ can be maintained.

Technically, this test is as described in Section 4.2. Equation (4.11) is estimated by ordinary least squares, and the residuals are computed. These residuals are regressed on inc_t, inf_t and their own values lagged up to five times, and the coefficient of determination for this regression is computed. The *LM* and the *LMF* statistics may now be calculated according to the formulae given in Section 4.2 (see Hendry (1989, p.55), or Harvey (1990, p.278)). Hence, in this case, the *LM* statistic has a χ^2 (5) distribution and the *LMF* statistic has an $F(5, 64)$ distribution. For the model considered here, both statistics are significant (*LM* = 41.583 and *LMF* = 18.093), so that we may reject the hypothesis that all five autocorrelation coefficients are jointly equal to zero. Inspection of the values of the autocorrelation coefficients of MODEL 4.5 suggests that the fourth order autocorrelation coefficient, equal to 0.81795, may contribute a lot towards this rejection of the null hypothesis.

Having established the presence of autocorrelation in the errors of equation (4.11), it is reasonable to enquire whether this is a result of the fact that the valid model is an autoregressive distributed lag model with common factors. If we start from the general *ADL*(5, 5, 1) model introduced in the previous section, with five lags for consumption and income, and one for the inflation variable, then there can be at most one common factor in the model. From the discussion of case 10 in Section 4.1, we may recall that common factors reflect common roots in the lag polynomials of each variable. Thus there cannot be more common factors than the order of the lag distribution with the smallest number of lags. If we work with a model with a single lag on the inflation variable, then even if a common factor is found, model simplification on this account can only be to move to a model which omits the longest lag on each variable and which exhibits first order autocorrelated errors.

However, given that up to fifth order autocorrelation in the residuals of the static model have been detected, it will be more interesting to start from an *ADL*(5) model, with five lags on each variable. This model can have up to five common factors present, and will allow us to test whether a static equation with fifth order autocorrelated errors (the simplest form potentially equivalent to the general *ADL*(5) model) is an acceptable simplification of the general model.

That is, consider the *ADL*(5) model:

$$cons_t = \sum_{i=1}^{5} \alpha_i cons_{t-i} + \sum_{i=0}^{5} \beta_i inc_{t-i} + \sum_{i=0}^{5} \gamma_i inf_{t-i} + error \quad . \tag{4.12}$$

We would like to determine what simplifications of equation (4.12) might be possible due to the existence of common factors in the lag polynomials of this equation, and whether, in the limit, the empirical evidence is consistent with the data having been generated from the static consumption function (equation (4.11)) with fifth order autocorrelated errors:

$$u_t = \sum_{j=1}^{5} \rho_j u_{t-j} + \varepsilon_t \quad . \tag{4.13}$$

To help resolve these issues, a series of common factor tests are performed. First, a test for one common factor is carried out. If this is not rejected, then a further test for a second common factor is performed, and so on. Only if all five common factor tests are not rejected will we not be able to reject the simplified model (equation (4.11) with (4.13)). These common factor tests are undertaken using COMFAC WALD (W) Chi^2 tests. The relevant statistics to study are those of the *incremental* values of the Wald statistics which are independent of each other, rather than the cumulative values. For tests at the 5% level of significance each incremental value is compared in turn with the tabulated χ^2 (2) value of 5.991. Thus, the incremental value for one common factor is compared with 5.991. If the calculated incremental value is larger than this tabulated figure, the hypothesis of one common factor may be rejected. Only if the calculated value is smaller than the tabulated value can one proceed to test for a second common factor, by comparing the incremental value for this second factor with the same tabulated value.

Empirical results illustrating this test are given in Section 4.6 under MODEL 4.6. Although we do not present the full results here, we may note in passing that the more restricted $ADL(5, 5, 1)$ model used in the previous section, with a single lagged inflation variable, cannot be rejected as a specific form of the $ADL(5)$ model in the form of equation (4.12). The Lagrange Multiplier F test for the joint significance of the four lagged inflation variables inf_{t-2} to inf_{t-5} is only 1.16, and is not significant. MODEL 4.6 also presents the COMFAC WALD (W) Chi^2 test statistics needed to test for common factors. By looking at each incremental χ^2 p-value, we cannot reject the null hypothesis that three common factors are present, but can reject four (or more) at the 5% significance level. Hence, the empirical evidence does not support a static consumption function with fifth order autocorrelated errors. Despite this, some model simplification (for example, the use of a model with two period lags on each variable and a third order autoregressive process for the errors) might be suggested. Whilst Harvey (1990, p.287) points to some difficulties in using the results of *COMFAC* analysis to determine model specification precisely, it may still be a useful part of a general to specific modelling sequence.

4.5 General to Specific Modelling and Data Mining

The message of this chapter is that in econometric model building, in order to derive credible models, it is preferable to start with a general model and attempt to reduce it by a sequence of tests of economically sensible restrictions. In the example in Section 4.3, the sequence of restrictions imposed (or model reductions) was directed by knowledge of the specific form (the *DHSY* formulation of the aggregate consumption function) which was ultimately to be tested. However, there need not be a unique model reduction sequence that leads from a general model to a specific form. For example, we moved to the *DHSY* specification in two steps, whilst a similar analysis carried out by Hendry, Muellbauer and Murphy (1990) involved a sequence of nine steps. In the special case where the sequence of tests is properly nested (contained within each other) it is possible to compute the true significance level α^* (see Section 2.2) for the jth test in the sequence by the following expression:

$$\alpha^* = 1 - (1 - \alpha_1) \cdot (1 - \alpha_2) \cdot ... \cdot (1 - \alpha_j) \ ,$$

where α_i, $i = 1, 2, ..., j$, is the significance level used in the ith test (see Maddala (1988, p.425)). For instance, for a sequence of three nested reductions, at a nominal significance level of 5%, the true significance level of the last test is $1 - (0.95)^2 = 0.143$.

In practice, the restrictions to be tested may not be nested one within the other so as to allow such a sequence of tests to be performed. For example, the Lagrange Multiplier tests for the joint significance of each lag in Section 4.3 are not nested within each other. There seems to be no theoretical reason for believing that in the general ADL model, all variables lagged one period, or two periods, etc. should be zero rather than any other particular combination of lags on these variables. Thus we must admit to some arbitrariness in the initial selection of zero restrictions to be tested. The tests of the joint significance for either lag two or lag three may be reasonable given the insignificance of these terms in the estimated unrestricted equation (MODEL 4.1 in Section 4.6) but to decide on the sequence of tests to be performed in this way is of course subject to the strictures on preliminary tests of significance discussed in Section 2.3.

The charge of data mining that can be directed against the general to specific methodology seems to be potentially more serious where the investigator does not have a clear idea as to the specific form that the investigation should lead to. Thus, for example, in Section 4.1 there were ten economically plausible models presented which could be derived from a simple $ADL(1)$ model. If the investigator were interested in only one of these, then the situation would be as existed in Section 4.3, where the specific form of the general model was known. However, if the investigator has no firm view as to the specific form of the final model to be considered, the interesting question remains as to whether general to specific modelling can be viewed as a method of model simplification, that is as a method of discovery, rather than of confirmation. There is a clear dilemma here. With a number of economic theories acceptable to the investigator, it seems inevitable that a data mining problem exists. General to specific modelling (model reduction through the testing of restrictions) may well lead to multiple admissible models not nested within each other. (Chapter 8 will consider the testing of non-nested models.) There is no systematic way of ordering the sequence of tests in general (though Pagan (1987) suggests that $COMFAC$ analysis provides a systematic way of choosing the dynamics of a system), but the particular sequence adopted could be crucial in the selection of the specific form finally accepted.

On the positive side, however, general to specific modelling does seem to represent a major advance over 'bottom up' or 'simple to general' approaches, where models are successively complicated or altered in response to indications of model misspecification. Thus, for example, there is little theoretical justification for the common practice of adding new variables to a model because of evidence of serial correlation in the errors of a fitted equation. Not only are conventional test statistics normally invalid in models with omitted variables, but there is no reason why two investigators starting from the same simple model will converge on the same final equation. If a test suggests an extension to a model, and subsequently another test on this extended model indicates some misspecification, then clearly the original decision to change the model in the way indicated was wrong. Accordingly, the entire approach is questionable. The major problem of 'simple to general' approaches to econometric modelling is that if one starts with a misspecified model, then the attempt to improve upon this model by extending it on the basis of statistical tests is likely to be based on erroneous statistical procedures. As was noted in Chapters 1 and 2, it was unstructured data mining and 'bottom up' modelling that led to the existence of a plethora of alternative models which so undermined the credibility of econometrics to many people.

The strength of general to specific modelling is that model construction proceeds from a very general model in a more structured, ordered (and statistically valid) fashion, and in this way avoids the worst excesses of data mining.

4.6 Stylized Computer Output (*PC-GIVE*)

Generalized *ADL* model for *cons*
MODEL 4.1: Modelling lc by OLS (equation (4.5) in text)
The present sample is: 1958 (2) to 1975 (4)

Variable	Coefficient	Std.Error	t-value
lc_1	-0.00136675	0.116107	-0.012
lc_2	0.00382734	.0289187	0.132
lc_3	-0.0329994	0.0284422	-1.160
lc_4	0.9511110	0.0316388	30.06
lc_5	0.0037529	0.1189240	0.032
li	0.2896970	0.0439468	6.592
li_1	0.1923160	0.0604884	3.179
li_2	-0.0390069	0.0513462	-0.760
li_3	0.0435061	0.0516025	0.843
li_4	-0.1905530	0.0559407	-3.406
li_5	-0.2198780	0.0622507	-3.532
inf	-0.3106290	0.0898343	-3.458
inf_1	0.1823840	0.0977310	1.866

$R^2 = 0.9999996$ $\sigma = 0.006471094$ DW $= 2.25$
* R^2 does NOT allow for the mean *
RSS $= 0.0024287531698$ for 13 variables and 71 observations

Solved Static Long Run equation
lc $=$ 1.005 li   -1.695 inf
(SE)   (0.010798)   (0.61923)

Tests on the significance of each set of variables

variable	F(num,denom)	Value[Probability]
lc	F(5, 58)	229.34 [0.0000] **
li	F(6, 58)	14.142 [0.0000] **
inf	F(2, 58)	11.446 [0.0001] **

Tests on the significance of each lag

Lag	F(num,denom)	Value[Probability]
1	F(3, 58)	4.9313[0.0041] **
2	F(2, 58)	0.709715 [0.4960]
3	F(2, 58)	0.700668 [0.5004]
4	F(2, 58)	648.49[0.0000]**
5	F(2, 58)	11.007[0.0001] **

First stage of testing restrictions: elimination of lags 2 and 3
MODEL 4.2: Modelling lc by OLS (equation (4.6) in text)
The present sample is: 1958 (2) to 1975 (4)

Variable	Coefficient	Std.Error	t-value
lc_1	-0.001765	0.1129420	-0.016
lc_4	0.945760	0.0298532	31.68
lc_5	0.009840	0.1139590	0.090
li	0.289977	0.0434100	6.680
li_1	0.176910	0.0573048	3.087
li_4	-0.194459	0.0489405	-3.973
li_5	-0.225464	0.0603603	-3.735
inf	-0.314417	0.0869449	-3.616
inf_1	0.208728	0.0951586	2.193

$R^2 = 0.9999995$ $\sigma = 0.006405109$ DW = 2.23
* R^2 does NOT allow for the mean *
RSS = 0.0025435762289 for 9 variables and 71 observations

Progress to date for modelling lc:

model	T	k	df	RSS
2	71	9	62	0.00254358
1	71	13	58	0.00242875
model	T	k	df	σ
2	71	9	62	0.00640511
1	71	13	58	0.00647109

Tests of model reduction
Model 1 --> 2: F(4, 59) = 0.697329 [0.5968]

Second stage of testing restrictions: seasonal differences and error correction
The DHSY model re-estimated without DO variable

MODEL 4.3: Modelling d4lc by OLS (equation (4.7) in text)
The present sample is: 1958 (2) to 1975 (4)

Variable	Coefficient	Std.Error	t-value
d4li	0.494884	0.0313028	15.81
dd4li	-0.210731	0.0417670	-5.045
lc_li_4	-0.087091	0.0130465	-6.675
inf	-0.112609	0.0243328	-4.628
dinf	-0.235723	0.0932488	-2.528

$R^2 = 0.9455928$ $\sigma = 0.00661662$ DW = 2.22
* R^2 does NOT allow for the mean *
RSS = 0.0028894571761 for 5 variables and 71 observations

The DHSY model in an equivalent form
MODEL 4.4: Modelling d4lc by OLS (equation (4.9) in text)
The present sample is: 1958 (2) to 1975 (4)

Variable	Coefficient	Std.Error	t-value
d4li	0.284153	0.0372289	7.633
d4li_1	0.210731	0.0417670	5.045
lc_li_4	-0.087091	0.0130465	-6.675
inf	-0.112609	0.0243328	-4.628
dinf	-0.235723	0.0932488	-2.528

$R^2 = 0.9455928$ $\sigma = 0.00661662$ DW = 2.22
* R^2 does NOT allow for the mean *
RSS = 0.0028894571761 for 5 variables and 71 observations

Progress to date for modelling lc:

model	T	k	df	RSS
3	71	5	66	0.00288946
2	71	9	62	0.00254358
1	71	13	58	0.00242875
model	T	k	df	σ
3	71	5	66	0.00661662
2	71	9	62	0.00640511
1	71	13	58	0.00647109

Tests of model reduction
Model 1 --> 2: F(4, 59) = 0.697329 [0.5968]
Model 1 --> 3: F(8, 59) = 1.3989 [0.2160]
Model 2 --> 3: F(4, 63) = 2.1417 [0.0860]

Estimation of a static consumption function
MODEL 4.5: Modelling lc by OLS (equation (4.11) in text)
The present sample is: 1958 (2) to 1975 (4)

Variable	Coefficient	Std.Error	t-value
li	0.984661	0.0007366	1336.76
inf	-0.564255	0.0864649	-6.52582

$R^2 = 0.999985$ $\sigma = 0.03473765$ DW = 1.53
* R^2 does NOT allow for the mean *
RSS = 0.083262603827 for 2 variables and 71 observations

Testing for Error Autocorrelation from lags 1 to 5
$Chi^2(5) = 41.583$ [0.0000] ** and F-Form(5, 64) = 18.093 [0.0000] **

Error Autocorrelation Coefficients:
	Lag 1	Lag 2	Lag 3	Lag 4	Lag 5
Coeff	0.45785	0.035383	-0.10362	0.81795	-0.43221

ADL(5) model estimated for further COMFAC analysis
MODEL 4.6: Modelling lc by OLS (equation (4.12) in text)
The present sample is: 1959 (2) to 1975 (4)

Variable	Coefficient	Std.Error	t-value
lc_1	-0.0830125	0.1233400	-0.673
lc_2	0.0049316	0.0313661	0.157
lc_3	-0.0219453	0.0311122	-0.705
lc_4	0.9380720	0.0339404	27.639
lc_5	0.0700182	0.1242680	0.563
li	0.2923640	0.0456152	6.409
li_1	0.2268210	0.0644192	3.521
li_2	-0.0408716	0.0564780	-0.724
li_3	0.0155646	0.0569171	0.273
li_4	-0.1801140	0.0573704	-3.139
li_5	-0.2217270	0.0628024	-3.531
inf	-0.3420160	0.1175960	-2.908
inf_1	0.2400120	0.1785850	1.344
inf_2	-0.0788621	0.1432810	-0.550

inf_3	-0.0908498	0.1320530	-0.688
inf_4	0.0518677	0.1367070	0.379
inf_5	0.1247240	0.1041260	1.198

$R^2 = 0.9999996$ $\sigma = 0.006449985$ DW = 2.29

$* R^2$ does NOT allow for the mean $*$

RSS = 0.0020801155352 for 17 variables and 67 observations

Solved Static Long Run equation

lc = +1.001 li   -1.035 inf

(SE)   (0.0094635)   (0.36228)

Tests on the significance of each variable

variable	F(num,denom)	Value Probability
lc	F(5, 50)	172.49 [0.0000] **
li	F(6, 50)	14.103 [0.0000] **
inf	F(6, 50)	4.9054 [0.0005] **

Tests on the significance of each lag

Lag	F(num,denom)	Value Probability
1	F(3, 50)	4.9263 [0.0045] **
2	F(3, 50)	0.4610230 [0.7108]
3	F(3, 50)	0.4525370 [0.7166]
4	F(3, 50)	373.33 [0.0000] **
5	F(3, 50)	6.4254 [0.0009] **

COMFAC WALD test statistic table

Order	Chi^2 df	Value[pval]	Incr Chi^2df	Value[pval]
5	2	0.104901 [0.9489]	2	0.104901 [0.9489]
4	4	0.324254 [0.9882]	2	0.219352 [0.8961]
3	6	1.1379 [0.9798]	2	0.81368 [0.6658]
2	8	18.121 [0.0203] *	2	16.983 [0.0002] **
1	10	24.702 [0.0059] **	2	6.5809 [0.0372] *

4.7 Suggestions for Further Reading

Full details of general to specific modelling are in fact more complex and rigorous than described above and go beyond the scope of this book (for a quite sophisticated description see Hendry (1983, 1987); much simpler presentations of this approach are those given in Pagan (1987), Cuthbertson (1985), Gilbert (1986) and Cuthbertson, Hall and Taylor (1992)). A development to general to specific Bayesian methodology can be found in Lubrano and Marimotou (1988). Traditional 'bottom up' and general to specific modelling are compared in Maddala (1988, pp. 423-425) and Gilbert (1989, pp. 122-125).

General to specific modelling has been criticized by Darnell (1986, 1988) and Darnell and Evans (1990), mainly on the grounds of a lack of a proper interpretation of the dynamic long run solution. It has, however, been defended by Phillips (1988a) who evaluated it positively as a tool for achieving an optimal inference procedure. More advanced description and references can be found in Hendry (1995) and in Keuzenkamp and McAleer (1995).

For Lagrange Multiplier, Likelihood Ratio and Wald tests, more advanced references are those of Judge *et al.* (1985, pp. 182-187), Amemiya (1985, pp. 141-146), Engle (1984) and Spanos (1986, pp. 328-336). An examination of the practical importance of the sensitivity of the Wald test to the form in which nonlinear restrictions are expressed has been given by Gregory and Veall (1986), and Lafontaine and White (1986).

Spanos (1988) examines the general to specific methodology within the broader context of constructing a coherent methodological framework for econometrics. Empirical applications using the general to specific approach are still scarce. Muscatelli (1989) has used it for modelling money demand in the UK. Applications of *ADL* models to East European parallel markets are given in Charemza (1990b, 1991), and to modelling financial markets in India in Ghatak and Charemza (1989) and Italy in Muscatelli and Papi (1988). An example of dynamic econometric modelling considered in the light of the general to specific approach has been given by Spanos (1986, pp. 553-570).

Chapter 5

Cointegration Analysis

5.1 Introductory Concepts

Cointegration analysis in time series econometrics was introduced in the mid 1980s, and has been regarded by many econometricians as the most important recent development in empirical modelling. The basic computational ideas of applied cointegration analysis are simple to understand and to use, as they require only the application of the method of ordinary least squares. The theory behind the computations is not so straightforward. In this chapter we concentrate entirely on those ideas which can be understood without the need for complex mathematics and which can be used without resorting to sophisticated computer software. Nevertheless, it is necessary to start with a description of some elementary concepts of stochastic processes and time series analysis. Those already familiar with the basic concepts of stochastic processes may ignore the first two sections of this chapter and move straight to Section 5.3.

We start with a definition of a *stochastic process*. By a stochastic process we will mean a family of real valued random variables, indexed by t, where t represents time. Since a random variable is usually denoted by a capital letter, say X, a stochastic process will be denoted as the set $\{X_t\}$. Simply put, each element $X_1, X_2, ..., X_t$ of the stochastic process $\{X_t\}$ is a random variable. In order to conform with econometric practice, and if there is no room for misunderstanding, we will refer to the stochastic process $\{X_t\}$ as X_t.

If all the random variables X_t have means (expected values), we may describe the *mean of a stochastic process* $\{X_t\}$ as a series of means (expected values) for particular X_t s or as a function of t. By analogy with the notation used for describing a single random variable, where μ conventionally denotes a mean, we may denote the mean of a stochastic process by μ_t. Analogously, the variance of a stochastic process is denoted by σ_t^2 and the covariance between two of the variables, say X_t and X_{t+j}, which belong to the stochastic process by $\sigma_{t,t+j}$.

The concept of a mean being a function of time is illustrated in Figure 5.1, where some random variables of a stochastic process $\{X_t\}$, for $t = 1, 2,$

3, ..., etc. are shown. The figure illustrates a case in which the means μ_1, μ_2, etc. are an increasing function of time.

Fig. 5.1: Stochastic process with nonstationary mean

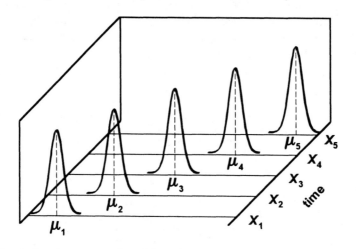

A stochastic process is said to be *stationary* (or, more precisely, is *stationary in a strict or strong sense*), if the joint and conditional probability distributions of the process are unchanged if displaced in time. In practice, it is more usual to deal with *weak sense* or *covariance* stationarity, restricting attention to the means, variances and covariances of the process (see Spanos (1986, pp.137-140)). Then, a stochastic process $\{X_t\}$ is said to be stationary if:

means are constant over time

$$E(X_t) = \text{constant} = \mu \quad ; \quad Var(X_t) = \text{constant} = \sigma^2 \quad ;$$

Variances of the random variables are the same over time

and:

$$Cov(X_t, X_{t+j}) = \sigma_j .$$

Covariance betw. 2 periods determined only by the gap betw. periods

Thus the means and the variances of the process are constant over time, while the value of the covariance between two periods depends only on the gap between the periods, and not the actual time at which this covariance is considered. If one or more of the conditions above are not fulfilled, the process is *nonstationary*. Hence, the process shown in Figure 5.1 would appear to be nonstationary because its means seem to be an increasing function of time. The stochastic process depicted by Figure 5.2 *may* be stationary, although we cannot say for certain whether or not it really is. It appears that its means are constant (identical for different *t*s) and the variances of the random variables also look to be the same. We cannot say anything about the covariance, since it cannot be shown on a diagram such as this.

An important form of a nonstationary variable is illustrated below by a simple and not (we hope) very realistic example. Suppose we are between two bars and we are trying to decide which one to use by tossing a coin. If it is a head, we move two steps to the right; if it is a tail we move two steps to the left. After moving, we repeat the tossing of the coin, etc. (for simplicity assume that the number of steps to each of the bars is infinite, which may be realistic if we had visited a couple of bars already). Let us describe our journey as a series of random variables Z_t. Each of the random variables Z_t takes the value -2 if we move towards the bar to the left and $+2$ if we decide to move towards the bar to the right.

Fig. 5.2: Stochastic process with stationary mean

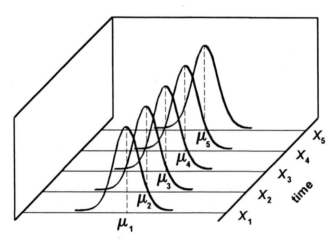

That is:

$$Z_t = \begin{cases} -2 & \text{with probability } 0.5 \\ +2 & \text{with probability } 0.5 \end{cases}.$$

Each of the random variables Z_t has its mean equal to zero and its variance equal to four and is independent from every other variable in the series, that is from Z_{t+j} for any $j \neq 0$. The stochastic process describing the 'bar-or-bar' dilemma (that is the position reached relative to the starting position after the ith toss of the coin) is then given as:

$$X_1 = Z_1 \quad , \quad X_2 = X_1 + Z_2 \quad , \quad X_3 = X_2 + Z_3 \quad , \quad \text{etc.} \quad ,$$

or more generally as:

$$X_t = X_{t-1} + Z_t \quad . \tag{5.1}$$

The fact that all the variables Z_t are identical and independent does not mean that the process described by (5.1) is stationary. Although in the above example $E(X_t) = 0$ (since the expected value of Z_t is zero), the variance of X_t can be expressed as:

$$Var(X_1) = Var(Z_1) = 4 \quad ,$$

$$Var(X_2) = Var(X_1) + Var(Z_2) = 8 \quad ,$$

or, in general:

$$Var(X_t) = 4 \cdot t \quad .$$

As we can see, the variance of this process is a linear function of time and the stochastic process X_t is nonstationary.

The 'bar-or-bar' example is a special case of an important nonstationary stochastic process called *a random walk*. A random walk is usually described in the form of equation (5.1), where Z_t represents a series of identical and independent random variables. They may not necessarily be discrete variables; for instance, Z_t may represent a series of identically and normally distributed random variables. In a similar fashion to our example, random walk stochastic processes are nonstationary. In the example above, the process was nonstationary as the variance of X_t was not constant. It is easy to check that if the mean of Z_t is not zero (as would be the case in our example where the coin tossed is biased), the mean of X_t is also a function of t.

Another, quite similar, example of a nonstationary stochastic process is:

$$X_t = \mu + X_{t-1} + Z_t \quad , \quad \mu \neq 0 \quad , \tag{5.2}$$

where Z_t is defined as before as a series of identically distributed independent random variables and μ is a constant. The difference between (5.1) and (5.2) is that in (5.1), $\mu = 0$. Referring to the 'bar-or-bar' example, if μ was equal to 1, the bar visitor takes one step towards the right before each toss of the coin. Consequently, there is a tendency for him (her) to float towards the right. Not surprisingly, the stochastic process given by (5.2) is called a *random walk with drift*.

In the literature, the concept of a *time series* is often used alongside the concept of a stochastic process. There is some ambiguity here. According to some authors a stochastic process and a time series are the same provided only that t can be interpreted as time, whilst according to some others a time series is a single realization of a stochastic process. In the case of an economic investigation, this distinction does not really matter, since what we usually observe is a sequence of data ordered in time. If we understand the time series to be a single realization of a stochastic process, then such a single realization can be as depicted in Figure 5.3.

Fig. 5.3: Single realization of a stochastic process

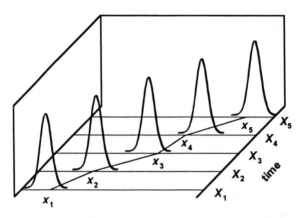

Let us assume, for simplicity, that a stochastic process and a time series are the same. Unfortunately, conventional economic time series analysis uses a slightly different notation from that of the calculus of probability. To be consistent with econometric textbooks, and also with the other chapters of this book, let us use the symbol ε_t to denote a series of identically distributed continuous random variables with zero means (that is ε_t replaces Z_t) and y_t (instead of X_t) to denote a time series. If in addition the errors ε_t are independently distributed, then the stochastic process $\{\varepsilon_t\}$ is called a 'white noise' process. In this case, instead of (5.1) we will use:

$$y_t = y_{t-1} + \varepsilon_t \ , \tag{5.3}$$

as a description of a random walk process, and instead of (5.2) use:

$$y_t = \mu + y_{t-1} + \varepsilon_t \ , \tag{5.4}$$

to represent a random walk with drift.

In economics, the form of nonstationarity in a time series may well be evident from an examination of the series. If the form of nonstationarity is a propensity of the series to move in one direction, we will call this tendency a *trend*.

A series may drift slowly upwards or downwards purely as a result of the effects of stochastic or random shocks. This is true for the random walk process. We have seen that the variance of this process increases over time, but so too does the correlation between neighbouring values (see Cryer (1986, pp. 11-13)). These results imply that there may be long periods in which the process takes values well away from its mean value. In Figure 5.3 there is a clear (stochastic) tendency for such movement and consequently this series is called a time series with a *stochastic trend*. A formal definition of a stochastic trend may be found in Harvey (1990, p.31).

Another example of a developing tendency in a nonstationary stochastic process is where the mean of the process is itself a specific function of time. If such a function is linear then the process can be described as:

$$y_t = \mu_t + \varepsilon_t \quad ,$$

where:

$$\mu_t = \alpha + \beta \cdot t \quad ,$$

or:

$$y_t = \alpha + \beta \cdot t + \varepsilon \quad . \tag{5.5}$$

In this case it is said that the process has a *deterministic trend*. A mixed stochastic-deterministic trend process is also possible. That is, the process can be described as:

$$y_t = \alpha + \beta \cdot t + y_{t-1} + \varepsilon_t \quad .$$

In these expressions, it has been assumed that the expected values of ε_t are zero and that the stochastic process $\{\varepsilon_t\}$ is white noise, but these conditions may be relaxed to allow for autocorrelation in the series of ε_t. If the ε_t s are autocorrelated, the processes (5.3) and (5.4) can no longer be called random walks. The variable y_t will still be nonstationary.

It is very important to clearly distinguish between stochastic trends with and without drift, and also between deterministic and stochastic trends. The differences are illustrated in Figures 5.4 and 5.5. Figure 5.4 shows a simulated series of 500 observations on series with and without drift. They have been simulated as:

$$y_t = y_{t-1} + \tilde{\varepsilon}_t \quad ,$$

(stochastic trend without drift) where $\tilde{\varepsilon}_t$ represents random numbers generated from the standard normal distribution, $t = 1, 2, ..., 500$, and :

$$y_t = 0.5 + y_{t-1} + \tilde{\varepsilon}_t \quad ,$$

(stochastic trend with drift). For a better comparison, the random numbers $\tilde{\varepsilon}_t$ were chosen to be identical for both processes. The starting values y_0 were also identical and equal to 1. It can be seen that, despite the fact that identical numbers were used to generate the two series, their dynamics are quite different. The presence of the drift parameter (0.5) predisposes y_t to develop, more or less systematically, upwards, compared to the stochastic process with no drift. Similarly, a negative constant (drift component) would cause the series to move downwards.

Fig. 5.4: Stochastic trend with and without drift

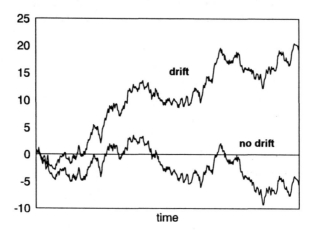

Figure 5.5 compares the stochastic trend model with drift, generated as above, with the following deterministic trend:

$$y_t = 0.5 \cdot t + \tilde{\varepsilon}_t \quad ,$$

where the random numbers $\tilde{\varepsilon}_t$ are identical to those adopted for the stochastic processes above. In the case of the deterministic trend, the deviations from the trend values or nonstationary mean are purely random, and die away quickly. They do not contribute to the long-run development of the series which is entirely determined by the trend component, $0.5 \cdot t$. In the case of the stochastic trend, however, the purely random component directly affects (contributes to) the long-run tendency of the development of y_t.

A mixed stochastic-deterministic trend process is also possible. That is, the process may be described as:

$$y_t = \alpha + \beta \cdot t + y_{t-1} + \varepsilon_t \quad .$$

One should not confuse a random walk process with a stochastic trend. A random walk is in fact a special case of a stochastic trend, where in the model:

$$y_t = y_{t-1} + \varepsilon_t \quad ,$$

the terms ε_t are identically and independently distributed for every t. For a stochastic trend, the ε_t terms need not necessarily be independent as long as they are stationary. For instance, the following is admissible as a stochastic trend:

$$y_t = y_{t-1} + \varepsilon_t \quad , \quad \varepsilon_t = \rho\varepsilon_{t-1} + \xi_t \quad ,$$

where $|\rho| < 1$ and ξ_t is a series of identically and independently distributed random variables. The above definitions are valid only for so-called first-order nonstationary processes, where there is a single lagged variable. A brief outline of higher-order processes will be presented later in the text.

Fig. 5.5: Stochastic and deterministic trend

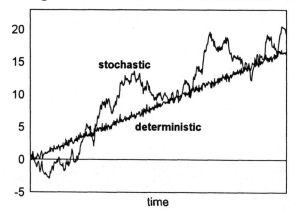

The processes we have been discussing can also be viewed as special cases from another class of processes. We can re-write the equation above as:

$$y_t = \theta y_{t-1} + \varepsilon_t \quad ,$$

where $\theta = 1$. Therefore the process above is often called a *unit root process* or, strictly speaking, a *process with one unit root*.

Another important type of nonstationary process is that which may be useful for modelling seasonality. Consider a process in which the variable y_t has a unit root for its own values lagged by more than one period, that is:

$$y_t = y_{t-s} + \varepsilon_t \quad .$$

If s represents a seasonal frequency of an economic time series (e.g. is equal to 4 or 12 for quarterly or monthly data respectively) then the values of y_t repeat what happened in periods $t-s$, $t-2s$, ..., etc. subject to the effect of the error term, creating a seasonal pattern or effect. Analogously to the concept of a stochastic trend, such a process is said to exhibit *stochastic seasonality*.

The differences between stochastic and deterministic seasonality are analogous to those between stochastic and deterministic trends. As an illustration, consider two simulated series each of length 500, generated with the use of identical random numbers. The first four values of each series are

$y_1 = -3$, $y_2 = 0$, $y_3 = 1$, $y_4 = -2$. Further observations on the series exhibiting stochastic seasonality are determined from:

$$y_t = y_{t-4} + \tilde{\varepsilon}_t \quad,$$

whilst observations on the series representing deterministic seasonality are obtained from:

$$y_t = y_1 Q1_t + y_2 Q2_t + y_3 Q3_t + y_4 Q4_t + \tilde{\varepsilon}_t \quad,$$

where the Qi_t variables are seasonal dummy variables such that:

$$Qi_t = \begin{cases} 1 \text{ for quarter } i \text{ observations} \\ 0 \text{ otherwise} \end{cases} \quad, \quad i = 1, 2, 3, 4.$$

Fig. 5.6: Stochastic and deterministic seasonality

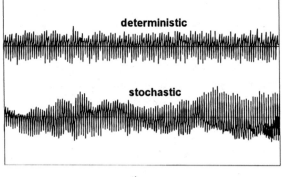

time

Figure 5.6 compares these series. Note that the amplitude of the process representing deterministic seasonality is, on average, constant over time, and that this series fluctuates around a constant. In contrast, the process exhibiting stochastic seasonality does not fluctuate around a constant, and has variable seasonal fluctuations which depend on the previous values of the series from corresponding quarters.

5.2 Nonstationary Series and Integrated Processes

Nonstationarity of time series has always been regarded as a problem in econometric analysis. It has been shown in a number of theoretical works (for example Phillips (1986)) that, in general, the statistical properties of regression analysis using nonstationary time series are dubious. Without going into this theory, we will indicate that if series are nonstationary one is likely to finish up with a model showing promising diagnostic test statistics even in the case where there is no sense in the regression analysis.

This point is illustrated below by a rather silly regression of a linear on a quadratic trend. Let a variable y_t be defined as: $y_1 = 1$, $y_2 = 2$, ..., $y_n = n$, and a variable x_t as: $x_1 = 1$, $x_2 = 4$, ..., $x_n = n^2$. For $n = 30$, the results of regressing y_t on x_t are as follows:

$$y_t = 5.92 + 0.030 \cdot x_t \quad ,$$
$$\quad (9.9) \quad (21.2)$$

where Student-t ratios are given in brackets below the estimates, the coefficient of determination $R^2 = 0.94$, and the Durbin-Watson statistic $DW = 0.06$.

If an investigator 'forgets' to report the Durbin-Watson statistic, the regression equation looks quite interesting, although in fact it represents a totally spurious relationship. Indeed, the only sign that something may be wrong in this regression is the very low Durbin-Watson statistic. As is evident from Figure 5.7, the observed and fitted values have no common pattern in their development over time. This somewhat extreme case shows the danger in interpreting regression results for two deterministically trended variables which diverge in time.

Fig: 5.7: Regression of a linear on a quadratic trend

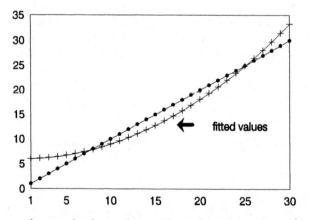

The second example shows the problem of spurious relationships in the case where the variables are subject to stochastic rather than deterministic trends. This example is essentially the same as one particular simulation exercise given in Newbold and Davies (1978) and repeated in Granger and Newbold (1986), but using a much greater number of replications. Suppose that two variables, y_t and x_t, are independently generated by random walk processes:

$$y_t = y_{t-1} + \varepsilon_{1t} \quad ,$$

$$x_t = x_{t-1} + \varepsilon_{2t} \quad ,$$

where ε_{1t}, ε_{2t} are independent standard normal random variables. That is, they are independent normally distributed random variables having zero means and variances equal to unity. Consider regression equations between ε_{2t} and ε_{1t} and between x_t and y_t of the form:

$$\varepsilon_{2t} = \gamma \cdot \varepsilon_{1t} + v_{1t} \quad ,$$

and

$$x_t = \beta \cdot y_t + v_{2t} \quad ,$$

in which the true values of γ and β are zero.

50,000 samples of size 50 each were generated for ε_{1t} and ε_{2t} and using these, values of x_t and y_t were computed for the random walk processes of each variable using starting values of zero for each. First we ran 50,000 regressions of ε_{2t} on ε_{1t} and tested for the significance of the regression coefficient using the Student-t significance test. This experiment is referred to as Case A. Next, we ran another 50,000 regressions of x_t on y_t and again used the Student-t test for the regression coefficient (Case B). For each regression we also computed the Durbin-Watson first-order autocorrelation statistic. The empirical distributions of the computed t-statistics are characterized by the usual descriptive measures (mean, standard deviation, and moment coefficients of skewness and kurtosis). Additionally, the 2.5% fractile of the empirical distributions as well as the percentages of the rejections of the hypothesis that the regression coefficient is equal to zero at the 5% significance level hypothesis are computed. Table 5.1 summarizes the results and compares them with the theoretical findings for the Student-t distribution with 49 degrees of freedom.

Table 5.1: Summary of the Newbold-Davies experiment (50,000 replications)

	Theoretical	Case A	Case B
Student-*t* statistics:			
Mean	0.000	0.000	-0.018
St. dev.	1.021	1.021	5.137
Skewness	0.000	0.006	-0.001
Kurtosis	3.125	3.162	4.039
2.5% fractile	-2.010	-2.010	-10.472
% of 'significant' results at 5% level	5.000	5.040	66.106
Regression statistics:			
Average Durbin-Watson	2.000	2.001	0.334

For case A, the theoretical and empirical results are very much in accord with each other. The estimates in the regression of ε_{2t} on ε_{1t} are unbiased (since the mean is equal to zero), skewness is negligible and the percentage of rejections of the hypothesis that the regression coefficient is equal to zero at the 5% level of significance is near to its theoretical value, that is close to 5%. Hence, the empirical distribution is very close to the theoretical Student-t distribution.

The picture given by Case B, describing the regression of x_t on y_t is totally different. First of all, the shape of the empirical distribution is now far from being similar to that of the Student-t distribution. Although still symmetric, its standard deviation is now much greater than that of the Student-t distribution and the coefficient of kurtosis indicates substantial deviation in shape from the theoretical distribution. Despite the fact that the series x_t and y_t are independently generated, the percentage of 'significant' regressions has risen to 66%. The 2.5% empirical fractile of the empirical distribution of the Student-t statistics, equal to -10.472, is now very remote from the figure read from tables of the Student-t distribution (-2.01). Hence, if one is using the conventional tables of the Student-t statistic for testing the significance of the regression of two series which are subject to stochastic trends, one has the about 2/3 chance that his/her regression will appear to be 'good' (significant) even if there is no relation between the series whatsoever. A warning that something may be amiss is to be found in the Durbin-Watson statistics being usually very low (in our case equal to 0.334 on average) which indicates very strong first order autocorrelation and tells the researcher that there is something seriously wrong with the results.

The above two examples show why economists do not like performing regressions on time series which are subject to stochastic or deterministic trends. These regressions often give apparently good results, and therefore may make it impossible to determine whether or not an economic relationship suggested by a theory has in fact any support from the data.

If one argues, for instance, that aggregate consumption in the UK is predominantly related to a random walk process with drift, it is possible to get some support from the following regression. $CONS_t$ is the original data for aggregate consumption for the period of 1957 (second quarter) to 1975 (fourth quarter) that was used for estimating versions of the Absolute and Permanent Income Hypotheses in Chapter 3. The variable x_t is a random walk with drift generated from the model:

$$x_t = 1 + x_{t-1} + v_t \ ,$$

where the series v_t consists of pseudo-random numbers generated from the standard normal distribution. Regress $CONS_t$ on x_t, an intercept, and three seasonal dummy variables, $Q1_t$, $Q2_t$ and $Q3_t$. The result looks remarkably good:

$$CONS_t = 5578 + 42.68x_t - 741Q1_t - 386Q2_t - 311Q3_t \quad,$$
$$\quad\ (112.7)\ (47.0)\quad (-14.6)\quad (-7.7)\quad (-6.2)$$

$$R^2 = 0.972\ ,\quad DW = 0.67\ ,$$

where Student-t values are given in brackets, R^2 is the conventionally calculated coefficient of determination and DW is the Durbin-Watson statistic. Apart from the Durbin-Watson statistic, the equation looks very promising, but obviously the way the computer generates its random numbers does not have a lot in common with UK aggregate consumption. It is worth noting that *no* data mining was undertaken for the above 'modelling'; the reported results are the very first that came out of the computer, for the first set of 72 random numbers generated.

The discussion above implies that regression analysis makes sense only for data which are not subject to a trend. Since almost all economic data series contain trends, it follows that these series have to be *detrended* before any sensible regression analysis can be performed. It was shown in Chapter 3 that a convenient way of getting rid of a trend in a series is by using first differences (that is, the difference between successive observations) rather than levels of the variables. For a time series with a stochastic trend of the type (5.3):

$$y_t = y_{t-1} + \varepsilon_t \quad,$$

we define the detrended variable:

$$\Delta y_t = y_t - y_{t-1} = \varepsilon_t \quad,$$

and Δy_t is evidently stationary. Similarly, for a random walk with drift (5.4) we have:

$$\Delta y_t = y_t - y_{t-1} = \mu + \varepsilon_t \quad.$$

and, again, Δy_t is stationary.

It is not necessary for a series to be a random walk for its differencing to achieve stationarity. The variables ε_t can be correlated with each other, that is they may not constitute a white noise process. For instance, if the process is of the type:

$$y_t = y_{t-1} + \varepsilon_t \quad,$$

with $\varepsilon_t = \rho \cdot \varepsilon_{t-1} + \xi_t \quad,$

where ξ_t is a white noise variable, first differencing of y_t gives a stationary series, provided that $|\rho| < 1$.

Sometimes it is necessary to difference a series more than once in order to achieve stationarity. In this context it is convenient to use the concept of an *integrated series*. Following Engle and Granger (1987) we may define such a series as follows:

Definition: A nonstationary series which can be transformed to a stationary series by differencing d times is said to be *integrated of order d*.

A series x_t integrated of order d is conventionally denoted as:

$$x_t \sim I(d) \quad .$$

Thus, for example, if $x_t \sim I(2)$, the first differences of the first differences of x_t achieve stationarity, that is:

$$\Delta\Delta x_t = \Delta(x_t - x_{t-1}) = (x_t - x_{t-1}) - (x_{t-1} - x_{t-2}) = x_t - 2x_{t-1} + x_{t-2} \quad .$$

This operation will be termed second (order) differencing, and the resulting variables called second differences. It is important to note that this operation is not the same as taking the difference between the observations on the variable x_t at time periods t and $t-2$. In general, $\Delta\Delta x_t = \Delta^2 x_t \neq x_t - x_{t-2}$.

If x_t is stationary, then no differencing is necessary; that is $x_t \sim I(0)$. If we have two series, x_{1t} and x_{2t} and $x_{1t} \sim I(0)$ while $x_{2t} \sim I(1)$, then $(x_{1t} + x_{2t}) \sim I(1)$. Also, if $x_t \sim I(d)$ then $(\alpha + \beta \cdot x_t) \sim I(d)$ where α and β are constants.

The definition, and indeed the entire problem of enquiry into stationarity, becomes more complex in the case where the series x_t is subject to seasonality. For a series measured s times per annum (so $s = 4$ for quarterly data and $s = 12$ for monthly data), if the series has a seasonal pattern then the differencing which removes seasonality should be s rather than one. That is, an operator $x_t - x_{t-s}$ should be applied rather than $x_t - x_{t-1}$. The difference $x_t - x_{t-s}$ is termed a seasonal difference, and the operation in which these variables are obtained is called *seasonal differencing*, or *s-differencing*. (A numerical example of this operation was given in Chapter 3.) Very occasionally, s-differencing may have to be performed more than once on the data to remove the seasonal pattern. Often (and contrary to the impression given in many textbooks) s-differencing also removes a trend, but where the trend is nonlinear, first differencing of the s-differences may be necessary in order to make the series stationary. Hence, the definition of a *seasonally integrated* series is the following. (This is a somewhat simplified version of a definition given by Engle, Granger and Hallman (1989)).

Definition: A nonstationary series is said to be *seasonally integrated* of order (d, D), denoted $SI_s(d, D)$ if it can be transformed to a stationary series by applying s-differences D times and then differencing the resulting series d times using first differences.

Normally, the value of s is known *a priori*, being equal to 4 in a series of quarterly data and equal to 12 in a series of monthly data. Therefore the subscript s can be safely omitted in order to keep the notation simple.

To reiterate, many series (for example those with additive seasonality) can be transformed to stationary series by applying only seasonal differencing. That is, they are $SI_4(0, 1)$) for quarterly data, or $SI_{12}(0, 1)$ for monthly data even if the nonseasonal component of the series is $I(1)$. However, in some situations, further nonseasonal (normally first) differencing is necessary. Such a procedure is required if there is multiplicative seasonality and (or) the nonseasonal component of the series is integrated of order greater than one, which could be the case for a nonlinear trend.

5.3 Testing for the Order of Integration

Before any sensible regression analysis can be performed, it is essential to identify the order of integration of each variable (provided, of course, that the variable can be transformed into a stationary variable through differencing). Two simple tests are described below.

Suppose that we wish to test the hypothesis that a nonseasonal variable y_t (for example a variable measured annually or one with no seasonal pattern) is integrated of order one, that is that y_t is generated by:

$$y_t = y_{t-1} + \varepsilon_t \ ,$$

where ε_t represents a series of identically distributed stationary variables with zero means.

At first sight, a straightforward procedure would seem to be to test for $\rho = 1$ in the autoregressive equation:

$$y_t = \rho \cdot y_{t-1} + \varepsilon_t \ . \tag{5.6}$$

If the error term in equation (5.6) is a white noise process, then this equation represents a random walk process when $\rho = 1$. We have already seen that such a process generating y_t is nonstationary. However, if $|\rho| < 1$, then the process generating y_t in (5.6) is integrated of order zero and is stationary (see Granger and Newbold (1986, pp. 8-10)). It is tempting to estimate equation (5.6) by ordinary least squares, and to test the hypothesis that $\rho = 1$ by a Student-t test. However, this is not the test used. Under the null hypothesis the equation estimated by (5.6) is nonstationary. Hence, the testing procedure based on the ordinary least squares estimation of non-stationary series might be misleading by showing spurious significance, as shown by the Newbold and Davies example in Section 5.2.

The testing procedure should therefore be conducted with the use of a model which is stationary when estimated under the null hypothesis. An appropriate and simple method of testing the order of integration of y_t in (5.6) has been proposed by Dickey and Fuller (1979), hereafter called the *DF* test. Strictly speaking, the *DF* test is a test of the null hypothesis that in (5.6) $\rho - 1 = 0$, the so-called *unit root test*. This test is based on the estimation of an equivalent regression equation to (5.6), namely:

$$\Delta y_t = \delta \cdot y_{t-1} + \varepsilon_t \ . \tag{5.7}$$

Equation (5.7) can be re-written as:

$$y_t = (1+\delta) \cdot y_{t-1} + \varepsilon_t \ ,$$

which is the same as (5.6) with $\rho = (1+\delta)$. Hence, if in (5.7) δ is negative, then in (5.6) ρ becomes smaller than one. The Dickey-Fuller test consists of testing the negativity of δ in the ordinary least squares regression of (5.7). Rejection of the null hypothesis: $\delta = 0$ in favour of the alternative: $\delta < 0$ implies that $\rho < 1$ and that y_t is integrated of order zero.

In order to test the null hypothesis it is necessary to know the distribution of the statistic used for the test and the associated critical region for its evaluation. Since in (5.7) we want to evaluate a hypothesis which concerns only a single parameter, the natural choice would seem to be that of a Student-t ratio, namely the ratio of the ordinary least squares estimate of δ to its ordinary least squares standard error.

Evidently, since the dependent variable in (5.7) is stationary (since $y_t \sim I(1))$, there is no danger of spurious significance due to stochastic trends. Unfortunately, despite the fact that under the null hypothesis the left-hand side variable in the regression equation (5.7) is stationary, this ratio or statistic does not have the familiar Student-t distribution. If $y_t \sim I(1)$, as implied by the null hypothesis, equation (5.7) represents a regression of an $I(0)$ variable on a $I(1)$ variable. Not surprisingly, in such a case the t-ratio does not have a limiting normal distribution. This is shown by Figures 5.8 and 5.9 where the distributions (frequencies) of 50,000 simulated Dickey-Fuller statistics are shown. These distributions have been computed in the following way.

For a process without drift, the variable y_t has been generated from:

$$y_t = y_{t-1} + \widetilde{\varepsilon}_t \ ,$$

where the $\widetilde{\varepsilon}_t$ are random numbers generated from the standard normal distribution and with initial value $y_0 = \widetilde{\varepsilon}_0$. For $t = 1, 2, ..., 50$, this generates a series of 50 'observations' on the variable y_t. For these 50 observations, the Dickey-Fuller test statistic in the form of the Student-t ratio is computed. Using a different set of random numbers for the error term $\widetilde{\varepsilon}_t$ for each replication, this procedure is repeated 50,000 times. The end result is 50,000 Dickey-Fuller test statistics which have been gathered together into the frequency distribution given as Figure 5.8. Figure 5.9 shows the distribution of computed *DF* statistics where equation (5.7) includes an intercept, for a process with a unitary drift coefficient, that is where y_t is generated from:

$$y_t = 1 + y_{t-1} + \widetilde{\varepsilon}_t \quad .$$

Fig. 5.8: Empirical distribution of the Dickey-Fuller statistic without drift

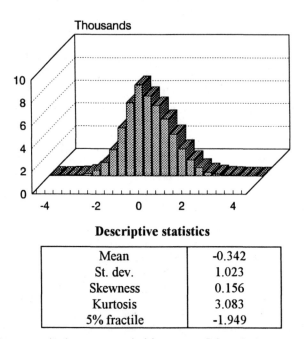

Descriptive statistics

Mean	-0.342
St. dev.	1.023
Skewness	0.156
Kurtosis	3.083
5% fractile	-1.949

Each of these graphs is accompanied by a set of descriptive statistics analogous to those used for explaining the Newbold-Davies experiment. In order to facilitate comparison between the cases of processes without and with drift, the same sets of random numbers for the error terms were used in each case. It is clear from Figures 5.8 and 5.9 that the simulated distributions are not like that of the Student-t distribution, which is symmetric and centered at zero. The distributions of the Dickey-Fuller statistics are visibly positively skewed, and in both cases have means which are negative rather than equal to zero. It is also evident that those two distributions are not identical. Hence, the presence or absence of a drift plays a crucial role in the Dickey-Fuller testing procedure.

Fig. 5.9: Empirical distribution of the Dickey-Fuller statistic with drift

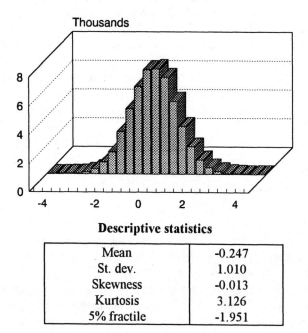

Descriptive statistics

Mean	-0.247
St. dev.	1.010
Skewness	-0.013
Kurtosis	3.126
5% fractile	-1.951

Since the distributions of Dickey-Fuller statistics are complicated and, in general, do not have known analytical forms, there are difficulties in finding exact critical values for the tests. Fortunately, critical values may be approximated through simulation. In the tables below Figures 5.8 and 5.9, the 5% fractiles, that is the simulated values which divide the lowest 5% of the statistics from the other 95%, are given. In the case of no drift, the value of −1.949 is the average between the 2500th and 2501st lowest values in the 50,000 statistics. Since the values of y_t were generated under the assumption that there is a unit root in the series, the value of −1.949 can be regarded as the 'critical value' at the level of significance of 5%. That is, if one uses this value for the evaluation of the null hypothesis that a series contains a unit root, and the unit root really exists in the series, then the mistake of rejecting the null hypothesis will be made, on average, no more than five times in 100 such cases. Evidently, the value of −1.949 is not the absolutely accurate representation of the 5% fractile, since the distribution of Dickey-Fuller statistic is simulated rather than derived analytically. For instance, where we repeated the simulation with a different set of random numbers, the 5% percentile value of the 50,000 statistics was −1.952 rather than −1.949. Although the difference is not substantial, it adds some uncertainty to the results.

Table 1 in the Appendix, which reports critical values (percentiles) for the distribution of the Student-*t* statistic for the Dickey-Fuller regression equation (5.7), has been constructed in a similar (though more precise) way to the above. It is constructed differently to other tables available (for instance Fuller (1976), Guilkey and Schmidt (1989) and MacKinnon (1991)). (For a more detailed description of the simulation technique used and the generation of initial values both for this table and Table 2 to Table 9 see Blangiewicz and Charemza (1990) and the Technical Notes to the statistical tables given in the Appendix). Table 1 in the Appendix reflects the fact that the percentiles computed for simulated distributions are empirical rather than theoretical and therefore have to be regarded with some uncertainty. This uncertainty is reflected by reporting a range for the critical values denoted by *lower* and *upper* values. For testing integration using the Dickey-Fuller test, the values denoted *lower* and *upper* in Column A are used in the following way. If the computed Student-*t* statistic is smaller (more negative) than the lower critical value for a particular number of observations (n), the null (unit root) hypothesis has to be rejected and the alternative of stationarity of y_t accepted. When reading the tables remember that the minus sign is omitted from each entry; hence 1.99, for the lower limit of the 5% critical value for the number of observations equal to 50 stands for −1.99, etc. If the calculated Student-*t* statistic is greater than the upper critical value, the null hypothesis cannot be rejected. There is an inconclusive range between the lower and upper limits which is due to the fact that we are using empirical (simulated) percentiles as the critical values rather than the analytical ones. Since the true critical value is unknown, if the calculated statistic falls within this range, then one is unsure whether or not to reject the null hypothesis.

But what if the null hypothesis that $\delta = 0$ in equation (5.7) cannot be rejected? In such a case the variable y_t might be integrated of order higher than zero, or might not be integrated at all. Consequently, the next step would be to test whether the order of integration is one. If $y_t \sim I(1)$, then $\Delta y_t \sim I(0)$. Hence we can repeat the test using Δy_t instead of y_t. The Dickey-Fuller equation is now:

$$\Delta\Delta y_t = \delta \cdot \Delta y_{t-1} + \varepsilon_t \ ,$$

and again our interest is in testing the negativity of δ. If the null hypothesis that $\delta = 0$ is rejected and the alternative $\delta < 0$ can be accepted, the series Δy_t is stationary and $y_t \sim I(1)$. If the null hypothesis cannot be rejected, we may subsequently test whether $y_t \sim I(2)$. That is, we run the Dickey-Fuller regression using $\Delta\Delta\Delta y_t$ as the left–hand–side variable and $\Delta\Delta y_{t-1}$ as the right-hand-side variable. In theory, we can continue the process until we establish an order of integration for y_t, or until we realize that y_t cannot be made stationary by differencing. In practice, it is unusual for economic series to be integrated of an order greater than two. Obviously it might be the case that the series is not integrated at all, so that no differencing of any order will transform it into a stationary series. It is also possible that a series is integrated of some order, but the tests applied fail to give a clear indication of this order. In both cases there is a danger of *overdifferencing*, that is of applying the difference operator too many times. Overdifferencing normally results in a very high positive (instead of negative) value of the *DF* test accompanied by a very high coefficient of determination for the fitted regression. Consider the following typical but fictitious example. Suppose that the *DF* statistic computed for a series x_t is 1.23, which obviously is not 'significantly negative', so we apply the test for first differences. For the differenced series Δx_t the *DF* statistic becomes -1.00, which is still not significantly negative so we move to second differences. However, for the series $\Delta\Delta x_t$, the *DF* statistic becomes 8.2 (positive!) and the coefficient of determination for the regression of $\Delta\Delta\Delta x_t$ on $\Delta\Delta x_{t-1}$ is 0.991. This is a clear indication of overdifferencing, and either the series x_t is $I(1)$ but the test has failed to discover this, or the series is not an integrated time series and differencing cannot transform it into a stationary series.

The Dickey-Fuller test can also be used for testing the order of integration for a variable generated as a stochastic process with drift, that is by tests on the equation:

$$\Delta y_t - \mu + \delta \cdot y_{t-1} + \varepsilon_t \ , \tag{5.8}$$

where μ is a constant or intercept representing drift (see equation (5.4)). The technique is analogous to that described before, but since the distribution of the Student-t statistic for δ is different (compare Figures 5.8 and 5.9), different tables of critical values should be used. In this case the values under Column B in Table 1 are appropriate. In practice, it is often unclear when one should use this test, and when one should use the *DF* test without an intercept. Experience suggests that tests with the intercept sometimes give unexpected results that are hard to interpret. (We consider general questions regarding the inclusion or otherwise of an intercept (and/or a trend term) in integration tests more fully in Section 5.4 below.)

Statistical inference about a stochastic trend is often combined with a deterministic trend. A straightforward modification of the Dickey-Fuller equation which accounts for both drift and a linear deterministic trend is the following:

$$\Delta y_t = \mu + \alpha \cdot t + \delta \cdot y_{t-1} + \varepsilon_t \ . \tag{5.9}$$

In the above equation it is possible to test simultaneously for the absence of a stochastic trend ($\delta < 0$) and the existence of a deterministic trend ($\alpha \neq 0$). Since in this case the null hypothesis involves more than one parameter, an appropriate test is the Lagrange Multiplier test, again with non-conventional critical values (see Dickey and Fuller (1981) or Guilkey and Schmidt (1989)). A simpler approach to the testing of the order of integration of a variable, conditional on the presence of a deterministic trend in the underlying process of that variable, is a straightforward Dickey-Fuller test on the negativity of δ in equation (5.9). Column C in Table 1 of the Appendix reports lower and upper bound values for this test.

A substantial weakness of the original Dickey-Fuller test is that it does not take account of possible autocorrelation in the error process ε_t. If ε_t is autocorrelated (that is, it is not white noise) then the ordinary least squares estimates of equation (5.7), and of its variants described above, are not efficient. A simple solution, advocated by Dickey and Fuller (1981), is to use lagged left–hand–side variables as additional explanatory variables to approximate the autocorrelation. This test, called the Augmented Dickey-Fuller test, and denoted conventionally as *ADF*, is generally regarded as being the most efficient test from among the simple tests for integration and is at present the most widely used in practice.

The *ADF* equivalent of (5.7) is the following:

$$\Delta y_t = \delta \cdot y_{t-1} + \sum_{i=1}^{k} \delta_i \cdot \Delta y_{t-i} + \varepsilon_t \ . \tag{5.10}$$

The testing procedure is the same as before, with an examination of the Student-t ratio for δ. The critical values of the test are the same as for the corresponding Dickey-Fuller test (as reported in Table 1 in the Appendix). It is straightforward to augment equations (5.8) and (5.9) analogously, by adding lagged left–hand–side variables to the set of regressors. Again, this should not affect the critical values of the test. The comments made earlier relating to overdifferencing apply equally to the *ADF* test.

In practice the choice of augmentation (that is, of the length and elements of the autoregressive component in (5.10)) is of the utmost importance and is often neglected in the literature. Since the primary goal of the inclusion of the augmentation terms is to secure a white noise property for ε_t, the emphasis should be put into applying a battery of tests for ensuring that the series ε_t is indeed independently and identically distributed. The minimum requirement here is to conduct thorough autocorrelation tests. The application of the Durbin-Watson test is not enough. This should be supported at least by a Lagrange Multiplier test for joint autocorrelation up to a given order (see the *COMFAC* example in

Chapter 4). It is also important not to have too many augmentation terms in the *ADF* equation. Whilst having too few augmentations affects the size of the test (the null hypothesis of the series being $I(1)$ can be rejected too often), too many augmentations result in diminishing power of the test, resulting in not rejecting the null hypothesis often enough. A simple guide for choosing the appropriate augmentation terms is to apply the *general to specific* procedure: start by selecting a reasonably large value of k in (5.10) and then systematically reduce the number of augmentations by imposing and testing zero restrictions and testing for autocorrelation in the restricted model. In most cases the deletion of insignificant augmentations does not affect the property of lack of autocorrelation of the residuals. Hence, it is normally possible to finish up with a model where only significant augmentations remain and, at the same time, no autocorrelation is present in the residuals. It is therefore important to remember that, if the total length of augmentation is k, the actual number of augmentation terms which appear in the equation might be smaller than k, since some of the coefficients δ_i can be zeros.

If only a quick guide is needed as to whether a variable is integrated of order zero, a useful tool is a simple test developed on the basis of the Durbin-Watson statistic. Instead of running the regressions needed for the *DF* and *ADF* tests, we may compute for the variable y_t a Durbin-Watson type statistic (the *integration Durbin-Watson statistic, IDW*):

$$IDW = \frac{\sum (y_t - y_{t-1})^2}{\sum (y_t - \bar{y}_t)^2} , \tag{5.11}$$

where $\bar{y}_t$ stands for the arithmetic mean of y_t. If $\rho = 1$ in (5.6), the numerator in (5.11) is equal to $\sum \varepsilon_t^2$. In other words, y_{t-1} represents the 'fitted' value for a regression of y_t on y_{t-1} under the restriction that the coefficient on y_{t-1} is equal to one. Intuitively, in such a case the value of *IDW* should be close to zero.

The *IDW* test should provide a rough guide to the stationarity of a variable. If it is low (say lower than 0.5), one might suspect that the variable in question is not stationary and that further, more thorough testing is required. If the value of *IDW* is close to two, the stationarity of the examined variable might be relatively safely assumed, without the need for further investigation.

Testing for seasonal integration is more complicated. From the various tests proposed, the simplest is probably that suggested by Dickey, Hasza and Fuller (1984) and modified by Osborn *et al.* (1988), denoted *DHF* hereafter. It resembles a generalization of the *ADF* test. For a series measured s times per annum, the original test is based on the Student-t statistic for the *OLS* estimate of the parameter δ in the regression equation:

$$\Delta_s z_t = \delta \cdot z_{t-s} + \sum_{i=1}^{k} \delta_i \cdot \Delta_s y_{t-i} + \varepsilon_t \ , \qquad (5.12)$$

where the variable z_{t-s} is constructed in the following way. First, regress $\Delta_s y_t$ (where $\Delta_s y_t = y_t - y_{t-s}$) on its own values, lagged up to h periods. That is, estimate the equation:

$$\Delta_s y_t = \sum_{i=1}^{h} \lambda_i \cdot \Delta_s y_{t-i} + \xi_t \ . \qquad (5.13)$$

Next, use the *OLS* estimates of $\lambda_1, \lambda_2, ..., \lambda_h$, (denoted accordingly as $\hat{\lambda}_1, \hat{\lambda}_2, ..., \hat{\lambda}_h$) to construct the variable z_t from $y_t, y_{t-1}, ..., y_{t-h}$ as:

$$z_t = y_t - \sum_{i=1}^{h} \hat{\lambda}_i \cdot y_{t-i} \ .$$

Finally, substitute the lagged value of z_t, namely z_{t-s}, into (5.12), estimate the equation and compute the Student-t statistic for δ. A modification suggested by Osborn *et al.* (1988, p.365) is to use $\Delta_s y_t$ rather than $\Delta_s z_t$ as the dependent variable in equation (5.12) that is, to estimate the equation:

$$\Delta_s y_t = \delta \cdot z_{t-s} + \sum_{i=1}^{k} \delta_i \cdot \Delta_s y_{t-i} + \varepsilon_t \ .$$

It is interesting to note that if in (5.13) $h = 0$, the *DHF* equation reduces to a straightforward analogue of the *ADF* equation, that is to:

$$\Delta_s y_t = \delta \cdot y_{t-s} + \sum_{i=1}^{k} \delta_i \cdot \Delta_s y_{t-i} + \varepsilon_t \ .$$

Computation of the *DHF* test with the use of econometric packages such as *PC-GIVE* is feasible, as the example in Section 5.8 illustrates. The choice of h and k in (5.13) and (5.12) should be done analogously to the way the degree of augmentation in the *ADF* test is determined. In other words, h and k should be selected as those values for which the white noise hypotheses for ε_t and ξ_t can be maintained. Again, the general to specific procedure can be applied, together with the Lagrange Multiplier test for autocorrelation of a reasonably high order. The critical values for the test for monthly and quarterly data, both with and without a constant (intercept) in the test equation, are given in Table 5 in the Appendix. The way the tables are constructed is analogous to that of the Dickey-Fuller tables; there are lower and upper values for each number of observations (n), with an inconclusive region between them. If the estimate of δ in (5.12) is significantly negative (that is, below the lower critical value; remember that the minus sign is omitted in the tables!), the null hypothesis of the existence of a seasonally integrated process may be rejected in favour of the alternative hypothesis that either there is no stochastic seasonality, or that stochastic seasonality which can be removed by using s-differences does not exist.

If the null hypothesis is not rejected, it is usual to consider the order of nonseasonal differencing required to achieve stationarity, rather than consider higher orders of seasonal differencing. That is, economic data series are generally expected to be $SI_s(0,0)$ or $SI_s(0,1)$ or $SI_s(d,1)$ so that, at most, using s-differences once is expected to remove seasonal nonstationarity. Hence, if the null ($\delta = 0$) in (5.12) above is not rejected (that is, the null hypothesis that the variable is $SI_s(0,1)$ cannot be rejected), the next step is to consider whether the variable is $SI_s(1,1)$ rather than $SI_s(0,1)$ with the former representing the new null hypothesis, and the latter the new alternative hypothesis. Hence, the following equation is constructed and estimated in the same way as the ADF test above:

$$\Delta\Delta_s y_t = \delta \cdot \Delta_s y_{t-1} + \sum_{i=1}^{k} \delta_i \cdot \Delta\Delta_s y_{t-i} + \varepsilon_t \ ,$$

and the significant negativity or otherwise of δ is examined. If the null hypothesis that the variable is $SI_s(1,1)$ is not rejected, then this forms the next alternative hypothesis. The new null is that the variable is $SI_s(2,1)$, which is examined by a test on the negativity of δ in the equation:

$$\Delta\Delta\Delta_s y_t = \delta \cdot \Delta\Delta_s y_{t-1} + \sum_{i=1}^{k} \delta_i \cdot \Delta\Delta\Delta_s y_{t-i} + \varepsilon_t \ ,$$

and so on. Note that the constructed variable z_t is needed only for the DHF test for the order of seasonal integration. It is not used in the later tests for the order of nonseasonal integration. In Section 5.8, an example of testing for seasonal integration as well as for the order of non-seasonal integration is given, using the DHF and ADF approaches for the principal variables in the $DHSY$ model.

A more general test, which allows for cyclical movements at different frequencies and therefore gives a richer insight into the nature of the seasonal pattern for a variable, is the test for seasonal integration proposed by Hylleberg, Engle, Granger and Yoo (1990), hereafter termed the $HEGY$ test. To discuss this test more fully, it will be useful to recall from Chapter 4 the concept of the lag operator L, where $Ly_t = y_{t-1}$ and $L^j y_t = y_{t-j}$. In this notation, a seasonal difference may be written as $(1-L^s)y_t$. The simple $HEGY$ tests for quarterly data use the representation:

$$\Delta_4 y_t = \sum_{i=1}^{4} \pi_i Y_{i,t-1} + \varepsilon_t \ , \tag{5.14}$$

where the $Y_{i,t}$ variables are constructed from the series on y_t as:

$$Y_{1,t} = (1+L)(1+L^2) \cdot y_t \qquad = y_t + y_{t-1} + y_{t-2} + y_{t-3} \quad ;$$

$$Y_{2,t} = -(1-L)(1+L^2) \cdot y_t \qquad = -y_t + y_{t-1} - y_{t-2} + y_{t-3} \quad ;$$

$$Y_{3,t} = -(1-L)(1+L) \cdot y_t \qquad = -y_t + y_{t-2} \quad ;$$

$$Y_{4,t} = -(L)(1-L)(1+L) \cdot y_t \qquad = Y_{3,t-1} = -y_{t-1} + y_{t-3} \quad .$$

The *HEGY* model may be estimated by ordinary least squares. If the null hypothesis of stochastic seasonality is true (that is, if the variable is seasonally integrated), then all π_is will be equal to zero. Correspondingly, though slightly imprecisely (see Hylleberg *et al.* (1990, p.223)), we may also say that a series will have no unit roots at all, and will therefore be stationary, only if each of the π_is are different from zero. Each negative π_i has a different interpretation. In particular, if only π_1 is negative, then there is no nonseasonal stochastic stationary component (that is no component corresponding to an $I(0)$ process). If only π_2 is negative, then there is no semi-annual cycle. Both π_3 and π_4 are related to the annual cycle, and may be tested jointly, with the use of the Lagrange Multiplier *F*-test. Thus the presence of unit roots at the zero, biannual and annual frequencies imply that $\pi_1 = 0$, $\pi_2 = 0$ and $\pi_3 = \pi_4 = 0$ respectively. Critical values for the *t*-statistics for the parameters π_1 and π_2, as well as for the Lagrange Multiplier *F*-statistic for testing the joint hypothesis: $\pi_3 = \pi_4 = 0$ are given in Table 7 in the Appendix. The way these values have been determined and are used is analogous to that described previously for the Dickey-Fuller and the *DHF* test statistics. If calculated values of the *t*-statistics are below those tabulated in Table 7 or the calculated *F*-statistic is above that tabulated in the same table, then the corresponding null hypotheses of zero values for the π_i parameters can be rejected at the chosen level of significance.

In order to justify the *HEGY* tests, those mathematically inclined may wish to check that the expression $(1-L^4)$ may be factorized as:

$$1-L^4 = (1-L)(1+L)(1+L^2) = (1-L)(1+L)(1-i \cdot L)(1+i \cdot L) \quad ,$$

where i is an imaginary part of a complex number such that $i^2 = -1$.

Technically, this factorization shows that a quarterly stochastic seasonal unit root process has four roots of modulus one. One root $(1-L)$ described as being at 'zero frequency' removes the trend. The three other roots $(1+L)$, and $(1 \pm i \cdot L)$ which remove the seasonal structure imply stochastic cycles of semi-annual and annual periodicity. For a more detailed explanation of the concepts of seasonal frequencies and seasonal fluctuations see Granger and Newbold (1986, Chapter 2). An elegant introduction to complex numbers and complex number dynamics can be found in Dhrymes (1970a, Mathematical Appendix).

Straightforward generalisations of the *HEGY* test can be made through an inclusion of a constant term in (5.14):

$$\Delta_4 y_t = \pi_0 + \sum_{i=1}^{4} \pi_i Y_{i,t-1} + \varepsilon_t \quad ,$$

or the inclusion of deterministic seasonality:

$$\Delta_4 y_t = \sum_{i=1}^{4} \pi_i Y_{i,t-1} + \sum_{i=1}^{4} b_i Q i_t + \varepsilon_t \quad ,$$

where $Q i_t$ denote seasonal dummy variables. The latter equation corresponds to the hypothesis that the variable y_t contains both deterministic and stochastic seasonal components. Tables of critical values for the cases where there is either a constant (intercept) or deterministic seasonality in the *HEGY* equation are given in the Appendix in Tables 8 and 9 respectively. Normally, some augmentation analogous to that of the Augmented Dickey-Fuller test is added to the *HEGY* equation in order to ensure that the residuals can be regarded as being white noise. With such augmentation, the simple *HEGY* test (without the constant and without seasonality) becomes:

$$\Delta_4 y_t = \sum_{i=1}^{4} \pi_i Y_{i,t-1} + \sum_{i=1}^{k} \delta_i \cdot \Delta_4 y_{t-i} + \varepsilon_t \quad .$$

As in the case of the *ADF* test, the addition of augmentation terms does not affect the distribution of the statistics and the critical values used in this case are the same as for the model without augmentation.

A much simpler model for quarterly data which can be useful in practical investigations is where it assumed that the process may have been generated by a combination of stochastic trend and deterministic seasonality of the type:

$$y_t = y_{t-1} + \sum_{i=1}^{4} \alpha_i Q i_t + \varepsilon_t \quad , \tag{5.15}$$

where the $Q i_t$ are seasonal dummy variables. In such a model, the order of integration can be tested by a conventional *DF* or *ADF* test. However, the distribution of the Student-*t* statistic is different and the critical values should be taken from Table 1 in the Appendix.

5.4 Further Considerations in the Testing for the Order of Integration

Whilst the Dickey-Fuller and Augmented Dickey-Fuller tests discussed in Section 5.3 remain popular methods in the testing for the order of integration of a series, some aspects of these tests have received criticism and alternative approaches have been suggested. In particular, some problems may arise from the use of Dickey-Fuller type tests which start by considering whether a series is integrated of order zero or not. If not, attention turns to whether it is integrated of order one, and so on. It has been established that this particular sequence of tests is not necessarily the best way in which to proceed and a different approach is discussed in section (a). In section (b), we investigate more fully questions raised earlier in Section (5.3) with respect to the inclusion of constant and trend terms in equations formulated to test for the order of integration of a series. Finally, in section (c) we indicate why Dickey-Fuller type tests may be unreliable in establishing the order of integration of a series which has been subject to a structural break. We examine one particular alternative (but related) approach that has been proposed for this situation.

(a) The Dickey-Pantula Test

In the Dickey-Fuller type tests we considered in the previous section, testing proceeds 'upwards'; that is, an investigator starts by deciding whether or not a variable is $I(0)$. If not $I(0)$, the next step would be to decide whether it is $I(1)$ or not, and so on. Thus the investigation starts from the lowest possible order of integration and moves upwards towards increasingly higher orders of integration. This is not necessarily the best way to proceed. We noted in Chapter 4 where the concept of general to specific modelling was discussed, that statistical tests may have better properties if one starts from the most *general* hypothesis and works downwards towards more *specific* hypotheses, an approach which might be described as 'testing downwards'.

The idea of testing downwards has been captured by Dickey and Pantula (1987) in their approach to determining the order of integration of a series. The sequence of tests starts from the highest sensible order of integration for a series and moves downwards towards lower orders of integration. Since Dickey-Fuller tests are based on the assumption of a series having at most one unit root, the first few tests in an 'upwards' testing direction would be theoretically invalid if the series in fact contained more than one unit root (i.e. was integrated of an order greater than one). The Dickey and Pantula method offers a simple remedy to this problem.

It is in fact unusual for an economic series to be integrated of a higher order than two. In order to understand the Dickey-Pantula test where this is the highest envisaged order of integration of a series, it is useful to start by considering an autoregressive model of order two:

$$(1 - \rho_1 L)(1 - \rho_2 L)y_t = u_t \quad ,$$

where L is the lag operator and u_t is a stochastic error term. The roots of this equation (r_1 and r_2) are the solutions (values of L) to:

$$(1 - \rho_1 L)(1 - \rho_2 L) = 0 \quad , \text{ so that either } \quad L = 1/\rho_1 \quad \text{or} \quad L = 1/\rho_2 \quad ,$$

$$\text{or} \quad r_1 = 1/\rho_1 \text{ and } r_2 = 1/\rho_2 \quad .$$

Stationarity of the process for y_t would require the absolute values of both roots to be greater than unity (e.g. see Granger and Newbold (1986, p.9)). These conditions for stationarity are often described in the literature as requiring that the roots 'lie outside the unit circle'.

The autoregressive equation may be re-written as:

$$y_t = (\rho_1 + \rho_2)y_{t-1} - \rho_1 \rho_2 y_{t-2} + u_t \quad . \tag{5.16}$$

Recalling that $\Delta^2 y_t = \Delta \Delta y_t = \Delta(y_t - y_{t-1}) = (y_t - y_{t-1}) - (y_{t-1} - y_{t-2})$ and that $\Delta y_{t-1} = y_{t-1} - y_{t-2}$, then equation (5.16) above may be re-written as:

$$\Delta^2 y_t = (\rho_1 \rho_2 - 1)\Delta y_{t-1} - (1 - \rho_1)(1 - \rho_2)y_{t-1} + u_t \quad ,$$

$$\text{or} \quad \Delta^2 y_t = \beta_1 \Delta y_{t-1} + \beta_2 y_{t-1} + u_t \quad , \tag{5.17}$$

where $\beta_1 = \rho_1 \rho_2 - 1$ and $\beta_2 = -(1 - \rho_1)(1 - \rho_2)$.

The initial null hypothesis is that the series on y_t is $I(2)$, in which case there are two unit roots ($r_1 = r_2 = 1$ and hence $\rho_1 = \rho_2 = 1$) so that in equation (5.17), $\beta_1 = \beta_2 = 0$. The initial alternative hypothesis is that $y_t \sim I(1)$, so that one of the roots, r_1 or r_2, is unity, and the other root has an absolute value greater than unity. Examination of the expressions for β_1 and β_2 above shows that for this alternative hypothesis, $\beta_2 = 0$ and $\beta_1 < 0$. Thus $\beta_2 = 0$ under both null and alternative hypotheses. A test of the null that $y_t \sim I(2)$ is accordingly performed by estimating equation 5.17 with the constraint $\beta_2 = 0$ imposed, that is by estimating:

$$\Delta^2 y_t = \beta_1 \Delta y_{t-1} + u_t \quad , \tag{5.18}$$

and testing whether the estimated β_1 coefficient is 'significantly negative'. This test can be carried out in an identical fashion to that discussed for the Dickey-Fuller test, namely by comparing the Student-t value associated with the estimate of β_1 with the critical values in column A in Table 1 in the Appendix. (Indeed, this was the test suggested in Section 5.3 for testing the null hypothesis that a series was integrated of order of at least two against the alternative hypothesis that it was $I(1)$).

If the initial null that $y_t \sim I(2)$ is rejected, then interest passes to testing the new null that $y_t \sim I(1)$. For this new null, the alternative hypothesis is that $y_t \sim I(0)$. If there is only one unit root as the new null specifies, then in equation 5.17, $\beta_2 = 0$ and $\beta_1 < 0$. The alternative hypothesis implies that $\beta_1 < 0$ and $\beta_2 < 0$ as stationarity of the process for y_t requires both $|\rho_1| < 1$ and $|\rho_2| < 1$.

The general equation (5.17) can now be estimated and the 'significant negativity' of the regression coefficient estimate of β_2 tested using the critical values in column A in Table 1. If the estimate of β_2 is not significantly negative, the null that $y_t \sim I(1)$ cannot be rejected. If the null is rejected, then the conclusion is that y_t is stationary, that is it is integrated of order zero. Note the difference between this sequence of tests and the Dickey-Fuller 'upward' testing approach. In the Dickey-Pantula approach when the null is that the series is $I(1)$, it means precisely $I(1)$ and not higher since hypotheses concerning higher orders of integration will have been tested previously. That is, the series contains at most one unit root. As pointed out above, however, non-rejection of the null that the series is $I(1)$ with the Dickey-Fuller approach is consistent with the series being integrated of order one *or higher* (at least one unit root) which is the source of the potential statistical weakness of this approach.

The test equations may include augmentations to allow for the possibility of serially correlated errors as in the Augmented Dickey-Fuller test, when again column A in Table 1 in the Appendix may be used. The test equations may also include a constant and/or a time trend. Appropriate tables of critical values would need to be applied in each case. These tables are the same as would be used for Dickey-Fuller tests with constant and/or trend (e.g. columns B and C in Table 1 in the Appendix). The Dickey-Pantula procedure may also be extended to test for higher orders of integration than two: (see Enders (1995), pp. 227-228). In practice it will often be the case that the Dickey-Pantula procedure will require fewer regressions to be run than in the Dickey-Fuller approach, and will lead one to the appropriate order of integration of a series more rapidly and efficiently.

(b) Integration Tests and the Presence of a Constant and Trend

In Section 5.3 it was noted that Dickey-Fuller type tests can also be applied when it is assumed that the stochastic process which has generated the data contains an intercept (constant) and/or a time trend (equations (5.8) and (5.9)). Similarly, as indicated above, the Dickey-Pantula test may be modified to allow for the presence of one or both of these effects. If the appropriate form of the process which generated the data was known, then tests would be performed using the tables of critical values corresponding to the process utilized with or without a constant. In practice, of course, the appropriate process to be adopted (i.e. equation (5.7), (5.8) or (5.9)) is unknown and the question arises as to the consequences of conducting unit root tests using an incorrectly assumed process, that is, the inclusion of a constant where the 'true' process does not have it or *vice versa*. This is too wide a subject to be examined fully here, but a flavour of the considerations and problems that arise in this situation can be given by considering whether or not an intercept should be included in the stochastic trend model.

Suppose that the actual process which generated the data was a stochastic trend with drift:

$$y_t = \mu + y_{t-1} + e_t \ , \tag{5.19}$$

or

$$\Delta y_t = \mu + e_t \ .$$

Mistakenly, an investigator omits the intercept or constant when estimating the process in order to carry out a Dickey-Fuller test, and estimates:

$$\Delta y_t = \delta y_{t-1} + \varepsilon_t \ . \tag{5.20}$$

The consequences of using the misspecified equation to test for a unit root in the data can be illustrated by simulation. Ten thousand samples of size 50 each were generated for the variable y_t by drawing values for e_t independently from a standard normal distribution and computing y_t from equation (5.19) with the value of μ fixed at 0.5. (A starting value of y_0 of zero was used in each case.) Equation (5.20) was then estimated for each of the 10,000 samples and an empirical distribution of the estimated Student-t values for the parameter δ obtained. The 5 percentile value of these Student-t values , that is the Student-t value for which 5% of the 10,000 values were less and 95% were more, was then calculated and found to be 1.27. The investigator believes that the process which has generated the data does not contain an intercept, so that the 5% critical value for the unit root test which will be used will be obtained from column A in Table 1 in the Appendix. For a sample size of 50, the lower and upper tabulated values are -1.99 and -1.91 respectively. Consequently, as the 5 percentile value of the empirical distribution of the test statistic used is, in this example, so much higher than the tabulated values, an investigator who incorrectly omits the intercept term in the equation estimated to perform the unit root test will hardly ever be in a position to reject the null of a unit root (non-stationarity) even when this is false. In statistical terminology, it can be said that the power of the test in this case is very low, where power is defined as the probability of rejecting a false null hypothesis. The power of the test will fall whenever the estimated equation includes a redundant constant, but by how much power will be reduced will depend on the size of the constant in the *DGP*.

However, one also has to consider the opposite case where the true null does not contain an intercept, but where the investigator mistakenly includes one in the equation estimated to perform a unit root test. That is, the data are now generated by the process:

$$y_t = y_{t-1} + e_t \quad ,$$

but the equation mistakenly estimated as representing the null is:

$$\Delta y_t = \delta_0 + \delta_1 y_{t-1} + \varepsilon_t \quad , \tag{5.21}$$

which involves a redundant constant δ_0.

Again, 10,000 samples of size 50 were generated for y_t, this time from equation (5.20). Each sample was used to estimate equation (5.21), and the 5 percentile value for the Student-t statistics on the estimated parameter δ_1 calculated. This had the value -2.92. In this case, the investigator erroneously believes that the null contains an intercept, so that unit root tests would be conducted by comparing the estimated Student-t value on δ_1 from any sample with the critical values from column B in Table 1 in the Appendix. For a sample of size 50, the 5% critical values reported in this table are -1.96 (lower) and -1.87 (upper). As the 5 percentile value is less than the lower tabulated value, then the null hypothesis of a unit root will tend to be rejected in error more often than the 5 cases out of 100 on average which was intended. The Type-1 error (the probability of falsely rejecting a true null hypothesis) is greater than the 5% value the investigator imagines he or she is working with. This could be considered a worse problem than the lack of power encountered in the first case, as with a fixed sample size, it is usual to set up a statistical test to meet a pre-specified Type-1 error (or size of the test).

The problem is compounded if the analysis is extended to cover time trends in the data generating process as well (e.g. equation (5.9)). Campbell and Perron (1991) report that the power of unit root tests fall even further if a time trend is included unneccessarily in the equation estimated to conduct the test. Omitting relevant deterministic regressors or including irrelevant ones can both lead to problems in properly identifying the presence or otherwise of a unit root in a series. Algorithms (sequences of steps to be followed) to help guide the investigator where there are no firm reasons to choose one data generating process rather than another have been provided by Dolado, Jenkinson and Sosvilla-Rivero (1990), Holden and Perman (1994) and Enders (1995).

(c) The Perron Test for a Unit Root in the Presence of a Structural Change

In Section 5.3 we introduced (equation (5.4)) the concept of a random walk with drift, namely:

$$y_t = \mu + y_{t-1} + \varepsilon_t \; . \tag{5.4}$$

The constant, μ, may be interpreted as a deterministic trend in this series, as can be demonstrated as follows.

Let y_0 be the starting value for the process at time period $t = 0$. Then:

$$y_1 = \mu + y_0 + \varepsilon_1 \; ,$$

and

$$y_2 = \mu + y_1 + \varepsilon_2$$
$$= 2\mu + y_0 + \sum_{i=1}^{2} \varepsilon_i \; .$$

In general,

$$y_t = \mu t + y_0 + \sum_{i=1}^{t} \varepsilon_i \; ,$$

so that the constant term μ in this $I(1)$ process represents a deterministic trend.

Consider this same process but which is subject to a structural break or change at some known point $t = b$. That is, there is some external event which occurs at time $t = b$ which causes a significant alteration to the process. Such an event is often termed an 'intervention'. The variable DO_t introduced in Chapter 3 to capture the effects of expenditure switching between two periods was an example of an intervention effect modelled by a dummy variable. Clearly, the effect of an intervention on a series could take many forms. For example, the effect of the introduction of seat belt legislation on the number of serious injuries and fatalities in car accidents could have both an immediate effect and other effects which might build up over time. On the other hand, the effects of a flash flood may appear simply as a single outlying point in a series relating to the number of car journeys made on a certain road over time. Since interventions are often of a qualitative rather than a quantitative nature, there are often problems in expressing the effects numerically. In practice, the effects of interventions on data series are usually modelled by a combination of 'step' and 'pulse' functions. The former refer to dummy variables which take the value of zero prior to the event happening, and unity afterwards, and could therefore reflect the idea of a law change which is sustained which may be expected to lead to a permanent effect on the level of a series. A pulse variable is a dummy variable which takes the value of unity only at the moment of intervention, and zero otherwise. Normally, such a variable is used to describe the effect of an intervention on a variable which is transitory or temporary. In the random walk with drift model, however, even a pulse or 'blip' at one period (usually called an 'additive outlier') will have a permanent effect on the series.

Thus if:

$$y_t = \mu + \delta P_t + y_{t-1} + \varepsilon_t \quad , \tag{5.22}$$

where P_t is a pulse variable such that

$$P_t = \begin{cases} 1 & \text{if } t = b \\ 0 & \text{otherwise} \end{cases} ,$$

and where b is the time period where the event occurs, then in the period before the intervention,

$$y_{b-1} = \mu + y_{b-2} + \varepsilon_{b-1}$$

$$= (b-1)\mu + y_0 + \sum_{i=1}^{b-1} \varepsilon_i \quad ,$$

where, as before, y_0 is the starting value of y_t. At the intervention period, $t = b$:

$$y_b = \mu + \delta + y_{b-1} + \varepsilon_b$$

$$= b\mu + \delta + y_0 + \sum_{i=1}^{b} \varepsilon_i \quad .$$

In the period following the intervention, $t = b+1$,

$$y_{b+1} = \mu + y_b + \varepsilon_{b+1}$$

$$= (b+1)\mu + \delta + y_0 + \sum_{i=1}^{b+1} \varepsilon_i \quad , \tag{5.23}$$

and so on, illustrating that the effect of a single pulse on an $I(1)$ series is permanent. In general, Equation (5.23) may be re-written as:

$$y_t = \mu t + \delta S_t + y_0 + \sum_{i=1}^{t} \varepsilon_i \quad ,$$

where S_t is a 'step function' such that:

$$S_t = \begin{cases} 1 & \text{if } t \geq b \\ 0 & \text{otherwise} \end{cases} .$$

The permanent effect of a pulse on an $I(1)$ series can be illustrated by means of a simulation example in which the variable y_t is determined from the model:

$$y_t = 0.5 + 100P_t + y_{t-1} + \varepsilon_t \quad , \tag{5.24}$$

where $y_0 = 1$ and

$$P_t = \begin{cases} 1 & \text{if } t = 250 \\ 0 & \text{otherwise} \end{cases} .$$

Five hundred values ($t = 1, ..., 500$) of ε_t were generated independently from a standard normal distribution and used with the initial value of y_t to produce the values which are displayed in Figure 5.10. Series both with and without the pulse effect are shown, and the permanent effect of the pulse is clear.

The effect of a 'blip' or pulse intervention effect on a stationary ($I(0)$) series is quite different, however. If the process generating the variable y_t had been:

$$y_t = \mu + \delta P_t + \alpha y_{t-1} + \varepsilon_t \qquad |\alpha| < 1 \quad ,$$

where P_t is the pulse variable defined earlier, then at $t = b - 1$:

$$y_{b-1} = \mu + \alpha y_{b-2} + \varepsilon_{b-1} \quad ,$$

at $t = b$:

$$y_b = \mu + \delta + \alpha y_{b-1} + \varepsilon_b$$
$$= \mu(1+\alpha) + \delta + \alpha^2 y_{b-2} + \sum_{i=0}^{1} \alpha^i \varepsilon_{b-i} \quad ,$$

at $t = b + 1$:

$$y_{b+1} = \mu + \alpha y_b + \varepsilon_{b+1}$$
$$= \mu(1+\alpha+\alpha^2) + \alpha\delta + \alpha^3 y_{b-2} + \sum_{i=0}^{2} \alpha^i \varepsilon_{b+1-i} \quad ,$$

and at $t = b + 2$:

$$y_{b+2} = \mu + \alpha y_{b+1} + \varepsilon_{b+2}$$
$$= \mu(1+\alpha+\alpha^2+\alpha^3) + \alpha^2\delta + \alpha^4 y_{b-2} + \sum_{i=0}^{3} \alpha^i \varepsilon_{b+2-i} \quad , \quad \text{etc.}$$

Fig. 5.10 Random walk process and a pulse effect

time

Inspection of these equations reveals that the greater the distance is in time from the intervention period, the less the effect of that intervention. The parameter δ measures the instantaneous effect of the pulse variable on y_t at the break period ($t = b$). A necessary and sufficient condition for this process to be stationary is that $|\alpha| < 1$. As the process develops, the influence of the intervention diminishes as periods after the break period ($t = b + i$) contain the term $\alpha^i \delta$ rather than δ. Thus an intervention in a stationary model will have temporary rather than permanent effects.

Intervention effects represent 'extraordinary' events in the history of a process. However, stochastic processes are by definition processes which display the effects of 'ordinary' or normal error shocks on a variable, captured by the ε_t terms in the equations above. In precisely the same way as we distinguished between the temporary and permanent nature of intervention effects on $I(0)$ and $I(1)$ processes, we can demonstrate that these same effects hold with respect to the usual error shocks to a process.

Thus for an $I(1)$ process at time t,

$$y_t = y_{t-1} + \varepsilon_t \quad,$$

and at time $t + 1$,

$$y_{t+1} = y_t + \varepsilon_{t+1}$$
$$= y_{t-1} + \varepsilon_t + \varepsilon_{t+1} \quad,$$

so that the full effect of the shock at ε_t carries over into the next and all succeeding periods. This is in contrast with the effects of the same shock ε_t on a stationary process:

$$y_t = \alpha y_{t-1} + \varepsilon_t \quad, \qquad |\alpha| < 1 \quad,$$

which at time $t+1$ becomes

$$y_{t+1} = \alpha y_t + \varepsilon_{t+1}$$
$$= \alpha^2 y_t + \varepsilon_{t+1} + \alpha \varepsilon_t \quad ,$$

so that the effect of the error ε_t dies away over time (i.e. is temporary rather than permanent).

In practice, it could be important to distinguish between temporary and permanent effects of shocks on the economy. Following the work of Nelson and Plosser (1982), there was a general acceptance that most macroeconomic variables exhibited some form of stochastic nonstationarity - e.g. could be modelled as unit root processes. In this case, as just explained, shocks to the economy could be thought of as having permanent effects on the economy, and this finding in turn could influence the way in which macroeconomic theorists viewed the working of an economy. Quite different conclusions might be reached if macroeconomic variables were in fact stationary (strictly speaking, exhibiting stationary fluctuations around a deterministic component such as a deterministic trend) which had been subject to a structural break over the period of interest. Apart from the permanent alteration to the mean level of the process due to the structural break, the effect of any shocks to the system would be temporary.

The potential presence of structural breaks makes the testing for the order of integration of a series by Dickey-Fuller type tests unreliable. Perron (1989, 1990) and Perron and Vogelsang (1992) have shown that a structural change in the mean of a stationary variable will tend to bias the usual Dickey-Fuller and augmented Dickey-Fuller tests towards non-rejection of the null of a unit root in the process. That is, in the presence of such a break, one may well conclude that a process is $I(1)$ whereas in fact it is $I(0)$ (albeit with a change in mean at some known point). Figure 5.11 indicates why such a mistake might be made.

Fig. 5.11: An $I(1)$ process and an $I(0)$ process with a mean shift

The process is actually an $I(0)$ process with a structural break; that is it is made up of two periods in which the data are stationary linked by a single intervention. However, it is clear that for the data as a whole, a linear deterministic trend:

$$y_t = \alpha_0 + \alpha_1 t + \varepsilon_t \ , \qquad\qquad t = 1, \ldots, n \ ,$$

would fit this data set quite well as all the low values are at the start of the data period, and all the high values at the end. Similarly, a first order autoregressive process:

$$y_t = \beta_0 + \beta_1 y_{t-1} + \varepsilon_t \ ,$$

would also fit the data well as low values are generally followed by low values and high followed by high. If $\beta_1 = 1$, then the equation describes a random walk with drift. We have already noted at the start of this section that a random walk with drift model is equivalent to a model which displays a deterministic trend. Thus the autoregressive equation will tend to reflect the essential properties of the trend equation by biasing the parameter β_1 towards unity. Hence, in the presence of a structural break in an $I(0)$ series, Dickey-Fuller type tests will tend to falsely accept the null hypothesis of a unit root even when the process is stationary each side of the structural break point.

In his paper, Perron (1989) suggested a series of tests for investigating stationarity in the presence of various types of shocks. The particular Perron test considered here (the 'additive outlier' test) has been developed to establish the order of integration of a variable where the alternative processes considered are a non-stationary stochastic process subject to a single pulse intervention at a known date, $t = b$, (which we have seen leads to a permanent effect on the series from that date) and a stationary process subject to this same intervention which also leads to a permanently higher mean level of the process. That is, the null hypothesis is that of a non-stationary process:

$$H_0: \quad y_t = \mu + \gamma P_t + y_{t-1} + \varepsilon_t \ , \qquad\qquad (5.25)$$

where

$$P_t = \begin{cases} 1 & \text{if } t = b \\ 0 & \text{otherwise} \end{cases} \ ,$$

and the alternative hypothesis is that of a stationary process subject to a shift:

$$H_1: \quad y_t = \mu + \delta S_t + \varepsilon_t \ , \qquad\qquad (5.26)$$

where

$$S_t = \begin{cases} 1 & \text{if } t \geq b \\ 0 & \text{otherwise} \end{cases}$$

At first sight, it may seem natural to apply a Dickey-Fuller test to equation (5.25), that is to estimate:

$$\Delta y_t = \mu + \gamma P_t + \delta y_{t-1} + \varepsilon_t \quad ,$$

and to test for the negativity of δ. However, if the null hypothesis is rejected, the implicit alternative hypothesis that would be accepted would be that y_t is stationary with a pulse rather than a step as in equation (5.26). Hence, Perron suggested a two-stage procedure where the possible 'step' which might exist in the series under the null is first removed from the series. In order to conduct the test, first the Ordinary Least Squares residuals (e_t) from the regression under the alternative hypothesis are computed as:

$$e_t = y_t - \hat{\mu} - \hat{\delta} S_t \quad ,$$

where $\hat{\mu}$ and $\hat{\delta}$ are the Ordinary Least Squares regression estimates of μ and δ. If the alternative hypothesis represented by equation (5.26) is true, then this regression should yield residuals which have been 'purged' of the influence of the intervention, so that accepting the stationarity of these residuals is also in favour of this alternative hypothesis. However, evidence of non-stationary behaviour in the residuals is also evidence in favour of the null hypothesis of nonstationarity represented by equation (5.25). Hence, in order to test the order of integration of the series on y_t, these residuals are then used in turn in the second stage regression:

$$e_t = \omega P_t + \alpha e_{t-1} + v_t \quad , \tag{5.27}$$

or equivalently,

$$\Delta e_t = \omega P_t + \alpha^* e_{t-1} + v_t \quad , \tag{5.28}$$

where $\alpha^* = \alpha - 1$ and where v_t is an error term. Diagnostic tests on whether or not the residuals from this second stage regression exhibit autocorrelated errors may be performed in the usual way and augmentation of the second stage regression by the use of lagged values of the dependent variable can be adopted if necessary. Perron and Vogelsang (1992) have shown that inclusion of the pulse term in equation (5.27) yields a test statistic which is invariant to the presence of 'nuisance parameters', which can arise from the particular correlation structure of the series on y_t. The test for the stationarity of the residuals is simply whether the regression estimate of α in equation (5.27) is significantly less than one, or using the normal form for these tests, whether the regression estimate of α^* in equation (5.28) is 'significantly negative'. If α^* is significantly negative, the null hypothesis is rejected in favour of the alternative stationary hypothesis represented by equation (5.26). Tables of critical values to perform this test on α^* are included in the Appendix as Table 6. They are used in the same way as the original Dickey-Fuller tables, except that they involve one extra parameter (λ) which represents the proportion that the data sample up to and including the break point is relative to the whole sample size. Thus if the sample size was 90 and the break point occurred at observation 30, λ would be taken as 0.33. The tables are symmetrical so that, for example, tabulated values for $\lambda = x$ and for $\lambda = 1 - x$ are identical. Thus only tables for values of λ up to $\lambda = 0.5$ are included in the Appendix. An example of the use of this test is included in Section 5.8.

5.5 The Concept of Cointegration

The main message from Section 5.2 was that trended data can be regarded as potentially a major problem for empirical econometrics. Trends, either stochastic or deterministic, may give rise to spurious regressions, uninterpretable Student-t values and other statistics, goodness of fit measures which are 'too high' and, in general, make regression results extremely difficult to evaluate.

The grim fact is that, in economics, most time series (data ordered by time) are subject to some type of trend. Section 5.3 suggested one remedy, namely to difference a series successively until stationarity is achieved. Nevertheless, this does not seem to be an ideal solution. It was shown earlier (Chapter 3) that applying first differences to the variables in the *DHSY* consumption function (or, strictly speaking, to logarithms of the variables), led to the loss of long-run properties, since the model in differences did not have a long run solution. The desire to evaluate models which combine both short run and long run properties and which at the same time maintain stationarity in all of the variables, has prompted a reconsideration of the problem of regression using variables measured in their levels.

The focus of attention has recently been concentrated on economic data series which, although nonstationary, can be combined together (through a linear combination) into a single series which is itself stationary. Series which exhibit such a property are called *cointegrated series*.

In order to illustrate the concept of cointegration, let us consider the following simple processes generating the series y_t and x_t.

$$y_t = 10 + x_t + u_t \quad , \tag{5.29a}$$

2 nonstationary series combined into 1 stationary one
= Cointegrated

and:

$$x_t = 0.5 + x_{t-1} + \varepsilon_t \quad , \tag{5.29b}$$

where ε_t is a white noise process. The series u_t is also stochastic. We can represent u_t as a simple linear combination of y_t and x_t, namely:

$$u_t = a \cdot y_t + b \cdot x_t - 10 \quad ,$$

where $a = 1$ and $b = -1$. Suppose that the process which generates u_t is given by:

$$u_t = 0.5 + u_{t-1} + \varepsilon_{1t} \quad , \tag{5.29c}$$

where ε_{1t} is also a white noise process. Evidently, both series x_t and u_t are random walk series (with drift). Figure 5.12 depicts the simulated series y_t and x_t for $t = 1, ..., 100$ using the processes (5.29a), (5.29b) and (5.29c), starting from initial values of x_t and u_t both being equal to zero. The generated series y_t is clearly nonstationary, as intuitively expected, since it is a combination of two other nonstationary ($I(1)$) series. Since the u_t term in (5.29a), is nonstationary, the series y_t and x_t are 'drifting apart' in time. The linear combination of y_t and x_t, $(1 \cdot y_t - 1 \cdot x_t - 10)$ is nonstationary. We will later call such series *not cointegrated.*

Fig. 5.12: Example of series whose linear combination
$$y_t - x_t \text{ is nonstationary}$$

time

Suppose, however, that we replace equation (5.29c) by:

$$u_t = 0.5 + 0.8u_{t-1} + \varepsilon_{1t} \quad , \tag{5.29d}$$

where the process which generates u_t, albeit strongly autoregressive, is stationary ($I(0)$). Figure 5.13 shows the series y_t and x_t generated by the process (5.29a), (5.29b) and (5.29d), using the same set of random numbers and starting values, as previously. The main difference between the processes in Figures 5.12 and 5.13 is that in the latter there is a *stationary* combination $(1 \cdot y_t - 1 \cdot x_t - 10)$ of two *non-stationary* series y_t and x_t. This combination, equal to u_t does not change systematically in time. The series y_t and x_t are drifting together in time. In such a case we will be saying that the series y_t and x_t *are cointegrated*.

Fig. 5.13: Example of series whose linear combination
$y_t - x_t$ **is stationary**

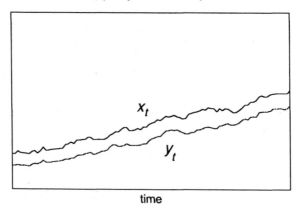

time

    Figure 5.13 illustrates the concept of cointegration. Equation (5.29a) can be regarded as a simple economic long run relationship (for example, where y_t might represent the logarithm of consumption, x_t the logarithm of income and where the long run income elasticity of consumption is equal to unity with autonomous consumption equal to 10). The above example could be replaced by a more general long run relationship with nonstationary variables but not necessarily having unitary coefficients. As long as the deviations from the long run path are stationary, the variables in question are again said to be cointegrated. Note that according to these figures, two time series can be cointegrated only if they are integrated of the same order. It is important to stress that if the linear combination of the nonstationary variables have coefficients different from 1 and −1, then the variables themselves might not appear to be 'drifting together in time'. One of them might grow faster then the other. However, if they are cointegrated, their linear combination (or the deviations from the long run path) will be stationary.

The formal definition of *cointegration of two variables*, developed by Engle and Granger (1987) is as follows:

Definition: Time series x_t and y_t are said to be *cointegrated of order d, b* where $d \geq b \geq 0$, written as:

$$x_t, y_t \sim CI(d, b) \quad,$$

if:

1. both series are integrated of order d,
2. there exists a linear combination of these variables, say $\alpha_1 \cdot x_t + \alpha_2 \cdot y_t$, which is integrated of order $d - b$.

The vector $[\alpha_1, \alpha_2]$ is called a *cointegrating vector*.

A straightforward generalization of the above definition for the case of n variables is the following. If x_t denotes an $n \times 1$ vector of series $x_{1t}, x_{2t}, ..., x_{nt}$ and:

a) each x_{it} is $I(d)$,

b) there exists an $n \times 1$ vector α such that $x_t' \cdot \alpha \sim I(d - b)$, then:

$x_t' \cdot \alpha \sim CI(d, b)$. (It is shown later that there are special cases where condition *a*) above can be relaxed.)

For empirical econometrics, the most interesting case is where the series transformed with the use of the cointegrating vector become stationary, that is where $d = b$, and the cointegrating coefficients (the coefficients which constitute the cointegrating vector) can be identified with parameters in the long run relationship between the variables. In this chapter we will concentrate on such situations, that is where $x_t' \cdot \alpha \sim CI(d, d)$.

Let us suppose that x_t, y_t are both $I(1)$ and that the long run relationship between them is given by:

$$y_t^* = \beta \cdot x_t \quad.$$

An important situation occurs if the variables x_t, y_t are $CI(1, 1)$ and have the cointegrating vector $[\beta, -1]$, so that the deviations of y_t from its long run path y_t^* are $I(0)$. If this is the case, a model in first differences incorporating an error correction mechanism can be sensibly developed (see Chapter 3). Specifically for the equation:

$$\Delta y_t = \beta_1 \Delta x_t + \beta_2 (y_{t-1} - \beta \cdot x_{t-1}) + \varepsilon_t \quad, \tag{5.30}$$

both the dependent variable Δy_t and the regressors Δx_t and $(y_{t-1} - \beta \cdot x_{t-1})$ are $I(0)$. Thus there is no danger of estimating a spurious regression because of the presence of stochastic or deterministic trends in the data. The model incorporates both a long run solution and has an error correction mechanism (*ECM*) when β_2 is negative.

As explained in Chapter 3 above, the starting point for deriving model (5.30) is a static equation with a single explanatory variable. Let the stochastic variable u_t represent deviations of y_t from its long run path y_t^*, that is:

$$ECM = y_t - y_t^* = y_t - \beta \cdot x_t = u_t \ ,$$

or:

$$y_t = \beta \cdot x_t + u_t \ . \tag{5.31}$$

Hence, u_t in (5.31) can be viewed in the same light as the term $(y_{t-1} - \beta \cdot x_{t-1})$ which appears in (5.30) to reflect the error correction aspect of that equation.

Let us consider various possibilities of integration and cointegration in (5.31).

1. if $y_t \sim I(1)$, and $x_t \sim I(0)$, then $u_t \sim I(1)$ and the variables x_t, y_t are not cointegrated;
2. if $y_t \sim I(1)$ and $x_t \sim I(1)$ then it *may* be that $u_t \sim I(0)$ and the variables x_t and y_t are cointegrated, *only if* $[\beta, -1]$ constitutes a cointegrating vector;
3. if $y_t \sim I(0)$ and $x_t \sim I(0)$ then $u_t \sim I(0)$ and the enquiry about cointegration does not really make sense;
4. if $y_t \sim I(0)$ and $x_t \sim I(1)$ then $u_t \sim I(1)$ and the variables x_t, y_t are not cointegrated.

Consequently, in a long run relationship between two variables both must be integrated of the same order if the error term is to be $I(0)$). Stationarity of the error term is especially important if one is going to examine models incorporating error correction mechanisms such as equation (5.30).

If the number of variables involved in the long run relationship increases, the problem becomes much more complicated than that implied by the definition above. Consider, for example, a three variable case:

$$y_t = \beta_1 x_{1t} + \beta_2 x_{2t} + u_t \ . \tag{5.32}$$

Now *it is* possible for the variables to be integrated of different orders and for the error term u_t to be stationary (later in the text we will assume, rather imprecisely, that stationarity is a synonym for $I(0)$). Suppose that $y_t \sim I(0)$, $x_{1t} \sim I(1)$ and $x_{2t} \sim I(1)$. By analogy with the previous analysis we might expect that in such a case $u_t \sim I(1)$. It may happen, however, that

$[\beta_1, \beta_2]$ constitutes a cointegrating vector for x_{1t}, x_{2t}, so that the linear combination $(\beta_1 x_{1t} + \beta_2 x_{2t}) \sim I(0)$ since x_{1t}, x_{2t} are integrated of the same order. If this is the case, u_t will be stationary, since $y_t \sim I(0)$ and also $(\beta_1 x_{1t} + \beta_2 x_{2t}) \sim I(0)$.

In economics a more common situation would be for $y_t \sim I(1)$, $x_{1t} \sim I(2)$ and) $x_{2t} \sim I(2)$. Despite the different orders of integration, the error term could still be stationary provided $(\beta_1 x_{1t} + \beta_2 x_{2t}) \sim I(1)$; that is, if $x_{1t}, x_{2t} \sim CI(2,1)$ with the cointegrating vector $[\beta_1, \beta_2]$. This leads to a major complication of the entire concept of cointegration in a long run relationship and in the stationarity of the error term, but there is a practical hint that can simplify testing procedures. If variables in a long run relationship are of a different order of integration and the order of integration of the dependent variable is lower than the highest order of integration of the explanatory variables, there must be at least two explanatory variables integrated of this highest order if the necessary condition for stationarity of the error term is to be met.

Where seasonal data are used, the entire concept of cointegration becomes more difficult. Section 5.3 outlined tests that could be used to investigate the seasonal integration properties of a series. The *HEGY* representation stresses the possibility that series may be transformed into stationary series by seasonal and/or other differencing. For cointegration analysis, this means additional complications. Let us say that the null hypothesis is that the variables x_t and y_t are not cointegrated, so that $u_t = y_t - \beta \cdot x_t$ is not stationary. In the case of seasonality this could mean that either $u_t \sim SI_s(0,1)$, or $u_t \sim SI_s(1,0)$ or $u_t \sim SI_s(1,1)$ to mention only the most straightforward possibilities. As for integration analysis, each case requires further analysis based on different lengths of differences.

5.6 Testing for Cointegration

Consider firstly the problem of testing for nonseasonal cointegration. Technically, the test for cointegration of the type $CI(d,b)$ for $b = d$, is analogous to testing for integration. A Dickey-Fuller, Augmented Dickey-Fuller or Durbin-Watson statistic can be used in order to determine whether the linear combination of two (or more) variables is $I(0)$. Cases of the type $CI(d,b)$ for $b < d$, are not of primary interest, since for $b < d$ the cointegrating vector is not stationary and does not have a straightforward economic interpretation. Nevertheless, special care is required since the distribution of the Student-t values, and consequently the critical values of the cointegration test, both depend heavily on the number of *unknown* cointegrating coefficients. A two-step algorithm for testing for cointegration in a long run relationship is given below. This algorithm is derived for a 'classical' Engle-Granger type enquiry into cointegration described more fully in Section 5.7.

Step 1:
Test for the order of integration of the variables involved in the postulated long run relationship (for example, equation (5.31)). If only two variables appear in the long run relation, both have to be of the same order of integration. If the number of variables is greater than two (that is if there is more than one explanatory variable), the order of integration of the dependent variable cannot be higher than the order of integration of any of the explanatory variables. Moreover, there must be either none or at least two explanatory variables integrated to an identical order higher than the order of integration of the dependent variable.

Step 2:
Decide whether the cointegrating vector is known, or has to be estimated. Sometimes the cointegrating vector may be known *a priori*. For instance, suppose one assumes that in a consumption function, where $cons_t$ denotes the logarithm of consumption and inc_t stands for the logarithm of income, the long run income elasticity of consumption is equal to unity. One form of the long run consumption function consistent with this is simply:

$$cons_t^* = inc_t ,$$

where long run consumption ($cons_t^*$) is equal to income. If this is believed to be the appropriate form of the long run function the cointegrating vector would be $(1, -1)$. In the general case, however, the long run relationship is of the form of equations (5.31) or (5.32) and the cointegrating vector is given by $(1, -\beta_1)$ or $(1, -\beta_1, -\beta_2)$ respectively. Coefficients in these vectors have to be estimated, usually by ordinary least squares. Hence, we have two cases at step 2:

Step 2a:
The cointegrating vector is known *a priori*. In this case the procedure is the same as that described earlier for testing the order of integration. In equations (5.7), (5.10) or (5.11) we have to replace y_t by the appropriate linear combination of the variables which we expect to be stationary. As an example, consider the consumption model mentioned above. The hypothesis to be tested is whether $cons_t, inc_t \sim CI(1, 1)$ with the known *a priori* cointegrating vector $(1, -1)$. Let us assume that the integration test (step 1) reveals that $cons_t \sim I(1)$ and $inc_t \sim I(1)$. The Dickey-Fuller cointegration

test, by analogy with (5.7), consists in testing the significance of the Student-t ratio for δ in the ordinary least squares regression:

$$\Delta u_t = \delta \cdot u_{t-1} + \varepsilon_t \ . \qquad (5.33)$$

where $u_t = cons_t - inc_t$. The critical values of the test are the same as used for testing integration. That is, they may be read from Table 1 in the Appendix. Analogously, the Augmented Dickey-Fuller test uses the Student-t ratio for δ from the equation:

$$\Delta u_t = \delta \cdot u_{t-1} + \sum_{i=1}^{k} \delta_i \cdot \Delta u_{t-i} + \varepsilon_t \ , \qquad (5.34)$$

Step 2b:
The cointegrating vector is not known *a priori*. That is, we are dealing with a long run relationship of the type:

$$y_t = \beta_1 x_{1t} + \beta_2 x_{2t} + ... + \beta_m x_{mt} + v_t \ , \qquad (5.35)$$

and the cointegrating vector $(1, -\beta_1, -\beta_2, ..., -\beta_m)$ is not known and has to be estimated. Computationally, little changes; we use the Dickey-Fuller or Augmented Dickey-Fuller equations like (5.33) and (5.34), with the estimated residuals from (5.35) instead of u_t so that:

$$\Delta \hat{v}_t = \delta \cdot \hat{v}_{t-1} + \xi_t \ , \qquad (5.36)$$

(Dickey-Fuller), or:

$$\Delta \hat{v}_t = \delta \cdot \hat{v}_{t-1} + \sum_{i=1}^{k} \delta_i \cdot \Delta \hat{v}_{t-i} + \xi_t \ , \qquad (5.37)$$

(Augmented Dickey-Fuller), where the $\hat{v}_t$ are the ordinary least squares residuals in (5.35) and can be interpreted as the deviations of y_t from its long run path.

As was the case for the integration test, the Student-t ratio that results from the regression of an $I(0)$ variable on an $I(1)$ variable (as is (5.36) or (5.37)) does not have the conventional Student-t distribution if the null hypothesis is true. The important difference between Step 2a and Step 2b is the fact that in Step 2b, coefficients in the cointegrating vector are estimated and *the distribution of the Student-t ratio depends on the number of coefficients estimated*. In the integration test and in the cointegration test with the cointegrating vector known, the number of coefficients estimated is zero, and consequently one can read the critical values of the test from Table 1 in the Appendix. If there is a positive number (m) of estimated coefficients in the cointegrating vector, we have to use Table 2 (or Table 3 if an intercept is included in the test equation using the estimated residuals) to obtain the appropriate critical values. For instance, if a long run relationship is given by (5.32), where there are two explanatory variables, and the number of observations is equal to 30, the approximate critical values for the cointegration test from Table 2 are for the 5% level of significance: -3.82 (lower bound) and -3.73 (upper bound). One would reject the null hypothesis of no cointegration if the Student-t value for δ in equation (5.36) or (5.37) is below -3.82, would not reject the null if the value was above -3.73, and be unsure whether to reject or not if the value lies between -3.82 and -3.73 in the inconclusive region. Now, m is taken as two as there are two estimated coefficients in the cointegrating vector.

In the same way as was discussed for the case of testing for the order of integration, a Durbin-Watson analogue can be applied as a 'rough and ready' method for testing for cointegration. The *cointegration Durbin-Watson test* (*CIDW*) consists in computing a Durbin-Watson statistic for the estimated deviations from a long run path which, under the cointegration hypothesis, are stationary:

$$CIDW = \frac{\sum (\hat{v}_t - \hat{v}_{t-1})^2}{\sum (\hat{v}_t - \bar{v}_t)^2} \, , \tag{5.38}$$

where $\bar{v}_t$ is the arithmetic mean for the residuals $\hat{v}_t$. The distribution of *CIDW* has not been fully investigated yet and its critical values are not known. By analogy with *IDW*, we might expect that the smaller is *CIDW*, the greater is the chance that the hypothesis that the series are cointegrated should be rejected. It is known that the power of *CIDW* depends positively on the goodness of fit of the *OLS* estimate of the long run relationship (5.35). Hence, Banerjee *et al.* (1986) proposed a simple 'rule of thumb' for a quick evaluation of the cointegration hypothesis: if *CIDW* computed for $\hat{v}_t$ of an

equation like (5.35) is smaller than the coefficient of determination (R^2) for this equation, the cointegration hypothesis is likely to be false; otherwise, when $CIDW > R^2$, cointegration may occur. We may then state that if the conventional Durbin-Watson statistic, computed for the residuals of a static model representing a long run relationship, is close to 2, there is no danger of the lack of cointegration of the variables.

As has been mentioned earlier, the testing for cointegration and the estimation of cointegrating vectors when one is dealing with seasonal data is more problematic than that for annual data, and this area is still in the process of development. Some progress has been made, however. Testing for cointegration and the estimation of a long run cointegrating model using seasonal data may be performed in a number of ways. Engle, Granger and Hallman (1989) have pointed out that the use of seasonal data to estimate the long run model may give rise to inconsistent estimates of the long run parameters. Annual data could be used to estimate these long run parameters thereby avoiding the need to model the seasonality, and the standard tests for cointegration applied. Alternatively, seasonal data may be used provided the series which may be cointegrated are 'filtered' or 'seasonally adjusted' first. Once the data is seasonally adjusted, one of the tests outlined in Step 2b above (for example, the *ADF* test of equation (5.37)) may be applied to the seasonally adjusted data. There are several suggested approaches to this seasonal adjustment. For instance, if there are two series x_t and y_t which have been shown to be seasonally integrated of the same order, then applying the operator $(1-L^s)/(1-L)$ to each series will yield seasonally adjusted series which can be tested for non-seasonal cointegration. Alternatively, the *HEGY* tests outlined above may identify the seasonal roots that should be extracted from the raw data before cointegration tests are applied. A straightforward (but probably generally sub-optimal) procedure is to assume that stochastic seasonality can be approximated by deterministic seasonal dummy variables, and include these in the long run relationship, or long run cointegrating vector. In such a case, Table 4 in the Appendix can be used for quarterly data, where m is the number of estimated coefficients in the long run cointegrating vector excluding those for the intercept and seasonal dummies. An example of this approach is given in Section 5.8 below.

The testing of seasonal cointegration and the estimation of seasonal cointegrating vectors is probably best approached by an extension of the Johansen method which is discussed in Chapter 6. Currently, there is little published work in this field, although an example of the technique has been provided by Kunst (1990). No doubt further examples will become available when this extension is incorporated in standard econometric software packages.

5.7 Modelling Cointegrated Series through Error Correction Models

This section describes how cointegrated nonstationary variables can be used to formulate and estimate a model with an error correction mechanism. The fact that variables are cointegrated implies that there is some adjustment process which prevents the errors in the long run relationship becoming larger and larger. Engle and Granger (1987) have shown that any cointegrated series have an error correction representation. The 'Granger Representation Theorem' which establishes this result is outlined in Chapter 6. The converse is also true, in that cointegration is a necessary condition for error correction models to hold (see Engle and Granger (1991, pp. 7-8)). A detailed analysis of cointegration and error correction mechanisms is given by Hylleberg and Mizon (1989). Phillips and Loretan (1991) have considered a variety of ways of representing cointegrated systems with particular emphasis on error correction model representations. Such models currently represent the most common approach to situations where it is wished to incorporate both the economic theory relating to the long run relationship between variables, and short run disequilibrium behaviour. Two of the simplest and most widely used procedures will be described, which require only the use of ordinary least squares estimation (for references to more complicated methods see the suggested further reading at the end of this chapter, and also at the end of Chapter 6).

The first approach was originally suggested by Engle and Granger (1987). It is particularly convenient for the case in which the variables appearing in the long run relation are all $I(1)$, or where the dependent variable is $I(1)$, and the explanatory variables are $CI(d+1, d)$. For simplicity we will only consider the case with a single explanatory variable in the long run relation. (The extension to the multivariate case is direct.) Thus, reconsider equation (5.31),

$$y_t = \beta \cdot x_t + u_t \ , \tag{5.39}$$

where both y_t and x_t are $I(1)$. Suppose that the coefficient β is unknown, but for its *OLS* estimate $\hat{\beta}$ the Dickey-Fuller and/or Augmented Dickey-Fuller tests indicate stationarity of the *OLS* residuals $\hat{u}_t$. In other words, cointegration of y_t and x_t of order $(1, 1)$ with the cointegrating vector $(1, -\hat{\beta})$ can be positively accepted. Logically, the next move would be to switch to a short run model with an error correction mechanism:

$$\Delta y_t = \alpha_1 \Delta x_t + \alpha_2 (y_{t-1} - \beta \cdot x_{t-1}) + \varepsilon_t \ , \tag{5.40}$$

where ε_t is an error term and α_2 is negative. It is tempting to estimate (5.40) by unrestricted ordinary least squares, since the parameters in the unrestricted version of (5.40) are exactly identified. That is, they may be recovered from the regression:

$$\Delta y_t = \alpha_1 \Delta x_t + \alpha_2 y_{t-1} - \alpha_2 \beta \cdot x_{t-1} + \varepsilon_t \ . \tag{5.41}$$

However, direct estimation of (5.41) probably would not be the best way forward. Firstly, in addition to $\hat{\beta}$ obtained from the regression of equation (5.39), we would now have another estimate of β, say $\tilde{\beta}$, and we do not know whether $\tilde{\beta}$ is a cointegrating coefficient for y_t and x_t. Secondly, and more important, is the fact that in (5.41) the variables have, by assumption, different orders of integration. Both Δy_t and Δx_t are $I(0)$ while y_{t-1} and x_{t-1} are $I(1)$. Unless an additional restriction: $(\alpha_2 y_t - \alpha_2 \beta \cdot x_t) \sim I(0)$ is met, these different orders of integration imply a 'hidden' assumption for ε_t, namely that $\varepsilon_t \sim I(1)$. In other words, the error term is nonstationary.

The Engle-Granger remedy consists of a two-step procedure. *First* estimate (5.39) by ordinary least squares and test for stationarity of the residuals. *Second*, if this is not rejected, estimate (5.40) replacing β by its previously computed *OLS* estimate $\hat{\beta}$. Now the condition of the identical order of integration for the variables in (5.40) is met. Δy_t, Δx_t and $(y_{t-1} - \hat{\beta} \cdot x_{t-1})$ are all $I(0)$ and consequently, provided the model is properly specified, ε_t is also $I(0)$.

One doubt about the Engle-Granger procedure concerns its first step. The variables y_t and x_t are nonstationary. Hence, what is the sense of estimating (5.39) by ordinary least squares? Further investigation has shown that the properties of the *OLS* estimators are not all bad. Indeed, under some general assumptions they are consistent. Unfortunately, the *OLS* estimate of the standard error of $\hat{\beta}$ is not consistent in this case and most researchers do not even bother to report it. (For a method better than *OLS* for computing standard errors for a regression with nonstationary variables, see West (1988).)

When using the Engle-Granger method, we must be aware of the fact that *we do not prove that the relation* (5.39) *is really a long run one*. This is an assumption and cannot be statistically verified. We have to have a strong belief in a long run equilibrium relationship between the variables that is supported by relevant economic theory. It may be that the theory suggests a convenient assumption about a long run relationship. In Section 5.6 we considered an example where we assumed the theory suggested that long run consumption and income were equal. Consequently in (5.39), $\beta = 1$ if y_t stands for the logarithm of consumption and x_t for the logarithm of income. In this case the Engle-Granger method simplifies to a direct estimation of:

$$\Delta y_t = \alpha_1 \Delta x_t + \alpha_2 (y_{t-1} - x_{t-1}) + \varepsilon_t \ ,$$

provided that y_t, $x_t \sim CI(1,1)$ with the cointegrating vector $(1,-1)$.

There may be other views about how the long run relationship (5.39) should be estimated (see Phillips and Loretan (1991)). For example, this could be approached through the use of an autoregressive distributed lag model (*ADL* models were introduced in Chapter 4). The unrestricted *ADL(n)* model for the variables y_t and x_t is formulated as:

$$y_t = \sum_{i=1}^{n} \alpha_i y_{t-i} + \sum_{i=0}^{n} \beta_i x_{t-i} + \varepsilon_t \ , \tag{5.42}$$

where α_i, β_i are coefficients and ε_t is an error term. Equation (5.42) can be estimated instead of (5.39) by *OLS* and then the long run coefficient β^* (when $y_t = y_{t-i}$ and $x_t = x_{t-i}$ for all i) is derived from the estimated *OLS* coefficients as:

$$\beta^* = \frac{\sum_{i=0}^{n} \hat{\beta}_i}{1 - \sum_{i=1}^{n} \hat{\alpha}_i} \,. \tag{5.43}$$

After testing for cointegration of y_t, x_t with the cointegrating vector $(1, -\beta^*)$, the model (5.40) can now be estimated by *OLS*, substituting β^* in place of β.

The general idea of the Engle-Granger and *ADL* methods is the same. Both methods start from the estimation of the long run relationship (5.39), either directly in the case of Engle-Granger or by using (5.42) in the *ADL* method, and then insert the deviations from the long run path, lagged appropriately, as the error correction mechanism in the short run equation. The difference consists in the method of estimation of the long run relationship.

5.8 An Example of Cointegration Analysis

In this section we examine the orders of integration and possible cointegration of the variables which appear in the *DHSY* aggregate consumption model, using the same sample data as in that study (Davidson *et al.* (1978)). The tests presented below were not available at the time this paper was published. Following the steps suggested in the previous sections, we start with testing for the order of integration of the variables involved, namely: $cons_t$ (logarithm of consumption), inc_t (logarithm of income) and inf_t (inflation measured as the seasonal difference of the logarithm of the price deflator, or $\Delta_4 p_t$). In the computer output below, these are denoted as 'lc', 'li' and 'inf' respectively.

First, we determine the order of seasonal integration of each variable using the Dickey-Hasza-Fuller (*DHF*) test. This is followed by testing whether first differences used once and twice after seasonal differencing make the variables stationary. In other words, for each variable we test the hypothesis that the variable is $SI_4(0, 1)$, then $SI_4(1, 1)$ and then $SI_4(2, 1)$ as the alternatives. Next we show the use of the *HEGY* test on the consumption variable, and also illustrate an application of the Perron test for the level of integration of a variable subject to a hypothesized structural break.

After we have considered these aspects relating to the integration properties of the variables, we turn to cointegration. We test whether a postulated equality in the long run relationship between consumption and income gives a stationary error. In order to develop a model with an error correction mechanism, we estimate an autoregressive distributed lag (*ADL*) model for consumption, income and inflation and use the long run solution of this model for constructing possible cointegrating coefficients. The errors from this long run model are in turn tested for stationarity, that is for the cointegration of $cons_t$, inc_t and inf_t, with the cointegrating vector estimated from the *ADL* long run solution. Only the long run and not seasonal cointegrating vectors are considered.

We start by testing for seasonal integration using the Dickey-Hasza-Fuller test. MODEL 5.1 in the computer output given in Section 5.9 shows the initial stage in the *DHF* procedure for the consumption variable ($cons_t$). This (general) model which contains four lagged values of $\Delta_4 cons_t$ may be reduced to the (specific) MODEL 5.2 by eliminating the lagged variables which have insignificant coefficients, namely those at lags 2, 3 and 4. (Note that the Chi^2 and *F*-form of the error autocorrelation test statistics reported below MODEL 5.1 do not reveal a problem with autocorrelated errors with this model so that the attempt to eliminate variables using the estimated Student-*t* values is reasonable.) The model reduction test noted below MODEL 5.2 shows that the reduction of the model from four lags to one is statistically acceptable. The restricted model also shows no problem of autocorrelated errors.

The estimated coefficients in the restricted model may now be used to create the z_t variable used in the *DHF* test as shown in the computer output. MODEL 5.3 provides the initial results from which the *DHF* test for the consumption variable may be performed. Eliminating the lagged variables at lags 2, 3 and 4 gives rise to the restricted model, MODEL 5.4. For this restricted model, the *t*-value on z_{t-4} is positive (2.029) so that it cannot possibly be 'significantly negative' in relation to the critical values of Table 5. Thus we cannot reject the null hypothesis that the consumption variable is seasonally integrated, and hence seasonal differencing (at least) of this variable is required for stationarity. As explained in Section 5.3, the next move is to see whether any nonseasonal differencing is required in addition to seasonal differencing.

MODEL 5.5 in Section 5.9 presents the results of an *ADF* test using the first differences of the seasonal differences of the consumption variable ($\Delta\Delta_4 cons_t$) as the dependent variable and incorporating four lags of the dependent variable as augmentation. Again, this model may be reduced to a more parsimonious form which does not exhibit signs of autocorrelated errors (MODEL 5.6) by the exclusion of variables with 'low' *t*-values. The *ADF* test concerns itself with the *t*-value on the variable $\Delta_4 cons_{t-1}$ (written as d4lc_1 in the computer output) which can be seen to take the value −1.47 in the reduced model. This value must be compared with the critical values in Table 1 in the Appendix to see if it is 'significantly negative'. From Table 1, at the 5% significance level and with 66 observations the tabulated lower and upper values are −1.98 and −1.91 respectively when no intercept is used in the test equation. As the calculated *t*-value is above (greater) than the upper limit critical values, the null hypothesis of the presence of a unit root for the seasonally differenced consumption variable cannot be rejected. That is, $\Delta_4 cons_t$ needs first differencing (at least) to achieve stationarity. Attention now turns to whether first differencing of the first differences of the seasonally differenced consumption data (that is $\Delta\Delta_4 cons_t$) is necessary to achieve stationarity. Students should note that both for expository reasons and because we are using quarterly (seasonal) data, we are using the 'upward testing' *ADF* procedure rather than the Dickey-Pantula test described in Section 5.4 to establish the order of integration of the variables. You may wish to confirm our conclusions using the Dickey-Pantula approach using seasonally differenced variables.

MODEL 5.7 in Section 5.9 reports the next stage of testing. The null hypothesis is now that differencing of at least the form $\Delta\Delta_4 cons_t$ is necessary to achieve stationarity of the consumption variable. MODEL 5.7 may be reduced to MODEL 5.8 by the omission of the fourth period lag of the dependent variable. However, this resulting model may not be further reduced by eliminating further lagged variables without leading to a perceived problem of autocorrelated errors. In MODEL 5.8 the *t*-value on $\Delta\Delta_4 cons_{t-1}$ is −5.488 which is 'significantly negative' using the critical values in Table 1. We can therefore reject the null hypothesis and conclude that first differences of the seasonal differences of $cons_t$ is a stationary variable. That is, the variable $cons_t$ is $SI_4(1,1)$.

Similar calculations were carried out for both the income and inflation variables, inc_t and inf_t, with the following results:

INTEGRATION ORDER TEST STATISTICS

	$cons_t$	inc_t	inf_t
DHF	2.029	1.566	−0.110
	$\Delta_4 cons_t$	$\Delta_4 inc_t$	$\Delta_4 inf_t$
ADF	−1.473	−1.915	−1.430
	$\Delta\Delta_4 cons_t$	$\Delta\Delta_4 inc_t$	$\Delta\Delta_4 inf_t$
ADF	−5.488	−6.330	−3.443

The results for the inflation variable in the table above are based on four fewer observations than for the other two variables due to the way this variable is constructed from the price deflator series.

From these results, we can conclude at the 5% significance level that all series ($cons_t$, inc_t and inf_t) are $SI_4(1,1)$, that is they may be transformed to stationary series by first differencing the seasonal differences. For both $\Delta_4 cons_t$ and $\Delta_4 inf_t$ the *ADF* statistics lie above the upper level critical values from Table 1. The *ADF* value for $\Delta_4 inc_t$ lies in the inconclusive range. However, first differencing the seasonal differences gives rise to calculated *ADF* values well below the lower level critical values in Table 1 in every case.

Before we proceed to the cointegration analysis, it is interesting to see whether or not the integration DurbinWatson test, *IDW* (see equation (5.11)) would give us similar results. As was stated in Section 5.3, the lower is the value of the Durbin-Watson statistic computed for a tested variable, the more it is likely that the variable is nonstationary. Given below are the values of the *IDW* statistic computed for all three variables for their seasonal differences and first differences of the seasonal differences.

IDW TEST STATISTICS

	$cons_t$	inc_t	inf_t
Δ_4	0.56	0.73	0.30
$\Delta\Delta_4$	2.20	2.26	1.67

For all the variables the message is clearly the same as that from the *ADF* testing. That is, low values of the *IDW* statistic for seasonal differences and higher for the first differences of the seasonal differences indicate nonstationarity of the former and stationarity of the latter.

We can look further into the seasonal pattern of the consumption variable by conducting a *HEGY* test as outlined in Section 5.9. The simplest *HEGY* tests we discussed in Section 5.3 for a variable y_t measured quarterly were based on the model:

$$\Delta_4 y_t = \sum_{i=1}^{4} \pi_i Y_{i,t-1} + \sum_{i=1}^{k} \delta_i \cdot \Delta_4 y_{t-i} + \varepsilon_t \quad ,$$

where the $Y_{i,t}$ variables were constructed variables. Firstly, these constructed variables were computed as detailed in the computer output above MODEL 5.9. These variables were then included in the regression given as MODEL 5.9. This model was reduced to MODEL 5.10 by the elimination of the lagged variables at lags 2 and 3 in the same way as was undertaken in the *ADF* modelling procedure earlier. The presence of unit roots at the zero, biannual and annual frequencies implied that $\pi_1 = 0$, $\pi_2 = 0$ and $\pi_3 = \pi_4 = 0$

respectively. The computer output for MODEL 5.10 allows us to carry out tests on these null hypotheses directly. Table 7 in the Appendix details the critical values for these tests. At the 5% level of significance and with 68 observations, the bounds for testing the null hypothesis that $\pi_1 = 0$ are -1.95 (lower) and -1.87 (upper). In this case, these also happen to be the same bounds relevant for testing the null hypothesis that $\pi_2 = 0$. To test the joint hypothesis that $\pi_3 = \pi_4 = 0$, the appropriate critical values from Table 7 are those in the column marked 'F' and are 3.17 (lower) and 3.35 (upper). Inspection of the computer output for MODEL 5.10 reveals that none of the three null hypotheses can be rejected. The calculated t-values for π_1 and π_2 are 2.672 and 0.068 respectively (that is, both are positive), and the calculated F-value for the joint test (the Wald test for linear restrictions) is 0.35618. Thus the calculated t-values are above the upper level critical values and the calculated F-value below the tabulated value. We conclude that the consumption variable contains unit roots at zero, semi-annual and annual frequencies. This implies that there is a seasonal unit root (that is, the series is seasonally integrated), confirming our result using the *DHF* methodology. Smith and Taylor (1995) arrive at a similar conclusion in their analysis of UK non-durable consumption expenditure between 1955(1) and 1992(1).

To illustrate the Perron approach to establishing the order of integration of a variable subject to an intervention or shock, we will consider the inflation series (inf_t). In Chapter 3 we noted that there was some advance warning of possible purchase tax increases to come in the second quarter of 1968. Some expenditure switching to the first quarter of that year was expected, and this may in addition have led to an increase in the rate of inflation from that time. We will treat the first quarter of 1968 as one in which there was a 'pulse' or one period shock to the inflation series, and conduct a Perron test on the lines explained in Section 5.4. We are attempting to decide whether the inflation series is a stationary series subject to a permanent increase in its mean at the break point (1968(1)), or a nonstationary series which was subject to a one-period shock at this same point. MODEL 5.11 gives the result of regressing the inflation variable on a step dummy (as equation (5.26) in the text). The residuals from this model are then used to estimate an equation on the lines of equation (5.28) in the text to give the results under MODEL 5.12.

The Perron test in this case relates to the examination of the t-value on the lagged residual, which can be seen to take the value of 0.217. The critical values appropriate in this case are in Table 6 in the Appendix. For a test at the 5% significance level with 71 observations and a value of $\lambda = 0.4$, the lower and upper bounds critical values are -3.47 and -3.39 respectively. In this case, the postulated break point lies 41/72 parts (or 0.569) through the sample data (the break is at 1968(1) and the sample data runs from 1958(1) to 1975(4)). Hence, the value of λ may be taken as $(1 - 0.6)$ or 0.4 as explained in Section 5.4. The calculated t-value lies above the upper level critical value for the test, so that the null hypothesis that the inflation series is nonstationary cannot be rejected, a finding consistent with the ADF tests carried out earlier.

Despite being unable to confirm that the appropriate differencing for the variables in the $DHSY$ model was as presented by $DHSY$, provided the variables $cons_t$, inc_t and inf_t are integrated of the same order (which they seem to be) there is a chance that their linear combination is stationary. We therefore turn our attention to cointegration analysis.

Let us first consider the $DHSY$ model that excluded inflation (equation (3.11)) which is equivalent to assuming values for the long run cointegrating vector (Step 2a in Section 5.6). The error correction term in this function (ignoring the lag) is of the form:

$$cons_t - inc_t \quad .$$

If the entire $DHSY$ function is to be stationary (assuming, for the sake of argument, that the other terms in the $DHSY$ function have been differenced appropriately), the term above must also be stationary. That is, the variables $cons_t$ and inc_t should be cointegrated of order $(1,1)$ with the cointegrating vector $(1,-1)$.

MODEL 5.13 shows the output for the ADF cointegration test for consumption and income, or equivalently, the integration test for the variable defined as $cons_t - inc_t$. In the computer output, this variable is denoted as lc_li , with a first difference dlc_li. MODEL 5.13 may be reduced to MODEL 5.14 by eliminating the variables at lags 5 and 6. The computed Student-t value, which is the value for the ADF cointegration test, is equal to 1.895. Formally, we should compare this value with the critical values given in Table 1 in the Appendix since no estimated coefficients were needed in order to define the cointegrating vector. However, the value of the test is so visibly positive that we can spare ourselves the effort of looking into the tables to find out whether 1.895 is 'significantly negative'. It is definitely not.

The conclusion is that the error correction mechanism of the $DHSY$ model is not stationary. In other words, the variables $cons_t$ and inc_t are not cointegrated $(1,1)$ with the cointegrating vector $(1,-1)$. This is confirmed by a relatively low value of the cointegration Durbin-Watson test statistic ($CIDW$) of 0.79 which may be computed for $cons_t - inc_t$. This, as far as testing nonstationarity is concerned, is not very low, but it looks rather suspicious.

Let us now consider the testing of long run cointegration in the $DHSY$ model where the coefficients in the potential long run cointegrating vector are unknown (Step 2b in Section 5.6). In order to extend the analysis, the long run model will be taken to be trivariate rather than bivariate (see equation (5.32) above), so that the inflation variable is also considered. An unrestricted $ADL(5, 5, 1)$ model for $cons_t$, inc_t and inf_t (that is five lags for both consumption and income, and a single lag for inflation) has been estimated and the results given in Section 5.9 as MODEL 5.15. Note that this model also includes seasonal dummy variables to approximate stochastic seasonality for the reasons outlined in Section 5.6 above. The estimated coefficients are then used to compute the long run parameters in a similar fashion to (5.43). They are directly computed by *PC-GIVE* and printed together with their asymptotic standard errors. Since they are equal to 0.943 for inc_t and -1.294 for inf_t, the error correction mechanism, representing deviations of $cons_t$ from its long run path, is computed as:

$$ECM = cons_t - 0.943 \cdot inc_t + 1.294 \cdot inf_t$$
$$- intercept \ and \ seasonal \ dummy \ variables \quad .$$

MODEL 5.16 gives the results of the initial *ADF* testing of this error term (denoted by ecm and its first differences by decm). This model may be reduced to MODEL 5.17 in the usual way. In this model, the t-value or test statistic on the lagged error correction term is equal to 0.206, which is clearly not 'significantly negative'. Formally, the appropriate critical values in this case are to be found in Table 4 in the Appendix for $m = 2$. This is the appropriate value for m as the tested cointegrating vector is now $(1, -0.943, 1.294,$ intercept and seasonal coefficients), that is it contains two estimated coefficients apart from the coefficients representing the deterministic seasonality. The tabulated values for a test at the 5% level of significance and 63 observations are (interpolating) -3.88 (lower) and -3.71 (upper) so that clearly the t-value in this case lies above the upper level critical value. Our conclusion is that the consumption, income and inflation series in the *DHSY* model are not (nonseasonally) cointegrated, if the cointegrating vector is that of the long run solution to an *ADL* model. Hylleberg *et al.* (1990) found no cointegration between the logarithm of consumption and the logarithm of income between 1955(1) and 1984(4) using the cointegrating vector $(1, -1)$.

However, Hendry, Muellbauer and Murphy (1990) found a cointegrating vector for the variables which appeared in the *DHSY* model using techniques which will be described in Chapter 6.

5.9 Stylized Computer Output (*PC-GIVE*)

Initial estimates for Dickey-Hasza-Fuller test
MODEL 5.1: Modelling d4lc by OLS
The present sample is: 1959 (1) to 1975 (4)

Variable	Coefficient	Std.Error	t-value
d4lc_1	0.843370	0.124901	6.752
d4lc_2	0.0948817	0.164701	0.576

d4lc_3	0.0254122	0.162428	0.156
d4lc_4	-0.0489343	0.127740	-0.383

$R^2 = 0.8340714$ $\sigma = 0.01163445$ DW = 1.97
* R^2 does NOT allow for the mean *
RSS = 0.0086630625602 for 4 variables and 68 observations

Testing for Error Autocorrelation from lags 1 to 5
$Chi^2(5) = 7.9781$ [0.1574] and F-Form(5, 59) = 1.5684 [0.1831]

MODEL 5.2: Modelling d4lc by OLS
The present sample is: 1959 (1) to 1975 (4)

Variable	Coefficient	Std.Error	t-value
d4lc_1	0.912540	0.0499746	18.260

$R^2 = 0.8326801$ $\sigma = 0.01141856$ DW = 2.14
* R^2 does NOT allow for the mean *
RSS = 0.0087357022974 for 1 variables and 68 observations

Testing for Error Autocorrelation from lags 1 to 5
$Chi^2(5) = 5.4717$ [0.3611] and F-Form(5, 62) = 1.0851 [0.3775]

Tests of model reduction
Model 1 --> 2: F(3, 65) = 0.181675 [0.9085]

Creating variable z for the Dickey-Hasza-Fuller test
d4lc_1 = lag(d4lc, 1);
lc_1 - lag(lc, 1);
lam*lc_1 = lc_1 * 0.91254;
z = lc - lam*lc_1;

MODEL 5.3: Modelling d4lc by OLS
The present sample is: 1959 (1) to 1975 (4)

Variable	Coefficient	Std.Error	t-value
d4lc_1	0.761449	0.124682	6.107
d4lc_2	0.0618682	0.159058	0.389
d4lc_3	-0.0167149	0.157235	-0.106
d4lc_4	-0.168533	0.132109	-1.276
z_4	0.0103009	0.00416765	2.472

$R^2 = 0.8487388$ $\sigma = 0.01119615$ DW = 1.94
* R^2 does NOT allow for the mean *

RSS = 0.0078972855429 for 5 variables and 68 observations

Testing for Error Autocorrelation from lags 1 to 5
$Chi^2(5) = 3.753$ [0.5855]   and F-Form(5, 58) = 0.677625 [0.6421]

MODEL 5.4: Modelling d4lc by OLS
The present sample is: 1959 (1) to 1975 (4)

Variable	Coefficient	Std.Error	t-value
d4lc_1	0.758745	0.0901771	8.414
z_4	0.00650415	0.00320561	2.029

$R^2 = 0.842504$ $\sigma = 0.01116189$ DW = 1.95
* R^2 does NOT allow for the mean *
RSS = 0.0082227978437 for 2 variables and 68 observations

Testing for Error Autocorrelation from lags 1 to 5
$Chi^2(5) = 4.771$ [0.4445]   and F-Form(5, 61) = 0.920559 [0.4739]

Augmented Dickey-Fuller test for $SI(0,1)$, consumption

MODEL 5.5: Modelling dd4lc by OLS
The present sample is: 1959 (2) to 1975 (4)

Variable	Coefficient	Std.Error	t-value
dd4lc_1	-0.0762641	0.122609	-0.622
dd4lc_2	0.00631618	0.125311	0.050
dd4lc_3	-0.00156628	0.127726	-0.012
dd4lc_4	-0.298163	0.124142	-2.402
d4lc_1	-0.0657502	0.0530884	-1.239

$R^2 = 0.1338828$ $\sigma = 0.01129085$ DW = 1.97
* R^2 does NOT allow for the mean *
RSS = 0.0079039677638 for 5 variables and 67 observations

Testing for Error Autocorrelation from lags 1 to 5
$Chi^2(5) = 1.8024$ [0.8758]   and F-Form(5, 57) = 0.315146 [0.9019]

MODEL 5.6: Modelling dd4lc by OLS
The present sample is: 1959 (2) to 1975 (4)

Variable	Coefficient	Std.Error	t-value
dd4lc_4	-0.297168	0.119387	-2.489
d4lc_1	-0.0722229	0.0490262	-1.473

$R^2 = 0.1281411$ $\sigma = 0.01106371$ DW = 2.11

* R^2 does NOT allow for the mean *

RSS = 0.0079563651198 for 2 variables and 67 observations

Testing for Error Autocorrelation from lags 1 to 5
$Chi^2(5) = 1.3577$ [0.9289]   and F-Form(5, 60) = 0.248201 [0.9391]

Augmented Dickey-Fuller test for *SI*(1, 1), consumption
ddd4lc = diff(dd4lc, 1);

MODEL 5.7: Modelling ddd4lc by OLS
The present sample is: 1959 (3) to 1975 (4)

Variable	Coefficient	Std.Error	t-value
ddd4lc_1	0.368868	0.281403	1.311
ddd4lc_2	0.346524	0.242055	1.432
ddd4lc_3	0.302401	0.195028	1.551
ddd4lc_4	0.00332254	0.129806	0.026
dd4lc_1	-1.4885	0.332579	-4.476

$R^2 = 0.6109555$ $\sigma = 0.01130684$ DW = 1.98

* R^2 does NOT allow for the mean *

RSS = 0.0077985273352 for 5 variables and 66 observations

Testing for Error Autocorrelation from lags 1 to 5
$Chi^2(5) = 4.6389$ [0.4615]   and F-Form(5, 56) = 0.846722 [0.5226]

MODEL 5.8:Modelling ddd4lc by OLS
The present sample is: 1959 (3) to 1975 (4)

Variable	Coefficient	Std.Error	t-value
ddd4lc_1	0.365001	0.235487	1.550
ddd4lc_2	0.342657	0.187601	1.827
ddd4lc_3	0.298540	0.122651	2.434
dd4lc_1	-1.4837	0.270339	-5.488

$R^2 = 0.6109513$ $\sigma = 0.01121535$ DW = 1.98

* R^2 does NOT allow for the mean *

RSS = 0.007798611094 for 4 variables and 66 observations

Testing for Error Autocorrelation from lags 1 to 5
$Chi^2(5) = 4.4258$ [0.4899]   and F-Form(5, 57) = 0.819403 [0.5410]

Creation of *HEGY* variables

lc_1 = lag(lc, 1);
lc_2 = lag(lc, 2);
lc_3 = lag(lc, 3);
y11 = lc + lc_1;
y111 = lc_1 - lc;
y12 = y11 + lc_2;
y1 = y12 + lc_3;
y21 = y111 - lc_2;
y2 = y21 + lc_3;
y3 = lc_2 - lc;

MODEL 5.9: Modelling d4lc by OLS
The present sample is: 1959 (1) to 1975 (4)

Variable	Coefficient	Std.Error	t-value
d4lc_1	0.733083	0.131472	5.576
d4lc_2	0.0766295	0.163468	0.469
d4lc_3	0.00154841	0.161610	0.010
d4lc_4	-0.193602	0.135958	-1.424
y1_1	0.000238737	9.4441e-005	2.528
y2_1	0.000592194	0.0139780	0.042
y3_1	-0.0190537	0.0223154	-0.854
y3_2	0.00649557	0.0222259	0.292

$R^2 = 0.8518258$ $\sigma = 0.01135496$ DW = 1.91
$* R^2$ does NOT allow for the mean *
RSS = 0.0077361111817 for 8 variables and 68 observations

Testing for Error Autocorrelation from lags 1 to 5
$Chi^2(5) = 3.9503$ [0.5566]   and F-Form(5, 55) = 0.678431 [0.6416]

MODEL 5.10: Modelling d4lc by OLS
The present sample is: 1959 (1) to 1975 (4)

Variable	Coefficient	Std.Error	t-value
d4lc_1	0.777738	0.0978865	7.945
d4lc_4	-0.168800	0.102637	-1.645
y1_1	0.000245376	9.1843e-005	2.672
y2_1	0.000940064	0.0137433	0.068
y3_1	-0.0174209	0.0215749	-0.807
y3_2	0.00524465	0.0217172	0.241

$R^2 = 0.8511585$ $\sigma = 0.01119544$ DW = 2.01
* R^2 does NOT allow for the mean *
RSS = 0.0077709525173 for 6 variables and 68 observations

Testing for Error Autocorrelation from lags 1 to 5
$Chi^2(5) = 3.5513$ [0.6156]   and F-Form(5, 57) = 0.628169 [0.6789]

Wald test for linear restrictions (Subset)

LinRes F(2, 62) = 0.35618 [0.7018]

Zero restrictions on: y3_1 y3_2

Perron test for inflation variable
dtb = ImpulseDummy(1968, 1);
du = StepDummy(1968, 1);

MODEL 5.11: Modelling inf by OLS
The present sample is: 1958 (1) to 1975 (4)

Variable	Coefficient	Std.Error	t-value
Constant	0.0311293	0.00593426	5.246
du	0.0625327	0.00890138	7.025

$R^2 = 0.4134967$ F(1, 70) = 49.351 [0.0000] $\sigma = 0.03753153$
DW = 0.1175
RSS = 0.098603112842 for 2 variables and 72 observations

e added to database
e = Residual; values of equation 1
de = diff(e, 1);

MODEL 5.12: Modelling de by OLS
The present sample is: 1958 (2) to 1975 (4)

Variable	Coefficient	Std.Error	t-value
e_1	0.00830378	0.0382138	0.217
dtb	-0.0555978	0.0110953	-5.011

$R^2 = 0.2681159$ $\sigma = 0.01108714$ DW = 1.52
* R^2 does NOT allow for the mean *
RSS = 0.0084817982634 for 2 variables and 71 observations

Testing for Error Autocorrelation from lags 1 to 5
$Chi^2(5) = 10.637 [0.0591]$ and F-Form$(5, 64) = 2.2556 [0.0593]$

Augmented Dickey-Fuller test for cointegration of cons and inc, with the cointegrating vector [1 , -1]

lc_li = lc - li;
dlc_li = diff(lc_li, 1);

MODEL 5.13: Modelling dlc_li by OLS
The present sample is: 1958 (4) to 1975 (4)

Variable	Coefficient	Std.Error	t-value
dlc_li_1	-0.730473	0.137468	-5.314
dlc_li_2	-0.588241	0.174190	-3.377
dlc_li_3	-0.575179	0.191983	-2.996
dlc_li_4	0.354610	0.190404	1.862
dlc_li_5	0.114331	0.171306	0.667
dlc_li_6	0.0485710	0.138469	0.351
lc_li_1	0.0224458	0.0163507	1.373

$R^2 = 0.8222645$ $\sigma = 0.0186059$ DW = 1.90
* R^2 does NOT allow for the mean *
RSS = 0.021463135149 for 7 variables and 69 observations

Testing for Error Autocorrelation from lags 1 to 5
$Chi^2(5) = 8.5486 [0.1285]$ and F-Form$(5, 57) = 1.6121 [0.1715]$

MODEL 5.14: Modelling dlc_li by OLS
The present sample is: 1958 (2) to 1975 (4)

Variable	Coefficient	Std.Error	t-value
dlc_li_1	-0.714707	0.131639	-5.429
dlc_li_2	-0.628712	0.137636	-4.568
dlc_li_3	-0.657293	0.135082	-4.866
dlc_li_4	0.268836	0.129119	2.082
lc_li_1	0.0267031	0.0140931	1.895

$R^2 = 0.8216575$ $\sigma = 0.01812147$ DW = 1.96
* R^2 does NOT allow for the mean *
RSS = 0.021673577946 for 5 variables and 71 observations

Testing for Error Autocorrelation from lags 1 to 5
$Chi^2(5) = 9.1002 [0.1051]$ and F-Form$(5, 61) = 1.7936 [0.1276]$

Unrestricted *ADL* model
MODEL 5.15: Modelling lc by OLS
The present sample is: 1958 (2) to 1975 (4)

Variable	Coefficient	Std.Error	t-value
lc_1	0.0305187	0.131125	0.233
lc_2	0.0139476	0.105446	0.132
lc_3	0.0791037	0.101820	0.777
lc_4	0.708311	0.104608	6.771
lc_5	0.0746747	0.126690	0.589
li	0.297103	0.0449884	6.604
li_1	0.162653	0.0621542	2.617
li_2	-0.0466777	0.0554264	-0.842
li_3	0.0484722	0.0536070	0.904
li_4	-0.164092	0.0571375	-2.872
li_5	-0.209375	0.0630411	-3.321
inf	-0.293451	0.0900713	-3.258
inf_1	0.172565	0.0982876	1.756
Constant	0.0661961	0.186013	0.356
Seasonal	-0.0364705	0.0157273	-2.319
Seasonal_1	-0.0147653	0.0116944	-1.263
Seasonal_2	-0.0211159	0.0154068	-1.371

$R^2 = 0.9980032$ F(16, 54) = 1686.8 [0.0000] $\sigma = 0.006352803$
DW = 2.21 RSS = 0.0021793380215 for 17 variables and 71 observations

Testing for Error Autocorrelation from lags 1 to 5
$Chi^2(5) = 11.532$ [0.0418] * and F-Form(5, 49) = 1.9004 [0.1113]

Solved Static Long Run equation

lc = +0.94263 li   -1.294 inf   +0.7084
(SE)   (0.18231)   (1.297)   (1.309)
-0.77427 Seasonal
(0.94937)

WALD test $Chi^2(3) = 160.6$ [0.0000] **

MODEL 5.16: Modelling decm by OLS
The present sample is: 1960 (2) to 1975 (4)

Variable	Coefficient	Std.Error	t-value
decm_1	-0.178257	0.131203	-1.359
decm_2	-0.0642325	0.133002	-0.483

decm_3	-0.104467	0.130134	-0.803
decm_4	0.434514	0.126951	3.423
decm_5	-0.0176592	0.137712	-0.128
decm_6	-0.144641	0.134932	-1.072
decm_7	-0.116399	0.136492	-0.853
decm_8	0.332555	0.130145	2.555
ecm_1	-0.0347973	0.0329290	-1.057

$R^2 = 0.9975986$ $\sigma = 0.0269318$ DW = 1.96
* R^2 does NOT allow for the mean *
RSS = 0.039167366686 for 9 variables and 63 observations

Testing for Error Autocorrelation from lags 1 to 5
$Chi^2(5) = 3.3871$ [0.6405] and F-Form(5, 49) = 0.55681 [0.7324]

MODEL 5.17: Modelling decm by OLS
The present sample is: 1960 (2) to 1975 (4)

Variable	Coefficient	Std.Error	t-value
decm_4	0.545077	0.106505	5.118
decm_8	0.449162	0.106997	4.198
ecm_1	0.00335816	0.0163221	0.206

$R^2 = 0.9973357$ $\sigma = 0.02691176$ DW = 2.26
* R^2 does NOT allow for the mean *
RSS = 0.0434545617 for 3 variables and 63 observations

Testing for Error Autocorrelation from lags 1 to 5
$Chi^2(5) = 5.7971$ [0.3265] and F-Form(5, 55) = 1.1148 [0.3633]

5.10 Suggestions for Further Reading

Problems of spurious regression and correlation have been recognized since the early days of statistics. A new perspective to these problems has been given by Granger and Newbold (1974, 1986). Desai (1981, Chapter 3) discusses spurious correlation within the general framework of testing economic theories. A thorough approach to this problem is highly complicated and formal (see Phillips (1986), or Stock and Watson (1988)). Methodological aspects of the lack of stationarity of variables in an econometric model are discussed by Charemza (1990a) and Nelson and Kang (1981). A useful and wide-ranging account of stochastic processes is that provided by Spanos (1986, Chapter 8).

For integration analysis (unit root testing) the seminal papers are those of Dickey and Fuller (1979, 1981) and, for the Durbin-Watson integration statistic, that by Sargan and Bhargava (1983). A more general model is discussed by Said and Dickey (1984). The first critical values for the *DF* and *ADF* tests were given by Fuller (1976), where a detailed statistical introduction to the problem of unit root analysis can be found. The widely known example of the empirical testing of stochastic and deterministic trends is that provided by Nelson and Plosser (1982) and a more sophisticated one has been provided by Perron (1989).

The foundations for cointegration analysis were given by Engle and Granger (1987), although their ideas had been known about since 1984, due to conference and discussion papers. Since 1986, the number of publications in this field has been growing rapidly. There were special issues of the journals *Oxford Bulletin of Economics and Statistics* (1986) and *Journal of Economic Dynamics and Control* (1988) devoted exclusively to the problems of cointegration. In the 1990s the increase in the literature on cointegration and related issues has been enormous. It is beyond the scope of this book to review this here. For a practitioner, relatively easy to read descriptions of cointegration techniques are given by Muscatelli and Hurn (1995) and especially Rao (1994), who presents a collection of comprehensible papers on various aspects of unit root and cointegration modelling. More advanced approaches can be found in a series of monographs and edited volumes of papers, most notably those of Granger (1990), Hatanaka (1996), Banerjee *et al.* (1993), Hargreaves (1994) and Hamilton (1994). From the numerous publications now available one might note the following. Applications of cointegration analysis which are relatively easy to read and follow can be found in the special issue of the *Oxford Bulletin of Economics and Statistics* (1986) mentioned above. Other applications are by Miller (1988) and Taylor (1988). The link between cointegration and error correction mechanisms is discussed in Mills (1990, pp. 273-274), Cuthbertson, Hall and Taylor (1992, pp. 133-134)) and Alogoskoufis and Smith (1995). An ingenious generalization of the interpretation of a cointegrating process as a drunkard's walk is given in Murray (1994). An interesting extension to the Engle-Granger two-step procedure is given by Engle and Yoo (1987) and an alternative by Wickens and Breusch (1988). Some theory and analysis of seasonal integration and cointegration can be found in Osborn *et al.* (1988), Engle, Granger and Hallman (1989), Kunst (1989, 1990) and Hylleberg *et al.* (1990). A collection of papers on modelling seasonality is that of Hylleberg (1992). Within the huge literature on seasonality, an important paper is that of Hylleberg (1995), where the relationship between general to specific modelling and integration testing is stressed. Selected papers on cointegration are published in the volume edited by Engle and Granger (1991). Important developments of statistical inference into cointegration are available in Park and Phillips (1988, 1989), Phillips (1988b), Phillips and Ouliaris (1990), Kwiatkowski *et al.* (1992) and Elliot, Rothenberg and Stock (1996). There is also a developed cointegration analysis within the vector autoregressive approach. This will be analysed in Chapter 6.

Chapter 6

Vector Autoregression: Forecasting, Causality and Cointegration

6.1 A Reconsideration of Structural Modelling

The previous chapters of this book have been directed towards the modelling of a single economic phenomenon which could be described by a single equation, with a single dependent variable. In this chapter (and also in Chapter 7) we will outline some problems and approaches of econometric modelling in situations where one is dealing with relationships described by a system of more than one equation. Before considering some relatively new approaches to multiple equation econometric modelling, it will be useful briefly to reconsider the traditional structural (Cowles Commission) method of constructing such models.

Structural multi-equation modelling is described in, for example, Goldberger (1964), Dhrymes (1978) or Johnston (1984) and only the central ideas will be outlined here. We will illustrate the main features of traditional structural multi-equation modelling by the use of two equation models, used widely in the literature. The first of these models is a simple Keynesian model, in which the Absolute Income Hypothesis (see Chapter 3) is complemented by an identity which defines the formation of income in a closed economy:

$$C_t = \alpha + \beta Y_t + \varepsilon_t \quad , \tag{6.1a}$$

$$Y_t = C_t + I_t \quad , \tag{6.1b}$$

where C_t stands for the level of aggregate consumption, Y_t is aggregate income, I_t is the level of investment, ε_t is an error term and α and β are coefficients. Completing the Absolute Income Hypothesis by the equilibrium condition (6.1b) that saving is equal to investment has an important consequence for the entire process of model estimation and use. Let us first make an *ad hoc* intuitive analysis of the effect of a sudden unexpected change in C_t through a change in ε_t. From (6.1a) it is clear that, for instance, a rise in ε_t causes a rise in C_t. At the same time a rise in C_t must also change Y_t through (6.1b). Hence, in the system of equations (6.1a - 6.1b), it is not possible to change C_t without causing Y_t to change. Similarly, it is not possible to change Y_t without affecting C_t. It is, however, possible to affect C_t and Y_t by a change in I_t but not the other way round; one may change

C_t and Y_t and leave I_t intact. Consequently, the variables C_t and Y_t in the system of equations (6.1a - 6.1b) are described as the *endogenous* variables (values determined within the system) whilst I_t is called an *exogenous* variable (its value is determined outside of the system). The endogenous variables are also described as being *jointly dependent* variables. It is usual to make a distinction between exogenous and lagged endogenous variables, despite the fact that the values of both can be considered as having been determined already for any time period of interest. Exogenous and lagged endogenous variables together make up what are described as the *predetermined* variables in a system. The distinction between the types of variable appearing in a multiple equation system is in sharp contrast with single equation structural modelling, where little attention is paid to the problem of endo-exogenous division of variables. Usually, what is on the left-hand side of a single equation structural model is simply treated as endogenous and what is on the right-hand side is treated as exogenous.

The observed simultaneity of C_t and Y_t has an important consequence for the entire process of econometric modelling. It is easy to show that in (6.1a) the right-hand side variable Y_t is correlated with the error term ε_t. This can be demonstrated by solving the system of equations (6.1a - 6.1b) for the endogenous variables:

$$C_t = \beta^* \alpha + \beta^* \beta I_t + \beta^* \varepsilon_t \quad , \tag{6.2a}$$

$$Y_t = \beta^* \alpha + \beta^* I_t + \beta^* \varepsilon_t \quad , \tag{6.2b}$$

where $\beta^* = \dfrac{1}{1-\beta}$. Clearly, Y_t is directly related to the error term, ε_t.

A structural model solved for the endogenous variables as functions of the predetermined variables only, like (6.2a - 6.2b), is usually called the *reduced form* of the model. However, to clarify what is to come, we will call a system of equations like (6.2a - 6.2b) a *restricted reduced form* and abbreviate, if necessary, as *RRF*. Coefficients of an *RRF* are often denoted as $\pi_{11}, \pi_{12}, \pi_{21}$, etc., so that in this notation, the restricted reduced form of (6.2a - 6.2b) would be written as:

$$C_t = \pi_{11} + \pi_{12} I_t + v_{1t} \quad , \tag{6.2c}$$

$$Y_t = \pi_{21} + \pi_{22} I_t + v_{2t} \quad . \tag{6.2d}$$

If (6.2a - 6.2b) and (6.2c - 6.2d) are compared, it can be seen that the form in which the coefficients enter into the former imply certain restrictions on the parameters in the latter, more general, notation. In this case, the restrictions are that $\pi_{11} = \pi_{21}$, and $(\pi_{22} - \pi_{12}) = 1$. The second restriction follows from noting that the coefficient on variable I_t in (6.2a) is β times the coefficient on I_t in (6.2b), and that β^* is a function of β.

It will be useful for what follows to note that knowledge of the true (not estimated) values of the restricted reduced form coefficients in (6.2c - 6.2d) would allow the coefficients in the original system (6.1a - 6.1b) to be retrieved. Specifically, $\beta = \pi_{12} / \pi_{22}$ and $\alpha = \pi_{21} / \pi_{22}$. The possibility of retrieving the coefficients of the original model from knowledge of the values of the restricted reduced form coefficients is termed *the identification problem*. We will return to this problem shortly.

The *unrestricted reduced form* (*URF*) is the set of linear equations expressing the jointly dependent variables as functions of the predetermined variables only, with no restrictions on the values of the coefficients in these equations. For the case of equations (6.1a - 6.1b) this gives:

$$C_t = \pi_{11}^* + \pi_{12}^* I_t + \varepsilon_{1t} \quad , \tag{6.3a}$$

$$Y_t = \pi_{21}^* + \pi_{22}^* I_t + \varepsilon_{2t} \quad , \tag{6.3b}$$

where no restrictions are imposed on the parameters π_{11}^*, π_{12}^*, π_{21}^* and π_{22}^*.

The original system (6.1a - 6.1b) is called the *structural form* of the model. As was noted above, in this structural form the covariance between Y_t and ε_t is not zero. It follows from equation (6.2b) that $E(Y_t \varepsilon_t) = \beta^* \sigma^2$, where σ^2 is the variance of ε_t. Consequently, equation (6.1a) cannot be consistently estimated by the ordinary least squares method, because the assumption that there is no correlation between the explanatory variable and the error term is violated. This fact, called *simultaneity bias* or *Haavelmo bias* (after the Cowles Commission member who first noted this problem) has been a persistent worry to structural modellers who, especially in the 1950s and 1960s, developed a great number of estimation methods to deal with this problem. One or more of these methods are thoroughly described in most textbooks of econometrics.

There is another problem of econometric inference in simultaneous equations structural models that was touched upon briefly above. This is the problem of the *identification* of structural parameters, that is the parameters which are present in the structural form of a model. Logically, this problem is prior to that of the estimation of the structural equations, in that estimation would not be sensible if the equation were not identified.

For example, consider a simple supply-demand system of two equations in which it is assumed that market clearing (equilibrium) is achieved in each period:

$$Q_t = \alpha_0 + \alpha_1 P_t + u_{1t} \quad , \tag{6.4a}$$

$$Q_t = \beta_0 + \beta_1 P_t + u_{2t} \quad . \tag{6.4b}$$

Here, equation (6.4a) represents a demand equation and (6.4b) a supply equation, Q_t is the quantity supplied and demanded of a good, and P_t is the price of the good. It is clear that the variables Q_t and P_t are jointly dependent, as were C_t and Y_t in (6.1a - 6.1b); one cannot change one of them independently of the other. Therefore, there is simultaneous equation bias in the system, since Q_t and P_t are correlated with both u_{1t} and u_{2t}. The model (6.4a - 6.4b) might be perfectly admissible from the point of view of economic theory, especially if we expect α_1 to be negative and β_1 to be positive. Nevertheless, intuition suggests that when it comes to estimation of the parameters α_0, α_1, β_0 and β_1 using two series of data for Q_t and P_t, something is wrong. How can we estimate four parameters from two series of data? Even, if we ignore the constant terms by, for instance, working with variables measured in deviations from their means, we are still left with two structural coefficients (α_1 and β_1) to be determined from the running of only one regression with a single explanatory (right-hand side) variable. If we run a regression of Q_t on P_t how will we know whether the result is a demand equation, a supply equation or a mixture of both? In this case, the equations (6.4a - 6.4b), and hence the model, are said to be *not identified* or *underidentified*.

Another way of seeing this is to note that it is not possible to recover the structural parameters α_0, α_1, β_0 and β_1 from knowledge of the *RRF* of the model, since the *RRF* contains only two coefficients and we have four structural parameters to determine. Even if we knew the true values of the restricted reduced form coefficients, there would be no way to determine or unscramble the values of the structural parameters from these known coefficients. This is in contrast to our result earlier for model (6.1a - 6.1b) which was identified, since knowing the four coefficients in the *RRF* (6.2a - 6.2b) it was possible to solve for the structural parameters α and β. Equations (6.4a - 6.4b) become identified if (on the grounds of economic theory) additional variables are added to the system, say an interest rate r_t to the demand equation and lagged price P_{t-1} to the supply equation. The model would then be given by:

$$Q_t = \alpha_0 + \alpha_1 P_t + \alpha_2 r_t + u_{1t} \quad , \tag{6.5a}$$

$$Q_t = \beta_0 + \beta_1 P_t + \beta_2 P_{t-1} + u_{2t} \quad . \tag{6.5b}$$

Note that in (6.5a - 6.5b) the division between endogenous and exogenous variables no longer corresponds with that of jointly dependent and predetermined variables. The jointly dependent (simultaneous) variables are still Q_t and P_t, but the predetermined variables are divided into the *lagged dependent* variables (in this case, just the one, P_{t-1}) and the *exogenous* variables (again, just one in this case, r_t). The structural parameters in (6.5a - 6.5b) are identified, since it is possible to solve for the structural parameters from knowledge of the values of the restricted reduced form coefficients of the model. Stewart and Wallis (1981, pp. 78-86) provide details of such a solution.

Structural models may be presented using matrix notation (see, for example, Goldberger (1964, Chapter 7) or Judge *et al.* (1985, Chapter 14)) as:

$$y_t'\Gamma + x_t'B = u_t' \quad , \tag{6.6}$$

where y_t' is a $(1 \times M)$ row vector of the observations at time t on the M jointly dependent variables, Γ is an $(M \times M)$ matrix of structural coefficients of the current jointly dependent (or endogenous) variables, x_t' is a $(1 \times H)$ row vector of the observations at time t on the H predetermined variables, B is an $H \times M$ matrix of coefficients on the predetermined variables, and u_t' is a $(1 \times M)$ row vector of disturbance terms. If lagged dependent variables are to be distinguished from the exogenous variables, the model may be written as:

$$y_t'\Gamma + x_t'^{*}B_0 + \sum_{i=1}^{k} y_{t-i}'B_i = u_t' \quad , \tag{6.7}$$

where k is the maximum lag length entertained for any of the endogenous variables. In this notation, $x_t'^{*}$ stands for the vector of observations on the exogenous rather than the predetermined variables at time t. For the sake of simplicity, we have assumed that there are no lagged exogenous variables in the model. If there were, either they could be simply included in the set of exogenous variables, or if a separate treatment of them was required, another set of terms on the lines of those introduced for the lagged endogenous variables could be introduced into (6.7).

For model (6.1a - 6.1b), the matrices Γ and B are:

$$\Gamma = \begin{bmatrix} 1 & -1 \\ -\beta & 1 \end{bmatrix} , \qquad B = \begin{bmatrix} \alpha & 0 \\ 0 & 1 \end{bmatrix} .$$

For model (6.4a - 6.4b) these matrices are:

$$\Gamma = \begin{bmatrix} 1 & 1 \\ -\alpha_1 & -\beta_1 \end{bmatrix} , \qquad B = \begin{bmatrix} -\alpha_0 & -\beta_0 \end{bmatrix} ,$$

and for model (6.5a - 6.5b):

$$\Gamma = \begin{bmatrix} 1 & 1 \\ -\alpha_1 & -\beta_1 \end{bmatrix} \ , \quad B = \begin{bmatrix} -\alpha_0 & -\beta_0 \\ -\alpha_2 & 0 \\ 0 & -\beta_2 \end{bmatrix} .$$

In model (6.5a - 6.5b) there is a lagged dependent variable. We may therefore split the set of predetermined variables into lagged endogenous (P_{t-1}) and exogenous (the intercept term and r_t) variables. The matrices of the parameters of (6.5a - 6.5b) in the form of equation (6.7) become:

$$\Gamma = \begin{bmatrix} 1 & 1 \\ -\alpha_1 & -\beta_1 \end{bmatrix} \ , \quad B_0 = \begin{bmatrix} -\alpha_0 & -\beta_0 \\ -\alpha_2 & 0 \end{bmatrix} \ , \quad B_1 = \begin{bmatrix} 0 & -\beta_2 \end{bmatrix} .$$

For equations (6.6), the restricted reduced form can be obtained by solving the matrix equation with respect to the variables in x_t :

$$y_t' = -x_t'\Pi + V_t \quad , \tag{6.8}$$

where $\Pi = B\Gamma^{-1}$, and $V_t = u_t'\Gamma^{-1}$. Analogously, for a model in the notation of equation (6.7), the *RRF* is defined as:

$$y_t' = -x_t'^{*}\Pi_0 - \sum_{i=1}^{k} y_{t-i}'\Pi_i + V_t \quad ,$$

where $\Pi_i = B_i\Gamma^{-1}$, $i = 0$, 1 , ..., k. The form of equations (6.6) and (6.8) indicates the restrictive nature of the identification problem in structural modelling. If a model is to be identified, it must be possible to recover the matrices of structural parameters Γ and B from the equation $\Pi = B\Gamma^{-1}$. Clearly, in general this is not possible. Intuitively, identification is more likely if the matrix Π contains a lot of zero elements or, more precisely, if the matrices Γ and B have zero elements in particular rows and columns. In structural econometrics, the existence of a zero element in the matrix Γ or B means that a *zero restriction* has been imposed for a particular variable. For instance, for model (6.5a - 6.5b), in matrix B we have zeros as elements {3, 1} and {2, 2}. This means that we know *a priori* that the variable P_{t-1} does not appear in the demand equation and the variable r_t does not appear in the supply equation. It is easy to check that without these restrictions model (6.5a - 6.5b) is not identified. Also, in order to identify parameters of endogenous and exogenous variables, it is necessary to establish prior to any econometric investigation which variable belongs to the set of the endogenous and which to the set of exogenous variables. In other words, the *endo-exogenous division* of the variables in a model has to be imposed. The technical 'order and rank' conditions which provide necessary and sufficient conditions for the identification of an equation in a simultaneous equation system are given in most econometric theory textbooks, and will not be pursued here.

6.2 Principles of Vector Autoregressive Modelling

Structural econometrics, and especially multi-equation modelling, attracted a lot of attention during the 1950s and 1960s. Theoretical advancements were mainly concerned with the development of estimation methods which took account of the 'simultaneous equation bias' that resulted from the correlation of error terms with some of the explanatory variables in an equation. Applications of multi-equation modelling were focused on the building of large and complicated models of economies, in some cases containing several thousand endogenous variables, which were used for forecasting and policy analysis. As was noted in Chapter 1, these models did not perform very well, and this sparked off widespread criticism of structural econometric modelling. As far as single equation models are concerned, the main cause of concern seems to be the practice of data mining (see Chapter 2). For multi-equation modelling, criticism has been mainly directed towards the assumption of zero restrictions and the endo-exogenous division of the variables.

The questioning of the role of zero restrictions imposed in order to achieve identification of a model started over thirty years ago (see Liu (1960)). The danger is that models may be formulated and estimated with some variables added to equations without much economic justification and other variables deleted (that is, zero restrictions imposed), in order to achieve identification. For instance, model (6.4a - 6.4b) may be perfectly supported by economic theory. Nevertheless this theory will never have any econometric confirmation because it is not identified. An investigator might be tempted to add extra, different variables to each equation, merely to satisfy the identification of each equation, even if the economic justification for such variables was weak.

The theoretical restrictions imposed on structural simultaneous equation models were viewed as 'incredible' in a seminal paper by Sims (1980), where the basis for the new methodology of vector autoregressive modelling was first formulated. The principal differences of the Sims modelling methodology from those formulated in the Cowles Commission structural approach are the following:

1. There is no *a priori* endo-exogenous division of variables;
2. No zero restrictions are imposed;
3. There is no strict (and prior to modelling) economic theory within which the model is grounded.

The above principles are quite revolutionary and have far reaching consequences. No zero restrictions and no specified exogenous variables means that the identification problem becomes ill defined. Principle 3 is in fact a consequence of the other two: if there is no variable excluded from any equation of a model and nothing is exogenous, it means that everything causes everything else and there is no room for assuming anything more than very general economic principles as a starting point. This is why the Sims methodology is often called by its critics *atheoretical macroeconometrics*. The standard defence of Sims' position is from an examination of the economist's example of a consumer maximizing his/her lifetime utility function. There is literally no variable which may not enter the consumer's demand and labour supply functions and there is no *a priori* reason to exclude any of them. It has to be stressed, however, that these 'atheoretical' postulates are regarded as testable hypotheses. It is shown later that further inference in a Sims type model may lead to a model form which is consistent with even highly detailed economic theories.

The starting point of modelling in the Sims methodology is the formulation of a *general (unrestricted) vector autoregressive (VAR) model*. As its name implies, this consists in regressing each current (non-lagged) variable in the model on all the variables in the model lagged a certain number of times. In order to stress the difference from structural modelling, suppose that we wish to develop a *VAR* alternative to the structural dynamic model described in matrix form by (6.7), that is a model containing vectors of current and lagged endogenous variables $y_t, y_{t-1}, \ldots, y_{t-k}$ and current exogenous variables x_t^*. For *VAR* modelling, this division is not relevant and it is also not relevant that there are no lagged exogenous variables. The unrestricted *VAR* alternative to model (6.7) can be described as:

$$Z_t = \sum_{i=1}^{k} A_i Z_{t-i} + \epsilon_t \quad , \tag{6.9}$$

where

$$Z_t = \begin{bmatrix} y_t \\ x_t^* \end{bmatrix} ,$$

is a column vector of observations on the current values of all the variables in the model. ϵ_t is a column vector of random errors which are usually assumed to be contemporaneously correlated but not autocorrelated, so that they have a non-diagonal covariance matrix. The matrices A_i do not contain any zero elements. There is some resemblance of (6.9) with the reduced form of a structural econometric model. In fact (6.9) constitutes an unrestricted reduced form of a structural model (in the sense defined in the previous section) for the case where there are no exogenous variables, that is where in (6.7) all elements in the B_0 matrix are zeros.

Since the *VAR* model involves only lagged variables on its right-hand side, and since these variables by definition are not correlated with the error term (assuming no autocorrelation), it can be consistently estimated, equation by equation, by ordinary least squares. However, since the multivariate error term ϵ_t was assumed above to have a non-diagonal covariance matrix, it would be natural to consider applying multivariate regression (or seemingly unrelated regressions) rather than ordinary least squares, in order to take account explicitly of the non-zero covariances of the error terms. In fact, as no restrictions are placed on the coefficients in (6.9), the multivariate least squares estimators are no more efficient than those of ordinary least squares (Harvey (1989, p.72)).

Often, particular equations in a general *VAR* model are completed by an additional set of deterministic components, such as intercept terms, deterministic trends and seasonal dummy variables. Also, the existence of stochastic trends (see Chapter 5) may be accommodated by allowing variables integrated of a given order to enter the *VAR* model after appropriate differencing. Harvey (1989, pp. 469-470), however, points out some difficulties with this if different series have different orders of integration. In addition, it is possible to allow for time varying elements in A_i by formulating the *VAR* model recursively and to impose some *a priori* knowledge concerning the variability of elements in A_i by assuming Bayesian priors. These types of inference are, however, beyond the scope of this book (for more information see the suggestions for further reading in Section 6.8).

One straightforward application of an unrestricted *VAR* model is for forecasting. A *VAR* forecaster does not worry about the economic theory underlying his or her *VAR* model and, more importantly, does not need to make any assumptions about the values of exogenous variables in the forecasting period. This is in contrast with standard econometric forecasting where forecasts have to be conditioned upon knowledge of exogenous variables.

For instance, suppose a single equation model, say:

$$y_t = \alpha x_t + \zeta_t \quad ,$$

is estimated for the period $t = 1, 2, ..., T$ and is to be used by an econometrician for *ex ante* forecasting for the period $t = T+1, ..., T^*$. Provided that the structural coefficient α is unchanged in the forecast period and that the model is an appropriate formulation of the way in which y_t is generated, an unbiased forecast of y_t, say y_t^f for a period t between $T+1$ and T^* is:

$$y_t^f = \alpha x_t \quad ,$$

that is, it is conditional on the information concerning x_t, the value of the exogenous variable in the forecast period. Quite evidently, the future data for x_t are not known, and it would be necessary to make some predictions concerning x_t and condition the forecast on these predictions rather than on the true but unknown values of x_t. Hence, the forecast of y_t will be heavily dependent on the predictions of x_t. In a *VAR* model, however, the problem of conditioning a forecast on an exogenous variable does not exist, since there are no exogenous variables.

If the contemporaneous correlation between the errors of the equations is ignored, a forecast in a *VAR* model can be made in a quite mechanical way. For the first forecast period, the forecasts in (6.9) are made conditional on the last observed values of the variables, as:

$$Z^f_{T+1} = \sum_{i=1}^{k} A_i Z_{T-i+1} \quad ,$$

and for the later periods recursively or sequentially, conditionally on the forecasts computed for periods for which true values are unknown. That is, in general:

$$Z^f_{T+j} = \sum_{i=1}^{k} A_i Z^f_{T+j-i} \quad ,$$

where:

$$Z^f_{T+j-i} = \begin{cases} Z^f_{T+j-i} & \text{for } j > i \\ Z_{T+j-i} & \text{for } j \leq i \end{cases} \quad .$$

In practice, it is not possible to avoid imposing some prior restrictions on a *VAR* system. There is always some limit on the number of variables which can be included in a *VAR* model as well as on the maximum number of lags. If we have, for instance, a system of six variables and we wish to impose five lags on each variable, the total number of regressors in each equation would be 30. This could make the entire modelling process impossible if we have only a small data sample. It may happen, then, that some variables have to be excluded prior to modelling. Especially important here is the choice of the appropriate length of the lags to be used. Whilst some quite sophisticated procedures for making this choice have been proposed (for example, see Hsiao (1979, 1981)), it seems of particular importance to establish the maximum lag length in relation to the possible existence of autocorrelation in the disturbances. Since a *VAR* model contains lagged dependent variables as regressors, autocorrelation of error terms can be very serious in that it may lead to inconsistent estimates of parameters if ordinary least squares or multivariate least squares methods are used for estimation. However, as was indicated in Chapter 5 where the role of augmentation for the Dickey-Fuller test was discussed, lagged dependent variables may provide a good approximation to an autoregressive process in the error terms. Hence an intuitive guide to establishing the best lag length in a *VAR* model is to choose such a k in (6.9) which results in estimated model residuals without significant autocorrelation.

An essential, but sometimes overlooked feature of a *VAR* model is that the multivariate error term in (6.9), ϵ_t, contains nonzero covariances. This feature allows the formulation of 'structural' alternatives to Cowles Commission type models, consistent with a particular economic theory and applicable for economic policy analysis.

In an attempt to make the interpretation of policy analysis in a *VAR* model more straightforward, it has become common practice to transform the model into one having 'orthogonal innovations'; that is to transform the model so that the error terms are no longer contemporaneously correlated. This may be illustrated by an example of a simple *VAR* model containing two variables x_t and y_t and two lags, so:

$$\begin{bmatrix} x_t \\ y_t \end{bmatrix} = \begin{bmatrix} a_1 & b_1 \\ c_1 & d_1 \end{bmatrix} \begin{bmatrix} x_{t-1} \\ y_{t-1} \end{bmatrix} + \begin{bmatrix} a_2 & b_2 \\ c_2 & d_2 \end{bmatrix} \begin{bmatrix} x_{t-2} \\ y_{t-2} \end{bmatrix} + \begin{bmatrix} \varepsilon_{1t} \\ \varepsilon_{2t} \end{bmatrix} , \tag{6.10}$$

where the error terms are contemporaneously correlated, that is;

$$E(\varepsilon_{1t}) = E(\varepsilon_{2t}) = 0; \quad E(\varepsilon_{1t}^2) = \sigma_{11}; \quad E(\varepsilon_{2t}^2) = \sigma_{22} ; \quad E(\varepsilon_{1t} \cdot \varepsilon_{2t}) = \sigma_{12} .$$

In order to obtain a model in which the error terms are contemporaneously uncorrelated we may multiply the first row of (6.10) by $\delta = \dfrac{\sigma_{12}}{\sigma_{11}}$ and subtract the result from the second row. The result is:

$$\begin{bmatrix} x_t \\ y_t - \delta x_t \end{bmatrix} = \begin{bmatrix} a_1 & b_1 \\ c_1^* & d_1^* \end{bmatrix} \begin{bmatrix} x_{t-1} \\ y_{t-1} \end{bmatrix} + \begin{bmatrix} a_2 & b_2 \\ c_2^* & d_2^* \end{bmatrix} \begin{bmatrix} x_{t-2} \\ y_{t-2} \end{bmatrix} + \begin{bmatrix} \varepsilon_{1t} \\ \varepsilon_{2t}^* \end{bmatrix} , \tag{6.11}$$

where:

$$c_i^* = (c_i - \delta a_i); \quad d_i^* = (d_i - \delta b_i); \quad \varepsilon_{2t}^* = (\varepsilon_{2t} - \delta \varepsilon_{1t}), \quad i = 1, 2 .$$

In (6.11) the error terms ε_{1t} and ε_{2t}^* are uncorrelated, since:

$$E(\varepsilon_{1t} \cdot \varepsilon_{2t}^*) = E(\varepsilon_{1t}(\varepsilon_{2t} - \delta \varepsilon_{1t}))$$
$$= E((\varepsilon_{1t} \cdot \varepsilon_{2t}) - (\sigma_{12} / \sigma_{11}) E(\varepsilon_{1t}^2))$$
$$= \sigma_{12} - \sigma_{12} = 0 .$$

As in general the σ_{ij} are unknown, sample values obtained from the residuals of the *VAR* equation estimates will be needed for further analysis. The idea behind making the error terms in (6.11) orthogonal to each other is to enable the equations which form (6.11) to be used separately for policy analysis. In this context, policy analysis refers to the impact of a known shock or 'orthogonal innovation' on the system. Section 6.3 develops this idea in more detail. One problem with such analysis is that the results may be sensitive to the ordering of the *VAR* equations, and another is that it is difficult to give a sensible meaning to an 'orthogonal innovation' (see Darnell and Evans (1990, pp. 120-123) or Cooley and LeRoy (1985, pp. 301-303)). In practice, it may be possible to decide on the ordering of the equations following the application of a series of *causality tests* of the type developed in Section 6.4.

In matrix notation, 'orthogonal innovations' may be obtained from (6.9) by multiplying it by the triangular matrix Φ with units on the main diagonal such that:

$$D = \Phi \cdot \Sigma \cdot \Phi' \ ,$$

where D is a diagonal matrix and Σ is the covariance matrix of the multi-variate error term ϵ_t. Hence, the *VAR* model becomes:

$$\Phi \cdot Z_t = \Phi \cdot \sum_{i=1}^{k} A_i Z_{t-i} + M_t \ , \tag{6.12}$$

where $M_t = \Phi \cdot \epsilon_t$. It can be shown that the random variables which constitute M_t are orthogonal to each other, so that $E(M_t M_t') = I$ where I is an identity matrix (see Johnston (1984, pp. 143-147)).

For large *VAR* systems, the procedure described above can be difficult since construction of the matrix Φ can be awkward and may require special ordering algorithms.

6.3 Impulse Response Analysis

One of the important applications of the orthogonalisation process discussed in Section 6.2 is that of dynamic simulation and projection. Suppose that one wishes to use the following simple two-equation *VAR*(1) system for dynamic policy simulation:

$$\begin{bmatrix} x_t \\ y_t \end{bmatrix} = \begin{bmatrix} a_1 & b_1 \\ c_1 & d_1 \end{bmatrix} \begin{bmatrix} x_{t-1} \\ y_{t-1} \end{bmatrix} + \begin{bmatrix} \epsilon_{1t} \\ \epsilon_{2t} \end{bmatrix} . \tag{6.13}$$

More specifically, the question asked is: 'what is the likely response of y at time t, $t+1$, $t+2$, etc., to a unitary exogenous shock in x at time t? That is, what is likely to happen to y_t over time if x_t changes by one unit at time t? From inspection of the first equation in (6.13) which determines x_t, it is clear that an alteration in ϵ_{1t} by one unit is equivalent to an alteration in x_t by one unit as both x_{t-1} and y_{t-1} are predetermined (already set). Hence the analysis is developed in terms of the effect of changes in the error term ϵ_{1t}. In the general case, where the covariance between ϵ_{1t} and ϵ_{2t} is nonzero and equal to σ_{12} , the above *VAR* representation is not a very attractive tool to be used for such an experiment. If the analyst changes ε_{1t} in the model by a unit, all that he/she can predict for time $t+1$ is that in time $t+1$ y should change by c_1 multiplied by the change in ε_{1t}, which is then just simply equal to c_1 . This result would be systematically wrong, since it would ignore the effect (d_1 times any change in y_t) which resulted from any change in ε_{2t}. Recall that ε_{1t} and ε_{2t} are correlated. If ε_{1t} changes, then it is likely that ε_{2t} will alter as well so that from the second equation in (6.13), y_t will alter by the same amount as ε_{2t} .

Clearly, a better tool for such an analysis would be the orthogonalized *VAR* where the error terms are not correlated, that is:

$$\begin{bmatrix} x_t \\ y_t - \delta x_t \end{bmatrix} = \begin{bmatrix} a_1 & b_1 \\ c_1^* & d_1^* \end{bmatrix} \begin{bmatrix} x_{t-1} \\ y_{t-1} \end{bmatrix} + \begin{bmatrix} \varepsilon_{1t} \\ \varepsilon_{2t}^* \end{bmatrix},$$

where:

$$c_1^* = (c_1 - \delta a_1); \quad d_1^* = (d_1 - \delta b_1); \quad \varepsilon_{2t}^* = (\varepsilon_{2t} - \delta \varepsilon_{1t}),$$

with $\delta = \sigma_{12} / \sigma_{11}$ and where σ_{11} is the variance of ε_{1t} and σ_{12} is the covariance between ε_{1t} and ε_{2t}.

In order to investigate the dynamics of this problem, let us consider the original *VAR*(1) model in the more general notation of equation (6.9):

$$Z_t = A_1 Z_{t-1} + \epsilon_t \quad .$$

Lagging the above equation as $Z_{t-1} = A_1 Z_{t-2} + \epsilon_{t-1}$ and substituting for Z_{t-1} gives:

$$\begin{aligned} Z_t &= A_1 Z_{t-1} + \epsilon_t \\ &= A_1 (A_1 Z_{t-2} + \epsilon_{t-1}) + \epsilon_t \\ &= A_1^2 Z_{t-2} + \epsilon_t + A_1 \epsilon_{t-1} \quad . \end{aligned}$$

Repeating the above n times, that is, successively substituting for Z_{t-2}, Z_{t-3}, etc., gives :

$$Z_t = \sum_{i=0}^{n} A_1^i \epsilon_{t-i} + A_1^{n+1} Z_{t-n+1} \quad .$$

If the condition: $\lim_{n \to \infty} A_1^n = 0$, called the *stability condition*, holds, then:

$$Z_t = \sum_{i=0}^{\infty} A_1^i \, \epsilon_{t-i} \quad .$$

Such a form representing a process which generates Z_t as an infinite sum of lagged random errors weighted by generally diminishing coefficients, is called, quite appropriately, a *vector moving-average representation*, denoted as *VMA*.

For the two-variable *VAR* model given by (6.13), the *VMA* representation is simply:

$$\begin{bmatrix} x_t \\ y_t \end{bmatrix} = \sum_{i=0}^{\infty} \begin{bmatrix} a_1 & b_1 \\ c_1 & d_1 \end{bmatrix}^i \begin{bmatrix} \varepsilon_{1t-i} \\ \varepsilon_{2t-i} \end{bmatrix} \quad .$$

This could have been used for the evaluation of time paths of responses of particular variables to a single unitary shock (and this is what simple policy analysis is about), if not for the unfortunate fact that, in general, the error terms ε_{1t-i} and ε_{2t-i} are correlated. In order to make the evaluation, again one can undertake orthogonalisation. From Section (6.2) we have:

$$\varepsilon_{2t}^* = \varepsilon_{2t} - \delta\varepsilon_{1t} \quad , \quad \text{where } \delta = \sigma_{12} / \sigma_{11}.$$

Thus:

$$\varepsilon_{2t} = \varepsilon_{2t}^* + \delta\varepsilon_{1t} \quad .$$

Hence, by substituting $\varepsilon_{2t-i}^* + \delta\varepsilon_{1t-i}$ for ε_{2t-i} in the *VMA* representation of the *VAR* model, one can write the *VMA* model as:

$$\begin{bmatrix} x_t \\ y_t \end{bmatrix} = \sum_{i=0}^{\infty} \begin{bmatrix} a_1 & b_1 \\ c_1 & d_1 \end{bmatrix}^i \begin{bmatrix} 1 & 0 \\ \delta & 1 \end{bmatrix} \begin{bmatrix} \varepsilon_{1t-i} \\ \varepsilon_{2t-i}^* \end{bmatrix} \quad ,$$

or, in a slightly different notation:

$$\begin{bmatrix} x_t \\ y_t \end{bmatrix} = \sum_{i=0}^{\infty} \begin{bmatrix} \phi_{11}^{(i)} & \phi_{12}^{(i)} \\ \phi_{21}^{(i)} & \phi_{22}^{(i)} \end{bmatrix} \begin{bmatrix} \varepsilon_{1t-i} \\ \varepsilon_{2t-i}^* \end{bmatrix} \quad .$$

Returning to the general notation of the *VAR*(1) model, the vector of variables Z_t can be represented in a form similar to the *VMA*:

$$Z_t = \sum_{i=0}^{\infty} \phi_i e_{t-i} \quad , \tag{6.14}$$

where:

$$\phi_i = \begin{bmatrix} \phi_{11}^{(i)} & \phi_{12}^{(i)} \\ \phi_{21}^{(i)} & \phi_{22}^{(i)} \end{bmatrix} ,$$

and:

$$e_t = \begin{bmatrix} \in_{1t} \\ \in_{2t}^* \end{bmatrix} .$$

The important difference between the *VMA* representation and (6.14) is that in (6.14) the residuals are orthogonal. Therefore, (6.14) can be used directly for tracking dynamic responses of particular variables to a shock in $\in_{1t}$. Matrices ϕ_i are called *impulse response functions*, since they represent the behaviour of the modelled series in response to shocks (innovations). Vector e_t is called the vector of *innovations*: this is a vector of impacts induced for particular variables where these impacts are independent from each other.

More precisely, the interpretation of particular elements of these matrices is the following:

$\phi_{21}^{(0)}$ is the expected instantaneous impact of a one-unit change in $\in_{1t}$ on y_t,

$\phi_{21}^{(1)}$ is expected one-period response of a one-unit change in $\in_{1t-1}$ on y_t,

etc.

The cumulated effect of a unit change in $\in_{1t}$ on the sequence of $\{y_{t+i}\}$, $i = 0, 1, 2, \cdots, p$ is given by:

$$\sum_{i=0}^{p} \phi_{21}^{(i)} .$$

Impulse responses are computed by most econometric packages which incorporate *VAR* analysis. An example of an impulse response analysis of the consumption-income-inflation model is given in Section 6.6.

6.4 Causality Inference

The general (unrestricted) *VAR* model containing a large number of estimated coefficients can usually be reduced in size by eliminating those coefficients for which the hypothesis that they are jointly equal to zero cannot be rejected (see Chapter 4 for a description of the Likelihood Ratio, Lagrange Multiplier and Wald tests for such hypotheses). In some situations, testing for zero coefficients can lead to economically relevant results. Often, testing zero restrictions in a *VAR* model is made within the context of *causality analysis*.

The notion of causality (and also of causal relations and causal ordering) is essentially a philosophical rather than an empirical matter. Philosophers do not agree on their understanding and definition of *a cause* and *outcome*. Theories vary from an extreme 'everything causes everything' (Democrit) to denying the existence of any causation whatsoever (Hume, Berkeley). Usually in modern philosophy the meaning of 'causation' is close to 'force' or 'produce'. In empirical econometrics the need for defining 'causality' is clear. One simply wants to know whether an increase of prices results in wages increasing when otherwise they would not have altered, or whether the relation works in the opposite direction, so that it is an increase of wages that results in an increase of prices. Consequently, there is a need to establish an operational and testable definition of causality. In econometrics, causality has a meaning more on the lines of 'to predict' rather than 'to produce'. Nevertheless, philosophical definitions have important influences on statistical counterparts. In particular, there are three important features of contemporary notions of causality. The first two may be summarized as:

1. 'instantaneous causation' does not exist, since there is always a time difference between independent actions,
2. for similar reasons, there is no such thing as 'simultaneous causation'.

In practice, however, it is necessary to speak about 'instantaneous' and 'simultaneous' causation simply because we are unable to maintain continuous observation and we can only analyse data related to a particular time interval or moment. The notion that ' x causes y and simultaneously y causes x ' is nothing but a simplification; due to discontinuity of observations, we are unable to define the cause and outcome.

The third notion can be stated as:

3. the future cannot 'cause' the present. This is perhaps the most straightforward of the features of the contemporary concept of causality and, as is shown below, plays an important role in testing for the presence of a causal relation.

In econometrics the most widely used *operational definition* of causality is the *Wiener-Granger* or *Granger definition of causality* (see Granger (1969)). It can be formulated in a simplified way as follows:

Definition:
x is a *Granger cause* of y (denoted as $x \rightarrow y$), if present y can be predicted with better accuracy by using *past* values of x rather than by not doing so, other information being identical.

This definition can be extended to *instantaneous causation*, denoted as $x \Rightarrow y$. Instantaneous causation exists if present y can be predicted better by using *present and past* values of x, *ceteris paribus*. The concepts of Granger causality and Granger instantaneous causality between two variables may be defined in a more formal way. Let us introduce the following notation:

U_t – the set of all past and present information existing at time t;

X_t – the set of all past and present information on a variable x existing at time t, that is $X_t = \{x_1, x_2, ..., x_t\}$. Evidently, X_t is a subset of U_t, or (since we may have more information than just for a single variable):

$$X_t \subset U_t \; ;$$

y_t – the current value of a variable y $(y_t \in U_t)$;

$\tilde{y}_t$ – an unbiased prediction of y_t .

With the use of the above notation, the definitions can be formulated as:

Granger causality:

if $MSE(\tilde{y}_t | U_{t-1}) < MSE(\tilde{y}_t | U_{t-1} \setminus X_{t-1})$ then $x \to y$,

Granger instantaneous causality:

if $MSE(\tilde{y}_t | U_t \setminus y_t) < MSE(\tilde{y}_t | U_t \setminus X_t, y_t)$ then $x \Rightarrow y$,

where MSE stands for the mean square error of prediction and $"|"$ and $"\setminus"$ are the conventional logical operators; that is $"A|B"$ means 'A conditional on B' and $"A \setminus B"$ means 'all elements of A which are not B' (if $B \subset A$).

In the above definitions, there is the rather vague notion of *all information*. Since the set of *all information* is not well defined, it is up to a researcher to decide which information to use, and which to ignore. Hence, for practical purposes, the notion of 'all information' has to be replaced by 'all relevant information', and which information is 'relevant' is always arbitrary.

To make progress, let us assume that 'all relevant information' is that which is included in an econometric model. The model may also include 'irrelevant information' and hence we may suppose that a general unrestricted *VAR* may be suitable for our purpose. In light of the above definitions, the problem of testing whether $x \to y$ reduces to a question of whether x can be eliminated from that part of a *VAR* model which describes y. In the literature on this subject, various tests for causality which use this principle have been proposed. We describe two of the most widely used tests below. These tests are complements rather than substitutes for each other.

The first of these tests, which is called a *Granger* test, is a straightforward and simple modification suggested by Sargent (1976) of the test originally suggested by Granger (1969). Consider an equation describing y_t in an unrestricted bivariate *VAR* model, that is one describing relations between two variables, x and y. This equation may be written as:

$$y_t = A_0 D_t + \sum_{j=1}^{k} \alpha_j y_{t-j} + \sum_{j=1}^{k} \beta_j x_{t-j} + \varepsilon_t \ , \tag{6.15}$$

where D_t denotes the deterministic (non-stochastic) variables of the equation (intercept, deterministic trend, seasonals, etc.) and A_0 is a vector of parameters. Formally, it has to be assumed that all the variables in the above equation are stationary or, more precisely, integrated of order zero. If $\beta_1 = \beta_2 = ... = \beta_k = 0$ then, in light of the above definition, x does not Granger cause y. A straightforward test for testing the restriction $\beta_1 = \beta_2 = ... = \beta_k = 0$ would be an F test or the Lagrange Multiplier LM test. For equation (6.15), the hypothesis $\beta_1 = \beta_2 = ... = \beta_k = 0$ can be tested by the LM test in the following way:

1. Regress y_t on all the deterministic components of (6.15) and on $y_{t-1}, y_{t-2}, ..., y_{t-k}$;
2. Compute the residuals of the above regression, denoted by u_t^* ;
3. Regress u_t^* on the entire set of explanatory variables which appear in (6.15), that is the variables used in step 1 and additionally $x_{t-1}, x_{t-2}, ..., x_{t-k}$;
4. Calculate the coefficient of determination for the above regression, say R_0^2 ;
5. Test the hypothesis by one of the following Lagrange multiplier statistics:

$$LM = T \cdot R_0^2 \ ,$$

which under the null hypothesis has a $\chi^2(k)$ distribution, or:

$$LMF = \frac{T-h}{k} \cdot \frac{R_0^2}{1-R_0^2} \ ,$$

which under the null hypothesis has an $F(k, T-h)$ distribution (T is the sample size and h is the number of variables in (6.15) including those for the variables in D_t). As has been mentioned in Chapter 4, it is normally preferable to use the LMF rather than the LM statistic.

The second of the causality tests described here has its origins in a paper by Sims (1972) who cleverly used the feature of the general concept of causality that the future cannot cause the present. The test was developed by Geweke, Meese and Dent (1983) and is called here the Sims-GMD test. Suppose, as before, that we wish to test whether x is a Granger cause for y (in our notation $x \to y$). Instead of equation (6.15), consider the following equation explaining x_t:

$$x_t = A_0 D_t + \sum_{j=1}^{k} \gamma_j x_{t-j} + \sum_{j=-m}^{k} \delta_j y_{t-j} + v_t \quad . \tag{6.16}$$

Equation (6.16) looks like the part of a *VAR* model describing x_t apart from the fact that it contains *leading* values of y_t; note the negative lower summation limit for the variable y_{t-j} which means that in equation (6.16), the variables $y_{t+1}, y_{t+2}, ..., y_{t+m}$ appear as well as lagged values of y_t ($j = 0$ must be excluded from the summation of the y_{t-j} terms). Evidently, if the coefficients of the leading ys are all zeros, that is if $\delta_{-1} = \delta_{-2} = ... = \delta_{-m} = 0$, we have a typical *VAR* equation for x_t.

But what if the hypothesis that $\delta_{-1} = \delta_{-2} = ... = \delta_{-m} = 0$ is rejected? Since the future cannot cause the present, future ys cannot cause the current x. Indeed, a necessary condition for x not to cause y is that the leading y_t terms in equation (6.16) have zero coefficients (see Greenberg and Webster (1983, pp. 149-151)). Thus the logical conclusion of finding nonzero coefficients on leading y_t terms, that is if $\delta_{-1}, \delta_{-2}, ..., \delta_{-m}$ are not jointly equal to zero, is that x *is a Granger cause for* y.

The technique for computing the Lagrange Multiplier test in this case is analogous to that described for the Granger test. The 'omitted variables' are now leading ys, $y_{t+1}, y_{t+2}, ..., y_{t+m}$:

1. Regress x_t on all the explanatory variables in equation (6.16) with the exception of $y_{t+1}, y_{t+2}, ..., y_{t+m}$;
2. Calculate residuals v_t^*;
3. Regress v_t^* on the full set of explanatory variables, inclusive of $y_{t+1}, y_{t+2}, ..., y_{t+m}$;
4. Compute the coefficient of determination of the above regression;
5. Using this coefficient of determination, compute the *LM* or *LMF* statistic, as described above.

It is difficult to say which of these two tests is better. Some Monte Carlo experiments (Guilkey and Salemi (1982)) show the Granger test to be superior. Also, the Sims-GMD test is more costly in terms of the loss of degrees of freedom, since for a given lag length there are more parameters to estimate (we also have leading variables in this case) and the number of observations used for estimation is smaller, since observations for the most recent periods of time are taken by the leading variables. Nevertheless, because of the different philosophical background of the tests, it seems advisable to use both rather than to choose one of them.

It should be stressed that these tests are strictly appropriate only where the variables are stationary. For nonstationary variables these tests are valid only approximately or, in some cases, may not be valid at all (see Lütkepohl (1991, p.379)). Indeed, from the Granger and Newbold results reported in Chapter 5, we know that it is generally unwise to use *LM*-type tests in models which contain $I(1)$ variables. It has been pointed out by Geweke (1984, pp. 1139-1140) that these causality tests may still be valid if the form of nonstationarity of the variables can be captured by the inclusion of deterministic trends and/or logarithmic transformations. Additionally, in practice it may be reasonable to consider the usually long lags of a *VAR* model as a convenient approximation to a unit root process. If this is the case, then the *LM* tests will be approximately valid. To illustrate this point, suppose that $y_t \sim I(1)$ and $x_t \sim I(0)$, and that an equation of a *VAR* model which explains y_t is given by:

$$y_t = \sum_{j=1}^{k} \alpha_j y_{t-j} + \sum_{j=1}^{k} \beta_j x_{t-j} + \varepsilon_t \quad .$$

If k is sufficiently large, it is possible that $y_t \approx \sum_{j=1}^{k} \alpha_j y_{t-j}$, so that the equation may be re-written as:

$$y_t \approx y_{t-1} + \sum_{j=1}^{k} \beta_j x_{t-j} + \varepsilon_t \quad ,$$

or:

$$\Delta y_t \approx \sum_{j=1}^{k} \beta_j x_{t-j} + \varepsilon_t \quad .$$

Since $y_t \sim I(1)$, the last equation contains only stationary variables. Thus if the above approximation for y_t is valid, the *OLS* estimates of β_j will exhibit the desirable properties of estimators from models with stationary variables, which will include approximately valid tests based on the assumption of stationarity.

As with any other method of statistical modelling, the validity of the tests and their interpretation in a *VAR* model depends on a proper specification, so that all relevant information is included in the model. This specification would involve the absence of autocorrelation in the error terms, and might imply the need for prior filtering or prewhitening of the data series (see Vandaele (1983, Chapter 11) or Greenberg and Webster (1983, pp. 149-155)). If autocorrelation is present, the Lagrange Multiplier statistics do not have the required distributions. One way of tackling the problem of autocorrelated errors is to ensure that the lag length adopted in the *VAR* model is long enough to approximate the possible autocorrelation, although Granger and Newbold (1986, p.252) suggest that this practice can lead to disappointing forecasts. As with any statistical tests, causality tests have to be viewed with caution.

One area in which these causality tests have been widely used is in the testing of monetarist and Keynesian theories of income determination and inflation, some examples of which are included in the further reading at the end of this chapter.

6.5 *VAR* and Cointegration Inference

In this section we will outline the linkage of cointegration analysis with *VAR* modelling. This linkage gives cointegration analysis an entirely new dimension and allows the analysis to be applied in a more general way than that described in Chapter 5. However, the analysis becomes computationally (and also conceptually) more complicated. Because of this complexity, we present only an introductory and highly simplified account of cointegration inference in a *VAR* model.

Consider the unrestricted *VAR* model, introduced in Section 6.2:

$$Z_t = \sum_{i=1}^{k} A_i Z_{t-i} + \epsilon_t \ , \tag{6.9}$$

where Z_t contains all n variables of the model and ϵ_t is a vector of random errors. We will use a straightforward vector generalization of the notation of integration and cointegration introduced in Chapter 5. The operator Δ in the expression of the type ΔW_t will denote first differencing of all the variables in a vector of variables W_t. Analogously, the notation $W_t \sim I(1)$ means that all the variables which constitute the vector of variables W_t are integrated of order one, that is their first differences are stationary. Notation ' $W_t \sim CI(1,1)$ with cointegrating vector γ ' means that the linear combination $\gamma' W_t \sim I(0)$. There might be more than one cointegrating vector; vectors $\gamma_1, \gamma_2, ..., \gamma_l$ may constitute a matrix γ such that $\gamma' W_t \sim I(0)$.

We will assume throughout this section that all the variables in Z_t are integrated of the same order, and that this order of integration is either zero or one. This assumption is in fact not very restrictive. If some variables which are integrated of order higher than one are of interest, we may consider their appropriate differences, which themselves are integrated of order one, to be included in the *VAR* model. For simplicity, the deterministic part of the *VAR* model (intercepts, deterministic trends, seasonals, etc.) are excluded.

The *VAR* model (6.9) can also be represented in the form:

$$\Delta Z_t = \Pi \cdot Z_{t-k} + \sum_{i=1}^{k-1} \Gamma_i \Delta Z_{t-i} + \epsilon_t \quad , \text{ for } k \geq 2 \quad , \tag{6.17}$$

where:

$$\Gamma_i = -I + A_1 + ... + A_i \quad (I \text{ is a unit matrix}) \ ,$$

$$\Pi = -(I - A_1 - ... - A_k) \ .$$

The equality of models (6.9) and (6.17) may be confirmed by adding $Z_{t-1}, Z_{t-2}, ..., Z_{t-k}$ and $A_1 Z_{t-2}, A_2 Z_{t-3}, ..., A_{k-1} Z_{t-k}$ to both sides of (6.9) and rearranging. We will call the transformation of a *VAR* model into the form of (6.17) a *cointegrating transformation*. (We are using notation consistent with that used in the literature on this subject. Please note, however, that in Section 6.1 the symbols Γ and Π have a different meaning from that here.)

Another, albeit similar, decomposition of (6.9) is the following:

$$\Delta Z_t = \Pi \cdot Z_{t-1} + \sum_{i=1}^{k-1} \Gamma_i^* \Delta Z_{t-i} + \epsilon_t \ , \tag{6.18}$$

where:

$$\Pi = -(I - A_1 - A_2 - ... - A_k) \quad ,$$

and:

$$\Gamma_i^* = -(A_{i+1} + A_{i+2} + ... + A_k) \quad , \quad i = 1, ..., k-1.$$

That is:

$$\Gamma_1^* = -(A_2 + A_3 + ... + A_k) \quad ,$$

$$\Gamma_2^* = -(A_3 + ... + A_k) \quad ,$$

$$\vdots$$

$$\Gamma_{k-1}^* = -A_k \quad .$$

It is important to observe the similarities and differences between (6.17) and (6.18). The similarities are obvious in that both contain the same set of variables, namely Zs in levels and in first differences. However, in (6.17) Zs in levels are lagged by the maximum lag, k, respectively to ΔZ_t, while in (6.18) Zs in levels are lagged by only one period. Despite this, the matrices (Π) of coefficients which reflect the impact of the lagged Zs on ΔZ_t are identical in (6.17) and (6.18). Hence, one must be careful when interpreting the elements of Π. Despite the fact that in (6.17) Zs in levels are lagged by as much as k, respectively to ΔZ_t, the matrix Π represents a constant dynamic adjustment of first differences of variables respectively to levels, regardless of the time difference.

In further analysis we will focus our attention on the matrix Π. In particular we will consider decompositions of matrices $\Pi \cdot Z_{t-1}$ (or $\Pi \cdot Z_{t-k}$), which are the essence of the so-called *Granger Representation Theorem*. This describes the conditions which have to be fulfilled if the variables in a *VAR* are to be cointegrated. Before we present the theorem, it will be advantageous to present an intuitive account of the problem using a simple three-dimensional *VAR* model:

$$
\begin{bmatrix} x_t \\ y_t \\ w_t \end{bmatrix} = A_1 \begin{bmatrix} x_{t-1} \\ y_{t-1} \\ w_{t-1} \end{bmatrix} + A_2 \begin{bmatrix} x_{t-2} \\ y_{t-2} \\ w_{t-2} \end{bmatrix} + \dots + A_k \begin{bmatrix} x_{t-k} \\ y_{t-k} \\ w_{t-k} \end{bmatrix} + \begin{bmatrix} \epsilon_{1t} \\ \epsilon_{2t} \\ \epsilon_{3t} \end{bmatrix} .
$$

Applying transformation (6.18), the above model can be represented as:

$$
\begin{bmatrix} \Delta x_t \\ \Delta y_t \\ \Delta w_t \end{bmatrix} = \Pi \cdot \begin{bmatrix} x_{t-1} \\ y_{t-1} \\ w_{t-1} \end{bmatrix} + \Gamma_1^* \cdot \begin{bmatrix} \Delta x_{t-1} \\ \Delta y_{t-1} \\ \Delta w_{t-1} \end{bmatrix} + \dots + \Gamma_{k-1}^* \cdot \begin{bmatrix} \Delta x_{t-k+1} \\ \Delta y_{t-k+1} \\ \Delta w_{t-k+1} \end{bmatrix} + \begin{bmatrix} \epsilon_{1t} \\ \epsilon_{2t} \\ \epsilon_{3t} \end{bmatrix} , \quad (6.19)
$$

The matrix Π, whose dimensions are 3×3, can be expressed as a product of two matrices:

$$ \Pi = \alpha \cdot \beta' . $$

Note that as Π is a square matrix, α and β must be of the same order as each other.

Our specific interest is in the evaluation of the rank of the matrix Π. The rank of a matrix A, denoted as $r(A)$, is the maximum number of linearly independent columns in the matrix (see Johnston (1984), Chapter 4). One of the important results of matrix algebra, to which we will refer shortly, is that, for two matrices, A and B, $r(A \cdot B) \leq \min\{r(A), r(B)\}$. Since matrix Π has three columns, its maximum rank is three and its minimum rank is zero. Let us consider all four possible cases.

Case 1: $r(\Pi) = 0$

In this case, Π contains zero elements only. Therefore, the *VAR* system in the form of (6.19) reduces to:

$$
\begin{bmatrix} \Delta x_t \\ \Delta y_t \\ \Delta w_t \end{bmatrix} = \Gamma_1^* \cdot \begin{bmatrix} \Delta x_{t-1} \\ \Delta y_{t-1} \\ \Delta w_{t-1} \end{bmatrix} + \dots + \Gamma_{k-1}^* \cdot \begin{bmatrix} \Delta x_{t-k+1} \\ \Delta y_{t-k+1} \\ \Delta w_{t-k+1} \end{bmatrix} + \begin{bmatrix} \epsilon_{1t} \\ \epsilon_{2t} \\ \epsilon_{3t} \end{bmatrix} .
$$

The result implies that, if the rank of the matrix Π is zero, then a *VAR* system of equations where all the variables are $I(1)$ can be estimated in first differences without any loss of relevant information. Since in such a case all variables in the estimated equations are stationary, test statistics such as the Student-*t* test, the *LM* test and the like, are valid in that sense that under the null hypothesis, distributions of these statistics have their well-defined (Student and F) distributions.

Case 2: $r(\Pi) = 1$

If the rank of matrix Π is one, then it can be represented as the product of two non-null vectors α and β'. This is a direct result of the above mentioned rule that $r(\alpha \cdot \beta') \leq \min\{r(\alpha), r(\beta)\}$. Since the rank of a non-null vector is one, from this inequality we infer that Π can be written as $\Pi = \alpha \cdot \beta'$. (For simplicity, in Cases 2 to 4 we will restrict our attention to α and β matrices which are of full rank.)

Substituting for Π, we have:

$$\Pi \cdot Z_{t-1} = \alpha \cdot \beta' \cdot Z_{t-1} = \begin{bmatrix} \alpha_{11} \\ \alpha_{21} \\ \alpha_{31} \end{bmatrix} \cdot \begin{bmatrix} \beta_{11} & \beta_{12} & \beta_{13} \end{bmatrix} \cdot \begin{bmatrix} x_{t-1} \\ y_{t-1} \\ w_{t-1} \end{bmatrix} \; .$$

The first row in the above expression is:

$$\alpha_{11} \cdot (\beta_{11}x_{t-1} + \beta_{12}y_{t-1} + \beta_{13}w_{t-1}) \quad ,$$

and consequently, the first equation in (6.19) can be written down as:

$$\Delta x_t = \alpha_{11} \cdot (\beta_{11}x_{t-1} + \beta_{12}y_{t-1} + \beta_{13}w_{t-1}) + f(\Delta x_{t-i}, \Delta y_{t-i}, \Delta w_{t-i}) + \epsilon_{1t} \quad ,$$

where $f(\Delta x_{t-i}, \Delta y_{t-i}, \Delta w_{t-i})$ represents all terms of (6.19) related to lagged variables in their first differences. The above equation looks very similar to that of a short-run model with an error-correction term along with some autoregressive elements as discussed in Chapter 5. Since the terms in $f(\Delta x_{t-i}, \Delta y_{t-i}, \Delta w_{t-i})$ are stationary, the entire equation is stationary only if the vector $\beta_{11}x_t + \beta_{12}y_t + \beta_{13}w_t$ is stationary. In fact, this must be stationary. Since the left-hand side in (6.19) is $I(0)$ by definition, so must be the right-hand side of it as well. Recalling the definition of cointegration, we can state that if $r(\Pi) = 1$, then the vector $\beta_{11}x_t + \beta_{12}y_t + \beta_{13}w_t$ is the cointegrating vector; that is:

$$(x_t, y_t, w_t) \sim CI(1,1), \text{ with cointegrating vector } [\beta_{11}, \beta_{12}, \beta_{13}].$$

Evidently, in the term $\beta_{11}x_t + \beta_{12}y_t + \beta_{13}w_t$, we do not know which variable is 'described' by this long-run process, or in other words, what is on the left-hand side of the cointegrating relationship. Despite the fact that due to the likely existence of a dynamic feedback process, the conditioning of the long-run process is somewhat arbitrary, we may for the sake of interpretation of the coefficients transform the short-run equation to a form where the error correction term is normalized with respect to x_t, namely:

$$\Delta x_t = \alpha_{11} \cdot (x_{t-1} - \gamma_{12} y_{t-1} - \gamma_{13} w_{t-1}) + f(\Delta x_{t-i}, \Delta y_{t-i}, \Delta w_{t-i}) + \epsilon_{1t} \quad ,$$

where:

$$\gamma_{12} = -\frac{\beta_{12}}{\beta_{11}} \quad , \quad \gamma_{13} = -\frac{\beta_{13}}{\beta_{11}} \quad .$$

The vector $[1, -\gamma_{12}, -\gamma_{13}]$ is called the normalized cointegrating vector.

We may conclude that, in Case 2, where $r(\Pi) = 1$ there is *one cointe-grating vector* which enters the three short-run equations of the *VAR* through the *adjustment coefficients* α_{11}, α_{21} and α_{31}. Note that in Case 1 there is no cointegrating vector.

Case 3: $r(\Pi) = 2$

Now, once more drawing conclusions from the rule that the rank of the product of two matrices cannot be greater than the rank of the individual matrices, again we can represent matrix Π as $\Pi = \alpha \cdot \beta'$. The difference from Case 2 is that α and β must be matrices of order 3×2 rather than vectors, since their ranks must be equal to 2. This gives:

$$\Pi \cdot Z_{t-1} = \alpha \cdot \beta' \cdot Z_{t-1} = \begin{bmatrix} \alpha_{11} & \alpha_{12} \\ \alpha_{21} & \alpha_{22} \\ \alpha_{31} & \alpha_{32} \end{bmatrix} \cdot \begin{bmatrix} \beta_{11} & \beta_{12} & \beta_{13} \\ \beta_{21} & \beta_{22} & \beta_{23} \end{bmatrix} \cdot \begin{bmatrix} x_{t-1} \\ y_{t-1} \\ w_{t-1} \end{bmatrix} \quad .$$

Consequently, in every equation of the short-run representation of the *VAR* model there are now two cointegrating vectors rather than one. That is, for the first equation we have:

$$\Delta x_t = \alpha_{11} \cdot (\beta_{11} x_{t-1} + \beta_{12} y_{t-1} + \beta_{13} w_{t-1}) + \alpha_{12} \cdot (\beta_{21} x_{t-1}$$
$$+ \beta_{22} y_{t-1} + \beta_{23} w_{t-1}) + f(\Delta x_{t-i}, \Delta y_{t-i}, \Delta w_{t-i}) + error \quad .$$

Case 4: $r(\Pi) = 3$

Since in Case 3, where $r(\Pi) = 2$, there were two cointegrating vectors, the obvious question to consider is whether there are 3 cointegrating vectors if the rank of the matrix Π is equal to three.

If there are three cointegrating vectors in a three-equations *VAR*, the normalized long run relationships would be written as:

$$x_t = \gamma_{12} y_t + \gamma_{13} w_t + u_{1t} \quad,$$

$$y_t = \gamma_{21} x_t + \gamma_{23} w_t + u_{2t} \quad,$$

$$w_t = \gamma_{31} x_t + \gamma_{32} y_t + u_{3t} \ .$$

and, since every cointegrating relationship is stationary, then it must be the case that $u_{1t} \sim I(0)$, $u_{2t} \sim I(0)$ and $u_{3t} \sim I(0)$. The above equations can be solved for x_t, y_t, w_t:

$$x_t = f_1(u_{1t}, u_{2t}, u_{3t}) \quad,$$

$$y_t = f_2(u_{1t}, u_{2t}, u_{3t}) \quad,$$

$$w_t = f_3(u_{1t}, u_{2t}, u_{3t}) \quad.$$

It is clear from the equations above that x_t, y_t, and w_t are functions of $I(0)$ variables only. Consequently, since there are no nonstationary terms on the right-hand sides of these equations, the left-hand sides must be stationary as well. Hence, if $r(\Pi) = 3$, then *all the variables in the VAR must be $I(0)$*. This is in contradiction with the initial assumption that all the variables in the VAR are $I(1)$. If matrix Π is of full rank, then this initial assumption cannot be valid.

This is different from Case 3 where, as indicated above, there were only two cointegrating relationships, namely:

$$x_t = \gamma_{12} y_t + \gamma_{13} w_t + u_{1t} \quad,$$

$$y_t = \gamma_{21} x_t + \gamma_{23} w_t + u_{2t} \quad.$$

These two equations cannot be solved for the three variables, x_t, y_t and w_t in terms of the u_{it} alone. If they are solved for two variables, say x_t and y_t, then the solutions are:

$$x_t = f_1(u_{1t}, u_{2t}, w_t) \quad,$$

$$y_t = f_2(u_{1t}, u_{2t}, w_t) \quad,$$

The right-hand sides of these equations involve w_t which is an $I(1)$ variable by assumption. Since the right-hand side contains one $I(1)$ variable, then the left-hand side, that is, variables x_t, y_t must be $I(1)$ as well.

A generalization of the above discussion leads to the *Granger Representation Theorem* (see Engle and Granger (1987), or Johansen (1989)). This theorem states that, under some general conditions:

(1) If the rank of matrix Π is equal to n, that is equal to the total number of variables explained in the *VAR* model, the vector process Z_t is stationary (that is all the variables in Z_t are integrated of order zero);

(2) If the rank of matrix Π is equal to $r < n$, there exists a representation of Π such that:

$$\Pi = \alpha \cdot \beta' , \qquad\qquad (6.20)$$

where α and β are both $n \times r$ matrices.

Matrix β is called the *cointegrating matrix* and has the property that $\beta' Z_t \sim I(0)$ while $Z_t \sim I(1)$. If the definition of cointegration is recalled from Chapter 5, the straightforward conclusion is that the variables in Z_t are cointegrated, with the cointegrating vectors $\beta_1, \beta_2, ..., \beta_r$ being particular columns of the cointegrating matrix β. Hence, in a *VAR* model explaining n variables there can be at most $r = n - 1$ cointegrating vectors.

We may note that model (6.17) can be regarded as a multivariate generalization of a model in differences with an error correction mechanism such as was discussed in Chapter 5. If the hypothesis concerning cointegration holds, that is if in (6.17) $\Pi = \alpha \cdot \beta'$, the matrix $\beta' Z_{t-k}$ constitutes a set of r error correction mechanisms separating out the long and short run responses in the model.

For empirical analysis, the essential problems are in the determination of r, that is in identifying the number of cointegrating vectors, and in estimating the cointegrating matrix β. The procedure outlined below is that of Johansen (1988, 1989). It is numerically quite complicated and we only describe the general principles. It consists of the following steps:

STEP 1: Regress ΔZ_t on $\Delta Z_{t-1}, \Delta Z_{t-2}, ..., \Delta Z_{t-k+1}$. Since there are n variables to explain in the *VAR* model, this is equivalent to performing n separate regressions. Construct the $n \times 1$ vector from the residual from each of these regressions at time t, and denote it by R_{0t}. Also, regress Z_{t-k} on $\Delta Z_{t-1}, \Delta Z_{t-2}, ..., \Delta Z_{t-k+1}$. Construct the $n \times 1$ vector of the residual from each of these regressions at time t, and denote it by R_{kt}.

STEP 2: Compute the four $n \times n$ matrices S_{00}, S_{0k}, S_{k0} and S_{kk} from the second moments and crossproducts of R_{0t} and R_{kt} as:

$$S_{ij} = T^{-1} \sum_{t=1}^{T} R_{it} R'_{jt} \quad , \; i, j = 0, k. \; (T = \text{sample size}).$$

STEP 3: Solve the equation:

$$| \mu S_{kk} - S_{k0} S_{00}^{-1} S_{0k} | = 0$$

That is, find the roots or eigenvalues of the polynomial equation in μ obtained from the determinant above. This is a non-standard form of the eigenvalue problem. The solution yields the eigenvalues $\hat{\mu}_1 > \hat{\mu}_2 > ... > \hat{\mu}_n$ (ordered from the largest to the smallest) and associated eigenvectors $\hat{v}_i$ which may be arranged into the matrix $\hat{V} = (\hat{v}_1 \; \hat{v}_2 ... \hat{v}_n)$. The eigenvectors are normalized such that $\hat{V}' S_{kk} \hat{V} = I$. Hall (1989, pp. 216-217) provides some guidance on the computational aspects of these calculations.

If the cointegrating matrix β is of rank $r < n$, the first r eigenvectors, $\hat{v}_1, \hat{v}_2, ..., \hat{v}_r$ are the cointegrating vectors, that is they are the columns of matrix β.

STEP 4: For each $\hat{\mu}_i$ compute the *LR* statistic:

$$LR = -T \cdot \sum_{i=r+1}^{n} ln(1 - \hat{\mu}_i) \; , \tag{6.21}$$

which, under the null hypothesis that there are at most r cointegrating vectors, has an asymptotic distribution whose quantiles are tabulated by Johansen (1988) and Osterwald-Lenum (1992). Normally testing starts from $r = 0$, that is from the hypothesis that there are no cointegrating vectors in a *VAR* model. If this cannot be rejected, the procedure stops since no confirmation of the existence of cointegrating vectors has been found. If it is rejected, it is possible to examine sequentially the hypotheses that $r \leq 1$, $r \leq 2$, etc. If the null hypothesis cannot be rejected for, say, $r \leq r_0$, but it has been rejected for $r \leq r_0 - 1$, the straightforward conclusion is that the number of cointegrating vectors or, in other words, the rank of β, is r_0. Johansen (1989) has shown that the first r estimated eigenvectors $\hat{v}_1, \hat{v}_2, ..., \hat{v}_r$ are the maximum likelihood estimates of the columns of β, the cointegrating vectors.

So far, we have concentrated on the elements of the matrix β in (6.20), since the columns of β have an economic interpretation as cointegrating vectors. That is, after normalization, they may be interpreted as long run parameters. The elements of α in (6.20) are straightforward to obtain once the matrix β is known, as the first r columns in the matrix $S_{0k} \hat{V}$. These elements also have an economic interpretation. In general, they measure the speed of adjustment of particular variables with respect to a disturbance in the equilibrium relation (see Johansen (1989, p.16)). Quite appropriately, the matrix α is called the *adjustment matrix* or, since we are dealing with a *VAR* model where the lagged values of the left-hand side variables enter the error correction mechanism, the *feedback matrix*.

In empirical applications of the Johansen method a major problem can be establishing the maximum lag length, that is k in (6.9). If an empirical analysis is concerned exclusively with the estimation and identification of a cointegrating vector, the problem is relatively simple. Since in (6.9), the random errors ϵ_t have to be free from autocorrelation, the usual practice is to allow for relatively long lags, since these might approximate the possible autocorrelation structure of the error terms. This argument parallels that used to justify the role of the length of augmentation in the augmented Dickey-Fuller test (see Chapter 5).

Testing and analyzing cointegration in a *VAR* model is often regarded as superior to the Engle-Granger single equation method described in Chapter 5. The statistical properties of the Johansen procedure are generally better and the power of the cointegration test is higher. However, it should be stressed that the Engle-Granger and Johansen procedures are grounded within different econometric methodologies. Most notably, in the Engle-Granger modelling approach, the endo-exogenous division of variables is assumed (and therefore there might be only one cointegrating relation) while in the Johansen approach, based on *VAR* modelling, there are no exogenous variables. It seems that the Johansen procedure can be used for single equation modelling as an auxiliary tool, checking the validity of the endo-exogenous variable division. Suppose, for instance, that the Johansen procedure indicates the existence of only one cointegrating vector. If the estimated cointegrating coefficients have, after normalization, economically sensible signs and are roughly similar in size to those estimated by the Engle-Granger method, this could be regarded as some confirmation of the single equation model to which the Engle-Granger method was applied. If, on the other hand, the number of cointegrating vectors found by the Johansen procedure is greater than one, it is likely that the endo-exogenous division of variables in this model is imperfect and that the model under consideration should consist of not one but two or more equations (see also the discussion of exogeneity in Chapter 7).

6.6 *VAR* Alternatives to the *DHSY* Model

(a) Impulse Responses
In order to illustrate the dynamic effects of the impact of unitary shocks on consumption, income and inflation, we consider the formulation of a *VAR* analogue to the *DHSY* model of aggregate consumption. The unrestricted *VAR* model is in the form of equation (6.9), with a deterministic component D_t, namely:

$$Z_t = A_0 D_t + \sum_{i=1}^{k} A_i Z_{t-i} + \epsilon_t \quad , \tag{6.22}$$

where $Z_t = \begin{bmatrix} cons_t & inc_t & inf_t \end{bmatrix}$. The deterministic components in this case consist of an intercept term, a deterministic linear trend and 3 seasonal dummy variables. The length of lag (the order of the *VAR* process) is assumed to be five (so that $k = 5$). This gives 60 parameters to be estimated in the *VAR*: fifteen as elements of the 3×5 matrix A_0 (we have five deterministic components in the model), and nine in each of the five 3×3 A_i matrices. The model is estimated by multivariate least squares. A selection from the computer output (from the *PC-FIML* part of the *PC-GIVE* package which is used for multi equation analysis) relating to the parameter estimates is shown in Section 6.7 under the heading MODEL 6.1. (In the *PC-GIVE* output a *VAR* model is called an *Unrestricted Reduced Form (URF)*. The goodness of fit measures reported here for the unrestricted reduced form estimates are the loglikelihood value (see Hendry (1989, p.66)), the logarithm of the determinant of Ω, denoted as $\log|\Omega|$, (Ω stands for the covariance matrix of the multivariate error term), and the correlation of actual and fitted values. The model is estimated using quarterly data from 1958 (1st quarter) to 1975 (4th quarter). It is worth noting from the results presented that the correlation between the residuals of the *VAR* model (denoted in the computer printout as the 'correlation of *URF* residuals') is substantial. Hence one would suspect that the impulse responses will differ from structural econometric dynamic multipliers.

Figures 6.1, 6.2 and 6.3 show the time paths or impulse responses to a unitary shock in consumption for the three modelled variables. For example, Figure 6.1 shows the responses of the consumption variable ($cons_t$) to its own unitary shock after zero periods, one period, two periods etc., up to the limit of thirty five periods. Unsurprisingly, the immediate (period zero) response of consumption to its unitary shock is equal to unity. Figures 6.2 and 6.3 also correctly show no responses at time zero for the other two variables in response to the unitary shock in consumption, but responses from period one onwards. Figures 6.4 - 6.6 and 6.7 - 6.9 are analogous, portraying the impulse responses of each of the three variables to unitary changes in the income and inflation variables respectively.

It appears from these figures that, eventually, all time paths resulting from the impulse response coefficients converge to zero. The absence of explosive responses to unitary shocks reflects the stability of the estimated model. For the individual variables, however, the way in which convergence is attained is quite different. For instance, impulse responses of consumption to a shock in both consumption and income exhibit a typical seasonal pattern. Income, however, grows initially after a consumption shock then declines from the second quarter. This decline lasts until the twelfth quarter after the shock is reached, from which point the responses again become positive. The interpretation of any of the other figures may be undertaken in a similar way.

(b) Forecasting

Following the claim made in Section 2 of this chapter on the convenience of using a *VAR* model for *ex ante* forecasting, consider the formulation of a *VAR* analogue to the *DHSY* model of aggregate consumption. In the same way as we approached the impulse response analysis, we will consider the unrestricted *VAR* model (6.22) where $Z_t = \begin{bmatrix} cons_t & inc_t & inf_t \end{bmatrix}$.

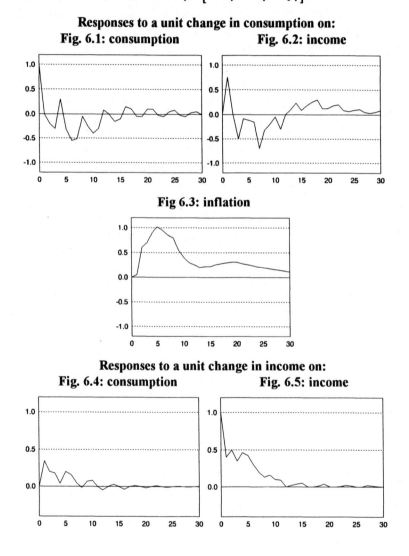

Responses to a unit change in consumption on:
Fig. 6.1: consumption   **Fig. 6.2: income**

Fig 6.3: inflation

Responses to a unit change in income on:
Fig. 6.4: consumption   **Fig. 6.5: income**

Fig 6.6: inflation

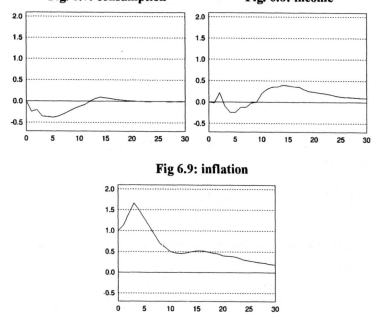

Responses to a unit change in inflation on:
Fig. 6.7: consumption   **Fig. 6.8: income**

Fig 6.9: inflation

The deterministic component (D_t) in this case, however, is only an in-tercept term. Since the model is to be used for an *ad hoc* mechanistic fore-cast, no adjustment to the data has been made, though from the results of Chapter 5 we know that the data are nonstationary. The length of lag (the order of the *VAR* process) is assumed to be five (so that $k = 5$). This gives 48 parameters to be estimated in the *VAR*: three as elements of the 3×1 vector A_0 (we have only one deterministic component in the model), and nine in each of the five 3×3 A_i matrices. The forecasts made are one–step–ahead forecasts where values for the periods up to and including period t are used for making predictions for period $t + 1$. As for the impulse response analysis, the model is estimated by multivariate least squares. A selection from the computer output relating to the parameter estimates and the forecasts is shown in Section 6.7 under the heading MODEL 6.2. The model is estimated using quarterly data from 1959 (2nd quarter) to 1970 (4th quarter) and forecasts from this model have been made for the period from 1971 (1st quarter) to 1975 (4th quarter) which are the same as were used by *DHSY* for evaluating the forecasting performance of the *DHSY* model.

Two types of forecasts have been made. The first are one–step–ahead forecasts, conditional on the observed values of lagged variables (that is, under the assumption that the forecaster making a forecast for period $t+1$ knows the realized values of the variables in period t).

The second type of forecasts for the next period ahead are dynamic or multi-step forecasts, where it is assumed that until the last quarter of 1970, the values of the variables are known, but after that period the forecasted values of the variables are used instead of the realizations of the particular variables. For instance, the forecasts for 1971 (1st quarter), denoted as $cons_{t+1}^f$, inc_{t+1}^f, inf_{t+1}^f are conditional on:

$$(cons_t, cons_{t-1}, cons_{t-2}, cons_{t-3}, cons_{t-4}, inc_t, inc_{t-1}, inc_{t-2}, inc_{t-3},$$
$$inc_{t-4}, inf_t, inf_{t-1}, inf_{t-2}, inf_{t-3}, inf_{t-4}),$$

where $t=1970$(4th quarter).

For 1971 (2nd quarter), the forecasts $cons_{t+2}^f$, inc_{t+2}^f, inf_{t+2}^f are conditional on:

$$(cons_{t+1}^f, cons_t, cons_{t-1}, cons_{t-2}, cons_{t-3}, inc_{t+1}^f, inc_t, inc_{t-1},$$
$$inc_{t-2}, inc_{t-3}, inf_{t+1}^f, inf_t, inf_{t-1}, inf_{t-2}, inf_{t-3}).$$

In the same way, for 1971 (3rd quarter) the forecasts are conditional on:

$$(cons_{t+2}^f, cons_{t+1}^f, cons_t, cons_{t-1}, cons_{t-2}, inc_{t+2}^f, inc_{t+1}^f, inc_t,$$
$$inc_{t-1}, inc_{t-2}, inf_{t+2}^f, inf_{t+1}^f, inf_t, inf_{t-1}, inf_{t-2}),$$

and so on.

Figures 6.10 to 6.12 show the one-step-ahead forecasts for consumption, income and inflation, together with realizations and forecast confidence intervals (equal to ($\pm$) two standard errors of forecast) whilst Figures 6.13 to 6.15. depict the dynamic or multi-step forecasts.

For interest, the two sets of forecasts obtained from the *VAR* model may be compared with those generated by a multivariate deterministic trend model with seasonal components, that is by:

$$Z_t = B_0 D_t + \zeta_t, \tag{6.23}$$

where $D_t = [Constant, Trend, Seasonal, Seasonal\_1, Seasonal\_2]$, Trend = 1, 2, ..., T , the variables *Seasonal, Seasonal_1* and *Seasonal_2* are seasonal dummy variables, and ζ_t is a vector of error terms. Estimates of equations (6.23) are summarized in Section 6.7 under MODEL 6.3. Figures 6.16 to 6.18 show the forecasts and realizations for this model for the same forecast period as the *VAR* model.

An inspection of the time paths of forecasts and realizations shows that none of the forecasts is fully admissible. In every figure some realizations lie outside the forecast confidence interval, with a tendency for all models to underpredict the series from 1973 onwards. The one-step *VAR* forecast is the only forecasting method which does not completely miss the huge rise in inflation which started from the beginning of 1974, a finding which is unsurprising given the nature of these forecasts. A comparison of parameter constancy forecast tests shows some superiority of the one-step *VAR* forecasts over those from the multivariate trend model. In each case, the test statistics for the one-step *VAR* forecasts lie below those for the multivariate trend model, though in virtually all cases the test statistics for the one-step forecasts are statistically significant at the 1% level. (Details of these test statistics are to be found in Doornik and Hendry (1994)).

The multi-step forecasts are not significantly better than either the one-step or multivariate trend models (for reasons of space, we do not report full output for this model). As with the other methods, realizations are within the confidence intervals at the start of the forecast period, but substantially underpredict both income and inflation towards the end (see Figures 6.13 to 6.15).

The forecasting diagnostics for the one-step *VAR* forecast for consumption are not as good as those computed for the *DHSY* model for the same period (see Chapter 3). However, it could be considered unfair to compare the multi-step *VAR* and *DHSY* forecasts directly as they are made under totally different assumptions. In particular, the forecasts analysed for the *DHSY* model in Chapter 3 were made under the rather unrealistic assumption that the time series of income and inflation were known for the forecasting period. Hence, this test was more a test for parameter constancy rather than a forecasting exercise. The multi-step *VAR* forecasts have been made under the more realistic assumption that values of income and inflation are unknown for the forecasting period and have to be predicted simultaneously with consumption.

(c) Causality

A *VAR* model may be used as the basis for testing causality (in the Granger sense) between consumption and inflation. As was mentioned in Chapter 3, the existence of a causal relation running from inflation to real consumption ($inf \rightarrow cons$) might result either from the existence of an unanticipated

One-step forecasts, *VAR*
Fig. 6.10: consumption

Fig. 6.11: income

Fig. 6.12: inflation

Multi-step forecasts, *VAR*
Fig. 6.13: consumption

Fig. 6.14: income

Fig. 6.15: inflation

Multivariate trend forecasts
Fig. 6.16: consumption

Fig. 6.17: income

Fig. 6.18: inflation

inflation effect or from a 'money illusion' effect. On the other hand, there could be a causal relation from real consumption to inflation ($cons \rightarrow inf$), if there is demand-pull inflation in the economy. Thus both types of causal relations might appear simultaneously, creating a feedback relation $inf \Leftrightarrow cons$. We have used two alternative *VAR* models to illustrate the testing of causality, both formulated for a three dimensional vector autoregressive process for the variables $cons_t$, inc_t, inf_t. Both of the models are *VAR*(5) models, incorporating up to five lags for each of the variables. The first set of equations is formulated in seasonal differences and with the deterministic part in each equation reduced to an intercept, or:

$$\Delta_4 Z_t = A_0 D_t + \sum_{i=1}^{5} A_i \Delta_4 Z_{t-i} + \epsilon_t \ , \tag{6.24}$$

where $D_t = [Constant]$.

The second set of equations is formulated in levels of the variables with a more fully developed deterministic part (constant, trend and seasonals):

$$Z_t = A_0 D_t + \sum_{i=1}^{5} A_i Z_{t-i} + \epsilon_t \ , \tag{6.25}$$

where $D_t = \left[Constant , Trend, Seasonal, Seasonal\_1, Seasonal\_2 \right]$.

It is worth emphasizing that testing for Granger causality in a model in levels is, for the case where variables are nonstationary, a popular but problematic exercise (see Harvey (1990, p.83) and the discussion in Section 6.4).

The equations in (6.24) correspond to the assumption that the seasonal components of the entire system are stochastic, while in (6.25) it is assumed that both trend and seasonal components are deterministic. Since our interest is in testing causality between consumption and inflation and the causality tests disregard covariances of the error terms, it is sufficient to base the analysis on the ordinary least squares estimates of the first and third equation of each model. Thus for the equations in (6.24) we consider:

$$\Delta_4 cons_t = \alpha_{c0} + \sum_{i=1}^{5} \alpha_{ci} \Delta_4 cons_{-i} + \sum_{i=1}^{5} \beta_{ci} \Delta_4 inc_{t-i} + \sum_{i=1}^{5} \gamma_{ci} \Delta_4 inf_{t-i} + \varepsilon_{ct} \ ,$$

$$\tag{6.26}$$

$$\Delta_4 inf_t = \alpha_{p0} + \sum_{i=1}^{5} \alpha_{pi} \Delta_4 cons_{-i} + \sum_{i=1}^{5} \beta_{pi} \Delta_4 inc_{t-i} + \sum_{i=1}^{5} \gamma_{pi} \Delta_4 inf_{t-i} + \varepsilon_{pt} \ ,$$

$$\tag{6.27}$$

and for those in (6.25) we consider:

$$cons_t = \alpha_{co} + \sum_{i=1}^{5} \alpha_{ci} cons_{t-i} + \sum_{i=1}^{5} \beta_{ci} inc_{t-i} + \sum_{i=1}^{5} \gamma_{ci} inf_{t-i}$$
$$+ 3 \text{ Seasonal Dummy Variables} + Trend + \varepsilon_{ct} \quad , \tag{6.28}$$

$$inf_t = \alpha_{po} + \sum_{i=1}^{5} \alpha_{pi} cons_{t-i} + \sum_{i=1}^{5} \beta_{pi} inc_{t-i} + \sum_{i=1}^{5} \gamma_{pi} inf_{t-i}$$
$$+ 3 \text{ Seasonal Dummy Variables} + Trend + \varepsilon_{pt} \quad . \tag{6.29}$$

For stationary variables, the Granger tests of the causal relations $inf \rightarrow cons$ or $\Delta_4 inf \rightarrow \Delta_4 cons$ consist of testing the hypothesis that in (6.28) or respectively in (6.26), $\gamma_{c1} = \gamma_{c2} = \gamma_{c3} = \gamma_{c4} = \gamma_{c5} = 0$. Analogously, the hypothesis that $cons \rightarrow inf$ is equivalent to testing whether in (6.29) $\alpha_{p1} = \alpha_{p2} = \alpha_{p3} = \alpha_{p4} = \alpha_{p5} = 0$, or similarly (for $\Delta_4 inf \rightarrow \Delta_4 cons$) in (6.27). Hence, the Granger test is simply a Lagrange Multiplier test for testing zero restrictions (see Chapter 5). Technically, this test can be computed in three different ways:

i) By estimating *an unrestricted* equation, with lags of particular variables formulated individually for each equation and then testing the (joint) *significance of each variable*. For instance, for the estimated equation (6.26) (MODEL 6.4 in Section 6.7) the *LMF* test statistic for significance of the variable d4inf (that is all the lagged inflation variables) is equal to 3.4848.

ii) By estimating a restricted equation, that is an equation with all the zero restrictions discussed above imposed, and then testing the omitted variables as *missing variables*. For the same example as *i)* above, the result of this test is given at the end of the computer output for MODEL 6.4 by the Wald test for linear restrictions (Subset). Again, the value of the test statistic is 3.4848.

iii) By performing a *model reduction* sequence in the way described in Chapter 4 as *general to specific* modelling. Regarding MODEL 6.4 as *general* and a model with the inflation variables omitted as *specific* would give the same F statistic of 3.4848 as the other two methods.

MODEL 6.4 in Section 6.7 shows the results of estimating equation (6.26) for testing $\Delta_4 inf \rightarrow \Delta_4 cons$ and MODEL 6.5 for testing the causality relation $\Delta_4 cons \rightarrow \Delta_4 inf$ from equation (6.27). MODELS 6.6 and 6.7 in Section 6.7 report the results of analogous Granger causality tests conducted on equations (6.28) and (6.29) which are in levels rather than seasonal differences.

For testing causality with the use of Sims-GMD method the approach described in *i)* requires leads of the variables to be constructed prior to modelling and these leads are regarded by *PC-GIVE* as separate variables. In *PC-GIVE*, leads are simply entered as negative lags. In Section 6.7, a one period lead in a variable is denoted by d4lc_–1, for example, in contrast to a one period lag written as d4lc_1.

The techniques of testing parallel those described above. However, it should be recalled that in the *VAR* model given as (6.24), the regression of $\Delta_4 inf_t$ on lagged $\Delta_4 inf_t$ s, lagged $\Delta_4 cons_t$ s and lagged $\Delta_4 inc_t$ s is now run and *leading* $\Delta_4 cons_t$ variables (that is $\Delta_4 cons_{t+1}$, $\Delta_4 cons_{t+2}$, $\Delta_4 cons_{t+3}$, $\Delta_4 cons_{t+4}$) are tested as missing variables for testing the hypothesis that $\Delta_4 inf \rightarrow \Delta_4 cons$ (MODEL 6.8). MODEL 6.9 shows the analogous results for testing the hypothesis that $\Delta_4 cons \rightarrow \Delta_4 inf$. Note that in the Sims-GMD test the sample finishes in 1974 (fourth quarter) and not 1975 (fourth quarter). The last four observations are discarded to allow for the formulation of leads in the variables. Similar computations for the *VAR* model (6.25) are shown in the computer output as MODELS 6.10 and 6.11. It should be noted that all the Durbin-Watson statistics computed for the above models are reasonably close to two. Although one must be aware of the possible bias of the Durbin-Watson statistic towards two in models containing lagged dependent variables, this is at least an indication that first order autocorrelation of the residuals is not likely to affect the validity of these Lagrange Multiplier statistics. It is interesting to note that the Sims-GMD method regards the equations of the *VAR* models as the restricted ones, while in the Granger method these are regarded as unrestricted. The unrestricted equations for the Sims-GMD method are those with the leading variables explicitly included, so that for (6.24) these are:

$$\Delta_4 Z_t = A_0 D_t + \sum_{i=-4}^{5} A_i \Delta_4 Z_{t-i} + \epsilon_t \ , \quad i \neq 0 \ ,$$

and for (6.25):

$$Z_t = A_0 D_t + \sum_{i=-4}^{5} A_i Z_{t-i} + \epsilon_t \ , \quad i \neq 0 \ .$$

The *LMF* statistics for testing causality between inflation and consumption are as follows:

For model (6.24):

$\Delta_4 inf \rightarrow \Delta_4 cons$: 3.48 (Granger), 2.69 (Sims-GMD)

$\Delta_4 cons \rightarrow \Delta_4 inf$: 1.92 (Granger), 6.35 (Sims-GMD)

For model (6.25):

$inf \rightarrow cons$: 2.92 (Granger), 3.93 (Sims-GMD)

$cons \rightarrow inf$: 1.57 (Granger), 6.92 (Sims-GMD)

The 5% critical values of the F distribution are 2.40 for $F(5 , 47)$ and 2.61 for $F(4 , 39)$. All the F statistics given above are significant apart from those for the Granger tests for $cons \rightarrow inf$ and $\Delta_4 cons \rightarrow \Delta_4 inf$. Conclusions cannot be very strong (especially for model (6.25)) since the assumption of stationarity for the variables in the model is, even in the presence of a deterministic trend and seasonals, a rather heroic one). Nevertheless, the results suggest the possibility of a feedback relation between inflation and consumption.

(d) Cointegration

In estimating cointegrating vectors and undertaking short run analysis in a *VAR* model describing consumption, income and inflation, one immediately encounters the problem of establishing the order of integration for the variables. It was suggested in Section 6.5 that cointegration analysis could be performed using the transformed model (6.17) and the Johansen procedure if all the variables which constitute the vector Z_t are integrated of order one.

As was discovered in Chapter 5, however, this is not the case for the data we are using. The variables are seasonally integrated, so that they become stationary after both seasonal differencing and first differencing. The discussion in Chapter 5 pointed out that seasonal cointegration analysis is still relatively undeveloped and complicated. For simplicity we have decided only to investigate long run cointegration. We also simplify the problem by assuming that the stochastic seasonality is approximated by deterministic seasonality and that the variables are integrated of order one conditionally on the presence of an intercept term and seasonal dummy variables in the nonstochastic part of the *VAR* model. Such a procedure has been used in practice in *VAR* cointegration analysis in models estimated with quarterly data by Johansen and Juselius (1990) and by Hendry, Muellbauer and Murphy (1990). Initially, we have estimated a *VAR* model with $k = 5$, denoted as *VAR*(5). The results of a similar exercise for a *VAR*(5) model but using a slightly different data sample are given in Hendry, Muellbauer and Murphy (1990, p.315).

The *VAR*(5) model is:

$$Z_t = A_0 D_t + \sum_{i=1}^{5} A_i Z_{t-i} + \epsilon_t \quad ,$$

(6.30)

where:

$$D_t = \left[Constant , Seasonal , Seasonal\_1 , Seasonal\_2 \right],$$

and

$$Z_t = \left[cons_t , inc_t , inf_t \right].$$

The results of estimating the equations in (6.30) are given in Section 6.7 under MODEL 6.12. In parallel with our discussion of cointegration in Section 5.8, it is worth considering whether we can reduce this *VAR(5)* system to a more parsimonious form by selective elimination of lagged variables. As a common lag length for each of the variables in the system is needed for the cointegration analysis, if a particular length of lag is excluded for the variables in one equation, this must also be done for the other equations. Thus a 'system reduction' approach is adopted in which at each stage of the process, the overall significance in the system of each regressor in turn is considered. One way of doing this is to examine the *F*-test statistics on the retained regressors presented in the computer output for MODEL 6.12. On the basis of these results it might be considered worthwhile eliminating all lagged variables in each equation at lag 2 as this lag is not significant at the 5% level for any of the three variables, $cons_t$, inc_t and inf_t. However, as with any problem where the variables are highly intercorrelated, considerable judgment has to be exercised in such an elimination. It would be quite usual in this case to consider eliminating variables at the longest lag first (see Vandaele (1983, p.131)), and if this was acceptable, to proceed to consider the next longest lag and so on. For MODEL 6.12, model reduction tests based on *F*-tests do not suggest any reductions are admissible from the original *VAR(5)* model (only the final results of these reduction tests are given under MODEL 6.12 to save space).

There are other model reduction criteria, however, three of which are routinely calculated by *PC-GIVE*. These tell a rather different story. These criteria are the loglikelihood values, and the Schwarz and Hannan-Quinn information criteria (see Lütkepohl (1991, p.132)). It can be seen that very little alteration in the values of these statistics occurs as, starting from the highest lags on each variable, one successively reduces the model from a *VAR(5)* model with 57 parameters (5 lags for each of 3 variables in 3 equations together with an intercept and three seasonal dummy variables in each equation) to a *VAR(1)* model with 21 parameters. However, there are large drops in the loglikelihood and information criteria values if one attempts to reduce each equation to simply an intercept and 3 seasonal dummy variables (12 parameters in all). These results suggest that the reduction of the *VAR(5)* to a *VAR(1)* system is not unreasonable. As our primary interest in this section is to illustrate the steps involved in a cointegration analysis, we will accordingly adopt the simpler *VAR(1)* model as our example.

The *VAR(1)* model may be written as:

$$\Delta Z_t = A_0 D_t + \Pi \cdot Z_{t-1} + \epsilon_t \quad . \tag{6.31}$$

The initial problem is the estimation of the number of cointegrating vectors and their elements. That is, one needs to decide on the order and elements of β in $\Pi = \alpha \cdot \beta'$. The results of applying the Johansen procedure for testing the order of the matrix β and estimating the elements of α and β for model (6.31) are given in Section 6.7 under MODEL 6.13. Three eigenvalues μ_i, $i = 1, 2, 3$, are printed at the beginning of this output. The *LR* statistics in the form of equation (6.21) for testing the hypothesis that there are at most r cointegrating vectors are given below. The figures in brackets are the critical values for a 5% significance test, as produced by *PC-GIVE*.

for $r \leq 2$:	0.0419	(3.8)
for $r \leq 1$:	8.119	(14.1)
for $r = 0$:	34.33	(21.0)

The results above suggest that the null hypothesis that there is no cointegrating vector should be rejected, since $34.33 > 21.0$. The next hypothesis, that the number of the cointegrating vectors is at most equal to one cannot be rejected, since 8.119 is not in the rejection region, that is $8.119 < 14.1$. The conclusion is that there is precisely one cointegrating vector in the estimated model and that the rank of the matrix Π is one. The first row of the β' matrix is:

1.000 −0.8296 0.1563 ,

which has been standardized so that its first element corresponds to the dependent variable ($cons_t$) in the first equation. This gives the following long run relationship:

$$cons_t = 0.8296 \cdot inc_t - 0.1563 \cdot inf_t \ .$$

The long run income elasticity of consumption is below unity, which is in line with findings concerning the market for nondurables in the UK by Bollerslev and Hylleberg (1985). The negative sign of the inflation variable is consistent with the hypothesis of an unanticipated inflation effect (see Chapter 3). The first element in the first row of the matrix α is negative, which is consistent with the hypothesis of an error correction mechanism given by the deviations from the long run consumption path.

One needs to exercise caution in interpreting the estimation results of the *VAR*(1) model. We noted at the outset that there was a question over the appropriate lag length to adopt for the *VAR* model. This conclusion is strengthened when the results of Hendry, Muellbauer and Murphy (1990) are considered. The *VAR*(5) model they adopted yielded long run coefficients of 0.93 for the income variable and −0.66 for the inflation variable. Their results suggest that the proper lag length for the *VAR* model adopted may be greater than one , in which case the *VAR*(1) model is misspecified.

6.7 Stylized Computer Output (*PC-GIVE*)

Impulse responses
MODEL 6.1: Estimating the unrestricted reduced form by OLS
(equation (6.22) in text)
The present sample is: 1959 (2) to 1975 (4)

URF Equation 1 for lc

Variable	Coefficient	Std.Error	t-value
lc_1	-0.018958	0.21968	-0.086
lc_2	-0.43548	0.20867	-2.087
lc_3	-0.32149	0.20442	-1.573
lc_4	0.44370	.20280	2.188
lc_5	-0.12746	0.19543	-0.652
li_1	0.33745	0.093342	3.615
li_2	0.11428	0.10761	1.062
li_3	0.12962	0.10069	1.287
li_4	0.069526	0.10066	0.691
li_5	-0.025030	0.10390	-0.241
inf_1	-0.25321	0.15185	-1.667
inf_2	0.14399	0.20534	0.701
inf_3	-0.37343	0.18710	-1.996
inf_4	0.13839	0.18535	0.747
inf_5	0.038185	0.15414	0.248
Constant	7.1203	2.6710	2.666
Trend	0.0040906	0.0015106	2.708
Seasonal	-0.039752	0.023045	-1.725
Seasonal_1	0.0074775	0.017924	0.417
Seasonal_2	-0.016490	0.022609	-0.729

$\sigma = 0.009226$ RSS = 0.004000596914

URF Equation 2 for li

Variable	Coefficient	Std.Error	t-value
lc_1	0.75945	0.49622	1.530
lc_2	-0.24036	0.47135	-0.510
lc_3	-0.44041	0.46174	-0.954
lc_4	0.089449	0.45810	0.195
lc_5	-0.70793	0.44144	-1.604
li_1	0.38522	0.21085	1.827
li_2	0.099744	0.24308	0.410
li_3	0.0091392	0.22745	0.040
li_4	0.36796	0.22738	1.618
li_5	0.10752	0.23469	0.458
inf_1	-0.047701	0.34301	-0.139

inf_2	0.46956	0.46382	1.012
inf_3	-0.59797	0.42262	-1.415
inf_4	0.062157	0.41868	0.148
inf_5	0.060152	0.34817	0.173
Constant	4.8863	6.0333	0.810
Trend	0.0032866	0.0034123	0.963
Seasonal	-0.0055049	0.052056	-0.106
Seasonal_1	0.045633	0.040487	1.127
Seasonal_2	0.030220	0.051071	0.592

$\sigma = 0.0208402$ RSS $= 0.02041277179$

URF Equation 3 for inf

Variable	Coefficient	Std.Error	t-value
lc_1	0.076948	0.18478	0.416
lc_2	0.48164	0.17552	2.744
lc_3	0.077023	0.17194	0.448
lc_4	0.27701	0.17059	1.624
lc_5	0.050183	0.16438	0.305
li_1	0.038948	0.078514	0.496
li_2	-0.048534	0.090517	-0.536
li_3	-0.042758	0.084696	-0.505
li_4	-0.091540	0.084670	-1.081
li_5	-0.22646	0.087393	-2.591
inf_1	1.2771	0.12773	9.999
inf_2	-0.20814	0.17272	-1.205
inf_3	0.25825	0.15737	1.641
inf_4	-0.46263	0.15590	-2.967
inf_5	0.28469	0.12965	2.196
Constant	-5.0642	2.2467	-2.254
Trend	-0.0028566	0.0012706	-2.248
Seasonal	0.018486	0.019384	0.954
Seasonal_1	-0.010351	0.015076	-0.687
Seasonal_2	0.031742	0.019018	1.669

$\sigma = 0.00776034$ RSS $= 0.002830474842$

correlation of URF residuals

	lc	li	inf
lc	1.000		
li	0.7427	1.000	
inf	-0.4424	-0.3567	1.000

standard deviations of URF residuals
      lc   li   inf
0.009226 0.02084 0.007760

loglik = 968.69315 log| Ω | = -28.9162 | Ω | = 2.76597e-013 T = 67

correlation of actual and fitted
      lc   li   inf
0.9977   0.9924   0.9913

Forecasting
MODEL 6.2: Estimating the unrestricted reduced form by OLS
(equation (6.22) in text)
The present sample is: 1959 (2) to 1975 (4) less 20 forecasts
The forecast period is: 1971 (1) to 1975 (4)

URF Equation 1 for lc

Variable	Coefficient	Std.Error	t-value
lc_1	-0.28835	0.22843	-1.262
lc_2	0.070067	0.060664	1.155
lc_3	-0.0024509	0.060189	-0.041
lc_4	1.0817	0.059236	18.261
lc_5	0.25349	0.23153	1.095
li_1	0.29535	0.10645	2.775
li_2	-0.13823	0.092566	-1.493
li_3	0.020281	0.093178	0.218
li_4	-0.11471	0.087632	-1.309
li_5	-0.18691	0.10300	-1.815
inf_1	-0.24049	0.21431	-1.122
inf_2	-0.043747	0.20941	-0.209
inf_3	-0.33918	0.19330	-1.755
inf_4	0.33864	0.18497	1.831
inf_5	0.15875	0.17620	0.901
Constant	0.13276	0.32552	0.408

σ = 0.0081746 RSS = 0.002071546815

URF Equation 2 for li

Variable	Coefficient	Std.Error	t-value
lc_1	-0.26748	0.50093	-0.534
lc_2	0.20638	0.13303	1.551
lc_3	0.056716	0.13199	0.430
lc_4	0.40816	0.12990	3.142
lc_5	0.18559	0.50772	0.366

li_1	0.47883	0.23343	2.051
li_2	-0.19303	0.20299	-0.951
li_3	0.0050211	0.20433	0.025
li_4	0.31521	0.19217	1.640
li_5	-0.10901	0.22588	-0.483
inf_1	-0.83984	0.46996	-1.787
inf_2	0.62266	0.45922	1.356
inf_3	-0.56250	0.42388	1.327
inf_4	0.36109	0.40563	0.890
inf_5	-0.068915	0.38640	-0.178
Constant	-0.63899	0.71383	-0.895

$\sigma = 0.0179262$ RSS $= 0.009961803871$

URF Equation 3 for inf

Variable	Coefficient	Std.Error	t-value
lc_1	0.36978	0.17506	2.112
lc_2	-0.024549	0.046489	-0.528
lc_3	-0.018012	0.046125	-0.391
lc_4	-0.0083565	0.045395	-0.184
lc_5	-0.29816	0.17743	-1.680
li_1	-0.068136	0.081573	-0.835
li_2	0.079353	0.070937	1.119
li_3	0.069341	0.071406	0.971
li_4	0.016263	0.067155	0.242
li_5	-0.059392	0.078935	-0.752
inf_1	1.0033	0.16423	6.109
inf_2	-0.16092	0.16048	-1.003
inf_3	0.35305	0.14813	2.383
inf_4	-0.48511	0.14175	-3.422
inf_5	0.015271	0.13503	0.113
Constant	-0.51302	0.24946	-2.057

$\sigma = 0.0062645$ RSS $= 0.001216562359$

correlation of URF residuals

	lc	li	inf
lc	1.000		
li	0.6626	1.000	
inf	-0.4000	-0.1959	1.000

standard deviations of URF residuals
    lc   li   inf
0.008175 0.01793 0.006264

loglik = 700.6126 log|Ω| = -29.8133 |Ω| = 1.12784e-013 T = 47

correlation of actual and fitted
    lc   li   inf
0.9969   0.9872   0.9558

1-step (ex post) forecast analysis 1971 (1) to 1975 (4)
Parameter constancy forecast tests:
using Ω $Chi^2(60)$= 526.76 [0.0000]** $F(60,31)$ = 8.7793 [0.0000]**
using V[e] $Chi^2(60)$= 153.99 [0.0000]** $F(60,31)$ = 2.5665 [0.0027]**
using V[E] $Chi^2(60)$= 120.62 [0.0000]** $F(60,31)$ = 2.0103 [0.0183]*

Multivariate trend model
MODEL 6.3: Estimating the unrestricted reduced form by OLS
(equation (6.23) in text)
The present sample is: 1958 (1) to 1975 (4) less 20 forecasts
The forecast period is: 1971 (1) to 1975 (4)

URF Equation 1 for lc

Variable	Coefficient	Std.Error	t-value
Seasonal	-0.10575	0.0052086	-20.302
Seasonal_1	-0.048202	0.0052013	-9.267
Seasonal_2	-0.037373	0.0051970	-7.191
Trend	0.0057834	0.00012273	47.122
Constant	8.6407	0.0053779	2e+003

σ = 0.0132461 RSS = 0.008246557339

URF Equation 2 for li

Variable	Coefficient	Std.Error	t-value
Seasonal	-0.048096	0.011058	-4.350
Seasonal_1	-0.016092	0.011042	1.457
Seasonal_2	-0.016780	0.011033	-1.521
Trend	0.0070892	0.00026056	27.208
Constant	8.7245	0.011417	764.163

σ = 0.028121 RSS = 0.0371671355

URF Equation 3 for inf

Variable	Coefficient	Std.Error	t-value
Seasonal	-0.00066652	0.0052230	-0.128
Seasonal_1	-0.00091895	0.0052158	-0.176
Seasonal_2	-0.0020372	0.0052114	-0.391
Trend	0.00073853	0.00012307	6.001
Constant	0.014716	0.0053928	2.729

$\sigma = 0.0132829$ RSS = 0.008292451247

correlation of URF residuals

	lc	li	inf
lc	1.000		
li	0.8526	1.000	
inf	-0.2833	-0.2047	1.000

standard deviations of URF residuals
lc	li	inf
0.01325	0.02812	0.01328

loglik = 679.21803 log$|\Omega|$ = -26.1238 $|\Omega|$ = 4.5143e-012 T = 52

correlation of actual and fitted
lc	li	inf
0.9917	0.9712	0.6607

1-step (ex post) forecast analysis 1971 (1) to 1975 (4)
Parameter constancy forecast tests:
using Ω Chi^2(60)= 776.3 [0.0000]** F(60,47)= 12.938 [0.0000]**
using V[e] Chi^2(60)= 632.94 [0.0000]** F(60,47)= 10.549 [0.0000]**
using V[E] Chi^2(60)= 416.96 [0.0000]** F(60,47)= 6.9493 [0.0000]**

Causality
Granger causality test for $\Delta_4 inf \rightarrow \Delta_4 cons$

MODEL 6.4: Modelling d4lc by OLS (equation (6.26) in text)
The present sample is: 1960 (2) to 1975 (4)

Variable	Coefficient	Std.Error	t-value
Constant	0.015619	0.0057597	2.712
d4lc_1	0.034751	0.19932	0.174
d4lc_2	-0.28197	0.21159	-1.333
d4lc_3	-0.11770	0.20546	-0.573
d4lc_4	-0.029644	0.20220	-0.147

d4lc_5	0.12369	0.18371	0.673
d4li_1	0.32437	0.084108	3.857
d4li_2	0.067616	0.095177	0.710
d4li_3	0.036323	0.090465	0.402
d4li_4	-0.096730	0.090568	-1.068
d4li_5	0.19179	0.091864	2.088
d4inf_1	-0.23291	0.11680	-1.994
d4inf_2	-0.042937	0.14307	-0.300
d4inf_3	-0.13320	0.13425	-0.992
d4inf_4	-0.042383	0.12680	-0.334
d4inf_5	0.090996	0.10725	0.848

$R^2 = 0.723966$ F(15, 47) = 268.8 [0.0000] σ = 0.00934465 DW = 1.96
RSS = 0.004104159517 for 16 variables and 63 observations

Tests on the significance of each variable

variable	F(num,denom)	Value	Unit Root t-test
d4lc	F(5, 47)	0.46027	-2.6583
Constant	F(1, 47)	7.3532 **	2.7117
d4li	F(5, 47)	3.6415**	2.2303
d4inf	F(5, 47)	3.4848**	-2.8901

Wald test for linear restrictions (Subset)
LinRes F(5, 47) =   3.4848 [0.0092] **

Zero restrictions on:
d4inf_1 d4inf_2 d4inf_3 d4inf_4 d4inf_5

Granger causality test for $\Delta_4 cons \rightarrow \Delta_4 inf$
MODEL 6.5: Modelling d4inf by OLS (equation (6.27) in text)
The present sample is: 1960 (2) to 1975 (4)

Variable	Coefficient	Std.Error	t-value
Constant	-0.011877	0.0061542	-1.930
d4inf_1	1.0729	0.12479	8.597
d4inf_2	-0.089762	0.15287	-0.587
d4inf_3	0.090814	0.14345	0.633
d4inf_4	-0.47131	0.13549	-3.479
d4inf_5	0.43003	0.11460	3.752
d4lc_1	-0.25748	0.21297	-1.209
d4lc_2	0.21033	0.22608	0.930
d4lc_3	0.11503	0.21953	0.524
d4lc_4	0.55115	0.21605	2.551
d4lc_5	0.19225	0.19630	0.979

d4li_1	0.081647	0.089868	0.909
d4li_2	0.078965	0.10170	0.776
d4li_3	0.017654	0.096661	0.183
d4li_4	-0.080967	0.096770	-0.837
d4li_5	-0.30838	0.098156	-3.142

$R^2 = 0.887462$ $F(15, 47) = 89.4$ [0.0000] $\sigma = 0.00998464$ DW $= 2.01$
RSS $= 0.004685576089$ for 16 variables and 63 observations

Tests on the significance of each variable

variable	F(num,denom)	Value	Unit Root t-test
d4inf	F(5, 47)	25.788**	0.24507
Constant	F(1, 47)	3.7246	-1.9299
d4lc	F(5, 47)	1.9233	1.5882
d4li	F(5, 47)	2.6351 *	0.84185

Wald test for linear restrictions (Subset)
LinRes F(5, 47) = 1.9233 [0.1082]

Zero restrictions on:
d4lc_1 d4lc_2 d4lc_3 d4lc_4 d4lc_5

Granger causality test for *inf* → *cons*
MODEL 6.6: Modelling lc by OLS (equation (6.28) in text)
The present sample is: 1959 (2) to 1975 (4)

Variable	Coefficient	Std.Error	t-value
Constant	7.1203	2.6710	2.666
lc_1	-0.018958	0.21968	-0.086
lc_2	-0.43548	0.20867	-2.087
lc_3	-0.32149	0.20442	-1.573
lc_4	0.44370	0.20280	2.188
lc_5	-0.12746	0.19543	-0.652
li_1	0.33745	0.093342	3.615
li_2	0.11428	0.10761	1.062
li_3	0.12962	0.10069	1.287
li_4	0.069526	0.10066	0.691
li_5	-0.025030	0.10390	-0.241
inf_1	-0.25321	0.15185	-1.667
inf_2	0.14399	0.20534	0.701
inf_3	-0.37343	0.18710	-1.996
inf_4	0.13839	0.18535	0.747
inf_5	0.038185	0.15414	0.248

Trend	0.0040906	0.0015106	2.708
Seasonal	-0.039752	0.023045	-1.725
Seasonal_1	0.0074775	0.017924	0.417
Seasonal_2	-0.016490	0.022609	-0.729

$R^2 = 0.9955$ F(19, 47) = 4.0364 [0.0001] σ = 0.009226 DW = 2.03
RSS = 0.004000596914 for 20 variables and 67 observations

Tests on the significance of each variable

variable	F(num,denom)	Value	Unit Root t-test
lc	F(5, 47)	4.0501**	-2.4884
Constant	F(1, 47)	7.1067*	2.6658
li	F(5, 47)	2.9906*	2.2094
inf	F(5, 47)	2.9217*	-2.3335
Trend	F(1, 47)	7.3328**	2.7079
Seasonal	F(3, 47)	1.4184	-0.94278

Wald test for linear restrictions (Subset)
LinRes F(5, 47) = 2.9217 [0.0223] *

Zero restrictions on:
inf_1 inf_2 inf_3 inf_4 inf_5

Granger causality test for *cons* → *inf*
MODEL 6.7: Modelling inf by OLS (equation (6.29) in text)
The present sample is: 1959 (2) to 1975 (4)

Variable	Coefficient	Std.Error	t-value
Constant	-5.0642	2.2467	-2.254
inf_1	1.2771	0.12773	9.999
inf_2	-0.20814	0.17272	-1.205
inf_3	0.25825	0.15737	1.641
inf_4	-0.46263	0.15590	-2.967
inf_5	0.28469	0.12965	2.196
li_1	0.038948	0.078514	0.496
li_2	-0.048534	0.090517	-0.536
li_3	-0.042758	0.084696	-0.505
li_4	-0.091540	0.084670	-1.081
li_5	-0.22646	0.087393	-2.591
lc_1	0.076948	0.18478	0.416
lc_2	0.48164	0.17552	2.744
lc_3	0.077023	0.17194	0.448
lc_4	0.27701	0.17059	1.624

lc_5	0.050183	0.16438	0.305
Trend	-0.0028566	0.0012706	-2.248
Seasonal	0.018486	0.019384	0.954
Seasonal_1	-0.010351	0.015076	-0.687
Seasonal_2	0.031742	0.019018	1.669

$R^2 = 0.9827$ F(19, 47) = 15.755 [0.0000] σ = 0.00776034 DW = 2.16
RSS = 0.002830474842 for 20 variables and 67 observations

Tests on the significance of each variable

variable	F(num,denom)	Value	Unit Root t-test
inf	F(5, 47)	53.977**	1.3532
Constant	F(1, 47)	5.081*	-2.2541
li	F(5, 47)	1.5663	-1.5544
lc	F(5, 47)	1.5729	1.9514
Trend	F(1, 47)	5.0541*	-2.2481
Seasonal	F(3, 47)	1.626	0.91653

Wald test for linear restrictions (Subset)
LinRes F(5, 47) =   1.5729 [0.1862]

Zero restrictions on:
lc_1 lc_2 lc_3 lc_4 lc_5

Sims causality test for $\Delta_4 inf \rightarrow \Delta_4 cons$
MODEL 6.8: Modelling d4inf by OLS
The present sample is: 1960 (2) to 1974 (4)

Variable	Coefficient	Std.Error	t-value
Constant	0.00060349	0.0076266	0.079
d4inf_1	0.95150	0.14362	6.625
d4inf_2	-0.11043	0.14703	-0.751
d4inf_3	0.13601	0.14547	0.935
d4inf_4	-0.42176	0.13375	-3.153
d4inf_5	0.38672	0.12569	3.077
d4li_1	0.11756	0.092868	1.266
d4li_2	0.098939	0.098245	1.007
d4li_3	0.038096	0.10060	0.379
d4li_4	0.0039309	0.10999	0.036
d4li_5	-0.27327	0.10698	-2.555
d4lc_1	-0.31538	0.21264	-1.483
d4lc_2	0.19283	0.22466	0.858
d4lc_3	0.017046	0.20959	0.081
d4lc_4	0.51107	0.23688	2.158

d4lc_5	0.057791	0.22883	0.253
d4lc_-1	-0.34256	0.14139	-2.423
d4lc_-2	0.060254	0.15877	0.380
d4lc_-3	-0.045351	0.16080	-0.282
d4lc_-4	-0.094773	0.13727	-0.690

$R^2 = 0.8935$ F(19, 39) = 88.291 [0.0000] σ = 0.00935796 DW = 2.21
RSS = 0.003415284791 for 20 variables and 59 observations

Wald test for linear restrictions (Subset)
LinRes F(4, 39) = 2.6923 [0.0449] *

Zero restrictions on:
d4lc_-1 d4lc_-2 d4lc_-3 d4lc_-4

Sims causality test for $\Delta_4 cons \rightarrow \Delta_4 inf$
MODEL 6.9: Modelling d4lc by OLS
The present sample is: 1960 (2) to 1974 (4)

Variable	Coefficient	Std.Error	t-value
Constant	0.018042	0.0060331	2.990
d4lc_1	-0.15465	0.18031	-0.858
d4lc_2	-0.22372	0.18983	-1.179
d4lc_3	-0.073904	0.18139	-0.407
d4lc_4	0.012108	0.19219	0.063
d4lc_5	-0.079686	0.17908	-0.445
d4li_1	0.30950	0.072456	4.272
d4li_2	0.15077	0.083957	1.796
d4li_3	0.18386	0.089688	2.050
d4li_4	-0.11066	0.095008	-1.165
d4li_5	0.058247	0.092781	0.628
d4inf_1	0.10325	0.16140	0.640
d4inf_2	0.0062847	0.13903	0.045
d4inf_3	-0.15252	0.12579	-1.212
d4inf_4	-0.085008	0.10804	-0.787
d4inf_5	0.14039	0.10064	1.395
d4inf_-1	-0.34808	0.15262	-2.281
d4inf_-2	0.00093993	0.16681	0.006
d4inf_-3	-0.030500	0.16930	-0.180
d4inf_-4	0.22343	0.10268	2.176

$R^2 = 0.7906$ F(19, 39) = 196.27 [0.0000] σ = 0.00772006 DW = 2.00
RSS = 0.002324376611 for 20 variables and 59 observations

Wald test for linear restrictions (Subset)
LinRes F(4, 39) = 6.3496 [0.0005] **

Zero restrictions on:
d4inf_-1 d4inf_-2 d4inf_-3 d4inf_-4

Sims causality test for *inf → cons*
MODEL 6.10: Modelling inf by OLS
The present sample is: 1959 (2) to 1974 (4)

Variable	Coefficient	Std.Error	t-value
Constant	0.65252	2.7209	0.240
inf_1	1.1461	0.12663	9.050
inf_2	-0.21287	0.15623	-1.363
inf_3	0.27246	0.14573	1.870
inf_4	-0.42442	0.14209	-2.987
inf_5	0.27888	0.12343	2.259
li_1	0.12220	0.078134	1.564
li_2	0.030811	0.088257	0.349
li_3	0.067230	0.092999	0.723
li_4	0.023691	0.088794	0.267
li_5	-0.23675	0.089000	-2.660
lc_1	-0.14713	0.18861	-0.780
lc_2	0.23274	0.19349	1.203
lc_3	0.091097	0.18286	0.498
lc_4	0.21019	0.16539	1.271
lc_5	-0.10165	0.17160	-0.592
lc_-1	-0.21964	0.11217	-1.958
lc_-2	-0.033361	0.12228	-0.273
lc_-4	-0.28164	0.095326	-2.954
lc_-3	0.16650	0.11837	1.407
Trend	0.00042296	0.0015503	0.273
Seasonal	0.0030470	0.021850	0.139
Seasonal_1	-0.016373	0.016969	-0.965
Seasonal_2	0.020929	0.020553	1.018

$R^2 = 0.9740$ F(23, 39) = 23.93 [0.0000] σ = 0.00694901 DW = 2.43
RSS = 0.001883260965 for 24 variables and 63 observations

Wald test for linear restrictions (Subset)
LinRes F(4, 39) = 3.9267 [0.0090] **

Zero restrictions on:
lc_-1 lc_-2 lc_-4 lc_-3

Sims causality test for *cons* → *inf*
MODEL 6.11: Modelling lc by OLS
The present sample is: 1959 (2) to 1974 (4)

Variable	Coefficient	Std.Error	t-value
Constant	7.1851	2.5311	2.839
lc_1	-0.11780	0.19212	-0.613
lc_2	-0.28030	0.19453	-1.441
lc_3	-0.31478	0.17943	-1.754
lc_4	0.44126	0.17306	2.550
lc_5	-0.17628	0.16961	-1.039
li_1	0.27560	0.078362	3.517
li_2	0.094041	0.090902	1.035
li_3	0.27401	0.092644	2.958
li_4	0.030952	0.092356	0.335
li_5	-0.066957	0.095728	-0.699
inf_1	0.067228	0.18836	0.357
inf_2	0.17626	0.16486	1.069
inf_3	-0.30945	0.14975	-2.067
inf_4	0.019201	0.14897	0.129
inf_5	0.11781	0.12904	0.913
inf_-1	-0.66420	0.16936	-3.922
inf_-2	0.28411	0.19703	1.442
inf_-3	-0.057162	0.20033	-0.285
inf_-4	0.18616	0.11827	1.574
Trend	0.0039665	0.0014319	2.770
Seasonal	-0.039740	0.020223	-1.965
Seasonal_1	-0.018310	0.016381	-1.118
Seasonal_2	-0.019479	0.018951	-1.028

$R^2 = 0.9974$ F(23, 39) = 2.2989 [0.0107] σ = 0.00714087 DW = 2.34
RSS = 0.001988687727 for 24 variables and 63 observations

Wald test for linear restrictions (Subset)
LinRes F(4, 39) = 6.9189 [0.0003] **

Zero restrictions on:
inf_-1 inf_-2 inf_-3 inf_-4

Cointegration
MODEL 6.12: Estimating the unrestricted reduced form by OLS
(equations (6.31) in text)
The present sample is: 1959 (2) to 1975 (4)

URF Equation 1 for lc

Variable	Coefficient	Std.Error	t-value
lc_1	0.28107	0.20181	1.393
lc_2	-0.057435	0.16500	-0.348
lc_3	0.054392	0.15965	0.341
lc_4	0.80616	0.16210	4.973
lc_5	-0.012072	0.20292	-0.059
li_1	0.27336	0.096063	2.846
li_2	-0.058713	0.092134	-0.637
li_3	-0.026182	0.087916	-0.298
li_4	-0.084540	0.088349	-0.957
li_5	-0.16346	0.096233	-1.699
inf_1	-0.21686	0.16093	-1.348
inf_2	0.20699	0.21705	0.954
inf_3	-0.35123	0.19886	-1.766
inf_4	0.22864	0.19398	1.179
inf_5	0.11667	0.16106	0.724
Constant	-0.074110	0.29207	-0.254
Seasonal	-0.042370	0.024497	-1.730
Seasonal_1	0.0081434	0.019068	0.427
Seasonal_2	-0.016985	0.024054	-0.706

$\sigma = 0.00981576$ RSS = 0.004624760655

URF Equation 2 for li

Variable	Coefficient	Std.Error	t-value
lc_1	1.0005	0.42816	2.337
lc_2	0.063379	0.35006	0.181
lc_3	-0.13841	0.33871	-0.409
lc_4	0.38067	0.34390	1.107
lc_5	-0.61522	0.43049	-1.429
li_1	0.33373	0.20380	1.638
li_2	-0.039245	0.19547	-0.201
li_3	-0.11604	0.18652	-0.622
li_4	0.24418	0.18744	1.303
li_5	-0.0037012	0.20416	-0.018
inf_1	-0.018498	0.34141	-0.054
inf_2	0.52018	0.46049	1.130
inf_3	-0.58013	0.42190	-1.375

inf_4	0.13467	0.41154	0.327
inf_5	0.12321	0.34170	0.361
Constant	-0.89408	0.61965	-1.443
Seasonal	-0.0076082	0.051971	-0.146
Seasonal_1	0.046168	0.040453	1.141
Seasonal_2	0.029822	0.051031	0.584

σ =.0208245 RSS = 0.0208156881

URF Equation 3 for inf

Variable	Coefficient	Std.Error	t-value
lc_1	-0.13257	0.16616	-0.798
lc_2	0.21765	0.13585	1.602
lc_3	-0.18546	0.13144	-1.411
lc_4	0.023893	0.13346	0.179
lc_5	-0.030391	0.16706	-0.182
li_1	0.083705	0.079090	1.058
li_2	0.072268	0.075855	0.953
li_3	0.066044	0.072382	0.912
li_4	0.016047	0.072739	0.221
li_5	-0.12979	0.079230	-1.638
inf_1	1.2517	0.13249	9.448
inf_2	-0.25214	0.17870	-1.411
inf_3	0.24275	0.16373	1.483
inf_4	-0.52566	0.15971	-3.291
inf_5	0.22988	0.13261	1.734
Constant	-0.040187	0.24047	-0.167
Seasonal	0.020314	0.020169	1.007
Seasonal_1	-0.010816	0.015699	-0.689
Seasonal_2	0.032088	0.019804	1.620

σ = 0.00808142 RSS = 0.003134847056

correlation of URF residuals

	lc	li	inf
lc	1.000		
li	0.7351	1.000	
inf	-0.5055	-0.3790	1.000

standard deviations of URF residuals
lc	li	inf
0.009816	0.02082	0.008081

loglik = 961.45658 log$|\Omega|$ = -28.7002 $|\Omega|$ = 3.43292e-013 T = 67

F-test against unrestricted regressors, $F(45, 137) = 62.001$ [0.0000] **
variables entered unrestricted:
Constant Seasonal Seasonal_1 Seasonal_2

F-tests on retained regressors, $F(3, 46)$

lc_1	1.82007	lc_2	1.05290
lc_3	1.00888	lc_4	15.4347**
lc_5	1.35866	li_1	5.38951**
li_2	0.352523	li_3	0.386219
li_4	3.11254*	li_5	4.60692**
inf_1	34.2827**	inf_2	0.782980
inf_3	1.14928	inf_4	3.78417*
inf_5	2.07506		

correlation of actual and fitted

lc	li	inf
0.9974	0.9923	0.9904

Progress to date

system	T	p		log-likelihood	Schwarz	Hannan-Quinn
6	67	12	OLS	657.051	-18.86	-19.10
5	67	21	OLS	894.776	-25.39	-25.81
4	67	30	OLS	902.738	-25.06	-25.66
3	67	39	OLS	915.364	-24.88	-25.65
2	67	48	OLS	939.872	-25.04	-26.00
1	67	57	OLS	961.457	-25.12	-26.26

Tests of model reduction
System 1 --> System 2: $F(9, 112) = 3.7754$ [0.0004] **

System 1 --> System 3: $F(18, 130) = 4.5457$ [0.0000] **
System 2 --> System 3: $F(9, 119) = 4.6523$ [0.0000] **

System 1 --> System 4: $F(27, 134) = 4.1117$ [0.0000] **
System 2 --> System 4: $F(18, 139) = 3.7072$ [0.0000] **
System 3 --> System 4: $F(9, 126) = 2.3581$ [0.0170] *

System 1 --> System 5: $F(36, 136) = 3.6492$ [0.0000] **
System 2 --> System 5: $F(27, 143) = 3.1174$ [0.0000] **
System 3 --> System 5: $F(18, 147) = 1.9896$ [0.0135] *
System 4 --> System 5: $F(9, 134) = 1.5273$ [0.1444]

System 1 --> System 6: F(45, 137) = 62.001 [0.0000] **
System 2 --> System 6: F(36, 145) = 66.348 [0.0000] **
System 3 --> System 6: F(27, 152) = 73.523 [0.0000] **
System 4 --> System 6: F(18, 156) = 107.23 [0.0000] **
System 5 --> System 6: F(9, 141) = 274.19 [0.0000] **

MODEL 6.13: Estimating the unrestricted reduced form by OLS
($VAR(1)$ system)
The present sample is: 1959 (2) to 1975 (4)

URF Equation 1 for lc

Variable	Coefficient	Std.Error	t-value
lc_1	0.93428	0.11911	7.844
li_1	0.035698	0.095120	0.375
inf_1	0.0089537	0.058452	0.153
Constant	0.30874	0.26655	1.158
Seasonal	-0.15261	0.0055054	-27.720
Seasonal_1	0.0077007	0.0069817	1.103
Seasonal_2	-0.032775	0.0045181	-7.254

σ = 0.0128055 RSS = 0.009838809692

URF Equation 2 for li

Variable	Coefficient	Std.Error	t-value
lc_1	0.82310	0.19218	4.283
li_1	0.31613	0.15348	2.060
inf_1	0.13982	0.094313	1.483
Constant	-1.0965	0.43008	-2.550
Seasonal	-0.089447	0.0088831	-10.069
Seasonal_1	0.039572	0.011265	3.513
Seasonal_2	-0.0094568	0.0072900	-1.297

σ = 0.0206619 RSS = 0.02561482682

URF Equation 3 for inf

Variable	Coefficient	Std.Error	t-value
lc_1	-0.12655	0.087436	-1.447
li_1	0.13033	0.069828	1.866
inf_1	0.96613	0.042910	22.515
Constant	-0.052679	0.19567	-0.269
Seasonal	0.0062514	0.0040416	1.547
Seasonal_1	-0.0018820	0.0051253	-0.367
Seasonal_2	0.0010745	0.0033167	0.324

σ = 0.00940057 RSS = 0.005302247598

correlation of URF residuals

	lc	li	inf
lc	1.000		
li	0.5960	1.000	
inf	-0.3490	-0.2346	1.000

standard deviations of URF residuals

lc	li	inf
0.01281	0.02066	0.009401

loglik = 894.77602 log|Ω| = -26.7097 |Ω| = 2.51253e-012 T = 67

F-test against unrestricted regressors, F(9, 141) = 274.19 [0.0000] **
variables entered unrestricted:
Constant Seasonal Seasonal_1 Seasonal_2

F-tests on retained regressors, F(3, 58)
lc_1 20.4994 [0.0000] **   li_1 3.30908 [0.0263] *
inf_1 189.047 [0.0000] **

correlation of actual and fitted

lc	li	inf
0.9945	0.9905	0.9836

Cointegration analysis 1959 (2) to 1975 (4)

eigenvalue μ_i	loglik	for rank
	873.529	0
0.400958	890.695	1
0.114131	894.755	2
0.000624358	894.776	3

Ho: rank=p	-Tlog(1-μ)	95%
p = 0	34.33**	21.0
p = 1	8.119	14.1
p = 2	0.04185	3.8

standardized β' eigenvectors

lc	li	inf
1.000	-0.8296	0.1563
-1.924	1.000	0.03819
-0.06198	-0.1832	1.000

standardized α coefficients

lc	-0.01172	0.02776	0.009726
li	0.8181	-0.002967	0.01203
inf	-0.2086	-0.04267	0.0003719

long-run matrix Po= $\alpha\beta'$, rank 3

	lc	li	inf
lc	-0.06572	0.03570	0.008954
li	0.8231	-0.6839	0.1398
inf	-0.1266	0.1303	-0.03387

Number of lags used in the analysis: 1
Variables entered unrestricted:
Constant Seasonal Seasonal_1 Seasonal_2

6.8 Suggestions for Further Reading

The seminal papers on *VAR* modelling are those of Sims (1980, 1982). An important development was made by Doan, Litterman and Sims (1984), where simple Bayesian priors were adopted for *VAR* modelling (see also Todd (1990)). Evaluation of the forecasting results from *VAR*s has not been consistent. Litterman (1986) found the results good, but Fair (1988) was less impressed. The best known sophisticated applications of *VAR* models for policy analysis are those of Bernanke (1986), Blanchard and Watson (1986), Blanchard and Quah (1989) and Quah and Vahey (1996). *VAR* models may be generalized to include moving average error terms, in which case they are described as *VARMA* models. Models of this type are discussed in Kendall and Ord (1990, Chapter 14) and Granger and Newbold (1986, Chapter 8). A comparison of *VAR* models with traditional macroeconometric models has been given by McNees (1986). Criticisms of *VAR* modelling are contained in Darnell and Evans (1990, Chapter 7), Epstein (1987, Chapter 7), Leamer (1985), Runckle (1987) and Pagan (1987). A recent development in *VAR* modelling is in their relationship to structural models as illustrated by Monfort and Rabemanjara (1990). *VAR* modelling was extended for use with panel (cross section and time series) data by Holtz-Eakin, Newey and Rosen (1988). A thorough statistical inquiry to the *VAR* approach, including cointegrated *VAR* models, is given by Lütkepohl (1991), Hamilton (1994) and Johansen (1995). More accessible introduction to *VAR* modelling is given by Enders (1995).

Causality analysis was developed prior to that of *VAR* modelling. Following the seminal paper of Granger (1969), a great amount of theoretical and empirical analysis was carried out. Apart from those mentioned in the text, noteworthy theoretical contributions are the papers of Geweke (1984), Wu (1983) and Zellner (1979). Conceptual difficulties of causality were discussed by Jacobs, Leamer and Ward (1979) and Spohn (1984). Various causality tests are compared in Geweke, Meese and Dent (1983) and Guilkey and Salemi (1982).

Among various applications of causality testing which are relatively straightforward are the following. Price-wage causality has been analysed by Shannon and Wallace (1985-86), Fosu and Huq (1988) and Charemza (1989). Causality between public expenditure and national income was evaluated by Singh and Sahni (1984), between velocity and growth of money by Fisher and Serletis (1989), and money and income by Hsiao (1981), Stock and Watson (1989), Williams, Goodhart and Gowland (1976) and Sims (1972). An example of a time series approach for investigating money and price causality is that of Deadman and Ghatak (1989). Published applications of the Johansen method are now in abundance. One may particularly note those of Johansen and Juselius (1990), Hall (1989), Hall and Henry (1988), and Hendry, Muellbauer and Murphy (1990). Also, it is important to note the work of Osterwald-Lenum (1992) discussing the problem of computing the critical values for the Johansen tests. The relationship between causation and cointegration has been investigated by Granger (1988).

Chapter 7

Exogeneity and Structural Invariance

7.1 Data Generating Processes

In Chapter 6 we outlined the principal assumptions of multi-equation modelling within the Cowles Commission framework, and introduced in greater detail, the 'atheoretical' *VAR* approach. We stated that the two principal assumptions of structural modelling, namely the endo-exogenous division of the variables and the zero restrictions imposed on a model's parameters, are abandoned in *VAR* modelling. There are no exogenous variables in the system and, due to the lack of zero restrictions, there is nothing like a 'structural form' of the model.

The *VAR* approach is quite difficult to apply in the real world. In practice, *VAR* modelling for more than four variables is rarely feasible. An investigator has to include many lags on many variables in each equation. The number of parameters to be estimated becomes large and even a single equation may become impossible to estimate, due to the shortage of observations. Moreover, the fact that the *VAR* approach is 'atheoretical' makes the development of an economically sensible model from a *VAR* system a quite difficult task (although, as shown in Chapter 6, not necessarily impossible).

The method of multi-equation modelling presented in this chapter, which we will call *exogeneity modelling*, can be thought of as a compromise in some respects between the need to keep the size of the model manageable and consistent with economic theory on the one hand, and the properties of the statistical data used for the modelling on the other. Generally speaking, exogeneity modelling still allows for some *a priori* zero restrictions to be imposed and therefore for control over the size of the model, but the endo-exogenous division between variables is not given *a priori* any more. This division constitutes a testable hypothesis and because of this it is, to some extent, connected with the former problem of zero restrictions. If a certain variable is not exogenous, it should be modelled within the system and therefore some of the hypothetical zero restrictions may not be valid.

Exogeneity modelling can be envisaged as bringing together elements from both structural and *VAR* modelling. It bears some resemblance to the concept of recursive systems (for example, see Wold (1954)), which were regarded in the 1950s as a criticism of simultaneous equation structural modelling. According to Wold, simultaneity does not exist in the economy as there is always a time lag between a cause and an outcome. Hence, models represented by the general form of equations (6.6) do not make sense.

However, exogeneity modelling is not as extreme as the early Wold theories would require. A system of simultaneous equations can be a valid part of the model, provided it is the result of a general to specific modelling exercise and survives the tests described in Chapters 3 and 4. Adapting slightly the notation of equation (6.7) in Chapter 6, this structural model may be written as:

$$y_t'\Gamma = z_t B_0 + \sum_{i=1}^{k} y_{t-i}' B_i + u_t' \ .$$ (7.1)

In structural modelling, the model specification stops here. In exogeneity modelling, however, the variables z_t can also be modelled, creating something like a recursive part of the system, as:

$$z_t = \sum_{i=1}^{g} C_i y_{t-i} + \sum_{i=1}^{l} D_i z_{t-i} + v_t \ .$$ (7.2)

The problem is to separate the parts of the model describing y_t and z_t in such a way that y_t can be modelled independently (but conditionally) on z_t. That is, no knowledge about the process generating z_t will be required for the modelling of y_t. Evidently for this to be the case, there should be no relation between the error terms u_t and v_t and no cross-restrictions between the parameters of the two parts of the model.

Exogeneity modelling can also be regarded as a method of inference in a *VAR* model. In the unrestricted *VAR* model, where the entire set of contemporaneous variables is denoted as Ψ_t:

$$\Psi_t = \sum_{i=1}^{k} A_i \Psi_{t-i} + \varepsilon_t \ ,$$

the problem is in the partitioning of Ψ_t into two sets of variables, say $[\Psi_t^1 \ \Psi_t^2]$, whose error terms are not correlated between the two sets. The part corresponding to Ψ_t^1 is then the *VAR* equivalent to (7.1), while the part corresponding to Ψ_t^2 is the *VAR* equivalent to (7.2).

Hence, the problem of distinguishing which variables should enter the vectors y_t and z_t plays a central role in exogeneity modelling. Before we move to the problems of establishing the partition between y_t and z_t, that is defining and testing for exogeneity, it will be useful to introduce the concept of a data generating process.

We start with some rather involved notation. Let x_t^* denote a vector of observations on n^* random variables at time t ($t = 1, 2, ..., T$). The matrix X_t^* denotes all observations on the n^* variables up to and including time t, that is $X_t^* = \left[x_1^* \, x_2^* \, ... x_t^* \right]$. The joint density function of the entire set of observations, current and past, is denoted herein as $D(\, x_1^*, x_2^*, ..., x_t^* \,|\, \theta^*)$ or $D(X_t^* \,|\, \theta^*)$ where θ^* is the vector of parameters of the joint density function. This joint density function is called the *Data Generating Process* (*DGP*). A working definition of this concept has been given by Spanos (1986, p.20) as 'the mechanism underlying the observable phenomena of interest'. An important decomposition of a *DGP* can be derived by representing it as a process of generating the data conditionally on the past, that is as:

$$D(X_T^* \,|\, \theta^*) = \prod_{t=1}^{T} D(x_t^* \,|\, X_{t-1}^* \,;\, \theta^*) \quad .$$ (7.3)

The notation of the type $D(\bullet \,|\, \bullet)$ used here bears a strong resemblance to that used for joint, conditional and marginal probability density functions. In fact, there are some formal differences between the analysis of probability distributions and *DGP*s, which we will ignore for simplicity. However, in order to avoid confusion when we use these concepts below, we will refer to 'processes' rather than to 'density functions'.

It is known from the foundations of probability theory (for example see Freund and Walpole (1987, pp. 102-127) or, at a more advanced level, Spanos (1986, pp. 78-95)) that if a *joint probability density* function of two continuous random variables, X and Y is $f(x, y)$ where x is a realization of X and y is a realization of Y, the *marginal distribution* of X has a density function:

$$g(x) = \int_y f(x, y) \, dy \quad ,$$

where the range of integration is the range of values of Y. Note that as this integration is with respect to y, the marginal distribution of x will not involve y (loosely, the variable y has been 'integrated out' of the joint probability distribution of x and y). The *conditional distribution* of y *given* x has its density function denoted as $f(y|x)$ and can be interpreted as the probability distribution of the random variable Y given that a realization of X is known to be x. The relationship between the joint, conditional and marginal distributions is:

$$f(x, y) = g(x) \cdot f(y|x) \quad .$$

As an example (adapted later in the text as EXAMPLE 7.1) consider the bivariate normal random variables (X, Y), that is random variables with a joint density function:

$$f(x, y) =$$

$$\frac{1}{\sqrt{1-\rho^2}\cdot 2\pi\cdot\sigma_1\sigma_2} exp\left\{-\frac{1}{2\cdot(1-\rho^2)}\left(\left[\frac{x-\mu_1}{\sigma_1}\right]^2\right.\right.$$

$$\left.\left.-2\cdot\rho\left[\frac{x-\mu_1}{\sigma_1}\right]\left[\frac{y-\mu_2}{\sigma_2}\right]+\left[\frac{y-\mu_2}{\sigma_2}\right]^2\right)\right\}$$

for $-\infty \le x \le \infty, -\infty \le y \le \infty, \sigma_1 > 0, \sigma_2 > 0$, and $-1 < \rho < 1$. The density function above has five parameters. In order to keep the notation conformable with most of the literature, we will denote the variance of x (that is σ_1^2) by σ_{11}, the variance of y (that is σ_2^2) by σ_{22} and the covariance of x and y by σ_{12}. In the case of the bivariate normal distribution this covariance is equal to $\rho\cdot\sigma_1\cdot\sigma_2$. The random variables having the above density function will be denoted in an abbreviated form as

$$(X, Y) \sim N_2(\mu_1, \mu_2, \sigma_{11}, \sigma_{22}, \rho).$$

The marginal density function for X can be derived from the bivariate distribution $N_2(\mu_1, \mu_2, \sigma_{11}, \sigma_{22}, \rho)$ by integrating it with respect to Y, giving:

$$g(x) = \frac{1}{\sqrt{2\pi}\cdot\sigma_1} exp\left\{-\frac{1}{2}\left[\frac{x-\mu_1}{\sigma_1}\right]^2\right\},$$

(see Spanos (1986, p.88)). Hence, the marginal distribution for X is nothing more than a univariate normal distribution with parameters μ_1, σ_{11}, or in conventional notation, $X \sim N(\mu_1, \sigma_{11})$.

Tedious but not particularly complicated algebra will lead to the following density function for the conditional distribution of Y on X (see Spanos (1986, p.93)):

$$f(y|x) =$$

$$\frac{1}{\sqrt{1-\rho^2}\cdot\sqrt{2\pi}\cdot\sigma_2} exp\left\{-\frac{1}{2\cdot(1-\rho^2)\cdot\sigma_{22}}\cdot[y-\mu_2-\rho\cdot\frac{\sigma_2}{\sigma_1}\cdot(x-\mu_1)]^2\right\}$$

which is in fact a density function for a univariate normal distribution with mean equal to $\mu_2 + \rho \cdot \dfrac{\sigma_2}{\sigma_1} \cdot (x - \mu_1)$ and variance $\sigma_{22} \cdot (1 - \rho^2)$. Hence, the conditional distribution of Y on X can be denoted as:

$$Y \mid X \sim N(\mu_2 + \rho \cdot \frac{\sigma_2}{\sigma_1} \cdot (x - \mu_1) , \sigma_{22} \cdot (1 - \rho^2)) \quad .$$

This result will be used in further examples throughout this chapter.

If we are dealing with three rather than two random variables, say X, Y and Z, the joint density function can be factorized as:

$$f(x , y , z) = s(z) \cdot h(y \mid z) \cdot f(x \mid y , z) \quad ,$$

where $s(z)$ is the marginal density of z (that is, it is equal to $\iint\limits_{x\,y} f(x , y , z) dy dx$ and $h(y \mid z)$, $f(x \mid y , z)$ are conditional densities. Equation (7.3) above can be thought of as an application and generalization of this result.

Having returned to the *DGP* and its representation, it is also interesting to note that the right-hand side conditional density processes $D(x_t^* \mid X_{t-1}^* ; \theta^*)$ bear a resemblance to a *VAR* model in that all the current observations are conditional on all the information from the past. However, for exogeneity modelling this is only the beginning. The size and complexity of (7.3) is in practical cases so big that any sensible inference on it is not possible. Hence, we would like to reduce (strictly speaking, to decompose) the *DGP* by distinguishing between the *redundant (irrelevant) variables* (w_t) which can be eliminated from (7.3) without affecting its entire structure, the *variables of interest* (y_t), which are subject to our economic inference, and the *extraneous variables* (z_t) which are in some sense not conditioned upon the variables of interest. Let us partition the vector of observations x_t^* into these three sets of variables $(w_t \; y_t \; z_t)$, and analogously let us partition X_t^* into $(W_t \; Y_t \; Z_t)$ and θ^* into $(\lambda_0 \; \lambda_1 \; \lambda_2)$. The idea of such notation is that variables denoted by lower case letters $(w_t \; y_t \; z_t)$ represent *contemporaneous* values of these variables at time t, while the capital letters $(W_t \; Y_t \; Z_t)$ correspond to *all past* values of particular variables *and* the contemporaneous ones. Generally, we may represent each factor on the right-hand side of (7.3) as:

$$D(x_t^* \mid X_{t-1}^* ; \theta^*) = D_0(w_t \mid W_{t-1} , Y_t , Z_t ; \lambda_0) \cdot D_1(y_t \mid W_{t-1} , Y_{t-1} , Z_t ; \lambda_1) \cdot$$
$$D_2(z_t \mid W_{t-1} , Y_{t-1} , Z_{t-1} ; \lambda_2) \quad .$$

However, if the variables w_t are redundant or irrelevant in relation to the remaining variables, they *may* depend on Y_t and Z_t, but y_t and z_t *may not* depend on W_t. The partition between the variables y_t and z_t is such that y_t depends on its own lagged values and the contemporaneous and lagged values of z_t, while z_t may depend on its own lagged values but only on lagged and not contemporaneous values of y_t. Hence, we may write (7.3) as (see Gilbert (1986)):

$$D(x_t^* \mid X_{t-1}^* ; \theta^*) = D_0(w_t \mid W_{t-1}, Y_t, Z_t ; \lambda_0)$$
$$\cdot D_1(y_t \mid Y_{t-1}, Z_t ; \lambda_1) \cdot D_2(z_t \mid Y_{t-1}, Z_{t-1} ; \lambda_2) \quad . \tag{7.4}$$

From now on we will ignore the redundant variables. The *general to specific* modelling approach, described in Chapter 4, shows one way of eliminating redundant variables from a model. Let us say that this has already been done and we are left with n variables (that is $n^* - n$ variables have been eliminated), which constitute the vector $x_t = (y_t \, z_t)$. Analogously, there is now a matrix X_t partitioned as $(Y_t \, Z_t)$, and the factorization in (7.4) can be simplified to:

$$D(x_t \mid X_{t-1} ; \theta) = D_1(y_t \mid Y_{t-1}, Z_t ; \lambda_1) \cdot D_2(z_t \mid Y_{t-1}, Z_{t-1} ; \lambda_2) \quad , \tag{7.5}$$

where θ denotes that part of θ^* which corresponds to X_t. The factor $D_1(\bullet \mid \bullet)$ in (7.5) is called a *conditional process* while the factor $D_2(\bullet \mid \bullet)$ is called, rather imprecisely, a *marginal process*. In general, the econometrician is particularly interested in obtaining the estimates of the parameters of the conditional process $D_1(\bullet \mid \bullet)$, especially its mean and variance, rather than the estimates of the marginal process for z_t.

It has to be stressed that a *DGP* itself is *not* an econometric model. As its name implies, it describes the way the data are generated, which does not necessarily correspond to any particular economic theory. An econometric model derived on the basis of a *DGP* might correspond either to its marginal or conditional process, depending on which is consistent with an economic theory.

One of the simplest examples of a model described by conditional and marginal processes is the case of two variables, z_t and y_t, which do not depend on any extraneous information and have no dynamics (EXAMPLE 7.1). They constitute bivariate normal random variables, that is:

$$z_t = \mu_1 + \varepsilon_{1t} \quad ,$$

$$y_t = \mu_2 + \varepsilon_{2t} \quad ,$$

where
$E(\varepsilon_{1t}) = E(\varepsilon_{2t}) = 0$, $Var(\varepsilon_{1t}) = \sigma_{11}$, $Var(\varepsilon_{2t}) = \sigma_{22}$, and $Cov(\varepsilon_{1t}\,\varepsilon_{2t}) = \sigma_{12}$.
Recalling the previously given result, in this example the joint process of z_t, y_t is $N_2(\mu_1, \mu_2, \sigma_{11}, \sigma_{22}, \rho)$ where $\rho = \sigma_{12}/(\sigma_{11}\cdot\sigma_{22})^{0.5}$ and N_2 stands for a bivariate normal distribution. The marginal processes of z_t, y_t are univariate normal processes, $N(\mu_1, \sigma_{11})$ and $N(\mu_2, \sigma_{22})$ respectively. The conditional process can be either that of y_t conditional on z_t, that is:

$$y_t \mid z_t \sim N(\alpha + \beta z_t, \sigma_y) \quad,$$

where $\alpha = \mu_2 - \beta\cdot\mu_1$, $\beta = \sigma_{12}/\sigma_{11}$, $\sigma_y = \sigma_{22} - \sigma_{12}^2/\sigma_{11}$, or analogously, that of z_t conditional on y_t. Returning to the general notation, $x_t = (z_t\ y_t)$, and, assuming the variable of interest is y_t then $y_t = (y_t)$, $z_t = (z_t)$, $Y_t = (y_1\ y_2...y_t)$, $Z_t = (z_1\ z_2...z_t)$, $X_t = (Y_t\ Z_t)$ and $\theta = (\mu_1, \mu_2, \sigma_{11}, \sigma_{22}, \rho)$. Hence, the *DGP* is given by:

$$D(X_T \mid \theta) = \prod_{t=1}^{T} D(x_t \mid X_{t-1}; \theta)$$

$$= \prod_{t=1}^{T} f_1(y_t \mid z_t; \alpha, \beta, \sigma_y)\cdot f_2(z_t \mid \mu_1, \sigma_{11}) \quad,$$

where $f_i(\bullet)$, $i = 1, 2$, denotes a density function of a normal random variable.

A straightforward extension of the above example is represented by a two equation model, consisting of two simple regression equations with contemporaneously correlated errors (EXAMPLE 7.2):

$$z_t = \alpha\cdot q_{1t} + \varepsilon_{1t} \quad,$$

$$y_t = \beta\cdot q_{2t} + \varepsilon_{2t} \quad,$$

where q_{1t} and q_{2t} are nonstochastic variables, and where, as before, $E(\varepsilon_{1t}) = E(\varepsilon_{2t}) = 0$, $Var(\varepsilon_{1t}) = \sigma_{11}$, $Var(\varepsilon_{2t}) = \sigma_{22}$, and $Cov(\varepsilon_{1t}\,\varepsilon_{2t}) = \sigma_{12}$.
The analysis is virtually the same as for EXAMPLE 7.1, with the only difference being that the mean of each marginal process, for z_t and y_t, is not constant but equal to $\alpha\cdot q_{1t}$ and $\beta\cdot q_{2t}$ respectively. The joint process of z_t and y_t is $N_2(\alpha\cdot q_{1t}, \beta\cdot q_{2t}, \sigma_{11}, \sigma_{22}, \rho)$ for each t where $\rho = \sigma_{12}/(\sigma_{11}\cdot\sigma_{22})^{0.5}$. The conditional process of y_t on z_t is:

$$y_t \mid z_t \sim N(\beta\cdot q_{2t} - \gamma\cdot\alpha\cdot q_{1t} + \gamma\cdot z_t, \sigma_y) \quad,$$

where $\gamma = \sigma_{12} / \sigma_{11}$, and $\sigma_y = \sigma_{22} - \sigma_{12}^2 / \sigma_{11}$. In the general notation:
$x_t = (z_t \ y_t \ q_{1t} \ q_{2t})$, $y_t = (y_t)$, $z_t = (z_t \ q_{1t} \ q_{2t})$, $Y_t = (y_1 \ y_2 ... y_t)$,
$Z_t = (z_1 \ z_2 ... z_t)$, $X_t = (Y_t \ Z_t)$, and $\theta = (\alpha, \beta, \sigma_{11}, \sigma_{22}, \rho)$.
Here, for convenience, we are regarding the q_{it} variables as random variables rather than complicate the notation even further by introducing another set of (nonrandom) variables. The *DGP* is:

$$D(X_T \mid \theta) = \prod_{t=1}^{T} D(x_t \mid X_{t-1}; \theta)$$

$$= \prod_{t=1}^{T} f_1(y_t \mid z_t, q_{1t}, q_{2t}; \alpha, \beta, \gamma, \sigma_y) \cdot f_2(z_t, q_{1t}, q_{2t} \mid \alpha, \sigma_{11}) \ .$$

To stress the generality of exogeneity modelling, we will show that the 'orthogonalization' of a *VAR* model, as discussed in Chapter 6, can also be regarded as a case of conditioning and marginalization of a *DGP*. For EXAMPLE 7.3, consider a two dimensional *VAR* model with two lags and contemporaneously correlated error terms, that is:

$$\begin{bmatrix} z_t \\ y_t \end{bmatrix} = \begin{bmatrix} a_1 & b_1 \\ c_1 & d_1 \end{bmatrix} \begin{bmatrix} z_{t-1} \\ y_{t-1} \end{bmatrix} + \begin{bmatrix} a_2 & b_2 \\ c_2 & d_2 \end{bmatrix} \begin{bmatrix} z_{t-2} \\ y_{t-2} \end{bmatrix} + \begin{bmatrix} \varepsilon_{1t} \\ \varepsilon_{2t} \end{bmatrix} ,$$

where
$E(\varepsilon_{1t}) = E(\varepsilon_{2t}) = 0$, $Var(\varepsilon_{1t}) = \sigma_{11}$, $Var(\varepsilon_{2t}) = \sigma_{22}$ and $Cov(\varepsilon_{1t} \ \varepsilon_{2t}) = \sigma_{12}$.
In order to develop a conditional process of y_t on z_t we may condition y_t on z_t, that is we multiply the first row of the above matrix by $\delta = \sigma_{12} / \sigma_{11}$ and subtract the result from the second row. As shown in Chapter 6, the result is:

$$\begin{bmatrix} z_t \\ y_t - \delta z_t \end{bmatrix} = \begin{bmatrix} a_1 & b_1 \\ c_1^* & d_1^* \end{bmatrix} \begin{bmatrix} z_{t-1} \\ y_{t-1} \end{bmatrix} + \begin{bmatrix} a_2 & b_2 \\ c_2^* & d_2^* \end{bmatrix} \begin{bmatrix} z_{t-2} \\ y_{t-2} \end{bmatrix} + \begin{bmatrix} \varepsilon_{1t} \\ \varepsilon_{2t}^* \end{bmatrix} ,$$

where $c_i^* = (c_i - \delta a_i)$; $d_i^* = (d_i - \delta b_i)$; $\varepsilon_{2t}^* = (\varepsilon_{2t} - \delta \varepsilon_{1t})$; $i = 1, 2$.
Note that the expression for z_t does not involve the current value of y_t. In addition, there is no contemporaneous correlation between the error terms in this 'orthogonalized' form of the equations.
Hence, the factorization of the *DGP* is given by:

$$D(X_T \mid \theta) = \prod_{t=1}^{T} D(x_t \mid X_{t-1} ; \theta)$$

$$= \prod_{t=1}^{T} f_1(y_t \mid z_t , z_{t-1} , y_{t-1} , z_{t-2} , y_{t-2} ; c_1^* , c_2^* , d_1^* , d_2^* , \delta)$$

$$\cdot f_2(z_t \mid z_{t-1} , y_{t-1} , z_{t-2} , y_{t-2} ; a_1 , a_2 , b_1 , b_2 , \sigma_{11}) \quad .$$

In EXAMPLES 7.1 and 7.2 we have shown that simple statistical bivariate models can be represented by a *DGP*. EXAMPLE 7.3 illustrated the factorization of a *VAR* model. Finally in this section, we will present an example (EXAMPLE 7.4) of a typical structural (Cowles-Commission type) model, often used to illustrate the so-called 'cobweb effect' in economic dynamics:

$$y_t = \alpha \cdot z_t + \varepsilon_{1t} \quad , \tag{7.6a}$$

$$z_t = \beta \cdot y_{t-1} + \varepsilon_{2t} \quad , \tag{7.6b}$$

where, as before, it is assumed that $\varepsilon_{1t} , \varepsilon_{2t}$ constitute a bivariate normal error process with $E(\varepsilon_{1t}) = E(\varepsilon_{2t}) = 0$, $Var(\varepsilon_{1t}) = \sigma_{11}$, $Var(\varepsilon_{2t}) = \sigma_{22}$, and $Cov(\varepsilon_{1t} \varepsilon_{2t}) = \sigma_{12}$. The marginal process of z_t is defined by (7.6b), being $N(\beta \cdot y_{t-1} , \sigma_{22})$, while the marginal process for y_t is a derived 'reduced form' equation for y_t, that is a process for an equation derived from (7.6a) after the substitution for z_t from (7.6b):

$$y_t = \alpha \cdot \beta \cdot y_{t-1} + v_t \quad , \tag{7.7}$$

where $v_t = \varepsilon_{1t} + \alpha \cdot \varepsilon_{2t}$. The expected value of v_t is zero and its variance is equal to $E(\varepsilon_{1t} + \alpha \cdot \varepsilon_{2t})^2 = \sigma_{11} + 2\alpha \cdot \sigma_{12} + \alpha^2 \sigma_{22}$, since $E(\varepsilon_{1t} \cdot \varepsilon_{2t}) = \sigma_{12}$. Hence, the covariance between the error terms of the marginal distributions, that is between v_t and ε_{2t}, is equal to $\sigma_{12} + \alpha \cdot \sigma_{22}$. By analogy to the previous examples, the conditional process of y_t on z_t can be derived from (7.7) and (7.6b) by defining $\delta = Cov(v_t \varepsilon_{2t}) / \sigma_{22} = \sigma_{12} / \sigma_{22} + \alpha$, multiplying (7.6b) by δ and subtracting the result from (7.7). This gives:

$$y_t = \delta \cdot z_t - (\sigma_{12} / \sigma_{22}) \cdot \beta \cdot y_{t-1} + u_t \quad , \tag{7.8}$$

where $u_t = \varepsilon_{1t} - (\sigma_{12} / \sigma_{22}) \cdot \varepsilon_{2t}$. The variance of u_t (say σ^2) is equal to $\sigma_{11} - (\sigma_{12}^2 / \sigma_{22})$. In fact (7.8) can be regarded as a regression equation:

$$y_t = a \cdot z_t + b \cdot y_{t-1} + u_t \quad , \tag{7.9}$$

where $a = (\alpha + \sigma_{12} / \sigma_{22})$ and $b = -(\sigma_{12} / \sigma_{22}) \cdot \beta$. It is easy to check that the error terms in the conditional equation (7.9) and the marginal equation (7.6b), that is u_t and ε_{2t}, are orthogonal. Finally, the *DGP* for (7.6a - 7.6b) can be written as:

$$
D(X_T \mid \theta) = \prod_{t=1}^{T} D(x_t \mid X_{t-1} ; \theta)
$$

$$
= \prod_{t=1}^{T} f_1(y_t \mid y_{t-1}, z_t ; a, b, \sigma^2) \cdot f_2(z_t \mid y_{t-1} ; \beta, \sigma_{22}) \quad .
$$

7.2 Weak and Strong Exogeneity

The arguments and examples in the previous section illustrate the idea of the division of the variables between those for which the conditioning is made (that is those which constitute the set y_t) and those for which the marginal processes are evaluated (that is z_t). This is connected with the much wider question of what are really the dependent and independent parts of the model.

Structural (Cowles Commission) econometrics distinguishes between the *endogenous* and *exogenous* variables of an econometric model. Generally, but not very precisely, the endogenous variables are those which are explained by the structure of the model and all the remaining variables are the exogenous variables. In so-called *full* econometric models (nearly all known structural econometric models are full) the number of endogenous variables is equal to the number of equations. As an illustration, recall the two structural models discussed in Chapter 6. The first one is a simple Keynesian model:

$$
C_t = \alpha + \beta Y_t + \varepsilon_t \quad ,
$$

$$
Y_t = C_t + I_t \quad ,
$$

where C_t is the level of consumption, Y_t is aggregate income, I_t is the level of investment, ε_t is an error term, and α and β are coefficients. In Chapter 6 it was postulated that the variables C_t and Y_t are endogenous and I_t exogenous. Since this model does not contain any lagged variables, the endogenous variables are also *jointly dependent* and the exogenous variable is *predetermined*. For estimation purposes, it is necessary to assume that the exogenous variable is not correlated with current (and indeed lagged) error terms.

The second example given in Chapter 6 is a supply-demand equilibrium model:

$$Q_t = \alpha_0 + \alpha_1 P_t + \alpha_2 r_t + u_{1t} \quad ,$$

$$Q_t = \beta_0 + \beta_1 P_t + \beta_2 P_{t-1} + u_{2t} \quad ,$$

where Q_t denotes the quantity transacted, P_t is the price, r_t is the interest rate and u_{1t}, u_{2t} are the error terms, assumed to be mutually and serially independent. In the above model the *current* endogenous variables are Q_t and P_t, which are also *jointly dependent*. P_{t-1} is the *lagged* endogenous variable which, together with r_t (the exogenous variable) creates the set of *predetermined* variables.

The above distinction between endogenous and exogenous variables is not sufficient for all purposes. For model estimation, some of the endogenous variables sometimes have to be treated more akin to exogenous rather than to endogenous variables. For instance, in the model discussed as EXAMPLE 7.4 in the previous section of this chapter, that is in:

$$y_t = \alpha \cdot z_t + \varepsilon_{1t} \quad , \tag{7.6a}$$

$$z_t = \beta \cdot y_{t-1} + \varepsilon_{2t} \quad , \tag{7.6b}$$

z_t and y_t are regarded as the jointly dependent or non-lagged endogenous variables, no matter whether the covariance of the error terms is zero or not. However, if the error terms are not contemporaneously correlated, the first of these equations can be consistently estimated by the ordinary least squares method, since z_t is not correlated with ε_{1t}. However, if ε_{1t} and ε_{2t} are contemporaneously correlated, z_t becomes correlated with ε_{1t} and ordinary least squares estimates of the equation for y_t are not consistent. Hence, the 'jointly dependent' variable z_t may be treated in the first case as an exogenous variable, and in the second case as an endogenous variable.

Further confusion arises when the model in EXAMPLE 7.4 is to be used for a dynamic enquiry (that is forecasting) for y_t. To make the example more interesting let us add an autoregressive process to the formation of z_t, so that the model becomes:

$$y_t = \alpha \cdot z_t + \varepsilon_{1t} \quad , \tag{7.10a}$$

$$z_t = \beta \cdot y_{t-1} + \gamma \cdot z_{t-1} + \varepsilon_{2t} \quad , \tag{7.10b}$$

Suppose, to keep things simple, that the error terms are neither serially nor contemporaneously correlated. If $\beta = 0$, the forecast values of y_t are simply conditional upon the set of observations for z_t. If $\beta \neq 0$, forecast values for y_t cannot be evaluated so straightforwardly from z_t since z_t depends on the lagged value of y_t and consequently, on the lagged ε_{1t}. Hence, despite the fact that y_t and z_t are formally endogenous, they have been treated differently, depending whether $\beta = 0$ or not.

Some of the problems encountered above may be dealt with by using the concepts of *predeterminedness* and *strict exogeneity*. It is said that a variable is predetermined in an equation of interest if it is independent of the *current* and *future* errors of that equation, while it is strictly exogenous if it is independent of the current, future and *past* errors of that equation. According to this, in model (7.10a) and (7.10b) the variable z_t is predetermined in equation (7.10a) if $\beta \neq 0$ (since it does depend on ε_{1t-1} through y_{t-1}) and is strictly endogenous if $\beta = 0$ since then it does not depend on the lagged errors of the equation (7.10a).

Although the concepts of predeterminedness and strict exogeneity are more precise than the traditional division of variables into endogenous and exogenous, it is still not precise enough to deal with all the potential ambiguities in defining econometric variables. In particular, it does not explicitly describe, *for what* an examining variable is to be exogenous. It can be easily shown that one's view of a variable can alter drastically, depending on which parameters of a model are of interest. (For a discussion of the concept of *parameters of interest* see Spanos (1986, pp. 418-421)). Returning to EXAMPLE 7.4 above (and retaining for the time being, the assumption that the error terms are independent), it is clear that if interest is in the estimation of the parameters of (7.6b), the role of the variable y_t is completely different from the case where interest is in the estimation of the parameters of (7.6a). This point may be exemplified by a problem posed by Pratt and Schlaifer (1984), which has subsequently been widely discussed in the literature. The model presented in this example is:

$$y_t = b \cdot z_t + u_t \quad ,$$

where $E(u_t \mid z_t) = 0$. Evidently, if this is a full model, z_t meets any of the criteria of exogeneity given above. However, suppose that the same model is rewritten as:

$$y_t = b^* \cdot z_t + u_t^* \quad ,$$

where $b^* = b + 1$ and $u_t^* = u_t - z_t$. Now the question of exogeneity of z_t looks much more complicated, since $E(u_t^* \mid z_t) \neq 0$. The problem becomes clearer if we decide whether our parameter of interest is b or b^*. If it is b, z_t is indeed exogenous (in the light of all the above definitions of exogeneity), but if the parameter of interest is b^*, z_t is not exogenous.

The idea of defining exogeneity for a given set of parameters of interest is central for the concepts of exogeneity proposed by Engle, Hendry and Richard (1983). They consider the following distinctions:

1. Between the variables which contain all necessary information for efficient estimation (static inference) of the parameters of interest conditionally on the values of these variables, and the remaining variables;

2. Between the variables whose values have to be known (be observed) in order to make a dynamic inference (forecast) from the estimated model using the parameters of interest, and those whose values may not be known;

3. Between the variables which do not alter the parameters of interest in a policy analysis experiment, and those which do.

The first of these divisions is connected with the concept of *weak exogeneity*, the second one with that of *strong exogeneity*, and the third with *super-exogeneity*. In this section we will discuss the first two of these concepts. Superexogeneity will be discussed in Section 7.3 below.

The concept of weak exogeneity is related to the problem of static inference in an econometric model, that is estimation. Generally, a variable z_t can be regarded as weakly exogenous for a set of parameters of interest, say ψ, if the marginal process for z_t contains no useful information for the estimation of ψ, that is if an inference for ψ can be efficiently made conditionally on z_t alone and its marginal process contains no relevant information. The concept can also be formulated in reverse. That is, z_t is weakly exogenous for the parameters of interest ψ, if knowledge of ψ is not required for inference on the marginal process of z_t (see Spanos (1986, pp. 376 and 421-422).

A slightly simplified (and therefore not entirely precise, but nevertheless sufficient for most practical purposes) definition of weak exogeneity is the following. The variable z_t is said to be weakly exogenous for ψ (the parameters of interest) if it is possible to write the *DGP* in terms of conditional and marginal processes as in (7.5), that is:

$$D(x_t \mid X_{t-1}; \theta) = D_1(y_t \mid Y_{t-1}, Z_t; \lambda_1) \cdot D_2(z_t \mid Y_{t-1}, Z_{t-1}; \lambda_2) \quad ,$$

and if:

1. ψ is a function of the parameters of the conditional process λ_1 alone (note that λ_1 itself *can* be a function of the parameters of the marginal process, that is of λ_2);

2. λ_1 and λ_2 are *variation free*, which means that, in particular, there cannot be any cross-restrictions between λ_1 and λ_2. In this case it

is still possible for λ_1 to be a function of λ_2 whilst λ_2 is not a function of λ_1.

Let us examine the existence of weak exogeneity for particular sets of parameters in the examples of *DGP*s introduced in Section 7.1. EXAMPLE 7.1 analyses the bivariate normal process:

$$z_t = \mu_1 + \varepsilon_{1t} \quad ,$$

$$y_t = \mu_2 + \varepsilon_{2t} \quad ,$$

where

$E(\varepsilon_{1t}) = E(\varepsilon_{2t}) = 0$, $Var(\varepsilon_{1t}) = \sigma_{11}$, $Var(\varepsilon_{2t}) = \sigma_{22}$, and $Cov(\varepsilon_{1t}\,\varepsilon_{2t}) = \sigma_{12}$.

The conditional process of y_t on z_t is:

$$y_t \,|\, z_t \sim N(\alpha + \beta z_t \,, \sigma_y) \quad ,$$

where $\alpha = \mu_2 - \beta \cdot \mu_1$, $\beta = \sigma_{12} / \sigma_{11}$, and $\sigma_y = \sigma_{22} - \sigma_{12}^2 / \sigma_{11}$. The *DGP* is given by:

$$D(X_T \,|\, \theta) = \prod_{t=1}^{T} D(x_t \,|\, X_{t-1} \,; \theta)$$

$$= \prod_{t=1}^{T} f_1(y_t \,|\, z_t \,; \alpha\,, \beta\,, \sigma_y) \cdot f_2(z_t \,|\, \mu_1\,, \sigma_{11}) \quad .$$

Let us say that the parameters of interest are those of the conditional process, so that $\psi = \lambda_1 = (\alpha\,, \beta\,, \sigma_y)$. Although the parameters in λ_1 are functions of the parameters $\lambda_2 = (\mu_1\,, \sigma_{11})$ in the marginal process, the parameters in λ_2 are not functions of those in λ_1, and there are no cross-restrictions between λ_1 and λ_2. Hence, z_t is weakly exogenous for $(\alpha\,, \beta\,, \sigma_y)$. In other words, the econometric model:

$$y_t = \alpha + \beta \cdot z_t + u_t \quad ,$$

can be sensibly derived from the *DGP* and consistently estimated, without any need for further inference concerning z_t. Note that formally the above equation is a part of a two equation model, since it should be accompanied by:

$$z_t = \mu_1 + \varepsilon_{1t} \quad .$$

EXAMPLE 7.2 is very similar to the above. The difference is that means of the processes are not constant and are functions of external variables q_{1t} and q_{2t} :

$$z_t = \alpha \cdot q_{1t} + \varepsilon_{1t} \quad,$$

$$y_t = \beta \cdot q_{2t} + \varepsilon_{2t} \quad,$$

where
$E(\varepsilon_{1t}) = E(\varepsilon_{2t}) = 0$, $Var(\varepsilon_{1t}) = \sigma_{11}$, $Var(\varepsilon_{2t}) = \sigma_{22}$, and $Cov(\varepsilon_{1t} \, \varepsilon_{2t}) = \sigma_{12}$.
The conditional process of y_t on z_t is:

$$y_t \mid z_t \sim N(a \cdot q_{1t} + b \cdot q_{2t} + c \cdot z_t , \sigma_y) \quad,$$

where $b = \beta$, $a = -(\sigma_{12} / \sigma_{22}) \cdot \alpha$, $c = \sigma_{12} / \sigma_{11}$, $\sigma_y = (\sigma_{22} - \sigma_{12}^2 / \sigma_{11})$ and
the *DGP* is:

$$D(X_t \mid \theta) = \prod_{t=1}^{T} D(x_t \mid X_{t-1} ; \theta)$$

$$= \prod_{t=1}^{T} f_1(y_t \mid z_t , q_{1t} , q_{2t} ; a , b , c , \sigma_y) \cdot f_2(z_t , q_{1t} , q_{2t} \mid \alpha , \sigma_{11}) \quad.$$

If the parameters of interest are (a , b , c , σ_y), then z_t is weakly exogenous for them, since there are no cross-restrictions between (a , b , c , σ_y) and (α , σ_{11}). Hence, the suggested econometric model is:

$$y_t = a \cdot q_{1t} + b \cdot q_{2t} + c \cdot z_t + u_t \quad,$$

$$z_t = \alpha \cdot q_{1t} + \varepsilon_{1t} \quad.$$

The problem of weak exogeneity becomes more complicated in the two remaining examples. In EXAMPLE 7.3 the *DGP* is a straightforward *VAR* process:

$$\begin{bmatrix} z_t \\ y_t \end{bmatrix} = \begin{bmatrix} a_1 & b_1 \\ c_1 & d_1 \end{bmatrix} \begin{bmatrix} z_{t-1} \\ y_{t-1} \end{bmatrix} + \begin{bmatrix} a_2 & b_2 \\ c_2 & d_2 \end{bmatrix} \begin{bmatrix} z_{t-2} \\ y_{t-2} \end{bmatrix} + \begin{bmatrix} \varepsilon_{1t} \\ \varepsilon_{2t} \end{bmatrix} \quad, \tag{7.11}$$

where
$E(\varepsilon_{1t}) = E(\varepsilon_{2t}) = 0$, $Var(\varepsilon_{1t}) = \sigma_{11}$, $Var(\varepsilon_{2t}) = \sigma_{22}$, and $Cov(\varepsilon_{1t} \, \varepsilon_{2t}) = \sigma_{12}$.
The conditional process of y_t on z_t together with the marginal process of z_t is:

$$\begin{bmatrix} z_t \\ y_t - \delta z_t \end{bmatrix} = \begin{bmatrix} a_1 & b_1 \\ c_1^* & d_1^* \end{bmatrix} \begin{bmatrix} z_{t-1} \\ y_{t-1} \end{bmatrix} + \begin{bmatrix} a_2 & b_2 \\ c_2^* & d_2^* \end{bmatrix} \begin{bmatrix} z_{t-2} \\ y_{t-2} \end{bmatrix} + \begin{bmatrix} \varepsilon_{1t} \\ \varepsilon_{2t}^* \end{bmatrix} \quad,$$

where

$$c_i^* = (c_i - \delta a_i) \, ; \, d_i^* = (d_i - \delta b_i) \, ; \, \varepsilon_{2t}^* = (\varepsilon_{2t} - \delta \varepsilon_{1t}) \, ; \, \delta = \sigma_{12} / \sigma_{11} \, ; \, i = 1, 2.$$

After reading EXAMPLES 7.1 and 7.2 it should be easy to check that z_t is weakly exogenous for the parameters of the conditional process of y_t on z_t, that is for c_i^* and d_i^* ($i = 1, 2$). Suppose, however, that interest is in a short run model for y_t with a cointegrated error correction mechanism developed from a *VAR*. Recalling the general results from Chapter 6, for a *VAR* model:

$$\xi_t = \sum_{i=1}^{k} A_i \xi_{t-1} + \epsilon_t \; ,$$

where ξ_t contains all n variables of the model and ϵ_t is a vector of random errors, the Johansen decomposition is:

$$\Delta\xi_t = \sum_{i=1}^{k-1} \Gamma_i \Delta\xi_{t-i} + \Pi \cdot \xi_{t-k} + \epsilon_t \; ,$$

where:
$$\Gamma_i = -I + A_1 + ...+A_i \quad (I \text{ is a unit matrix})$$
$$\Pi = -(I - A_1 - ....-A_k) \quad .$$

If there are r cointegrating vectors, the above equation can be rewritten as:

$$\Delta\xi_t = \sum_{i=1}^{k-1} \Gamma_i \Delta\xi_{t-i} + \alpha \cdot \beta' \cdot \xi_{t-k} + \epsilon_t \; ,$$

where β is a $n \times r$ matrix of cointegrating vectors and α is a $n \times r$ matrix of adjustment coefficients. The two dimensional *VAR* process with $k = 2$ given by (7.11) may be rewritten as:

$$\begin{bmatrix} \Delta z_t \\ \Delta y_t \end{bmatrix} = \begin{bmatrix} \bar{a}_1 & b_1 \\ c_1 & \bar{d}_1 \end{bmatrix} \begin{bmatrix} \Delta z_{t-1} \\ \Delta y_{t-1} \end{bmatrix} + \begin{bmatrix} \bar{a}_2 & \bar{b}_2 \\ \bar{c}_2 & \bar{d}_2 \end{bmatrix} \begin{bmatrix} z_{t-2} \\ y_{t-2} \end{bmatrix} + \begin{bmatrix} \varepsilon_{1t} \\ \varepsilon_{2t} \end{bmatrix} \; , \tag{7.12}$$

where:
$$\bar{a}_1 = a_1 - 1, \; \bar{d}_1 = d_1 - 1, \; \bar{a}_2 = a_1 + a_2 - 1, \; \bar{b}_2 = b_1 + b_2 \; ,$$
$$\bar{c}_2 = c_1 + c_2 \; , \; \bar{d}_2 = d_1 + d_2 - 1 \quad .$$

Suppose now that there is a cointegrating vector in the *VAR* (as may be recalled from Chapter 6, in a two dimensional *VAR* there cannot be more than one cointegrating vector), $\beta' = \begin{bmatrix} \beta_1 & \beta_2 \end{bmatrix}$, and a corresponding vector of adjustment coefficients $\alpha' = \begin{bmatrix} \alpha_1 & \alpha_2 \end{bmatrix}$, so that the elements of matrix $\Pi = \alpha \cdot \beta'$ become:

$$\bar{a}_2 = \alpha_1 \cdot \beta_1, \quad \bar{b}_2 = \alpha_1 \cdot \beta_2,$$
$$\bar{c}_2 = \alpha_2 \cdot \beta_1, \quad \bar{d}_2 = \alpha_2 \cdot \beta_2.$$

If we derive a conditional process for Δy_t on Δz_t (by multiplying the first equation by $\delta = \sigma_{12}/\sigma_{11}$ and subtracting the result from the second equation) the marginal process for Δz_t and the conditional process for Δy_t given Δz_t are:

$$\begin{bmatrix} \Delta z_t \\ \Delta y_t - \delta \Delta z_t \end{bmatrix} = \begin{bmatrix} \bar{a}_1 & b_1 \\ \bar{c}_1^* & \bar{d}_1^* \end{bmatrix} \begin{bmatrix} \Delta z_{t-1} \\ \Delta y_{t-1} \end{bmatrix} + \begin{bmatrix} \bar{a}_2 & \bar{b}_2 \\ \bar{c}_2^* & \bar{d}_2^* \end{bmatrix} \begin{bmatrix} z_{t-2} \\ y_{t-2} \end{bmatrix} + \begin{bmatrix} \varepsilon_{1t} \\ \varepsilon_{2t}^* \end{bmatrix},$$

where

$$\bar{c}_1^* = c_1 - \delta \cdot \bar{a}_1, \quad \bar{d}_1^* = \bar{d}_1 - \delta \cdot b_1, \quad \bar{c}_2^* = \bar{c}_2 - \delta \cdot \bar{a}_2,$$
$$\bar{d}_2^* = \bar{d}_2 - \delta \cdot \bar{b}_2, \quad \text{and } \varepsilon_{2t}^* = (\varepsilon_{2t} - \delta \cdot \varepsilon_{1t}).$$

As before, ε_{1t} and ε_{2t}^* are orthogonal, so that their covariance is zero. This does not mean, however, that z_t is weakly exogenous if the parameters of interest are those of the conditional process of Δy_t. The parameters of the conditional process are $\bar{c}_1^*, \bar{d}_1^*, \bar{c}_2^*$, and $\bar{d}_2^*$, and those of the marginal process are $\bar{a}_1, b_1, \bar{a}_2$ and $\bar{b}_2$. If there is one cointegrating vector in the process, it is clear that the parameters of the conditional and marginal processes are not variation free. Specifically:

$$\bar{a}_2 = \alpha_1 \cdot \beta_1; \quad \bar{c}_2^* = \alpha_2 \cdot \beta_1 - \delta \cdot \alpha_1 \cdot \beta_1,$$
$$\bar{b}_2 = \alpha_1 \cdot \beta_2; \quad \bar{d}_2^* = \alpha_2 \cdot \beta_2 - \delta \cdot \alpha_1 \cdot \beta_2.$$

Hence, there are two cross-restrictions between the parameters of the marginal and conditional distributions. It is not possible to alter the cointegrating coefficients β_1 and β_2 and the adjustment coefficient α_1 without affecting the coefficients of the marginal process. Only α_2 can be changed freely, since it does not enter the marginal process. It is important to note that z_t becomes weakly exogenous for $\delta, \bar{c}_1^*, \bar{d}_1^*, \bar{c}_2^*$, and $\bar{d}_2^*$ if $\alpha_1 = 0$ since in that case there are no cross-restrictions between the parameters of the marginal and conditional distributions.

There is some simple intuition behind the above example. There are two equations and only one error correction mechanism. If this mechanism enters both equations simultaneously, it is not possible to enquire about one of the equations separately from the other. The only possibility of separate inference is when one of the adjustment coefficients is equal to zero, so that the error correction mechanism enters only one of the equations. This exogeneity analysis in an error correction model is derived from the more general approach of Urbain (1991); a similar problem is briefly discussed by Hendry, Muellbauer and Murphy (1990).

EXAMPLE 7.4 analyses a *DGP* which corresponds to a cobweb model:

$$y_t = \alpha \cdot z_t + \varepsilon_{1t} \quad , \tag{7.6a}$$

$$z_t = \beta \cdot y_{t-1} + \varepsilon_{2t} \quad , \tag{7.6b}$$

where
$E(\varepsilon_{1t}) = E(\varepsilon_{2t}) = 0$, $Var(\varepsilon_{1t}) = \sigma_{11}$, $Var(\varepsilon_{2t}) = \sigma_{22}$, and $Cov(\varepsilon_{1t} \, \varepsilon_{2t}) = \sigma_{12}$.
The reduced form equation (marginal process) for y_t is:

$$y_t = \alpha \cdot \beta \cdot y_{t-1} + v_t \quad , \tag{7.7}$$

where
$v_t = \varepsilon_{1t} + \alpha \cdot \varepsilon_{2t}$, $Var(v_t) = E(\varepsilon_{1t} + \alpha \cdot \varepsilon_{2t})^2 = \sigma_{11} + 2\alpha \cdot \sigma_{12} + \alpha^2 \sigma_{22}$, and $Cov(v_t \, \varepsilon_{2t}) = \sigma_{12} + \alpha \cdot \sigma_{22}$. These results have been derived in Section 7.1 above, where it was also shown that the conditional process of y_t on z_t is:

$$y_t = \delta \cdot z_t - (\sigma_{12} / \sigma_{22}) \cdot \beta \cdot y_{t-1} + u_t \quad , \tag{7.8}$$

where $\delta = Cov(v_t \, \varepsilon_{2t}) / \sigma_{22} = (\sigma_{12} / \sigma_{22}) + \alpha$, $u_t = \varepsilon_{1t} - (\sigma_{12} / \sigma_{22}) \cdot \varepsilon_{2t}$
and $Var(u_t) = \sigma_{11} - (\sigma_{12}^2 / \sigma_{22}) = \sigma^2$, or:

$$y_t = a \cdot z_t + b \cdot y_{t-1} + u_t \quad , \tag{7.9}$$

where $a = \alpha + (\sigma_{12} / \sigma_{22})$ and $b = -(\sigma_{12} / \sigma_{22}) \cdot \beta$.

Suppose that the parameter of interest is the regression coefficient on z_t in equation (7.6a), that is α. The parameters of the conditional process of y_t on z_t are (a, b, σ^2) and those of the marginal process for z_t are (β, σ_{22}). It is not possible to recover α solely from the parameters of the conditional process since:

$$\alpha = a - (\sigma_{12} / \sigma_{22}) \quad ,$$

that is, additional knowledge on the parameter σ_{22} of the marginal process is required. We may relate this result to our earlier definition of weak exogeneity since the marginal process of z_t contains relevant information for the estimation of the parameter of interest. Hence, z_t is not weakly exogenous for the parameter of interest α. The condition for z_t to become weakly exogenous for α is that the covariance between ε_{1t} and ε_{2t} is zero. If

$\sigma_{12} = 0$, then $\alpha = a$ and no knowledge on the marginal process is needed for an enquiry concerning α.

The above examples suggest that testing for weak exogeneity is, in many cases, equivalent to testing for zero covariance of the error terms. In EXAMPLE 7.2 the *DGP* is:

$$z_t = \alpha \cdot q_{1t} + \varepsilon_{1t} \quad ,$$

$$y_t = \beta \cdot q_{2t} + \varepsilon_{2t} \quad ,$$

where
$E(\varepsilon_{1t}) = E(\varepsilon_{2t}) = 0$, $Var(\varepsilon_{1t}) = \sigma_{11}$, $Var(\varepsilon_{2t}) = \sigma_{22}$, and $Cov(\varepsilon_{1t}\,\varepsilon_{2t}) = \sigma_{12}$. If the null that $\sigma_{12} = 0$ is rejected, the next step is to move to a model where one of the variables is conditioned upon the other, for example to:

$$y_t = a \cdot q_{1t} + b \cdot q_{2t} + c \cdot z_t + u_t \quad ,$$

$$z_t = \alpha \cdot q_{1t} + \varepsilon_{1t} \quad .$$

However, we still do not know whether the above equations constitute a *DGP* (and hence the covariance between u_t and ε_{1t} is nonzero) or a marginal process for z_t and a conditional process for y_t (in this case the covariance between u_t and ε_{1t} is zero). A straightforward generalization of EXAMPLE 7.4 shows that if $Cov(u_t\,\varepsilon_{1t}) \neq 0$, z_t is not weakly exogenous for a, b and c. Hence the hypothesis of zero covariance between u_t and ε_{1t} has to be tested.

Technically, testing for zero covariance can be performed by the use of the Lagrange Multiplier test once again. We simply estimate the equation we think represents the marginal process by the method of ordinary least squares, compute the residuals and test these residuals as a missing variable in what we think is the conditional process. Since there is only one 'variable' (that is, the computed residuals) added to the regression, the traditional Student-t significance test is equivalent to the Lagrange Multiplier test. Such a procedure for testing weak exogeneity was originally suggested by Engle (1984, pp. 815-816).

EXAMPLE 7.3 shows, however, that in some cases the problem of weak exogeneity is more complex than this. If our interest is in the parameters of a short run equation with an error correction mechanism, it is essential that the marginal processes for the variables which appear in this short run equation do not contain the same error correction mechanism. If the equation for y_t is, for instance, a simple model with an error correction mechanism of the form introduced in Chapter 3, namely:

$$\Delta y_t = \alpha_1 \Delta z_t + \alpha_2 (y_{t-1} - \beta \cdot z_{t-1}) + \varepsilon_{1t} \quad ,$$

it is important in order for z_t to be weakly exogenous for the parameters in this equation that an equation explaining z_t (*i*) has its errors uncorrelated with ε_{1t} and (*ii*) does not contain the term $(y_{t-1} - \beta \cdot z_{t-1})$. If β is not specified *a priori*, it may be taken as having been estimated by the Engle-Granger (Chapter 5) or Johansen (Chapter 6) method. In any case, the testing procedure is more complex and consists firstly of testing (*ii*) in an equation for z_t, that is by an ordinary Student-*t* test. If the hypothesis of a zero regression coefficient for $(y_{t-1} - \beta \cdot z_{t-1})$ in the equation for z_t cannot be rejected, then the residuals of the equation for z_t with this term omitted may be computed and their significance in the equation for y_t may be tested. In the general case, the error correction terms may appear in the marginal model with various lags ($t-1, t-2$, and so on) so that the first stage in the testing procedure would be a joint test on the coefficients of the lagged error correction variables.

While the concept of weak exogeneity is primarily of a static nature, in that it deals with problems of static enquiry in a model (particularly estimation), the concept of *strong exogeneity* widens the issue by adding a dynamic aspect to it. Thus in forecasting, in order to avoid any feedback problems between the endogenous variables to be forecast and an 'exogenous' variable z_t, it would be necessary for the variable z_t not to be influenced by either the contemporaneous value of the endogenous variables or by the past or lagged values of these variables. Thus in EXAMPLE 7.4 above, forecast values of y_t outside of the sample period cannot be made conditionally on the values of z_t for these forecast periods, as these values of z_t will themselves depend upon lagged forecast values of y_t. Returning to our general notation, z_t should not be influenced either by the parameters of the conditional distribution of an endogenous variable y_t, or by the past values, y_{t-1}, y_{t-2}, etc. In other words, in this case, z_t is both weakly exogenous and is not preceded by any of the endogenous variables in the model. This suggests the following definition of strong exogeneity (see Engle, Hendry and Richard (1983) or Spanos (1986, p.505)):

Definition: A vector of variables z_t is strongly exogenous with respect to y_t for the parameters of interest ψ if:

1. z_t is weakly exogenous for ψ;
2. Y_{t-1} is not a Granger cause for z_t.

The definition of Granger causality as given in Section 6.4 states that y is a Granger cause for z if z_t can be predicted better with the use of information on past y (Y_{t-1}) rather than by not doing so, other information being identical. As a consequence, the Granger test for causality consists of testing that the coefficients of all lagged y_ts in equations explaining z_t are jointly zero.

Returning to the factorization of a *DGP* as (7.5):

$$D(x_t \mid X_{t-1} ; \theta) = D_1(y_t \mid Y_{t-1}, Z_t ; \lambda_1) \cdot D_2(z_t \mid Y_{t-1}, Z_{t-1} ; \lambda_2) \ ,$$

z_t is strongly exogenous with respect to y_t for the parameters of interest ψ if:

a) ψ is a function of λ_1 and not of λ_2,

b) λ_1 and λ_2 are variation free,

c) $D_2(z_t \mid Y_{t-1}, Z_{t-1} ; \lambda_2) = D_2(z_t \mid Z_{t-1} ; \lambda_2)$; that is Y_{t-1} is excluded from the set of variables explaining z_t.

Conditions a) and b) are those of weak exogeneity and condition c) defines Granger noncausality of y_t for z_t.

In EXAMPLES 7.1 and 7.2, the distinction between weak and strong exogeneity is irrelevant, since the processes are static. Granger causality does not appear and what is weakly exogenous is, at the same time, strongly exogenous. In EXAMPLE 7.3 when considering the exogeneity of z_t with respect to y_t with the parameters of interest being those of the conditional distribution, $\delta, c_1, c_2, d_1, d_2$ in:

$$\begin{bmatrix} z_t \\ y_t - \delta z_t \end{bmatrix} = \begin{bmatrix} a_1 & b_1 \\ c_1^* & d_1^* \end{bmatrix} \begin{bmatrix} z_{t-1} \\ y_{t-1} \end{bmatrix} + \begin{bmatrix} a_2 & b_2 \\ c_2^* & d_2^* \end{bmatrix} \begin{bmatrix} z_{t-2} \\ y_{t-2} \end{bmatrix} + \begin{bmatrix} \varepsilon_{1t} \\ \varepsilon_{2t}^* \end{bmatrix} \ ,$$

weak exogeneity requires that $Cov(\varepsilon_{1t} \varepsilon_{2t}^*) = 0$ and strong exogeneity requires, additionally, that $b_1 = b_2 = 0$, so that y_t does not Granger cause z_t.

In EXAMPLE 7.4 , that is for the model

$$y_t = \alpha \cdot z_t + \varepsilon_{1t} \ , \tag{7.6a}$$

$$z_t = \beta \cdot y_{t-1} + \varepsilon_{2t} \ , \tag{7.6b}$$

where the parameter of interest is α, the weak exogeneity requirement for z_t is that $Cov(\varepsilon_{1t} \varepsilon_{2t}) = 0$ and, additionally, for strong exogeneity, that $\beta = 0$. Obviously, if $\beta = 0$, the model can no longer be interpreted as a 'cobweb model'.

Testing for Granger causality has been described in detail in Chapter 6. Testing for strong exogeneity consists in testing for weak exogeneity as described above, and then separately for Granger causality. The difficulty with this is the fact that weak exogeneity in most cases is tested through estimation of an equation representing the conditional process while Granger causality requires inference on the marginal process. Since these processes are represented by two separate regression equations, estimated in most cases by ordinary least squares, both hypotheses cannot be tested jointly, but rather sequentially. As it is well known, this increases the probability of rejecting the true null hypothesis which is, in this case, the hypothesis of strong exogeneity.

7.3 Structural Invariance, Superexogeneity and the Lucas Critique

In the previous sections of this chapter it was assumed that the 'structure' of each model (that is the parameters of interest) was constant, both over time and with respect to changes in particular variables. Changes of parameters over time are not considered here as we have already outlined some methods of evaluating time constancy of parameters in Chapter 3 above. Instead, our interest is focused on the problem of possible variability in the parameters of a model generated by changes in variables. If there is no such variability in a model it is said that the model is *structurally invariant*. In particular, our interest is with evaluating the possibility of such changes with respect to variables likely to be used as 'policy instruments', that is variables whose changes depend on the decisions of policy makers (for instance, a central bank interest rate, the rate of VAT, or the level of import duties).

A simple illustration of the problem of structural invariance can be made with the use of a single equation model:

$$y_t = \alpha \cdot z_t + \varepsilon_t \ ,$$

where ε_t is an error term with $E(\varepsilon_t) = 0$, so that $E(y_t \mid z_t) = \alpha \cdot z_t$ where y_t and z_t are observed variables. Let us assume that this model represents all our economic knowledge (strictly speaking, that the marginal process of z_t is deterministic) and that the problem is to evaluate the expected response (output) of y_t if, in period T, z_t (the input) is changed from z_T to $z_T^{\bullet}$. We may say that by changing an input, in our case by changing z_T to $z_T^{\bullet}$, we are making *an intervention* in the model. If:

$$E(y_T \mid z_T^{\bullet}) = \alpha \cdot z_T^{\bullet} \ ,$$

that is:

$$E(y_T \mid z_T^{\bullet}) - E(y_T \mid z_T) = \alpha \cdot (z_T^{\bullet} - z_T) \ ,$$

then the model is structurally invariant. The structure (in this case, the parameter α) can be successfully used for evaluating the expected response of the dependent variable in a 'what if' type exercise (simulation, or policy analysis). If, however:

$$E(y_T \mid z_T^\bullet) = \alpha^* \cdot z_T^\bullet \quad ,$$

and $\alpha^* \neq \alpha$, the model is *not* structurally invariant. Since the lack of structural invariance of the model is reflected in the change of the parameter α with respect to a change in z_t, we say that the parameter α *is not structurally invariant with respect to* z_t. The lack of structural invariance is usually a sad message to a policy analyst. If a model intended for use is structurally invariant and data on y_t and z_t are available, the parameter α can be estimated by, say, ordinary least squares and the estimate can safely be used in a policy simulation experiment. If it is not structurally invariant, no knowledge can be retrieved from the sample relevant to α^*.

Generally, as described above the problem of structural invariance of an economic model is purely academic. Nobody would seriously argue that a model describing an economic phenomenon would be absolutely robust for changes in an input, irrespective of the size of these changes. If in the above model y_t represents consumption of non-durables and z_t is income, it is clear that the marginal propensity to consume *must* change if income changes by, say, 1,000%. We can make the problem of structural invariance operational if we narrow the class of potential changes in z_t. We may, for instance, say that although the structure of a model is not absolutely robust for *any* change in input, it is structurally invariant if such a change is relatively small. We may therefore narrow the concept of structural invariance to a *given class of input changes* (*interventions*).

In an econometric model, we are interested in identifying variables which can be used safely as instruments in policy analysis, that is which are at least weakly exogenous (without any feedback relations or cross-restrictions with the variable representing output) and whose changes (policy interventions) do not affect the parameters of interest. If these two conditions are fulfilled, that is if a variable z_t is weakly or strongly exogenous and the parameters of interest are structurally invariant with respect to z_t, then z_t is said to be *superexogenous*.

For a more formal definition of superexogeneity, recall the factorization of the data generating process (see equation (7.5) in Section 7.1):

$$D(x_t \mid X_{t-1}; \theta) = D_1(y_t \mid Y_{t-1}, Z_t; \lambda_1) \cdot D_2(z_t \mid Y_{t-1}, Z_{t-1}; \lambda_2) \quad .$$

Following Hendry, Muellbauer and Murphy (1990), z_t may be defined as being superexogenous for λ_1 (the parameters of interest) if:

a) it is weakly exogenous,
b) λ_1 is invariant to changes in λ_2.

It is worth noting that if z_t is to be regarded as a policy instrument and is represented by a proper non-degenerate marginal process, the policy interventions are represented by changes in the parameters of that marginal process, λ_2, rather than in z_t itself. For example, a change in the value of a variable can be seen as a change in the mean or variance of that process. EXAMPLE 7.1 was that of the bivariate normal distribution:

$$z_t = \mu_1 + \varepsilon_{1t} \quad ,$$

$$y_t = \mu_2 + \varepsilon_{2t} \quad ,$$

where
$E(\varepsilon_{1t}) = E(\varepsilon_{2t}) = 0, Var(\varepsilon_{1t}) = \sigma_{11}, Var(\varepsilon_{2t}) = \sigma_{22}$, and $Cov(\varepsilon_{1t} \varepsilon_{2t}) = \sigma_{12}$.
The parameters of the conditional process of y_t on z_t are: $\lambda_1 = (\alpha, \beta, \sigma_y)$,
where $\alpha = \mu_2 - \beta \cdot \mu_1$, $\beta = \sigma_{12} / \sigma_{11}$, $\sigma_y = \sigma_{22} - \sigma_{12}^2 / \sigma_{11}$, and of the
marginal process for z_t are $\lambda_2 = (\mu_1, \sigma_{11})$. It has already been noted that
z_t is weakly exogenous for the parameters of interest λ_1, since λ_1 and λ_2
are variation free. Nevertheless, z_t may not be superexogenous for λ_1, since
the parameters of the conditional process α, β and σ_y are functions of the
parameters of the marginal process for z_t. Hence, if a policy analyst wants to
perform an intervention on z_t by changing either μ_1 or σ_{11}, then provided
that σ_{12} remains constant, the parameters of the conditional process will
also change.

The problem of structural invariance and its relevance for policy analysis is the essence of what is called the *Lucas critique* of policy evaluation. Lucas (1976) questioned the appropriateness of using econometric models for policy simulation experiments by arguing that the structure of a model can be altered by the impact of expectations concerning the policy. Hence, even if a model is perfectly estimated and remarkably stable within the sample period, its structure may change once expectations concerning the policy become formulated. What is even more important, the Lucas critique states that in such a case, when a policy experiment is performed, the parameters of the marginal process must change, and often in a way unexpected to the policy maker. The Lucas critique is widely regarded as an important explanation of the failure of structural econometric models in policy simulation experiments.

To illustrate the Lucas critique, recall EXAMPLE 7.4. The *DGP* considered in that example was the following:

$$y_t = \alpha \cdot z_t + \varepsilon_{1t} \quad , \tag{7.6a}$$

$$z_t = \beta \cdot y_{t-1} + \varepsilon_{2t} \quad , \tag{7.6b}$$

where $E(\varepsilon_{1t}) = E(\varepsilon_{2t}) = 0$, $Var(\varepsilon_{1t}) = \sigma_{11}$, and $Var(\varepsilon_{2t}) = \sigma_{22}$. It was
shown in Section 7.2 that if $Cov(\varepsilon_{1t} \varepsilon_{2t}) = \sigma_{12} \neq 0$, z_t is not a weakly

exogenous variable for the parameter of interest α. If, however, $\sigma_{12} = 0$ then z_t becomes weakly exogenous *and* superexogenous, since the relationship between the parameters of the conditional process of y_t for z_t, namely a, b and σ^2 and these of the marginal distribution of z_t, are:

$$a = \alpha + (\sigma_{12}/\sigma_{22}), \quad b = -(\sigma_{12}/\sigma_{22})\cdot\beta, \quad \sigma^2 = \sigma_{11} - (\sigma_{12}^2/\sigma_{22}) \ .$$

Hence, if $\sigma_{12} = 0$, then $a = \alpha$, $b = 0$ and $\sigma^2 = \sigma_{11}$. This means that whatever change is made in the marginal distribution of z_t (that is alterations to either β or σ_{22}), the structure of the conditional distribution is unaffected. The variable z_t can be safely used as a policy instrument (if, of course, it makes economic sense).

Suppose, however, that it is not z_t which enters equation (7.6a), but rather its expected value conditional on relevant information available at time t. This 'relevant information' will be denoted by Ω_t. Hence:

$$y_t = \alpha \cdot E(z_t \,|\, \Omega_t) + \varepsilon_{1t} \ . \tag{7.6c}$$

What we will show below is that now, even when the covariance between the error terms of equations (7.6b - 7.6c) is zero, z_t is no longer superexogenous for α. According to (7.6b), the 'relevant information available at time t' is nothing but y_{t-1} and hence we have:

$$E(z_t \,|\, \Omega_t) = \beta \cdot y_{t-1} \ , \tag{7.6d}$$

or:

$$z_t = E(z_t \,|\, \Omega_t) + \varepsilon_{2t} \ .$$

It is easy to discover that if the model consists of equations (7.6b), (7.6c) and (7.6d), z_t is not superexogenous for α. If in (7.6c), $E(z_t \,|\, \Omega_t)$ is replaced by $z_t - \varepsilon_{2t}$ from (7.6d), orthogonalization of the equations:

$$y_t = \alpha \cdot z_t + \zeta_t \ ,$$

where $\zeta_t = \varepsilon_{1t} - \alpha \cdot \varepsilon_{2t}$, and (7.6b) gives:

$$y_t = \alpha \cdot \beta \cdot y_{t-1} + \eta_t \ , \tag{7.6e}$$

where $\eta_t = (\zeta_t + \alpha \cdot \varepsilon_{2t}) = \varepsilon_{1t}$. Although $Cov(\eta_t \ \varepsilon_{2t}) = 0$, z_t does not appear in (7.6e). Consequently, (7.6e) is a marginal process for y_t (strictly speaking, a process conditional on y_{t-1}) rather than a conditional process of y_t on z_t. Despite lacking z_t it does contain parameters from the marginal process of z_t. Therefore z_t is not superexogenous for the parameter of interest α.

The example below shows the difficulty in using an econometric model for policy analysis in the light of the Lucas critique. We again consider a consumption function with an unanticipated inflation effect. In contrast to the *DHSY* consumption function, we now assume that consumers can, at least to some extent, foresee a future inflation and are able to adjust their decisions accordingly. In simplified notation the consumption function is the following:

$$cons_t = \mu_t + \alpha \cdot (inf_t - E(inf_t \mid \Omega_t)) + u_{1t} \quad , \tag{7.13a}$$

where μ_t represents all the elements of the consumption function apart from the Deaton effect and u_{1t} is an error term. Hence, if consumers foresee the inflation correctly, there is no unanticipated inflation effect. The consumers' expectations of inflation at time t are assumed to be formed in a rational expectations fashion using all information available at time $t-1$. For simplicity we assume that all the relevant information at time $t-1$ is represented by a single variable g_{t-1}, so that:

$$E(inf_t \mid \Omega_t) = \beta \cdot g_{t-1} \quad , \tag{7.13b}$$

or:

$$inf_t = \beta \cdot g_{t-1} + u_{2t} \quad ,$$

where $E(u_{2t}) = 0$. Equations (7.13a - 7.13b) can be combined to eliminate the unobserved expectations variable as:

$$cons_t = \mu_t + \alpha \cdot inf_t - \alpha \cdot \beta \cdot g_{t-1} + u_{1t} \quad . \tag{7.14}$$

Suppose now that an econometrician is not aware of the model (7.13a) - (7.13b). He or she estimates the model:

$$cons_t = \mu_t + a \cdot inf_t + b \cdot g_{t-1} + v_t \quad . \tag{7.15}$$

Not surprisingly, if the true model is (7.13a - 7.13b), the ordinary least squares estimates of (7.15) are likely to be highly accurate. In fact $a = \alpha$, $b = -\alpha \cdot \beta$, and $v_t = u_{1t}$, and it is easy to check that for the parameters of interest a, b and $Var(v_t)$, inf_t is weakly exogenous. Suppose, however, that the econometrician wants to evaluate the expected response of consumption to a change of inf_t, from inf_t to $inf_t^{\bullet}$ by an amount δ_t. The intervention is:

$$inf_t^{\bullet} = \beta \cdot g_{t-1} + u_{2t} + \delta_t \quad .$$

The econometrician expects consumption to change by $a \cdot \delta_t$, that is he or she expects the simulated consumption to be:

$$cons_t^{sim} = \mu_t + a \cdot (inf_t + \delta_t) + b \cdot g_{t-1} \quad .$$

This, however, is not going to happen. According to (7.13b):

$$E((inf_t + \delta_t) \mid \Omega_t) = \beta^* \cdot g_{t-1} \quad ,$$

that is, if inf_t changes and g_{t-1} remains unchanged, the parameter β must change, otherwise (7.13b) will no longer be the expected value. Consequently, the true outcome of the simulation, in terms of its expected value, is:

$$cons_t^{true} = \mu_t + \alpha \cdot (inf_t + \delta_t) - \alpha \cdot \beta^* \cdot g_{t-1} \quad ,$$

and this is not what the econometrician would expect.

Testing for structural invariance and superexogeneity is generally not a simple task, since, as was stated before, the assertion of structural invariance is, in absolute terms, never valid. It can only be tested to some extent, assuming that the class of the interventions is known and usually equivalent to that of the variability of the exogenous variable or its predictions. Tests for superexogeneity are not yet firmly established in the econometric literature; nevertheless some guidance can be given.

Hendry, Muellbauer and Murphy (1990) assumed that 'historical' interventions (in other words the variation of the tested variable within a sample) affect the parameters of interest if there is no structural invariance. Hence, if there is a structural break in the conditional model, it should correspond to a structural break in the marginal model. The straightforward procedure is to test for structural breaks in both conditional and marginal processes (for example by examining one-step recursive residuals as described in Chapter 3) and to compare the eventual occurrences of structural breaks. If there are some structural breaks, it means that the parameters of the processes are not constant within the sample. If the structural breaks for the conditional and marginal processes coincide in time, that is they appear for the same time period, it is likely that the structural break in the conditional model has been caused by variability in the parameters of the marginal model. If this is the case, the hypothesis of structural invariance (or, if weak exogeneity holds, the hypothesis of superexogeneity) can be rejected.

Slightly more general tests can be developed by assuming that the parameter of interest can be regarded as a linear function of the variable tested for structural invariance. In the simplest case of a linear model with one weakly exogenous variable z_t :

$$y_t = \alpha \cdot z_t + \varepsilon_t \quad , \tag{7.16}$$

the parameter α can be expressed as:

$$\alpha = \alpha_0 + \alpha_1 z_t \quad . \tag{7.17}$$

If the superexogeneity hypothesis holds, $\alpha_1 = 0$, so that $\alpha = \alpha_0 =$ constant. If it does not hold, (7.16) can be tested for heteroscedasticity due to the omitted squares of the variable z_t. Substituting (7.17) into (7.16) gives:

$$y_t = \alpha_0 \cdot z_t + \alpha_1 \cdot z_t^2 + \varepsilon_t \quad ,$$

which means that in the model:

$$y_t = \alpha \cdot z_t + \zeta_t \quad ,$$

where $\zeta_t = \alpha_1 \cdot z_t^2 + \varepsilon_t$, there are heteroscedastic errors, proportional to the squares of z_t.

Alternatively, one may assume that variability in α is not due to the changes in z_t itself, but rather to the deviations of z_t from its conditional expected value (that is from the mean of its marginal process). Hence, it is assumed that:

$$\alpha = \alpha_0 + \alpha_1(z_t - \mu_t) \quad , \tag{7.18}$$

where μ_t is the conditional expected value of the marginal process of z_t. If we combine (7.18) with (7.16), we get:

$$y_t = \alpha_0 \cdot z_t + \alpha_1(z_t - \mu_t) \cdot z_t + \varepsilon_t \quad .$$

The expected value of $(z_t - \mu_t) \cdot z_t$ is the same as $E(z_t - \mu_t)^2$, which is the variance of the marginal process of z_t. This suggests testing the squared residuals $(\hat{u}_t^2)$ from the marginal process of z_t as an omitted variable in (7.16). If the null hypothesis that $\alpha_1 = 0$ is rejected in the regression:

$$y_t = \alpha_0 \cdot z_t + \alpha_1 \cdot \hat{u}_t^2 + \varepsilon_t \quad ,$$

the variable z_t cannot be regarded as superexogenous (see Engle and Hendry (1993)). The above procedure can be easily extended, for instance for allowing for a dynamic process in (7.18), that is:

$$\alpha = \alpha_0 + \sum_{i=0}^{k} \alpha_{i+1}(z_{t-i} - \mu_{t-i}) \quad ,$$

which eventually leads to testing the hypothesis that in the equation:

$$y_t = \alpha_0 \cdot z_t + \sum_{i=0}^{k} \alpha_{i+1} \hat{u}_{t-i}^2 + \varepsilon_t \quad ,$$

$\alpha_1 = \alpha_2 = ... = \alpha_k = 0$. This can be done with the use of a Lagrange Multiplier test (note, however, that some additional degrees of freedom are required, since the residuals of the marginal process are not known and have to be estimated).

Charemza and Király (1991) assumed that the set of 'admissible interventions' is that generated not by the variability of z_t, but rather by prediction errors made from the conditional process. Hence, if the variable z_t is not superexogenous and predictions (for instance one-step ahead recursive forecasts) have been made from the model with invariant parameters, the prediction errors are likely to be correlated with z_t. This suggests regressing the prediction errors on current and/or lagged z_t and testing their significance. If the hypothesis that the regression coefficients are equal to zero in such a regression is rejected, z_t is not superexogenous.

7.4 Exogeneity in the *DHSY* Model

In this section we will illustrate the use of the tests outlined above to investigate the exogeneity properties of the inflation variable included in the *DHSY* formulation of UK aggregate consumption (see Chapter 3). A similar analysis could also be performed for the income variable which appears in this model, but we do not pursue this here (see Hendry, Muellbauer and Murphy (1990) for such an analysis).

Irrespective of whether one is testing for weak, strong, or superexogeneity, the initial step is the formulation of a marginal model for inflation. There is no unique way of doing this, but from the arguments already presented in this book, one way would be to start from an equation for inflation from a quite general *VAR* representation of the variables appearing in the *DHSY* model. Chapter 5 considered the level of integration of the variables appearing in the *DHSY* model. From this it seems reasonable to use a differenced form of these variables, rather than their levels. Accordingly, estimation is started from a *VAR*(3, 5, 5) equation for Δinf_t, $\Delta_4 cons_t$ and $\Delta_4 inc_t$ respectively, that is from an equation with three lags for Δinf_t, and five lags for both $\Delta_4 cons_t$ and $\Delta_4 inc_t$. The ordinary least squares estimates of this *VAR* equation are given in Section 7.5 under MODEL 7.1. It is immediately apparent from this estimated model that at the 5% level of significance, no individual consumption or income coefficients are statistically significant, nor are the consumption or income coefficients taken together (the *F*-test values for these joint tests are only 0.476 and 1.153). This *VAR* equation was successively reduced to a simple autoregressive model of order one (an *AR*(1) model) by a sequence of model reduction tests. First one can test whether an autoregressive model of order three (that is, the regression of Δinf_t on Δinf_{t-1}, Δinf_{t-2} and Δinf_{t-3}) can be rejected as a specific case of the general *VAR*(3, 5, 5) equation. The computer output under MODEL 7.2 in Section 7.5 shows that the $F(10, 55)$ value for this model reduction is 2.08 which is right on the borderline of statistical significance. As the null hypothesis that the $AR(3)$ is a specific case of the $VAR(3, 5, 5)$ equation could not be clearly rejected, model reduction proceeded by omitting the terms Δinf_{t-2} and Δinf_{t-3} from MODEL 7.2. Compared with the general $VAR(3, 5, 5)$ equation, the simple $AR(1)$ model has the value for a model reduction $F(12, 55)$ test of 2.07 which is just significant at the 5% significance level, whereas the autoregressive model with both first and third order lagged variables (not reported here) has an $F(11, 55)$ value of 1.92 which is just not significant. Hence, both the simple $AR(1)$ model and the model containing both first and third order lagged variables are candidates for adoption as the marginal process for inflation (the conclusions drawn from either are identical). For simplicity (and to maximize the degrees of freedom available) we have chosen to give the results stemming from the estimation of the simple first order autoregressive model given as MODEL 7.3 in Section 7.5. This $AR(1)$ model has been taken to represent the marginal process for the inflation variable in the exogeneity testing which follows.

An important aspect of this marginal process is that it contains neither lagged consumption nor lagged income terms. This has some immediate consequences for both the concepts of exogeneity one may test for, and for the tests themselves. So far as weak exogeneity is concerned, despite the fact that the *DHSY* model contains an error correction mechanism, the absence of consumption and income in the marginal process means that there is no question as to whether error correction terms appear in the marginal process. Clearly they cannot. Hence, for testing weak exogeneity, one may simply investigate the possible covariance between the residuals of the marginal process (termed *unif* in the computer output) and the residuals of the conditional process, namely the *DHSY* model. However, since there are no lagged consumption terms in the marginal process, such a test is simultaneously a test for the strong exogeneity of inflation.

The *DHSY* model estimated for the same sample period as the $AR(1)$ model for the first difference of inflation is reported as MODEL 7.4 in Section 7.5. The test for the strong exogeneity of inflation may be carried out by a standard Student-t test or equivalent F-test on the residuals from the marginal process included as a variable in the *DHSY* model. This $F(1, 61)$ value reported in MODEL 7.4 is very small (0.033) and is clearly not significant. One can conclude that inflation may be taken as strongly exogenous for the parameters of interest of the conditional model, which in this case are the parameters of the *DHSY* model.

Let us now consider testing for the structural invariance of the *DHSY* model. Both the marginal process for inflation and the *DHSY* model were re-estimated by recursive least squares (see Chapter 3) and the one-step recursive residuals for each were calculated. Figures 7.1 and 7.2 are graphs of these residuals. Inspection of these graphs reveals no cases in which structural breaks in the marginal process coincide with breaks in the conditional

One-step residuals
Fig 7.1: consumption

Fig 7.2: inflation

or *DHSY* model. This is consistent with the *DHSY* model being structurally invariant, and with inflation being superexogenous in this model. The other tests for superexogeneity outlined in Section 7.3 above have also been carried out. MODEL 7.5 reports the results of testing the significance of current and lagged squared residuals in the *DHSY* model. The $F(2, 59)$ value for adding these squared residuals is 1.06 which, like the preceding test statistic, is not significant at the 5% level of significance. Taken together, MODELS 7.6 and 7.7 report the results of the Charemza-Király test. The prediction errors from the *DHSY* model (designated as *icons* in the computer output in Section 7.5) are regressed on the first difference of inflation and its lag. The low $F(2, 50)$ value for the joint significance of these regressors is in line with the previous test results which all point towards the structural invariance of the *DHSY* model and the superexogeneity of inflation.

7.5 Stylized Computer Output (*PC-GIVE*)

MODEL 7.1: Modelling dinf by OLS
The present sample is: 1959 (2) to 1975 (4)

Variable	Coefficient	Std.Error	t-value
dinf_1	0.293532	0.148738	1.973
dinf_2	0.0196022	0.138714	0.141
dinf_3	0.324431	0.136986	2.368
d4lc_1	-0.171610	0.167842	-1.022
d4lc_2	0.0706658	0.167175	0.423
d4lc_3	0.00127806	0.161807	0.008
d4lc_4	0.208086	0.163877	1.270
d4lc_5	-0.0791631	0.144997	-0.546
d4li_1	0.103909	0.0730584	1.422
d4li_2	0.0652503	0.0818650	0.797
d4li_3	0.0305726	0.0756883	0.404
d4li_4	-0.0416707	0.0754149	-0.553
d4li_5	-0.124372	0.0793809	-1.567

$R^2 = 0.4459066$ $\sigma = 0.008528365$ DW = 1.89
* R^2 does NOT allow for the mean *
RSS = 0.0039275827565 for 13 variables and 67 observations
Testing for Error Autocorrelation from lags 1 to 5
$Chi^2(5) = 6.1761$ [0.2895]   and F-Form(5, 49) = 0.9951 [0.4306]

Tests on the significance of each variable

variable	F(num,denom)	Value	Unit Root t-test
dinf	F(3, 54)	3.4265*	-1.4887
d4lc	F(5, 54)	0.476227	0.139146
d4li	F(5, 54)	1.1532	0.219036

MODEL 7.2: Modelling dinf by OLS
The present sample is: 1959 (2) to 1975 (4)

Variable	Coefficient	Std.Error	t-value
dinf_1	0.414979	0.114995	3.609
dinf_2	-0.0636988	0.113088	-0.563
dinf_3	0.202547	0.109775	1.845

$R^2 = 0.2363958$ $\sigma = 0.009196347$ DW = 1.99
* R^2 does NOT allow for the mean *
RSS = 0.0054126589476 for 3 variables and 67 observations

Testing for Error Autocorrelation from lags 1 to 5
$Chi^2(5) = 11.62$ [0.0404] * and F-Form(5, 59) = 2.4759 [0.0421] *

Error Autocorrelation Coefficients:

	Lag 1	Lag 2	Lag 3	Lag 4	Lag 5
Coeff.	0.18312	0.61277	-0.0095933	-0.25165	0.2314

Progress to date for modelling dinf:
Tests of model reduction
Model 1 --> 2: F(10, 55) = 2.0796 [0.0420] *

MODEL 7.3: Modelling dinf by OLS
The present sample is: 1959 (2) to 1975 (4)

Variable	Coefficient	Std.Error	t-value
dinf_1	0.431881	0.107839	4.005

$R^2 = 0.1955027$ $\sigma = 0.009295259$ DW = 2.10
* R^2 does NOT allow for the mean *
RSS = 0.0057025218199 for 1 variables and 67 observations

Testing for Error Autocorrelation from lags 1 to 5
$Chi^2(5) = 8.7546$ [0.1193] and F-Form(5, 61) = 1.8337 [0.1196]

Tests of model reduction
Model 1 --> 2: F(10, 55) = 2.0796 [0.0420] *

Model 1 --> 3: F(12, 55) = 2.0713 [0.0345] *
Model 2 --> 3: F(2, 65) = 1.7405 [0.1835]

uinf added to database
uinf = Residual values of equation 3
uinfsq = uinf * uinf;

MODEL 7.4: Modelling d4lc by OLS
(Test for strong exogeneity of inflation)
The present sample is: 1959 (2) to 1975 (4)

Variable	Coefficient	Std.Error	t-value
d4li	0.495576	0.0308767	16.050
dd4li	-0.217932	0.0413832	-5.266
lc_li_4	-0.0862625	0.0129346	-6.669
inf	-0.109619	0.0241520	-4.539
dinf	-0.297975	0.101727	-2.929

$R^2 = 0.949123$ $\sigma = 0.006519354$ DW = 2.28
* R^2 does NOT allow for the mean *
RSS = 0.0026351225285 for 5 variables and 67 observations

LM test for omitted variables
Add F(1, 61) = 0.0338521 [0.8546]

Added variables:
uinf

MODEL 7.5: Modelling d4lc by OLS
The present sample is: 1959 (3) to 1975 (4)

Variable	Coefficient	Std.Error	t-value
d4li	0.494228	0.0311907	15.845
dd4li	-0.217901	0.0416399	-5.233
lc_li_4	-0.0861245	0.0130179	-6.616
inf	-0.110004	0.0243145	-4.524
dinf	-0.283067	0.106818	-2.650

$R^2 = 0.9475849$ $\sigma = 0.006559779$ DW = 2.28
* R^2 does NOT allow for the mean *
RSS = 0.0026248731007 for 5 variables and 66 observations

LM test for omitted variables
Add F(2, 59) = 1.0586 [0.3534]

Added variables:
uinfsq uinfsq_1

MODEL 7.6: Modelling d4lc by RLS
The present sample is: 1959 (1) to 1975 (4)

Variable	Coefficient	Std.Error	t-value
d4li	0.495607	0.0306346	16.178
dd4li	-0.217579	0.0409818	-5.309
lc_li_4	-0.0861678	0.0128156	-6.724
inf	-0.109708	0.0239547	-4.580
dinf	-0.294364	0.0975668	-3.017

$R^2 = 0.9495123$ $\sigma = 0.006468408$ DW = 2.28
* R^2 does NOT allow for the mean *
RSS = 0.0026359393428 for 5 variables and 68 observations

icons added to database
icons = StdInn values of model 7.6

MODEL 7.7: Modelling icons by RLS
The present sample is: 1963 (1) to 1975 (4)

Variable	Coefficient	Std.Error	t-value
dinf	-0.0229279	0.110513	-0.207
dinf_1	0.0366982	0.110510	0.332

$R^2 = 0.00222362$ $\sigma = 0.006827318$ DW = 2.39
* R^2 does NOT allow for the mean *
RSS = 0.0023306138749 for 2 variables and 52 observations

Tests on the significance of each variable

variable	F(num,denom)	Value	Unit Root t-test
dinf	F(2, 50)	0.0557144	0.129724

7.6 Suggestions for Further Reading

Relatively little has been published on exogeneity analysis. Apart from the seminal paper of Engle, Hendry and Richard (1983), concepts of exogeneity have been considered by Wu (1983), Leamer (1985), Eichenbaum (1985), and Cooley and LeRoy (1985), mostly in relation to the concept of causality (also see Geweke (1984)). A survey of tests which can be useful for the testing of weak exogeneity is given by Pesaran and Smith (1990); see also the edited volume by Ericsson and Irons (1994). Empirical results of testing for exogeneity are given by Baba, Hendry and Starr (1992), Hendry and Ericsson (1991) and Ericsson and Irons (1995), An historical account of the development of the concept of exogeneity has been provided by Epstein (1987), and an enquiry into the origins of the concept of autonomy or structural invariance by Aldrich (1989). Spanos (1986) provides a systematic formalization of the use of data generating processes in econometric modelling.

Some advances in exogeneity analysis have been made within a Bayesian framework, for example by Lubrano, Pierse and Richard (1986), Steel (1987, 1989), and Steel and Richard (1989). Theoretical papers on superexogeneity and structural invariance include Engle and Hendry (1993), and Charemza (1988). Applications of weak and strong exogeneity testing include Charemza and Király (1990) and Hendry, Muellbauer and Murphy (1990). Theoretical and empirical works concerning the Lucas critique have mainly been conducted within the framework of encompassing analysis and therefore are referred to in Chapter 8.

Chapter 8

Non-nested Models, Encompassing and Model Selection

8.1 Problems in Choosing Between Models

In the earlier chapters we have suggested various methods of deriving an econometric model which, for one reason or another, may be regarded as 'good' practice. For instance, use of the general to specific methodology (Chapter 4) can result in a single equation model derived from an autoregressive distributed lag model in a systematic way, in that it survives a series of Lagrange Multiplier tests for various linear and/or nonlinear restrictions. On the other hand, one may construct a model using, say, the Engle-Granger approach (Chapter 5). In the multi-equation case, a model may be formulated from a Cowles Commission type structural model, a vector autoregressive model (Chapter 6), or a system of equations based on the principle of exogeneity modelling (Chapter 7). If it is not clear which is the best modelling approach on *a priori* grounds and various methodologies are applied to derive an empirical model, it is unlikely that one would finish up with identical models. An obvious question which arises in this context is: how can one select the best model?

The answer to the model selection problem is not necessarily obvious even if there is no question as to the modelling methodology believed to be appropriate. Suppose, for instance, that one starts from a simple autoregressive distributed lag model of order one which is regarded as a general model (see Chapter 4):

$$y_t = \alpha_1 y_{t-1} + \beta_0 x_t + \beta_1 x_{t-1} + \varepsilon_t \quad . \tag{8.1}$$

Imagine that one model derived from (8.1) through applying the general to specific methodology turns out to be a first order autoregressive process:

$$y_t = \alpha_1 y_{t-1} + \varepsilon_t \quad . \tag{8.2}$$

It was said in Chapter 4 that the general model (8.1) becomes the specific model (8.2), if it satisfies the restrictions:

$$\beta_0 = \beta_1 = 0 \quad .$$

Alternatively, from the same general *ADL* model (8.1) and using the same methodology, one may develop another specific form, for instance a finite distributed lag model:

$$y_t = \beta_0 x_t + \beta_1 x_{t-1} + \varepsilon_t \quad . \tag{8.3}$$

The restriction required to derive (8.3) from (8.1) is:

$$\alpha_1 = 0 \quad .$$

Evidently, both models (8.2) and (8.3) are special cases of (8.1). However, (8.2) is not a special case of (8.3), nor is (8.3) a special case of (8.2). We may write down the hypotheses concerning (8.1) and (8.2) in a way typical of traditional testing of statistical 'null' (H_0) and 'alternative' (H_A) hypotheses, as:

H_0: it is true that $\beta_0 = \beta_1 = 0$, or model (8.2) is true ;

H_A: it is *not* true that $\beta_0 = \beta_1 = 0$, or model (8.1) is true.

Similarly, the corresponding hypotheses concerning models (8.1) and (8.3) can be formulated. Hypothesis H_A above is a *composite* hypothesis, and as it covers all other possible values of the parameters other than those specified in H_0, it may be said to complement H_0 to the set of all *admissible* values of the parameters β_0 and β_1. The parameter space (the set of all admissible values of the parameters) has been effectively partitioned or divided by the null and alternative hypotheses into a rejection and a non-rejection region. Rejection of the null hypothesis in this case automatically implies acceptance of the alternative hypothesis. As model (8.2) is a special case of model (8.1) in that it can be derived from (8.1) by means of parametric restrictions, the testing of the null hypothesis that $\beta_0 = \beta_1 = 0$ is also an example of the testing of *nested* hypotheses. More generally, both models (8.2) and (8.3) may be said to be *nested* within (8.1) as they constitute special cases of model (8.1).

If we want to choose between models (8.2) and (8.3) however, we have to formulate the hypotheses in a noncomplementary way, so that they do not constitute together the set of all admissible values for α_1, β_0, and β_1. The hypotheses we want to test are:

H_1 : model (8.2) is true ,
H_2 : model (8.3) is true .

Since H_1 and H_2 do not constitute together the set of admissible hypotheses (or, in other words, neither is a special case of the other) we will call hypotheses like H_1 and H_2 *non-nested hypotheses* and the underlying models *non-nested models*. The problem of testing non-nested hypotheses is clearly different from that of testing nested hypotheses; if we treat H_1 as we treated H_0 and we reject it, it does not necessarily mean that H_2 is true. Our task is to evaluate whether model (8.2) is to be rejected in favour of (8.3) or *vice versa*, and the techniques applied will be different from those used for testing nested hypotheses.

It must be stressed that the problem of choosing between two (or more) different models can be seen in a wider context than that of selecting between 'specific' models derived from a 'general' one. For instance, (8.2) could be the result of testing Granger causality in a vector autoregressive modelling exercise, rather than a simplification of an *ADL* model. This will not change the statistical problem of selecting between (8.2) and (8.3).

A similar (and to a large extent overlapping) problem is that of the *encompassing* of econometric models. Generally, it is said that model *A* *encompasses* model *B* if it has the ability to account for the behaviour of model *B* or, in other words, if it can explain the behaviour of relevant characteristics of model *B* (see Mizon (1984), or Mizon and Richard (1986)). Since the 'relevant characteristics' may vary from one model to another, it is difficult to discuss encompassing in absolute terms. Instead one may speak of, for example, *variance encompassing* (where the variation of errors in model *B* can be explained by model *A*), or *forecast encompassing* (where the forecast errors from model *B* can be explained by model *A*). Although non-nested techniques are frequently used for testing hypotheses concerning encompassing (see Section 8.2 below), it does not mean that encompassing and testing non-nested hypotheses are the same. Consider, for instance, general to specific modelling. A comparison of a specific and a general model is a problem of testing nested hypotheses and therefore is not a non-nested problem. However, a specific model derived from a general model will have a larger error variance (since some of the variables have been dropped or restrictions imposed) and therefore the general model will encompass the specific one for variance. On the other hand, a specific model may encompass the general one for forecast. For instance, in the derivation of the *DHSY* model described in Chapter 3, it was the case that the forecast diagnostics for the specific model (MODEL 3.5) were superior to that of the general model (MODEL 3.6). Without any formal testing, it seems at least plausible that forecasts from the specific model may explain, to some extent, the forecast errors made by the general model.

8.2 Model Selection Tests

It was pointed out in Chapter 2 that traditional econometric criteria for selecting the 'best' model, such as the maximum R^2 (coefficient of determination) criterion, are far from being ideal especially if the model has been derived through data mining. Several other measures have been proposed, however, which aim to improve understanding of the overall characteristics of a model. The most widely used criteria for judging the goodness of fit of a particular model whilst taking into account the number of estimated parameters are:

i) The coefficient of determination, adjusted for the number of explanatory variables, $\overline{R}^2$:

$$\overline{R}^2 = 1 - \frac{T-1}{T-k} \cdot (1 - R^2) \quad ,$$

where R^2 is the coefficient of determination, T is the number of observations and k is the number of explanatory variables (including an intercept). This measure was introduced and discussed in Chapter 2, in the context of data mining.

ii) The Akaike information criterion *AIC* (see for example Harvey (1990, pp. 177-178), or Judge *et al.* (1985, pp. 243-245)), computed as:

$$AIC = (-2 \cdot lnL(\bullet) + 2 \cdot k) / T \quad ,$$

where $lnL(\bullet)$ is the value of the loglikelihood function of the estimated model. The idea behind the *AIC* criterion is to select the model which has the minimal loss of information (that is, the smallest *AIC*). For models with the same number of parameters and estimated using the same sample this leads to selecting the model with the smallest residual sum of squares or, in other words, with the largest R^2 (see Maddala (1988, p.426)). For models with different numbers of explanatory variables the *AIC* and $\overline{R}^2$ criteria may differ.

iii) The Schwarz Bayesian criterion *SC* (see Judge *et al.* (1985, pp. 245-246)):

$$SC = ln\hat{\sigma}^2 + \frac{k \cdot lnT}{T} \quad ,$$

where $\hat{\sigma}^2$ is an unbiased estimate of the residual variance. The formula above has been derived for the case of normally and independently distributed residuals and is the result of a Bayesian procedure of seeking the most probable (*a posteriori*) model. Model selection is on the basis of choosing the model with the smallest *SC* value.

iv) The Final Prediction Error *FPE* criterion (see Judge *et al.* (1985, pp. 243-245)):

$$FPE = \frac{T+k}{T-k} \cdot \hat{\sigma}^2 \quad .$$

This, as its name implies, leads to selecting a model with the smallest *ex-post* prediction error. That is, *FPE* is based on forecasts made using actual rather than estimated values of explanatory variables for forecast periods and using parameter estimates for the entire sample, inclusive of the forecast period. (For a slightly different definition of *ex-post* forecasts see

Klein (1971a, pp. 19-21).) Various modifications of the *FPE* criterion have been suggested in the literature, which are referred to in Judge *et al.* (1985, p.244).

The above criteria, as well as numerous modifications of them, are all based on the principle of minimizing the residual sum of squares as a guide for selecting the best model (see Maddala (1988, p.426)). Each criterion, however, has different underlying assumptions. The adjusted R^2 criterion assumes that a 'true' model exists and the task is in finding it, given the assumption that the 'best' model for this purpose is that which minimizes the residual sum of squares adjusted for the number of explanatory variables. The *FPE* adopts a more parsimonious position. According to this criterion, even a 'true' model should be reduced in size if this would lead to improving the predictive quality of the model. The aim of the *AIC* and *SC* criteria is the selection of the model with the maximum information available (where 'information' is a precisely defined probability concept; see Theil (1971, pp. 636-637) and again do not concern themselves as to whether a 'true' model exists or not. The *AIC* criterion is regarded as being inconsistent in the sense that it does not select the model with maximum information with probability tending to one as $T \to \infty$. This problem seems to be overcome by the *SC* criterion, which is recommended for large samples in place of the *AIC*.

All the above statistics can be calculated for individual models and, with all the reservations described in Chapter 2, can also be used for an *ad hoc* selection between models. They do not, however, answer the question as to which of the models is better in a direct comparison with each other, that is whether one of them should be rejected in favour of the other. As was shown in Section 8.1, in principle such a selection can be made by the formulation and testing of non-nested hypotheses. Describing the structure and formal properties of tests used in evaluating such hypotheses is beyond the scope of this book. It is also not necessary to give precise formulae for computing particular statistics, since most of them are calculated by contemporary econometric computer packages.

We will discuss some simple tests for the closely related problem of testing for encompassing, however. The non-nested test described here for variance encompassing is the J test, proposed by Davidson and MacKinnon (1981). Suppose that the models we wish to select from are those given by the hypotheses below:

$$H_1: \quad y_t = \alpha x_t + \varepsilon_{1t} \quad , \tag{8.4a}$$

$$H_2: \quad y_t = \beta z_t + \varepsilon_{2t} \quad . \tag{8.4b}$$

The fact that the above models are linear and that each of them has only one explanatory variable is for the sake of simplification only. In practice, the models considered may well be nonlinear and/or with many explanatory variables each. The J test consists in testing the hypothesis that H_2 is true by:

1. Estimating equation (8.4b), resulting in an estimate of the parameter β which may be denoted as $\hat{\beta}$ (for a linear equation this is just the ordinary least squares estimate);
2. Adding the predicted values $\hat{\beta}z_t$ from (8.4b) to equation (8.4a) and hence estimating (8.4a) as:

$$y_t = \alpha x_t + \theta \cdot \hat{\beta}z_t + \varepsilon_t \quad . \tag{8.5}$$

The test that (8.4b) encompasses (8.4a) for variance then simply consists of testing whether in (8.5) the *OLS* estimate of θ differs significantly from zero. This can be done, for instance, with the use of the Student-t test. When used for testing θ in an equation like (8.5), the Student-t statistic has only an asymptotic standard normal distribution and the test is not very powerful, especially for small samples.

The logical complement to the testing of whether (8.4b) encompasses (8.4a) is to test whether (8.4a) encompasses (8.4b). For this case, the test is for the null hypothesis that $\delta = 0$ in the regression equation:

$$y_t = \beta z_t + \delta \cdot \hat{\alpha}x_t + v_t \quad , \tag{8.6}$$

where $\hat{\alpha}x_t$ stands for the fitted values (predictions) from equation (8.4a). Since tests on (8.5) and (8.6) are performed independently, we cannot exclude the possibility of getting conflicting results. It may happen that in (8.5) θ is significant (so that (8.4b) encompasses (8.4a)) and, at the same time, in (8.6) δ is also significant (so that (8.4a) encompasses (8.4b)). This case is unlikely to occur except for very weak evidence. Analogously, we would not be pleased if both θ and δ appear to be insignificant, since this would mean that either both of our models are 'best', or (more likely) that both are equally bad. Ideally, we would like to have conclusive results such that if θ is significant, δ is not or *vice versa*, so that we would be able to make a clear selection of the better model.

As the J test is an asymptotic and not very powerful test, there have been numerous modifications and alternatives proposed, and one or more of these are computed by most of the specialized econometric packages. These tests include the Cox (1961) test, the adjusted Cox test (Godfrey and Pesaran (1983)), the Ericsson (1983) test, the Fisher and McAleer (1981) *JA* test and the 'encompassing' test (Mizon and Richard (1986); see also Maddala (1988, pp. 445-446)). Whilst the J and *JA* tests are asymptotically equivalent, Monte Carlo studies indicate that for small samples, the J test rejects the true hypothesis more often than it should, but that the *JA* test is less powerful than the J test when the models being compared have very different numbers of explanatory variables (see Kmenta (1986, pp. 595-598)).

The forecast encompassing test we present here is that introduced by Chong and Hendry (1986) and developed subsequently by Ericsson (1989) and Clements and Hendry (1991). The idea of the test is quite similar to that of the J test. Suppose that the model given by (8.4a) is the 'rival' model and that given by (8.4b) is 'our' model. The question is whether our model encompasses, in terms of forecast, the 'rival' model. Suppose further that for both models, series of one-step ahead forecasts are available. These can be, for instance, forecasts made with the use of recursive least squares estimates, that is:

$$\hat{y}_t = \hat{\alpha}_{t-1} x_t \ ,$$

$$\tilde{y}_t = \hat{\beta}_{t-1} z_t \ ,$$

where $\hat{\alpha}_{t-1}$ and $\hat{\beta}_{t-1}$ are the recursive least squares estimates obtained with the use of data up to (and inclusive of) time $t-1$. Both forecasts can be pooled together to give a compound forecast $\bar{y}_t$ and compared with the observed y_t giving:

$$\bar{y}_t = (1-\gamma) \cdot \hat{y}_t + \gamma \cdot \tilde{y}_t \ ,$$

or:

$$y_t = (1-\gamma) \cdot \hat{y}_t + \gamma \cdot \tilde{y}_t + \bar{u}_t \ , \tag{8.7}$$

where γ is a weight and $\bar{u}_t$ is the compound forecast error. If the 'rival' model is true and our model is not, then in (8.7) $\gamma = 0$ and $\bar{y}_t = \hat{y}_t$. This constitutes a testable hypothesis since from (8.7) we have:

$$\hat{u}_t = \gamma \cdot (\tilde{y}_t - \hat{y}_t) + \bar{u}_t \ , \tag{8.8}$$

where $\hat{u}_t = y_t - \hat{y}_t$ and is equal to the forecast error of the 'rival' model. Hence, the procedure consists of testing for the statistical significance of γ in the regression equation (8.8).

Chong and Hendry (1986) have shown that the Student-t test for γ is a valid test, at least for large samples, provided that both forecasts are made on an *ex-ante* basis. For this analysis, the concept of an *ex-ante* forecast means that although the values of the explanatory variables may be known for the forecast period (after reading Chapter 7 we should rather say 'weakly exogenous' rather than 'explanatory' variables), the coefficients used for computing the forecasts may be estimated from data prior to the forecast period rather than known.

One of the most important features of the forecast encompassing test above is its ease of use. The models under comparison can be large nonlinear systems of equations, separately estimated, and not necessarily by recursive methods. In fact it is not even necessary for us to know the 'rival' model (full specifications of models and statistical data used for estimation are rarely published). All we need to know in order to perform the test are the 'rival' *ex-ante* forecasts.

8.3 An Empirical Encompassing Exercise

As an empirical encompassing problem we have taken the comparison of the *DHSY* consumption function with an alternative derived from the Houthakker-Taylor dynamic demand model (*HT* herewith). The Houthakker and Taylor (1966, 1970) model was especially popular in the 1960s and 1970s and has been used widely for analysing consumption and savings in a number of countries (see for example Swamy (1968) or Portes and Winter (1978, 1980)). It appears that after Taylor and Houthakker's (1990) reconsideration of their model in light of the development of cointegration theory, interest in their model has been renewed.

From various modifications and variants of the Houthakker-Taylor dynamic demand consumption model, we have chosen one which has been used for the analysis of aggregate demand and is relatively straightforward in its specification. Following the formulation of the *DHSY* model used earlier, we express the variables in the Houthakker-Taylor model in logarithms and seasonal differences. This model is then given as:

$$\Delta_4 cons_t = \alpha_1 \Delta_4 sav_{t-1} + \alpha_2 \Delta\Delta_4 inc_t + \alpha_3 \Delta_4 inc_{t-1} + \xi_t \quad ,$$

where, as before, $cons_t$ stands for the logarithm of aggregate consumption of non-durables, inc_t for the logarithm of personal disposable income and $\Delta\Delta_4$ denotes first and fourth differences respectively. The new variable here is sav_{t-1}, which denotes the logarithm of personal saving (personal disposable income minus consumers' expenditure) at the end of the previous period. The Houthakker-Taylor theory suggests that α_1 should be negative, α_2 should lie between zero and one and α_3 should be equal to one. In order to impose the restriction that $\alpha_3 = 1$, we have reformulated the model by introducing a variable $\Delta_4 co_t^* in_{t-1}$ such that:

$$\Delta_4 co_t^* in_{t-1} = \Delta_4 cons_t - \Delta_4 inc_{t-1} \quad ,$$

and the model becomes:

$$\Delta_4 co_t^* in_{t-1} = \alpha_1 \Delta_4 sav_{t-1} + \alpha_2 \Delta\Delta_4 inc_t + \xi_t \quad . \tag{8.9}$$

The ordinary least squares estimates of (8.9) for the variables and sample period identical to that used in Chapter 3 for the estimation of the *DHSY* model are given as MODEL 8.1 in Section 8.4. The data for saving was derived from *Economic Trends, Annual Supplement*, 1981. (For simplicity, a very slight alteration to the data for one period was made to avoid a negative value for personal saving which would have precluded the use of logarithms.) In the computer output, the logarithm of saving is denoted by *ls*. In addition to the parameter estimates and the usual diagnostic statistics, also reported are the Schwarz Bayesian criterion *SC* and the final prediction error *FPE*. For comparison, for the *DHSY* model the *SC* value was -9.809 and the *FPE* value was 0.000047.

At first sight, the *HT* model looks definitely inferior to the *DHSY* model. Although the estimated coefficients are statistically significant, and have signs and magnitudes consistent with prior expectations, nevertheless the information criteria *SC* and *FPE* are not as good as those of the *DHSY* model. The Durbin-Watson statistic is very low (although greater than the R^2 coefficient and therefore consistent with the 'rule of thumb' for stationarity of the residuals - see Chapter 5). In particular, the forecasting properties of the model (*Forecast Chi*^{2} and the *Chow* test statistics) show that the hypothesis of the constancy of the parameters both for the period up to the end of 1971 and after that has to be rejected.

Does this mean that we have selected a 'straw man' and that without further analysis we can claim victory for the *DHSY* model over that of *HT*? Not necessarily. If we re-estimate the *HT* model by a method which explicitly accounts for the fact that the residuals display first order autocorrelation, we may note a substantial improvement in the forecasts. We have re-estimated the model by a maximum likelihood method which explicitly allows for first order autocorrelation. The properties and estimation details of this method (which is called *RALS*, for *r*th order Autoregressive Least Squares) are not discussed here; details can be found in Doornik and Hendry (1994). With the use of the *RALS* estimates, the *Forecast Chi*^{2} statistic and the *Chow* test (reported beneath the *OLS* results for MODEL 8.1) are much improved and do not lead to the outright rejection of the hypothesis of parameter constancy. Moreover, it has to be remembered that we cannot directly compare the *DHSY* and *HT* models, since the dependent variables are not the same. The *DHSY* model explains $\Delta_4 cons_t$, while the left-hand side variable in the *HT* model is $\Delta_4 co^*_t in_{t-1}$. Hence, further testing is needed in order to establish superiority.

We start with the *J* test for variance encompassing. As has been said already, this consists of testing the significance of the fitted values from one model when used as an additional explanatory variable in another. In our case, however, we have an additional problem, since the dependent variables in the estimated models are not the same. Before performing the *J* test, we have to transform the fitted values in order to ensure comparability. If we want to test the hypothesis that *HT* encompasses *DHSY*, we have to re-estimate the *DHSY* model using the fitted values from the *HT* model as an additional variable. However, the fitted value from the estimated *HT* model is (say) $\widetilde{\Delta}_4 co_t^* in_{t-1}$, that is it corresponds to $\Delta_4 co_t^* in_{t-1}$ rather than to $\Delta_4 cons_t$. We may recompute the 'fitted' value for $\Delta_4 cons_t$ from the *HT* model as:

$$\widetilde{\Delta}_4 cons_t = \widetilde{\Delta}_4 co_t^* in_{t-1} + \Delta_4 inc_{t-1} \quad .$$

MODEL 8.2 in Section 8.4, where the $\widetilde{\Delta}_4 cons_t$ variable is denoted as *htf*, shows that the Student-*t* statistic on the fitted values from the *HT* model is equal to -0.595, which is not significantly different from zero at conventional levels of significance. Hence, we have no evidence that *HT* encompasses *DHSY* for variance.

MODEL 8.3 in Section 8.4 shows the *J* test regression for the hypothesis that *DHSY* encompasses *HT*. Again, the fitted value of the *DHSY* model has to be transformed for comparability, that is $\Delta_4 inc_{t-1}$ has to be subtracted from the originally computed fitted value. The variable resulting from this manipulation is denoted by *dhf* in the computer printout. It is evident that the inclusion of *dhf* substantially changes the entire model. The originally significant variables $\Delta_4 sav_{t-1}$ and $\Delta\Delta_4 inc_t$ change their signs and become insignificant. The estimated coefficient for *dhf* is close to unity and highly significant. Moreover, the Durbin-Watson statistic does not suggest a problem with autocorrelation. Hence, it seems that the *DHSY* model does encompass the *HT* model for variance. If one accepts the traditional interpretation of autocorrelation in the residuals of a fitted model as the result of model misspecification due to missing variables, it looks as if what was missing from the *HT* model was the *DHSY* component.

For the forecast encompassing test we have computed one-step ahead forecasts using the recursive least squares method. Using *PC-GIVE*, this consists of estimating the equation by *RLS*, saving one-step ahead errors (called in the *PC-GIVE* menu, 'innovations') and using them for computing the forecast values. We may think of the series of one-step ahead forecasts as a series of systematically published one period ahead forecasts by a forecasting office, which we wish to check against our own results. It does not matter how large or how complicated the models are that have been used to generate these forecasts. All we have to know are the forecast values and realizations. Having these, we can easily recompute the forecast errors.

In the computer output in Section 8.4, the difference between the forecasts from the *DHSY* and *HT* models obtained by recursive regressions are denoted respectively as *dh_ht* and *ht_dh*. Analogously, the corresponding forecast errors are denoted by *dhru* and *htru*. MODELS 8.4 and 8.5 show the computed results of the forecast encompassing test. In MODEL 8.4, where the forecast errors of the *DHSY* model are regressed on the differences between the forecasts *ht_dh*, the Student-*t* ratio is insignificant. In MODEL 8.5, where the forecast errors of the *HT* model are regressed on the differences between the forecasts *dh_ht*, the Student-*t* ratio is significant. We have obtained an unambiguous result. That is we have found out that the *DHSY* model does encompass the forecasts from the *HT* model, and at the same time the *HT* model does not encompass the *DHSY* model. Thus both encompassing tests applied here, the variance and forecast encompassing tests, conclusively show the superiority of the *DHSY* model over the *HT* model.

8.4 Stylized Computer Output *(PC-GIVE)*

MODEL 8.1: Modelling d4lc_li1 by OLS
The Sample is 1958 (2) to 1975 (4) less 0 Forecasts

Variable	Coefficient	Std.Error	HCSE	t-value
d4ls1	-0.006	0.00244	0.00523	-2.6841
dd4li	0.5432	0.07877	0.09061	6.89683

$R^2 = 0.4722$ $\sigma = 0.016422$ F(2, 69) = 30.87 DW = 0.857
RSS = .0186092 for 2 Variables and 71 Observations
Information Criteria: SC = -8.126700; FPE = 0.000277

Tests Of Parameter CONSTANCY Over 1971 1 - 1975 4
Forecast $Chi^2(20)$ = 42.0[**]
CHOW TEST(20, 49)   = 2.07[*]

Modelling d4lc_li1 by RALS
Tests Of Parameter CONSTANCY Over 1971 1 - 1975 4
Forecast $Chi^2(20)$ = 35.0[*]
CHOW TEST(20, 47)   = 1.66

MODEL 8.2: Modelling d4lc by OLS
The Sample is 1958 (2) to 1975 (4) less 0 Forecasts

Variable	Coefficient	Std.Error	HCSE	t-value
d4li	0.5524	0.10168	0.10695	5.43296
dd4li	-0.222	0.04620	0.04532	-4.8098
lc_li 4	-0.090	0.01432	0.01362	-6.3208
inf	0.119	0.02703	0.02619	-4.4198
dinf	-0.234	0.09374	0.11404	-2.4982
htf	-0.077	0.13005	0.13864	-0.59516

$\sigma = 0.006649$ F(6, 65) =0 189.37 DW = 2.144

RSS = 0.0028737 for 6 Variables and 71 Observations
Information Criteria: SC = -9.754587; FPE = 0.000048

MODEL 8.3: Modelling d4lc_li1 by OLS
The Sample is 1958 (2) to 1975 (4) less 0 Forecasts

Variable	Coefficient	Std.Error	HCSE	t-value
d4ls1	0.0002	0.00103	0.00078	0.19798
dd4li	-0.001	0.04216	0.04214	-0.0245
dhf	1.003	0.05216	0.04563	19.240

σ = 0.006516 F(3, 68) =0 254.10 DW = 2.208
RSS = 0.0028877 for 3 Variables and 71 Observations
Information Criteria: SC = -9.929842; FPE = 0.000044

MODEL 8.4: Modelling dhru by OLS
The Sample is 1965 (4) to 1975 (4) less 0 Forecasts

Variable	Coefficient	Std.Error	HCSE	t-value
ht_dh	-0.0045	0.02106	0.01765	-0.21190

σ = 0.007568 F(1, 40) = 0.04 DW = 2.571
RSS = 0.0022909 for 1 Variable and 41 Observations
Information Criteria: SC = -9.701792; FPE = 0.000059

MODEL 8.5: Modelling htru by OLS
The Sample is 1965 (4) to 1975 (4) less 0 Forecasts

Variable	Coefficient	Std.Error	HCSE	t-value
dh_ht	0.2665	0.02799	0.02411	9.52167

σ = 0.010060 F(1, 40) = 90.66 DW = 2.108
RSS = 0.0040479 for 1 Variable and 41 Observations
Information Criteria: SC = -9.132548; FPE = 0.000104

8.5 Suggestions for Further Reading

The literature on non-nested hypotheses and related tests is quite abundant. Thorough discussions of the problem in an econometric context have been given by Pesaran (1974), Quandt (1974) and Pesaran and Deaton (1978). Reviews of the subject are included in MacKinnon (1983), Godfrey (1984) and McAleer and Pesaran (1986). Further developments of the J test can be found in Davidson and MacKinnon (1982) and, in a wider context, in Davidson and MacKinnon (1985). Godfrey (1989) reviews misspecification tests for nested models.

Not a great deal has been published on encompassing. Advanced papers on this subject are those of Mizon (1984) and Mizon and Richard (1986), where a detailed definition of encompassing is given, grounded in the concept of data generating processes (see Chapter 7). A simpler explanation and an example can be found in Hendry (1988a).

A straightforward example of an application of the Chong and Hendry forecast encompassing test is given by Charemza (1991), where the test is applied for a comparison of a large nonlinear structural model with a simple (naive) model. Holden and McGregor (1989) used encompassing tests for finding a good deflator for the *DHSY* model. The *J* test for choosing between different measures of money income was used by Cuthbertson and Taylor (1988). Various encompassing tests for analysing a model of a trade balance were applied by Ahumada (1985). An advanced empirical paper using encompassing to discriminate between a *VAR* and a structural model is that by Hendry and Mizon (1990).

A paper which considers the application of the use of encompassing for testing superexogeneity and the Lucas critique is that of Hendry (1988b). This idea has been further developed and applied to the analysis of consumption by Favero (1989).

Data Appendix

Year	Quarter	Consumption	Income	Prices
1957	1	5011	5657	61.8
	2	5368	6049	62.1
	3	5424	5914	63.1
	4	5718	6115	62.2
1958	1	5147	5836	63.2
	2	5439	6097	64.4
	3	5537	6052	64.4
	4	5818	6175	65.1
1959	1	5253	5955	64.9
	2	5669	6480	64.5
	3	5722	6387	64.9
	4	6069	6578	65.5
1960	1	5510	6330	64.9
	2	5913	6870	65.4
	3	5951	6821	65.9
	4	6246	7051	66.7
1961	1	5702	6693	66.6
	2	6062	7106	67.2
	3	6122	7168	68.5
	4	6380	7205	69.2
1962	1	5749	6734	70.1
	2	6154	7071	71.3
	3	6194	7181	71.4
	4	6489	7398	71.8
1963	1	5866	6933	72.1
	2	6367	7360	72.8
	3	6514	7605	72.4
	4	6718	7746	73.6
1964	1	6123	7366	73.7
	2	6520	7656	75.2
	3	6651	7779	75.5
	4	6895	7988	76.7

Year	Quarter	Consumption	Income	Prices
1965	1	6195	7607	77.6
	2	6592	7839	79.3
	3	6770	7902	79.6
	4	7005	8158	80.4
1966	1	6383	8167	81.0
	2	6816	7983	82.4
	3	6882	7913	82.9
	4	7068	8145	84.1
1967	1	6429	7802	84.5
	2	6865	8169	84.9
	3	7029	8291	85.0
	4	7310	8399	85.8
1968	1	6718	8323	86.8
	2	6968	8236	88.8
	3	7115	8263	89.8
	4	7430	8452	91.2
1969	1	6707	8248	93.0
	2	7077	8273	94.0
	3	7181	8364	94.8
	4	7617	8645	96.0
1970	1	6776	8313	98.0
	2	7221	8698	99.1
	3	7426	8796	100.2
	4	7786	8959	102.4
1971	1	6855	8589	104.9
	2	7335	8733	107.9
	3	7467	8941	109.2
	4	7952	9282	110.4
1972	1	7147	8972	112.9
	2	7636	9655	114.5
	3	7829	9584	116.9
	4	8332	10100	118.9
1973	1	7539	9750	122.3
	2	7948	10125	125.1
	3	8157	10241	127.6
	4	8691	10534	130.0

Year	Quarter	Consumption	Income	Prices
1974	1	7601	10001	137.0
	2	7985	9903	144.5
	3	8186	10507	150.0
	4	8798	11016	154.4
1975	1	7735	10473	165.0
	2	7984	10022	178.2
	3	8045	10224	186.5
	4	8646	10434	191.1

Description and sources of data:

Consumption:
Consumers' non-durable expenditure in the U.K. in 1970 prices;

Income:
Personal disposable income in the U.K. in 1970 prices;

Prices:
Consumers' expenditure deflator index, 1970=100,

Source: M. Pokorny (1987), *An Introduction to Econometrics*, page 408, Basil Blackwell Ltd. Original data source: Economic Trends, Annual Supplements, 1976 and 1981, HMSO.

Exercises for Discussion

Exercise 1 (Data mining)

Two independent researchers, A and B, presented regression equations to describe a variable y. Researcher A selected her equation by choosing two explanatory variables out of 10 'candidates' $x_1, x_2, ..., x_{10}$, while B selected his model with two explanatory variables out of four different 'candidates' z_1, z_2, z_3, z_4. There were 25 observations on each variable and the criteria for selecting explanatory variables to enter a model was on the basis of choosing those variables with the highest Student-t statistics. Assume that all the 'candidate' variables are orthogonal with respect to each other. The results are as follows:

Model selected by A:

$$y_t = \underset{(6.6)}{0.50} + \underset{(2.4)}{0.20 \cdot x_1} + \underset{(3.2)}{0.70 \cdot x_2}$$

Model selected by B:

$$y_t = \underset{(7.3)}{0.70} + \underset{(1.8)}{0.60 \cdot z_1} + \underset{(2.2)}{0.50 \cdot z_2}$$

where Student-t ratios are given in brackets. For the two equations above, compute the true significance levels if tests are conducted at a nominal 5% significance level. Is it possible to say which of the two results is more trustworthy?

Exercise 2 (Data mining)

Researcher 1, while trying to evaluate a relationship explaining a variable y, regressed it on the variable x_1, and then separately on x_2, x_3 and x_4 (that is four separate simple regressions were run). This researcher selected the model with the highest Student-t ratio on an explanatory variable, which was:

$$y_t = \underset{(2.91)}{0.25} - \underset{(4.12)}{5.31 \cdot x_3} + a \; residual$$

where the coefficient of determination $R^2 = 0.92$, and the Student-t statistics for coefficients are in parentheses. Independently, researcher 2 decided to regress y on variable x_2 only, without running any other regressions. The result was:

$$y_t = \underset{(2.91)}{0.31} - \underset{(2.12)}{3.26 \cdot x_2} + a \; residual$$

with $R^2 = 0.76$ Discuss whether it is possible to decide which of the results (that is of researchers 1 and 2) is better. Would you answer differently if

265

researcher 2 had decided to use x_3 rather than x_2 so that both researchers present the same final model? Comment on the possibility of 'Lovell bias' in these results.

Exercise 3 (The *DHSY* model)

The estimated *DHSY* aggregate consumption model for a certain country with the use of 70 quarterly observations is the following:

$$\Delta_4 cons_t = \underset{(15.3)}{0.30} \cdot \Delta_4 y_t - \underset{(4.0)}{0.10} \cdot \Delta\Delta_4 y_t + \underset{(2.2)}{0.127} \cdot (cons_{t-4} - y_{t-4})$$
$$+ \underset{(3.2)}{0.10} \cdot \Delta_4 p_t - \underset{(1.2)}{0.17} \cdot \Delta\Delta_4 p_t + a \ residual$$

where $cons_t$ is real aggregate consumption, y_t is total real disposable income and p_t is the price index (implicit price deflator). All variables are in natural logarithms, Student-t statistics for particular coefficients are in parentheses and Δ symbols are of the type $\Delta x_t = x_t - x_{t-1}$ and $\Delta_4 x_t = x_t - x_{t-4}$.

(i) Comment on the possible existence of an error correction mechanism in the above model.

(ii) Comment on the possible existence of Deaton's unanticipated inflation effect and/or the 'money illusion' effect.

Exercise 4 (General to specific modelling)

For the general unrestricted *ADL(2)* model, that is for:

$$y_t = a_1 y_{t-1} + a_2 y_{t-2} + b_0 x_t + b_1 x_{t-1} + b_2 x_{t-2} + an \ error \quad,$$

formulate a set of restrictions which generate the following specific models:

(i) A model in first differences with a second order error-correction mechanism, that is of the form:

$$\Delta y_t = \beta_1 \Delta x_t + \beta_2 (y_{t-1} - x_{t-1}) + \beta_3 (y_{t-2} - x_{t-2}) + an \ error \quad.$$

(ii) A specific model with two common factors, which is equivalent to a linear regression model with second-order autocorrelation in the errors, that is:

$$y_t = \alpha x_t + u_t \quad,$$

with:

$$u_t = \rho_1 u_{t-1} + \rho_2 u_{t-2} + \varepsilon_t \quad.$$

Exercise 5 (General to specific modelling)

In a process of single equation modelling with the use of the 'general to specific' methodology, the autoregressive distributed lag *(ADL)* model:

$$y_t = \alpha_1 y_{t-1} + \alpha_2 y_{t-2} + \beta_0 x_t + \beta_1 x_{t-1} + \beta_2 x_{t-2} + an\ error \quad ,$$

has been used as a general model. During the model reduction process the following specific models have been estimated:

Model A: $\underset{(3.73)}{y_t = 0.27 \cdot x_t} - \underset{(5.17)}{0.06 \cdot \cdot x_{t-1}} + a\ residual$

Model B: $\underset{(1.33)}{y_t = 0.73 \cdot y_{t-1}} + \underset{(3.34)}{0.15 \cdot \Delta x_t} + a\ residual$

where $\Delta x_t = x_t - x_{t-1}$ and Student-*t* statistics for the regression coefficients are in parentheses.

(i) Formulate restrictions on the parameters of the *ADL* model which have to be tested for the derivation of the specific models A and B.

(ii) Describe the procedure for testing the validity of the restrictions imposed (that is, formulate the null and alternative hypotheses and describe the computations for the particular steps in testing the restrictions).

(iii) Using the estimated models A and B evaluate, without formal testing, for which (if either) of the models the restrictions imposed on the general *ADL* model seem to be valid.

Exercise 6 (Testing for the order of integration)

For a series of quarterly, seasonally unadjusted data, the following ordinary least squares results were computed (with Student-*t* values given below the estimated parameters):

$$\underset{(3.31)}{\Delta_4 y_t = \alpha \cdot z_{t-4}} + augmentation \quad ,$$

$$\underset{(-2.81)}{\Delta \Delta_4 y_t = \beta \cdot \Delta_4 y_{t-1}} + augmentation \quad ,$$

$$\underset{(-4.33)}{\Delta \Delta \Delta_4 y_t = \gamma \cdot \Delta \Delta_4 y_{t-1}} + augmentation \quad ,$$

where the *OLS* estimates of particular parameters are denoted by α, β, γ and z_t is the variable transformed as in the Dickey-Hasza-Fuller test.

Decide what is the appropriate order of integration for the variable y_t.

Exercise 7 (Testing for the order of integration)

In order to decide on the order of integration of a series of 50 annual observations on a variable y_t the following Dickey-Fuller and Augmented Dickey-Fuller statistics have been computed (the OLS estimates of particular parameters are denoted by α, α_1, α_2, Student-*t* ratios are given in brackets below the symbols for the parameters, d denotes the Durbin-Watson autocorrelation statistic):

$$\Delta y_t = \underset{(3.3)}{\alpha} \cdot y_{t-1} \quad , \quad d = 1.03$$

$$\Delta y_t = \underset{(1.20)}{\alpha} \cdot y_{t-1} + \underset{(3.5)}{\alpha_1} \cdot \Delta y_{t-1} \quad , \quad d = 2.03$$

$$\Delta y_t = \underset{(-0.7)}{\alpha} \cdot y_{t-1} + \underset{(2.9)}{\alpha_1} \cdot \Delta y_{t-1} + \underset{(0.8)}{\alpha_2} \cdot \Delta y_{t-2} \quad , \quad d = 2.21$$

$$\Delta\Delta y_t = \underset{(-2.1)}{\alpha} \cdot \Delta y_{t-1} \quad , \quad d = 1.01$$

$$\Delta\Delta y_t = \underset{(-2.7)}{\alpha} \cdot \Delta y_{t-1} + \underset{(3.9)}{\alpha_1} \cdot \Delta\Delta y_{t-1} \quad , \quad d = 1.98$$

$$\Delta\Delta y_t = \underset{(-2.3)}{\alpha} \cdot \Delta y_{t-1} + \underset{(3.3)}{\alpha_1} \cdot \Delta\Delta y_{t-1} + \underset{(0.31)}{\alpha_2} \cdot \Delta\Delta y_{t-2} \quad , \quad d = 2.31$$

Given that the appropriate 5% critical value for the Dickey-Fuller and Augmented Dickey-Fuller statistics is 1.99 decide:

i)   What is the appropriate order of integration for the variable y_t ?

ii)   What is the appropriate length of augmentation for the test (if any)?

Exercise 8 (Integration and cointegration)
A simple wage-adjustment model is the following (w_t is a nominal wage, p_t is a price):

$$\Delta w_t = \alpha\Delta p_t + \beta(w_{t-1} - \gamma p_{t-1}) + u_t \quad .$$

Under the hypothesis of wage homogeneity, $\gamma = 1$. The *ADF* t-ratio statistics (computed without a constant term) using 30 observations, for levels and first differences of w_t and p_t are as follows:

w_t: 2.18 (levels); $- 3.37$ (first differences)

p_t: $- 0.25$ (levels); $- 8.11$ (first differences)

Under the assumption of wage homogeneity, that is where $\gamma = 1$, the cointegration of w_t and p_t was tested by the use of the ADF t-ratio statistic which took the value -4.97. Alternatively, where the assumption about homogeneity was dropped, w_t was regressed on p_t with the result:

$$w_t = \underset{(2.03)}{1.12} \cdot p_t + v_t, \quad ADF(v_t) = -0.58, \quad DW = 0.57, \quad R^2 = 0.85,$$

where $ADF(v_t)$ is the *ADF* statistic computed for the *OLS* residuals of the above equation, DW is the Durbin-Watson statistic, R^2 is the coefficient of determination and the Student-t ratio is in brackets below the estimated coefficient.

Answer the following questions:
(i)   What are the orders of integration of p_t and w_t?
(ii) Is the necessary condition for cointegration of p_t and w_t met?
(iii) Does the 'rule of thumb' for comparing R^2 and DW confirm the hypothesis about cointegration in the non-homogeneous model?
(iv) Does the ADF test confirm this hypothesis in the non-homogeneous model?
(v)   Are p_t and w_t cointegrated under the hypothesis of homogeneity?
(vi) For estimating the wage-adjustment equation, would you prefer to use the homogeneity assumption, or to apply the Engle-Granger procedure for the non-homogeneous model?

Exercise 9 (Integration and cointegration)

While analysing the relationship between money (m_t) and income (y_t), an econometrician estimated the following regression using ordinary least squares and 25 annual observations. (Data are in real terms, and in logarithms.)

$$m_t = \underset{(5.31)}{0.858} \cdot y_t + u_t$$

$$R^2 = 0.80 \quad , \quad DW = 0.75 \quad , \quad ADF(u_t) = -1.75 \quad ,$$
$$ADF(m_t) = -3.22 \quad , \quad ADF(y_t) = -4.31 \quad ,$$

where the Student-t statistic is given in brackets below the estimated parameter, R^2 is the coefficient of determination, DW is the Durbin-Watson statistic computed for the residuals u_t, and $ADF(\cdot)$ is the augmented Dickey-Fuller statistic computed for u_t, m_t and y_t respectively.

Using the results above, establish whether:
(i)   the series m_t and y_t are integrated of the same order;
(ii) the series m_t and y_t are cointegrated;
(iii) the model can be sensibly estimated in first differences, with or without an error correction mechanism.

Exercise 10 (Cointegration)

Decide, using the results below, whether it makes sense to test for cointegration of the dependent and explanatory variables in models (a) and (b). What are the necessary conditions for the existence of cointegration in these models and how can they be tested?

Model (a): $y_t = \alpha_1 x_{1t} + \alpha_2 x_{2t} + u_t$,

Model (b): $y_t = \alpha_1 x_{1t} + u_t$.

The Augmented Dickey-Fuller t-ratio statistics computed for levels and first differences of particular variables, using 50 observations and without a constant term in the ADF regression equation, are as follows:

y_t: -5.24 (levels); 11.63 (first differences)

x_{1t}: 1.21 (levels); -4.05 (first differences)

x_{2t}: -0.11(levels); -7.27 (first differences)

Exercise 11 (Cointegration)

The estimates of a static demand for money function, formulated in logarithms and based on 60 annual observations are (m_t = money, y_t = nominal income, r_t = interest rate, ε_t = error term, Student-t values are in parentheses):

$$m_t = \underset{(4.1)}{1.0} + \underset{(3.3)}{0.22\cdot y_t} - \underset{(-5.6)}{0.70\cdot r_t} + \varepsilon_t$$

$$R^2 = 0.71 \quad , \quad ADF(\varepsilon_t) = -6.20 \quad , \quad DW = 2.05 \quad ,$$

where R^2 is the coefficient of determination, ADF is the Augmented Dickey-Fuller statistic for the error term ε_t (in the form of the Student-t test) and DW is the Durbin-Watson statistic for the residuals. The Augmented Dickey-Fuller integration statistics (in the Student-t form) computed for all the variables are the following:

for m_t: 1.25 ;   for y_t: 3.11 ;   for r_t: 0.91 .

(i) Comment on the results. Is there a danger of spurious regression in the model?

(ii) Test and comment for the possible presence or absence of cointegration of the variables.

(iii) Discuss whether it is advisable to test further for the possible use of first differences of variables rather than levels and to introduce an error correction mechanism. If so, how would you proceed?

Exercise 12 (Cointegration)

For 30 annual observations, the estimated static regression of the logarithm of money (mon_t) on the logarithm of disposable income (y_t), and the logarithm of prices (p_t), gives the following result:

$$mon_t = 0.678y_t + 1.17p_t + \varepsilon_t \quad ,$$

$$R^2 = 0.77 \; ; \; DW = 0.45 \; ; \; ADF(\varepsilon_t) = -1.34$$

where R^2 is a coefficient of determination, DW is the Durbin-Watson statistic for the residuals ε_t and $ADF(\varepsilon_t)$ is the Augmented Dickey-Fuller statistic computed for the residuals. The 5% critical values for the lower limits for the ADF statistic for 30 observations are the following:

for $m = 0 : -1.99$; for $m = 1 : -3.82$;

for $m = 2 : -3.82$; for $m = 3 : -4.17$.

The hypothesis of money non-neutrality requires that in the above relationship the coefficient of p_t is equal to one. Under this restriction, the regression results are:

$$mon_t - p_t = 0.896 y_t + u_t \quad ,$$

$$R^2 = 0.77 \; ; DW = 0.45 \; ; ADF(u_t) = -3.14 ,$$

where $ADF(u_t)$ is the Augmented Dickey-Fuller statistic computed for the residuals. It is known that the order of integration of mon_t is two, of p_t is two, of y_t is one and of the difference between mon_t and p_t is one. Using these results, decide which of the relationships above (that is relationships assuming and not assuming the neutrality of money) can be regarded as the cointegrating relationship.

Exercise 13 (General to specific modelling and cointegration)
The 'general to specific' methodology has been applied for modelling the relationship between consumption, c_t and income, y_t using annual data in their natural logarithms. The procedure started from an unrestricted $ADL(2)$, model,

$$a(L)c_t = b(L)y_t + \varepsilon_t \quad ,$$

$$a(L) = 1 - \alpha_1 L - \alpha_2 L^2 \quad ,$$

$$b(L) = \beta_0 + \beta_1 L + \beta_2 L^2 \quad ,$$

where L is the lag operator and ε_t is an error term. After a series of reductions the following specific model has been derived:

$$\Delta c_t = \theta \Delta y_t + error$$

where Δ stands for the first difference operator. The estimation shows that $0 < \theta < 1$.

i) Describe the problem which arises in the economic interpretation of the model. Is it possible to find both long-run and steady-state (stable equilibrium) solutions in this model?

ii) Derive restrictions that must be imposed on the general model in order to derive the specific model given above.

iii) Noting that the error correction mechanism is absent from the specific equation, comment on the possibility of cointegration between c_t and y_t.

Exercise 14 (Cointegration)
While testing the purchasing power parity (*PPP*) hypothesis, a series of 30 annual observations on the logarithms of the nominal exchange rate, d_t , the domestic price index, p_t and the foreign country price level, p_t^*, have been examined. It is often claimed that, in order for the 'strong' version of the PPP hypothesis to hold, the real exchange rate, that is:

$$r_t = d_t - (p_t - p_t^*) \quad ,$$

must be stationary. The 'weak' PPP holds if the relationship:

$$d_t = \alpha + \beta(p_t - p_t^*) \quad ,$$

is stationary (where α and β are constant coeficients).

It has been found that the order of integration of the variables d_t , p_t and p_t^* is one. For r_t, the computed Augmented Dickey-Fuller (*ADF*) statistic is equal to -1.16. The regression of d_t on a constant and $(p_t - p_t^*)$ gives the following result:

$$d_t = 0.67 + 1.13(p_t - p_t^*) \quad ,$$

$$DW = 1.21 , \quad R^2 = 0.71 , \quad ADF(\varepsilon_t) = -4.18,$$

where *DW* denotes the Durbin-Watson autocorrelation statistic, R^2 is the coefficient of determination and $ADF(\varepsilon_t)$ is the Augmented Dickey-Fuller statistic computed for the residuals of this regression.

Using the results given above, decide in favour or against the weak and strong *PPP* hypotheses.

Describe how would you proceed if it is found that the order of integration of the variable d_t is one, but the variables p_t and p_t^* are each integrated of order two.

Exercise 15 (*VAR* and causality)
(i) Describe the main differences between multi-equation structural modelling (Cowles Commission methodology) and vector autoregressive (*VAR*) modelling.
(ii) In order to detect possible causality between inflation π_t and money supply m_t the following two equation *VAR* model was estimated using 80 quarterly observations:

$$\pi_t = \sum_{i=1}^{4} \alpha_{pi} \pi_{t-i} + \sum_{i=1}^{4} \beta_{pi} m_{t-i} + intercept + trend$$
$$+ 3 \; seasonal \; dummy \; variables + error \; term$$

$$m_t = \sum_{i=1}^{4} \alpha_{mi} \pi_{t-i} + \sum_{i=1}^{4} \beta_{mi} m_{t-i} + intercept + trend$$

$$+ 3 \ seasonal \ dummy \ variables + error \ term$$

The following Lagrange Multiplier (*LMF*) statistics were computed for testing the restrictions:

(a) $\beta_{p1} = \beta_{p2} = \beta_{p3} = \beta_{p4} = 0$: $LMF = 38.13$

(b) $\alpha_{m1} = \alpha_{m2} = \alpha_{m3} = \alpha_{m4} = 0$: $LMF = 1.16$

Determine at the 5% level of significance whether there is a one way causal relation from inflation to money, from money to inflation, or whether there is a feedback relation between money and inflation. What are the appropriate degrees of freedom for these *LMF* tests?

Exercise 16 (*VAR* and causality)
In order to investigate the money neutrality hypothesis, a researcher decides to start with a contegration analysis between money (m_t) and an industrial production index (p_t), followed by causality analysis. For this analysis 60 quarterly, seasonally adjusted observations in their natural logarithms are used. It is assumed that both m_t and p_t series are integrated of order one. The OLS estimation results of the long-run relationship are the following:

$$p_t = \underset{(18.22)}{0.321} + \underset{(3.56)}{0.014} m_t + u_t \quad,$$

$$R^2 = 0.876 \ , DW = 0.56 \ ,$$

where Student *t*-values are given in brackets, R^2 is the coefficient of determination, *DW* is the Durbin-Watson statistic and u_t are the residuals. The vector autoregressive model is the following:

$$\Delta p_t = \alpha_{11} \Delta p_{t-1} + \alpha_{12} \Delta p_{t-2} + \beta_{11} \Delta m_{t-1} + \beta_{12} \Delta m_{t-2} + residuals$$

$$\Delta m_t = \alpha_{21} \Delta p_{t-1} + \alpha_{22} \Delta p_{t-2} + \beta_{21} \Delta m_{t-1} + \beta_{22} \Delta m_{t-2} + residuals$$

The particular calculated Lagrange Multiplier statistics are the following:

for testing the hypothesis: $\beta_{11} = \beta_{12} = 0$: 8.43 *

for testing the hypothesis: $\alpha_{21} = \alpha_{22} = 0$: 2.11

The statistic significant at the 0.05 significance level is marked by a star.
Are money and industrial production cointegrated? How did you arrive at your conclusion?

Exercise 17 (*VAR* and causality)

(i) Describe the Granger concept of causality and its role in econometric modelling.

(ii) In order to investigate a relationship between GNP (denoted by y_t) and government spending (g_t), a two equation vector autoregressive (*VAR*) model was estimated by the ordinary least squares method, using 30 annual observations. The results were as follows:

$$y_t = \underset{(1.0)}{0.25} + \underset{(5.3)}{0.66} \cdot y_{t-1} + \underset{(1.3)}{0.37} \cdot g_{t-1} + \varepsilon_t \quad , \quad R^2 = 0.73$$

$$g_t = \underset{(5.0)}{0.87} + \underset{(3.0)}{0.18} \cdot y_{t-1} + \underset{(3.2)}{0.50} \cdot g_{t-1} + \varepsilon_t \quad , \quad R^2 = 0.90$$

where R^2 is the coefficient of determination and Student-t statistics are given in brackets below the parameter estimates. Using the results above, can you decide in favour of the Wagnerian hypothesis that GNP is a Granger cause for government expenditure, or in favour of the Keynesian hypothesis that government expenditures are a Granger cause for GNP, or for neither hypothesis?

Exercise 18 (*VAR*, causality and conditioning)

The following *VAR* model is formulated for the relationship between the rate of growth of GDP in country A (y_t) and the rate of growth of GDP in country B (x_t):

$$y_t = \alpha_{11} y_{t-1} + \beta_{11} x_{t-1} + u_{1t} \quad ,$$

$$x_t = \alpha_{21} y_{t-1} + \beta_{22} x_{t-1} + u_{2t} \quad ,$$

$$u_t = \begin{bmatrix} u_{1t} \\ u_{2t} \end{bmatrix} \sim IID\ N(0, \Sigma) \quad ,$$

where *IID N* stands for identically and independently distributed vectors of random normal variables with zero means and covariance matrix Σ:

$$\Sigma = \begin{bmatrix} \sigma_{11} & \sigma_{12} \\ \sigma_{21} & \sigma_{22} \end{bmatrix} .$$

i) What has to be assumed about the integration orders of y_t and x_t, if the above model is to be successfully estimated by the ordinary least squares method and subsequently used for Granger causality analysis?

ii) Transform the above *VAR* into a conditional model with orthogonalized innovations. Condition y_t for x_t (that is, make y_t be 'explained' directly by x_t)

Exercise 19 (*VAR*, causality and conditioning)

The following data generating process (*DGP*) is given:

$$y_t = \alpha_0 + u_{1t} \quad ,$$

$$x_t = \beta_0 + \beta_1 y_{t-1} + u_{2t} \quad ,$$

$$u_t = \begin{bmatrix} u_{1t} \\ u_{2t} \end{bmatrix} \sim IID\ N(0, \Sigma) \quad .$$

where *IID N* stands for identically and independently distributed vectors of random normal variables with zero means and covariance matrix Σ :

$$\Sigma = \begin{bmatrix} \sigma_{11} & \sigma_{12} \\ \sigma_{21} & \sigma_{22} \end{bmatrix} \quad .$$

i) Derive the conditional process of y_t for x_t (that is, make y_t be 'explained' directly by x_t through orthogonalization).

ii) Formulate the condition(s) which must be fulfilled in order for x_t to be weakly exogenous for y_t , with the parameters of interest being those of the conditional process.

iii) Formulate the condition(s) which must be fulfilled in order for x_t to be strongly exogenous for y_t.

Exercise 20 (*VAR* and cointegration)

Time series y_t and x_t evolve according to:

$$\begin{bmatrix} \Delta y_t \\ \Delta x_t \end{bmatrix} = \begin{bmatrix} -0.5 & 0.5 \\ -0.6 & 0.6 \end{bmatrix} \begin{bmatrix} y_{t-1} \\ x_{t-1} \end{bmatrix} + \begin{bmatrix} \varepsilon_{1t} \\ \varepsilon_{2t} \end{bmatrix}$$

where $\varepsilon_t = (\varepsilon_{1t}\ \varepsilon_{2t})' \sim IID\ N(0, \Sigma)$, and Σ is a diagonal matrix. Find the cointegrating vector.

Appendix: Statistical Tables

Technical Notes

Tables of critical values of particular test statistics have been prepared through simulation repeated n times (where n is sufficiently large) of a data generating process (DGP) which represents the process under the null hypothesis, computing the statistics n times and then analysing the percentiles of simulated distributions of particular test statistics. For each test the procedure (that is, the simulation of distributions of statistics formed using n computed test statistics) has been repeated for different sample sizes (that is, lengths of individual data series chosen for the DGP in each replication). This length of data series is denoted by T. Let the percentile computed for a distribution obtained from a DGP using samples of size T be denoted as π_T.

Since T varies, it is possible to smooth the percentiles through a regression approximation. It was found out that the most satisfactory approximation was given by a quadratic regression:

$$\pi_T = \alpha + \beta \frac{1}{\ln(T)} + \gamma \frac{1}{[\ln(T)]^2} + e_T \quad ,$$

where α, β and γ are the regression coefficients and e_T denotes residuals of the regression. Let the standard error of this regression be denoted as $s(e_T)$ and the fitted values as $\hat{\pi}_T$. Hence, upper and lower limits for the smoothed percentiles of distributions of particular statistics, regarded as the upper and lower limits for the critical values of test statistics and denoted as π_T^l and π_T^u respectively are given by:

$$\pi_T^l = \hat{\pi}_T - 2 \cdot [s(e_T) + s(\pi_T)] \quad ,$$

and

$$\pi_T^u = \hat{\pi}_T + 2 \cdot [s(e_T) + s(\pi_T)] \quad ,$$

where $s(\pi_T)$ is the David and Johnson (1954) estimate of the standard error of a particular percentile.

The computations have been programmed using the *GAUSS* 4.2 language and conducted on the CRAY CS6400 computer at the University of Manchester under the UNIX operating system.

Particular DGPs, sample sizes and numbers of replications used for the computations are described below:

Dickey-Fuller integration test:

DGP:

$$y_t = \alpha_0 + y_{t-1} + \alpha_1 t + \sum_{i=1}^{4} \delta_i Q i_t + \epsilon_t \quad , \quad y_0 \sim N(0,1) \quad ,$$

where $\epsilon_t \sim IID\ N(0,1)$ and $Q i_t$ s are seasonal (quarterly) dummy variables and $t = 1, 2, \ldots, T$. For each integration Dickey-Fuller statistic there were 24 different sample sizes used, namely $T = 15, 20, 25, 30, 40, 50, 75, 100, 125, 150, 175, 200, 225, 250, 275, 300, 325, 350, 375, 400, 425, 450, 475, 500$.

Restrictions, values of the particular *DGP* parameters and numbers of replications n were as follows:

1. Dickey-Fuller test without an intercept (critical values in Table 1, column A):
   $\alpha_0 = \alpha_1 = $ all $\delta_i s = 0$, $n = 50,000$ for each T (total number of replications is 1,200,000).

2. Dickey-Fuller test with an intercept (critical values in Table 1, column B):
   $\alpha_1 = $ all $\delta_i s = 0$, $\alpha_0 = 1$, $n = 50,000$ for each T (total number of replications is 1,200,000).

3. Dickey-Fuller test with an intercept and trend (critical values in Table 1, column C):
   all $\delta_i s = 0$, $\alpha_0 = 1$, $\alpha_1 = 1/T$, $n = 50,000$ for each T (total number of replications is 1,200,000).

4. Dickey-Fuller test with quarterly seasonals (critical values in Table 1, column D):
   $\alpha_0 = \alpha_1 = 0$, $\delta_1 = -0.1$, $\delta_2 = 0.1$, $\delta_3 = -0.1$, $\delta_4 = 0.1$, $n = 23,000$ for each T (total number of replications is 552,000).

Dickey-Fuller cointegration test:
   DGP:

$$y_t = \beta_0 + \sum_{i=1}^{m} \beta_i x_{i,t} + \sum_{i=1}^{4} \delta_i Q i_t + u_t \quad ,$$

$$u_t = u_{t-1} + \epsilon_{u,t} \quad , \quad u_0 \sim N(0,1) \quad ,$$

$$x_{i,t} = \alpha + x_{i,t-1} + \epsilon_{i,t} \quad , \quad x_{i,0} \sim N(0,1) \quad ,$$

$$\epsilon_{u,t} \sim IID\ N(0,1) \quad ,$$

$$\epsilon_{i,t} \sim IID\ N(0,1) \quad ,$$

$$\beta_i = 1/m \quad , \quad m = 1, 2, \ldots, 8 \quad , \quad t = 1, 2, \ldots, T \quad .$$

The 24 different sample sizes used were the same as for the integration Dickey-Fuller statistics. Restrictions, values of the particular *DGP* parameters and numbers of replications *n* were as follows:

5. Dickey-Fuller test without an intercept (critical values in Table 2):
   $\beta_0 = \alpha = $ all $\delta_i s = 0$, $n = 50,000$ for each T for $m = 1, 2, ..., 5$ (total number of replications is 1,200,000) and $n = 30,000$ for each T for $n = 6$, 7, 8 (total number of replications for every m is 720,000).

6. Dickey-Fuller test with an intercept (critical values in Table 3):
   $\beta_0 = \alpha = 1$, all $\delta_i s = 0$, $n = 50,000$ for each T for $m = 1, 2, ..., 5$ (total number of replications is 1,200,000) and $n = 30,000$ for each T for $n = 6$ 7, 8 (total number of replications for every m is 720,000).

7. Dickey-Fuller test with deterministic quarterly seasonality (critical values in Table 4):
   $\beta_0 = \alpha = 0$, $\delta_1 = -0.1$, $\delta_2 = 0.1$, $\delta_3 = -0.1$, $\delta_4 = 0.1$, $n = 25,000$ for each T and for each m (total number of replications for every m is 600,000).

Dickey-Hasza-Fuller seasonal integration test:
   DGP:

$$y_t = \alpha_0 + y_{t-s} + \epsilon_t \ , \ y_0 \sim N(0,1) \ , \ s = 4, 12 \ .$$

where $\epsilon_t \sim IID \ N(0,1)$ and $t = 1, 2, ..., T$. For quarterly data $(s = 4)$, $T = 25$, 30, 40, 50, 75, 100, 125, 150, 200, 300, 400, 500. For monthly data $(s = 12)$, $T = 100, 150, 200, 300, 400, 500, 600, 800, 1,000, 1,200, 1,400, 1,600$.
   Restrictions, values of the particular *DGP* parameters and numbers of replications *n* were as follows (all critical values are in Table 5):

8. Dickey-Hasza-Fuller test without an intercept for the quarterly data $(\alpha_0 = 0$, $s = 4$, $n = 50,000$ for each T (total number of replications is 600,000).

9. Dickey-Hasza-Fuller test without an intercept for monthly data:
   $\alpha_0 = 0$, $s = 12$, $n = 25,000$ for each T (total number of replications is 300,000).

10. Dickey-Hasza-Fuller test with an intercept for quarterly data:
    $\alpha_0 = 1$, $s = 4$, $n = 50,000$ for each T (total number of replications is 600,000).

11. Dickey-Hasza-Fuller test with an intercept for monthly data:
    $\alpha_0 = 1$, $s = 12$, $n = 20,000$ for each T (total number of replications is 240,000).

Perron additive outlier integration test:
  DGP:

$$y_t = y_{t-1} + dtb_t + \epsilon_t \quad, \quad y_0 \sim N(0, 1) \quad,$$

where $\epsilon_t \sim IID\ N(0, 1)$ and:

$$dtb_t = \begin{cases} 1 & \text{for} \quad t = T \cdot (\lambda + 1) \\ 0 & \text{otherwise} \end{cases} \quad,$$

$t = 1, 2, ..., T$ and $\lambda = 0.1, 0.2, 0.3, 0.4, 0.5$. For each λ there were 12 different sample sizes used: $T = 20, 25, 30, 40, 50, 75, 100, 125, 150, 200, 300, 500$. For each T and each λ there were 50,000 replications made (total number of replications for every λ is 600,000). All critical values are in Table 6.

HEGY seasonal integration test for quarterly data:
  DGP:

$$y_t = y_{t-4} + \epsilon_t \quad, \quad y_0 \sim N(0, 1).$$

where $\epsilon_t \sim IID\ N(0, 1)$ and $t = 1, 2, ..., T$, $T = 25, 30, 40, 50, 75, 100, 125, 150, 200, 300, 400, 500$. The same *DGP* has been used for all 3 *HEGY* tests, namely without an intercept (Table 7), with an intercept (Table 8) and with deterministic seasonality (Table 9). There is an inconsistency in the way these *HEGY* tables are constructed in comparison with the other tables, where the deterministic components in the *DGPs* (constant, trend and seasonals) are regarded as true rather than nuisance parameters. The reason for this change is the need for comparability between the tables presented here and the original ones, published in Hylleberg *et al.* (1990) which uses the above *DGP* (see also Smith and Taylor (1995)). For the tests with and without an intercept, the number of replications for each T was 50,000, which gives a total number of replications equal to 600,000, and for the tests with deterministic seasonality the number of replications for each T was 45,000 with a total number of replications equal to 540,000.

Table 1: Dickey-Fuller and Augmented Dickey-Fuller integration tests; critical values (minus sign omitted), 1% level of significance.

n	A lower	A upper	B lower	B upper	C lower	C upper	D lower	D upper
15	2.79	2.68	3.28	3.15	4.76	4.54	3.62	3.41
20	2.74	2.62	3.08	2.94	4.56	4.34	3.58	3.36
25	2.71	2.60	2.96	2.82	4.41	4.19	3.55	3.34
30	2.70	2.58	2.88	2.74	4.29	4.07	3.54	3.33
40	2.67	2.56	2.78	2.64	4.11	3.90	3.52	3.31
50	2.66	2.55	2.72	2.59	3.98	3.77	3.52	3.31
75	2.65	2.53	2.64	2.50	3.74	3.55	3.52	3.30
100	2.64	2.52	2.60	2.46	3.62	3.41	3.52	3.30
125	2.64	2.52	2.57	2.44	3.52	3.31	3.52	3.31
150	2.64	2.52	2.55	2.42	3.45	3.29	3.52	3.31
175	2.63	2.52	2.54	2.40	3.38	3.17	3.52	3.31
200	2.63	2.52	2.53	2.39	3.33	3.11	3.53	3.31
225	2.63	2.52	2.52	2.39	3.28	3.07	3.53	3.32
250	2.63	2.52	2.52	2.38	3.25	3.03	3.53	3.32
275	2.63	2.52	2.51	2.37	3.21	3.00	3.53	3.32
300	2.63	2.52	2.50	2.37	3.18	2.96	3.53	3.32
325	2.63	2.52	2.50	2.36	3.15	2.94	3.54	3.32
350	2.63	2.52	2.50	2.36	3.13	2.91	3.54	3.33
375	2.63	2.52	2.49	2.36	3.11	2.89	3.54	3.33
400	2.63	2.52	2.49	2.35	3.09	2.87	3.54	3.33
425	2.63	2.52	2.49	2.35	3.07	2.85	3.54	3.33
450	2.63	2.52	2.49	2.35	3.05	2.83	3.54	3.33
475	2.63	2.52	2.48	2.35	3.03	2.81	3.54	3.33
500	2.63	2.52	2.48	2.35	3.02	2.80	3.55	3.33

KEY: Column A: test equation without intercept
Column B: test equation with intercept
Column C: test equation with intercept and trend
Column D: test equation with quarterly seasonals

Table 1, *cntd*: Dickey-Fuller and Augmented Dickey-Fuller integration tests; critical values (minus sign omitted), 5% level of significance.

n	A		B		C		D	
	lower	upper	lower	upper	lower	upper	lower	upper
15	2.01	1.94	2.31	2.22	3.69	3.55	2.72	2.60
20	2.00	1.93	2.18	2.10	3.63	3.49	2.76	2.64
25	2.00	1.92	2.11	2.02	3.55	3.41	2.79	2.67
30	1.99	1.92	2.06	1.97	3.47	3.33	2.80	2.68
40	1.99	1.92	2.00	1.91	3.34	3.20	2.83	2.71
50	1.99	1.91	1.96	1.87	3.24	3.10	2.84	2.72
75	1.98	1.91	1.90	1.81	3.05	2.90	2.86	2.74
100	1.98	1.91	1.87	1.78	2.91	2.77	2.87	2.75
125	1.98	1.91	1.85	1.76	2.82	2.67	2.88	2.76
150	1.98	1.91	1.83	1.75	2.74	2.60	2.89	2.77
175	1.98	1.91	1.82	1.74	2.67	2.53	2.89	2.77
200	1.98	1.91	1.81	1.73	2.62	2.48	2.90	2.78
225	1.98	1.91	1.81	1.72	2.57	2.43	2.90	2.78
250	1.98	1.91	1.80	1.72	2.53	2.39	2.90	2.78
275	1.98	1.91	1.80	1.71	2.50	2.36	2.90	2.78
300	1.98	1.91	1.79	1.71	2.47	2.32	2.91	2.79
325	1.98	1.91	1.79	1.70	2.44	2.30	2.91	2.79
350	1.98	1.91	1.78	1.70	2.41	2.27	2.91	2.79
375	1.98	1.91	1.78	1.69	2.39	2.25	2.91	2.79
400	1.98	1.91	1.78	1.69	2.36	2.22	2.91	2.79
425	1.98	1.91	1.77	1.69	2.34	2.20	2.91	2.79
450	1.98	1.91	1.77	1.69	2.32	2.18	2.91	2.79
475	1.98	1.90	1.77	1.68	2.31	2.16	2.92	2.79
500	1.98	1.90	1.77	1.68	2.29	2.15	2.92	2.80

KEY: Column A: test equation without intercept
     Column B: test equation with intercept
     Column C: test equation with intercept and trend
     Column D: test equation with quarterly seasonals

**Table 1, *cntd.*: Dickey-Fuller and Augmented Dickey-Fuller
integration tests; critical values (minus sign omitted),
10% level of significance.**

n	A lower	A upper	B lower	B upper	C lower	C upper	D lower	D upper
15	1.64	1.57	1.85	1.78	3.24	3.11	2.31	2.23
20	1.64	1.58	1.76	1.69	3.21	3.09	2.38	2.30
25	1.65	1.58	1.70	1.63	3.15	3.03	2.43	2.34
30	1.65	1.58	1.66	1.59	3.09	2.97	2.45	2.37
40	1.65	1.58	1.61	1.54	2.97	2.85	2.49	2.41
50	1.65	1.58	1.57	1.51	2.87	2.75	2.51	2.43
75	1.65	1.58	1.52	1.46	2.68	2.56	2.54	2.46
100	1.65	1.58	1.49	1.43	2.55	2.43	2.56	2.48
125	1.65	1.58	1.48	1.41	2.45	2.33	2.57	2.48
150	1.65	1.58	1.46	1.39	2.38	2.25	2.57	2.49
175	1.65	1.58	1.45	1.38	2.31	2.19	2.58	2.50
200	1.65	1.58	1.44	1.38	2.26	2.13	2.58	2.50
225	1.65	1.58	1.43	1.37	2.21	2.09	2.59	2.50
250	1.65	1.58	1.43	1.36	2.17	2.05	2.59	2.51
275	1.65	1.58	1.42	1.36	2.13	2.01	2.59	2.51
300	1.65	1.58	1.42	1.35	2.10	1.98	2.59	2.51
325	1.65	1.58	1.42	1.35	2.07	1.95	2.59	2.51
350	1.65	1.58	1.41	1.34	2.04	1.92	2.59	2.51
375	1.65	1.58	1.41	1.34	2.02	1.89	2.60	2.51
400	1.65	1.58	1.40	1.34	1.99	1.87	2.60	2.52
425	1.65	1.58	1.40	1.33	1.97	1.85	2.60	2.52
450	1.65	1.58	1.40	1.33	1.95	1.83	2.60	2.52
475	1.65	1.58	1.40	1.33	1.93	1.81	2.60	2.52
500	1.65	1.58	1.39	1.33	1.91	1.79	2.60	2.52

KEY: Column A: test equation without intercept
Column B: test equation with intercept
Column C: test equation with intercept and trend
Column D: test equation with quarterly seasonals

**Table 2: Dickey-Fuller and Augmented Dickey-Fuller
cointegration tests;**
critical values (minus sign omitted), without intercept,
1% level of significance, m = 1,...,4

n	m=1		m=2		m=3		m=4	
	lower	upper	lower	upper	lower	upper	lower	upper
15	4.15	3.66	4.84	4.62	5.51	5.37	6.17	6.03
20	4.43	3.94	4.73	4.51	5.21	5.07	5.77	5.64
25	4.66	4.17	4.68	4.46	5.05	4.91	5.55	5.42
30	4.85	4.36	4.65	4.44	4.95	4.81	5.41	5.27
40	5.14	4.64	4.63	4.42	4.83	4.70	5.24	5.10
50	5.35	4.86	4.63	4.42	4.77	4.63	5.14	5.01
75	5.71	5.21	4.65	4.43	4.69	4.55	5.02	4.88
100	5.94	5.45	4.66	4.45	4.65	4.51	4.96	4.82
125	6.11	5.62	4.68	4.46	4.63	4.49	4.92	4.78
150	6.24	5.75	4.69	4.48	4.62	4.48	4.90	4.76
175	6.35	5.86	4.71	4.49	4.61	4.47	4.88	4.74
200	6.44	5.95	4.72	4.50	4.61	4.47	4.87	4.73
225	6.51	6.02	4.73	4.51	4.60	4.46	4.86	4.72
250	6.58	6.09	4.74	4.52	4.60	4.46	4.85	4.72
275	6.64	6.15	4.75	4.53	4.60	4.46	4.85	4.71
300	6.69	6.20	4.75	4.54	4.60	4.46	4.84	4.71
325	6.74	6.25	4.76	4.55	4.60	4.46	4.84	4.70
350	6.78	6.29	4.77	4.55	4.60	4.46	4.84	4.70
375	6.82	6.33	4.77	4.56	4.60	4.46	4.84	4.70
400	6.86	6.37	4.78	4.56	4.60	4.46	4.83	4.70
425	6.89	6.40	4.78	4.57	4.60	4.46	4.83	4.69
450	6.92	6.43	4.79	4.57	4.60	4.46	4.83	4.69
475	6.95	6.46	4.79	4.58	4.60	4.46	4.83	4.69
500	6.98	6.49	4.80	4.58	4.60	4.46	4.83	4.69

**Table 2, *cntd.*: Dickey-Fuller and Augmented Dickey-Fuller
cointegration tests;**
critical values (minus sign omitted), without intercept,
1% level of significance, m = 5,...,8

n	m=5		m=6		m=7		m=8	
	lower	upper	lower	upper	lower	upper	lower	upper
15	6.86	6.73	7.46	7.28	8.03	7.86	8.59	8.38
20	6.34	6.21	6.86	6.69	7.34	7.17	7.83	7.62
25	6.05	5.93	6.53	6.35	6.95	6.78	7.40	7.19
30	5.87	5.74	6.32	6.14	6.71	6.54	7.13	6.92
40	5.65	5.52	6.06	5.89	6.41	6.24	6.80	6.59
50	5.52	5.39	5.91	5.74	6.24	6.07	6.60	6.40
75	5.36	5.23	5.72	5.54	6.02	5.85	6.35	6.14
100	5.28	5.15	5.63	5.45	5.91	5.74	6.23	6.02
125	5.23	5.11	5.57	5.40	5.85	5.68	6.16	5.95
150	5.21	5.08	5.54	5.36	5.81	5.64	6.11	5.90
175	5.19	5.06	5.51	5.34	5.78	5.61	6.08	5.87
200	5.17	5.04	5.49	5.32	5.76	5.59	6.05	5.84
225	5.16	5.03	5.48	5.30	5.75	5.58	6.03	5.82
250	5.15	5.02	5.47	5.29	5.73	5.56	6.02	5.81
275	5.14	5.02	5.46	5.28	5.72	5.55	6.01	5.80
300	5.14	5.01	5.45	5.28	5.72	5.55	6.00	5.79
325	5.13	5.01	5.45	5.27	5.71	5.54	5.99	5.78
350	5.13	5.00	5.44	5.27	5.71	5.54	5.98	5.77
375	5.13	5.00	5.44	5.26	5.70	5.53	5.98	5.77
400	5.13	5.00	5.44	5.26	5.70	5.53	5.97	5.76
425	5.12	5.00	5.43	5.26	5.69	5.52	5.97	5.76
450	5.12	4.99	5.43	5.25	5.69	5.52	5.96	5.75
475	5.12	4.99	5.43	5.25	5.69	5.52	5.96	5.75
500	5.12	4.99	5.43	5.25	5.69	5.52	5.96	5.75

**Table 2, *cntd.*: Dickey-Fuller and Augmented Dickey-Fuller
cointegration tests;**
critical values (minus sign omitted), without intercept,
5% level of significance, m = 1,...,4

n	m=1		m=2		m=3		m=4	
	lower	upper	lower	upper	lower	upper	lower	upper
15	3.45	3.34	3.89	3.81	4.46	4.38	4.98	4.91
20	3.63	3.52	3.85	3.77	4.31	4.23	4.77	4.70
25	3.74	3.63	3.83	3.75	4.22	4.14	4.66	4.58
30	3.82	3.70	3.82	3.73	4.17	4.09	4.57	4.50
40	3.92	3.80	3.80	3.71	4.10	4.02	4.47	4.41
50	3.98	3.87	3.79	3.70	4.06	3.98	4.42	4.36
75	4.08	3.96	3.77	3.69	4.01	3.94	4.35	4.28
100	4.13	4.01	3.77	3.68	3.99	3.91	4.31	4.25
125	4.17	4.05	3.76	3.68	3.97	3.90	4.29	4.23
150	4.19	4.08	3.76	3.68	3.97	3.89	4.28	4.21
175	4.21	4.10	3.76	3.67	3.96	3.88	4.27	4.20
200	4.23	4.11	3.76	3.67	3.96	3.88	4.26	4.19
225	4.24	4.13	3.76	3.67	3.95	3.87	4.25	4.19
250	4.26	4.14	3.76	3.67	3.95	3.87	4.25	4.18
275	4.27	4.15	3.75	3.67	3.95	3.87	4.24	4.18
300	4.27	4.16	3.75	3.67	3.95	3.87	4.24	4.18
325	4.28	4.17	3.75	3.67	3.94	3.87	4.24	4.17
350	4.29	4.17	3.75	3.67	3.94	3.87	4.23	4.17
375	4.30	4.18	3.75	3.67	3.94	3.86	4.23	4.17
400	4.30	4.18	3.75	3.67	3.94	3.86	4.23	4.17
425	4.31	4.19	3.75	3.67	3.94	3.86	4.23	4.17
450	4.31	4.19	3.75	3.67	3.94	3.86	4.23	4.16
475	4.32	4.20	3.75	3.67	3.94	3.86	4.23	4.16
500	4.32	4.20	3.75	3.67	3.94	3.86	4.23	4.16

Table 2, *cntd.*: Dickey-Fuller and Augmented Dickey-Fuller cointegration tests;
critical values (minus sign omitted), without intercept,
5% level of significance, m = 5,...,8

n	m=5 lower	m=5 upper	m=6 lower	m=6 upper	m=7 lower	m=7 upper	m=8 lower	m=8 upper
15	5.51	5.45	6.04	5.94	6.54	6.46	7.03	6.92
20	5.23	5.16	5.69	5.60	6.12	6.04	6.55	6.45
25	5.07	5.01	5.50	5.40	5.89	5.80	6.29	6.18
30	4.97	4.90	5.37	5.28	5.74	5.65	6.11	6.01
40	4.85	4.78	5.22	5.12	5.55	5.47	5.90	5.80
50	4.78	4.71	5.13	5.04	5.45	5.36	5.78	5.67
75	4.68	4.61	5.01	4.92	5.31	5.22	5.62	5.51
100	4.63	4.56	4.96	4.86	5.24	5.16	5.54	5.43
125	4.61	4.54	4.92	4.83	5.20	5.12	5.49	5.39
150	4.59	4.52	4.90	4.81	5.17	5.09	5.46	5.35
175	4.57	4.50	4.88	4.79	5.15	5.07	5.44	5.33
200	4.56	4.49	4.87	4.78	5.14	5.06	5.42	5.31
225	4.56	4.49	4.86	4.77	5.13	5.05	5.41	5.30
250	4.55	4.48	4.86	4.76	5.12	5.04	5.40	5.29
275	4.54	4.48	4.85	4.76	5.11	5.03	5.39	5.28
300	4.54	4.47	4.85	4.75	5.11	5.03	5.38	5.27
325	4.54	4.47	4.84	4.75	5.10	5.02	5.38	5.27
350	4.53	4.46	4.84	4.74	5.10	5.02	5.37	5.26
375	4.53	4.46	4.84	4.74	5.10	5.01	5.37	5.26
400	4.53	4.46	4.83	4.74	5.09	5.01	5.36	5.26
425	4.53	4.46	4.83	4.74	5.09	5.01	5.36	5.25
450	4.53	4.46	4.83	4.74	5.09	5.01	5.36	5.25
475	4.52	4.45	4.83	4.73	5.09	5.00	5.35	5.25
500	4.52	4.45	4.83	4.73	5.09	5.00	5.35	5.25

Table 2, *cntd.*: Dickey-Fuller and Augmented Dickey-Fuller cointegration tests;
critical values (minus sign omitted), without intercept,
10% level of significance, m = 1,...,4

n	m=1		m=2		m=3		m=4	
	lower	upper	lower	upper	lower	upper	lower	upper
15	3.15	3.07	3.49	3.43	3.99	3.93	4.47	4.42
20	3.25	3.17	3.46	3.40	3.89	3.83	4.32	4.27
25	3.30	3.23	3.44	3.39	3.83	3.77	4.23	4.18
30	3.34	3.26	3.43	3.37	3.79	3.73	4.18	4.12
40	3.38	3.31	3.42	3.36	3.75	3.69	4.11	4.06
50	3.41	3.33	3.41	3.35	3.72	3.66	4.07	4.02
75	3.44	3.37	3.40	3.34	3.68	3.62	4.01	3.96
100	3.46	3.39	3.39	3.33	3.67	3.61	3.99	3.94
125	3.47	3.40	3.39	3.33	3.66	3.59	3.97	3.92
150	3.48	3.40	3.38	3.33	3.65	3.59	3.96	3.91
175	3.48	3.41	3.38	3.33	3.64	3.58	3.96	3.90
200	3.49	3.41	3.38	3.32	3.64	3.58	3.95	3.90
225	3.49	3.42	3.38	3.32	3.64	3.58	3.95	3.89
250	3.49	3.42	3.38	3.32	3.63	3.57	3.94	3.89
275	3.50	3.42	3.38	3.32	3.63	3.57	3.94	3.89
300	3.50	3.42	3.38	3.32	3.63	3.57	3.94	3.89
325	3.50	3.42	3.38	3.32	3.63	3.57	3.94	3.88
350	3.50	3.43	3.38	3.32	3.63	3.57	3.93	3.88
375	3.50	3.43	3.37	3.32	3.63	3.57	3.93	3.88
400	3.50	3.43	3.37	3.32	3.63	3.56	3.93	3.88
425	3.50	3.43	3.37	3.32	3.62	3.56	3.93	3.88
450	3.50	3.43	3.37	3.32	3.62	3.56	3.93	3.88
475	3.51	3.43	3.37	3.32	3.62	3.56	3.93	3.88
500	3.51	3.43	3.37	3.32	3.62	3.56	3.93	3.88

Table 2, *cntd.*: Dickey-Fuller and Augmented Dickey-Fuller cointegration tests;
critical values (minus sign omitted), without intercept,
10% level of significance, m = 5,...,8

n	m=5		m=6		m=7		m=8	
	lower	upper	lower	upper	lower	upper	lower	upper
15	4.96	4.89	5.43	5.35	5.90	5.83	6.32	6.24
20	4.75	4.69	5.17	5.09	5.59	5.51	5.97	5.88
25	4.63	4.58	5.03	4.95	5.41	5.34	5.77	5.68
30	4.56	4.50	4.94	4.86	5.30	5.22	5.64	5.56
40	4.47	4.41	4.83	4.75	5.16	5.08	5.48	5.40
50	4.41	4.36	4.76	4.68	5.08	5.00	5.39	5.30
75	4.34	4.29	4.67	4.59	4.97	4.90	5.27	5.18
100	4.31	4.25	4.63	4.55	4.92	4.84	5.20	5.12
125	4.29	4.23	4.61	4.53	4.88	4.81	5.17	5.08
150	4.28	4.22	4.59	4.51	4.86	4.79	5.14	5.06
175	4.27	4.21	4.58	4.50	4.85	4.77	5.12	5.04
200	4.26	4.20	4.57	4.49	4.84	4.76	5.11	5.02
225	4.25	4.19	4.56	4.48	4.83	4.75	5.10	5.01
250	4.25	4.19	4.55	4.47	4.82	4.74	5.09	5.00
275	4.24	4.19	4.55	4.47	4.81	4.74	5.08	5.00
300	4.24	4.18	4.55	4.47	4.81	4.73	5.08	4.99
325	4.24	4.18	4.54	4.46	4.81	4.73	5.07	4.99
350	4.24	4.18	4.54	4.46	4.80	4.73	5.07	4.98
375	4.23	4.18	4.54	4.46	4.80	4.72	5.06	4.98
400	4.23	4.18	4.54	4.46	4.80	4.72	5.06	4.97
425	4.23	4.17	4.53	4.45	4.79	4.72	5.06	4.97
450	4.23	4.17	4.53	4.45	4.79	4.72	5.05	4.97
475	4.23	4.17	4.53	4.45	4.79	4.71	5.05	4.97
500	4.23	4.17	4.53	4.45	4.79	4.71	5.05	4.96

**Table 3: Dickey-Fuller and Augmented Dickey-Fuller
cointegration tests;**
critical values (minus sign omitted), with intercept,
1% level of significance, m = 1,...,4

n	m=1		m=2		m=3		m=4	
	lower	upper	lower	upper	lower	upper	lower	upper
15	5.01	4.89	5.64	5.50	6.27	6.14	6.89	6.76
20	4.73	4.61	5.29	5.15	5.84	5.71	6.37	6.24
25	4.57	4.46	5.10	4.96	5.60	5.47	6.08	5.95
30	4.47	4.35	4.97	4.83	5.45	5.32	5.89	5.76
40	4.35	4.23	4.82	4.68	5.26	5.13	5.67	5.53
50	4.28	4.16	4.73	4.59	5.15	5.02	5.53	5.40
75	4.19	4.07	4.62	4.48	5.00	4.87	5.36	5.23
100	4.14	4.03	4.56	4.42	4.93	4.80	5.28	5.14
125	4.12	4.00	4.52	4.39	4.89	4.76	5.23	5.09
150	4.10	3.99	4.50	4.37	4.86	4.73	5.19	5.06
175	4.09	3.98	4.49	4.35	4.84	4.71	5.17	5.04
200	4.08	3.97	4.48	4.34	4.83	4.69	5.15	5.02
225	4.07	3.96	4.47	4.33	4.81	4.68	5.14	5.00
250	4.07	3.96	4.46	4.32	4.80	4.67	5.13	4.99
275	4.07	3.95	4.45	4.32	4.80	4.66	5.12	4.99
300	4.06	3.95	4.45	4.31	4.79	4.66	5.11	4.98
325	4.06	3.95	4.44	4.31	4.79	4.65	5.11	4.97
350	4.06	3.94	4.44	4.30	4.78	4.65	5.10	4.97
375	4.06	3.94	4.44	4.30	4.78	4.64	5.10	4.96
400	4.05	3.94	4.44	4.30	4.77	4.64	5.09	4.96
425	4.05	3.94	4.43	4.30	4.77	4.64	5.09	4.96
450	4.05	3.94	4.43	4.30	4.77	4.64	5.09	4.96
475	4.05	3.94	4.43	4.29	4.77	4.63	5.09	4.95
500	4.05	3.94	4.43	4.29	4.76	4.63	5.08	4.95

Table 3, *cntd.*: Dickey-Fuller and Augmented Dickey-Fuller cointegration tests;
critical values (minus sign omitted), with intercept,
1% level of significance, m = 5,...,8

n	m=5		m=6		m=7		m=8	
	lower	upper	lower	upper	lower	upper	lower	upper
15	7.46	7.31	8.13	7.95	8.68	8.48	9.07	8.91
20	6.87	6.71	7.39	7.21	7.88	7.68	8.25	8.10
25	6.53	6.37	6.99	6.81	7.43	7.23	7.79	7.64
30	6.31	6.16	6.73	6.55	7.14	6.94	7.49	7.34
40	6.05	5.90	6.42	6.24	6.80	6.60	7.13	6.98
50	5.90	5.75	6.24	6.06	6.60	6.40	6.92	6.76
75	5.70	5.56	6.01	5.83	6.34	6.14	6.64	6.48
100	5.61	5.45	5.90	5.72	6.21	6.01	6.49	6.34
125	5.55	5.39	5.84	5.66	6.14	5.94	6.41	6.25
150	5.51	5.36	5.80	5.62	6.09	5.89	6.35	6.20
175	5.48	5.33	5.77	5.59	6.06	5.86	6.31	6.16
200	5.46	5.31	5.75	5.57	6.03	5.83	6.28	6.13
225	5.45	5.29	5.74	5.56	6.01	5.81	6.26	6.10
250	5.44	5.28	5.73	5.55	6.00	5.80	6.24	6.08
275	5.43	5.27	5.72	5.54	5.99	5.79	6.22	6.07
300	5.42	5.26	5.71	5.53	5.98	5.78	6.21	6.05
325	5.41	5.26	5.71	5.53	5.97	5.77	6.20	6.04
350	5.41	5.25	5.70	5.52	5.96	5.76	6.19	6.03
375	5.40	5.25	5.70	5.52	5.96	5.76	6.18	6.03
400	5.40	5.24	5.69	5.51	5.95	5.75	6.17	6.02
425	5.39	5.24	5.69	5.51	5.95	5.75	6.17	6.01
450	5.39	5.24	5.69	5.51	5.95	5.75	6.16	6.01
475	5.39	5.23	5.69	5.51	5.94	5.74	6.16	6.00
500	5.39	5.23	5.69	5.51	5.94	5.74	6.15	6.00

Table 3, *cntd.*: Dickey-Fuller and Augmented Dickey-Fuller cointegration tests;
critical values (minus sign omitted), with intercept,
5% level of significance, m = 1,...,4

n	m=1		m=2		m=3		m=4	
	lower	upper	lower	upper	lower	upper	lower	upper
15	4.01	3.93	4.53	4.47	5.07	4.98	5.60	5.51
20	3.85	3.78	4.34	4.28	4.82	4.73	5.28	5.20
25	3.76	3.69	4.23	4.17	4.68	4.59	5.11	5.03
30	3.71	3.63	4.16	4.09	4.59	4.50	5.00	4.92
40	3.64	3.56	4.07	4.01	4.48	4.39	4.86	4.78
50	3.60	3.52	4.02	3.95	4.42	4.33	4.77	4.70
75	3.55	3.47	3.95	3.89	4.33	4.24	4.67	4.59
100	3.52	3.45	3.92	3.85	4.29	4.20	4.62	4.54
125	3.51	3.43	3.90	3.83	4.26	4.17	4.59	4.51
150	3.50	3.42	3.88	3.82	4.25	4.16	4.57	4.49
175	3.49	3.42	3.87	3.81	4.24	4.14	4.55	4.47
200	3.48	3.41	3.86	3.80	4.23	4.13	4.54	4.46
225	3.48	3.41	3.86	3.79	4.22	4.13	4.53	4.45
250	3.48	3.40	3.85	3.79	4.21	4.12	4.52	4.44
275	3.47	3.40	3.85	3.78	4.21	4.12	4.52	4.44
300	3.47	3.40	3.84	3.78	4.20	4.11	4.51	4.43
325	3.47	3.40	3.84	3.78	4.20	4.11	4.51	4.43
350	3.47	3.40	3.84	3.78	4.20	4.11	4.51	4.43
375	3.47	3.39	3.84	3.77	4.20	4.10	4.50	4.42
400	3.47	3.39	3.84	3.77	4.19	4.10	4.50	4.42
425	3.47	3.39	3.83	3.77	4.19	4.10	4.50	4.42
450	3.47	3.39	3.83	3.77	4.19	4.10	4.50	4.42
475	3.46	3.39	3.83	3.77	4.19	4.10	4.50	4.41
500	3.46	3.39	3.83	3.77	4.19	4.10	4.49	4.41

**Table 3, *cntd.*: Dickey-Fuller and Augmented Dickey-Fuller
cointegration tests;**
critical values (minus sign omitted), with intercept,
5% level of significance, m = 5,...,8

n	m=5		m=6		m=7		m=8	
	lower	upper	lower	upper	lower	upper	lower	upper
15	6.08	6.01	6.58	6.49	7.09	7.00	7.52	7.41
20	5.71	5.64	6.15	6.06	6.59	6.49	6.98	6.87
25	5.50	5.43	5.90	5.81	6.30	6.21	6.67	6.57
30	5.37	5.29	5.75	5.66	6.12	6.02	6.48	6.37
40	5.21	5.13	5.56	5.47	5.90	5.80	6.24	6.13
50	5.11	5.04	5.45	5.36	5.77	5.67	6.09	5.99
75	5.00	4.91	5.30	5.21	5.60	5.50	5.90	5.80
100	4.93	4.85	5.23	5.14	5.52	5.42	5.81	5.70
125	4.89	4.82	5.19	5.10	5.47	5.37	5.75	5.64
150	4.87	4.79	5.16	5.07	5.43	5.34	5.71	5.61
175	4.85	4.78	5.14	5.06	5.41	5.31	5.68	5.58
200	4.84	4.76	5.13	5.04	5.39	5.30	5.66	5.56
225	4.83	4.75	5.12	5.03	5.38	5.28	5.64	5.54
250	4.82	4.75	5.11	5.02	5.37	5.27	5.63	5.53
275	4.82	4.74	5.10	5.01	5.36	5.27	5.62	5.52
300	4.81	4.74	5.10	5.01	5.35	5.26	5.61	5.51
325	4.81	4.73	5.09	5.00	5.35	5.25	5.60	5.50
350	4.80	4.73	5.09	5.00	5.34	5.25	5.60	5.49
375	4.80	4.73	5.09	5.00	5.34	5.24	5.59	5.49
400	4.80	4.72	5.08	4.99	5.34	5.24	5.59	5.48
425	4.80	4.72	5.08	4.99	5.33	5.24	5.58	5.48
450	4.79	4.72	5.08	4.99	5.33	5.23	5.58	5.47
475	4.79	4.72	5.08	4.99	5.33	5.23	5.57	5.47
500	4.79	4.72	5.08	4.99	5.33	5.23	5.57	5.47

Table 3, *cntd.*: Dickey-Fuller and Augmented Dickey-Fuller cointegration tests;
critical values (minus sign omitted), with intercept,
10% level of significance, m = 1,...,4

n	m=1		m=2		m=3		m=4	
	lower	upper	lower	upper	lower	upper	lower	upper
15	3.55	3.50	4.05	4.00	4.56	4.49	5.03	4.96
20	3.44	3.38	3.91	3.86	4.37	4.30	4.80	4.73
25	3.38	3.32	3.83	3.78	4.26	4.19	4.66	4.60
30	3.34	3.28	3.78	3.73	4.19	4.12	4.58	4.52
40	3.29	3.24	3.71	3.66	4.10	4.04	4.48	4.41
50	3.26	3.21	3.67	3.63	4.06	3.99	4.42	4.35
75	3.22	3.17	3.62	3.57	3.99	3.93	4.34	4.27
100	3.21	3.15	3.60	3.55	3.96	3.89	4.30	4.23
125	3.20	3.14	3.58	3.53	3.94	3.88	4.27	4.21
150	3.19	3.14	3.57	3.52	3.93	3.86	4.25	4.19
175	3.18	3.13	3.56	3.51	3.92	3.85	4.24	4.18
200	3.18	3.13	3.56	3.51	3.91	3.75	4.23	4.17
225	3.18	3.13	3.55	3.50	3.91	3.84	4.23	4.16
250	3.18	3.12	3.55	3.50	3.91	3.84	4.22	4.16
275	3.17	3.12	3.55	3.50	3.90	3.84	4.22	4.15
300	3.17	3.12	3.54	3.49	3.90	3.83	4.21	4.15
325	3.17	3.12	3.54	3.49	3.90	3.83	4.21	4.15
350	3.17	3.12	3.54	3.49	3.90	3.83	4.21	4.15
375	3.17	3.12	3.54	3.49	3.89	3.83	4.21	4.14
400	3.17	3.12	3.54	3.49	3.89	3.83	4.20	4.14
425	3.17	3.12	3.54	3.49	3.89	3.83	4.20	4.14
450	3.17	3.12	3.53	3.49	3.89	3.82	4.20	4.14
475	3.17	3.11	3.53	3.48	3.89	3.82	4.20	4.14
500	3.17	3.11	3.53	3.48	3.89	3.82	4.20	4.13

**Table 3, *cntd.*: Dickey-Fuller and Augmented Dickey-Fuller
cointegration tests;**
critical values (minus sign omitted), with intercept,
10% level of significance, m = 5,...,8

n	m=5		m=6		m=7		m=8	
	lower	upper	lower	upper	lower	upper	lower	upper
15	5.48	5.43	5.93	5.85	6.37	6.30	6.78	6.69
20	5.20	5.15	5.60	5.53	5.99	5.92	6.37	6.28
25	5.04	4.99	5.42	5.34	5.77	5.71	6.14	6.05
30	4.94	4.88	5.30	5.23	5.64	5.57	5.98	5.90
40	4.81	4.76	5.16	5.08	5.47	5.40	5.80	5.71
50	4.74	4.69	5.07	5.00	5.37	5.30	5.69	5.60
75	4.64	4.59	4.96	4.89	5.24	5.17	5.54	5.45
100	4.60	4.55	4.91	4.83	5.18	5.11	5.47	5.38
125	4.57	4.52	4.87	4.80	5.14	5.07	5.42	5.33
150	4.55	4.50	4.85	4.78	5.11	5.05	5.39	5.30
175	4.54	4.49	4.84	4.76	5.09	5.03	5.37	5.28
200	4.53	4.48	4.82	4.75	5.08	5.01	5.35	5.26
225	4.52	4.47	4.82	4.74	5.07	5.00	5.34	5.25
250	4.51	4.46	4.81	4.73	5.06	4.99	5.32	5.24
275	4.51	4.46	4.80	4.73	5.05	4.99	5.32	5.23
300	4.50	4.45	4.80	4.72	5.05	4.98	5.31	5.22
325	4.50	4.45	4.79	4.72	5.04	4.98	5.30	5.21
350	4.50	4.45	4.79	4.71	5.04	4.97	5.30	5.21
375	4.50	4.44	4.79	4.71	5.04	4.97	5.29	5.20
400	4.49	4.44	4.78	4.71	5.03	4.97	5.29	5.20
425	4.49	4.44	4.78	4.71	5.03	4.96	5.28	5.19
450	4.49	4.44	4.78	4.70	5.03	4.96	5.28	5.19
475	4.49	4.44	4.78	4.70	5.03	4.96	5.28	5.19
500	4.49	4.44	4.78	4.70	5.02	4.96	5.27	5.19

**Table 4: Dickey-Fuller and Augmented Dickey-Fuller
cointegration tests with quarterly seasonals;
critical values (minus sign omitted)
1% level of significance, m = 1,...,5**

n	m=1		m=2		m=3		m=4		m=5	
	lower	upper	lower	upper	lower	upper	lower	upper	lower	upper
15	4.77	4.58	5.75	5.46	6.59	6.32	7.43	7.12	8.12	7.89
20	4.51	4.30	5.30	5.01	5.96	5.70	6.65	6.34	7.26	6.94
25	4.36	4.16	5.05	4.77	5.63	5.36	6.23	5.92	6.75	6.43
30	4.27	4.07	4.90	4.62	5.42	5.15	5.97	5.66	6.43	6.12
40	4.17	3.97	4.73	4.45	5.19	4.92	5.67	5.36	6.07	5.76
50	4.11	3.91	4.64	4.36	5.06	4.79	5.50	5.19	5.88	5.56
75	4.05	3.85	4.54	4.25	4.91	4.64	5.31	5.00	5.65	5.33
100	4.03	3.82	4.49	4.21	4.85	4.59	5.23	4.92	5.55	5.24
125	4.01	3.81	4.47	4.19	4.82	4.56	5.19	4.88	5.51	5.19
150	4.01	3.81	4.46	4.18	4.81	4.54	5.17	4.86	5.48	5.17
175	4.01	3.80	4.46	4.17	4.80	4.54	5.16	4.85	5.47	5.15
200	4.00	3.80	4.46	4.17	4.80	4.53	5.15	4.84	5.46	5.15
225	4.00	3.80	4.46	4.17	4.80	4.53	5.15	4.84	5.46	5.15
250	4.00	3.80	4.46	4.17	4.80	4.54	5.15	4.84	5.46	5.14
275	4.01	3.80	4.46	4.18	4.80	4.54	5.15	4.84	5.46	5.15
300	4.10	3.80	4.46	4.18	4.81	4.54	5.15	4.84	5.46	5.15
325	4.01	3.81	4.47	4.18	4.81	4.54	5.15	4.84	5.47	5.15
350	4.01	3.81	4.47	4.18	4.81	4.55	5.16	4.85	5.47	5.16
375	4.01	3.81	4.47	4.18	4.82	4.55	5.16	4.85	5.47	5.16
400	4.01	3.81	4.47	4.19	4.82	4.55	5.16	4.85	5.48	5.16
425	4.01	3.81	4.48	4.19	4.82	4.56	5.17	4.86	5.48	5.17
450	4.02	3.81	4.48	4.19	4.83	4.56	5.17	4.86	5.49	5.17
475	4.02	3.82	4.48	4.20	4.83	4.56	5.17	4.86	5.49	5.18
500	4.02	3.82	4.48	4.20	4.84	4.57	5.18	4.87	5.50	5.18

**Table 4, *cntd.*: Dickey-Fuller and Augmented Dickey-Fuller
cointegration tests with quarterly seasonals;**
critical values (minus sign omitted)
5% level of significance, m = 1,...,5

n	m=1		m=2		m=3		m=4		m=5	
	lower	upper	lower	upper	lower	upper	lower	upper	lower	upper
15	3.68	3.55	4.47	4.29	5.21	5.02	5.96	5.74	6.71	6.45
20	3.57	3.45	4.23	3.06	4.84	4.66	5.45	5.23	6.04	5.78
25	3.52	3.39	4.11	3.94	4.65	4.46	5.18	4.96	5.69	5.43
30	3.48	3.36	4.04	3.87	4.53	4.35	5.01	4.79	5.47	5.21
40	3.45	3.32	3.95	3.78	4.39	4.21	4.83	4.60	5.23	4.97
50	3.43	3.30	3.91	3.74	4.32	4.14	4.73	4.50	5.10	4.84
75	3.41	3.28	3.86	3.69	4.24	4.06	4.61	4.39	4.95	4.69
100	3.40	3.27	3.84	3.67	4.22	4.03	4.57	4.35	4.89	4.63
125	3.40	3.27	3.84	3.66	4.20	4.02	4.55	4.33	4.87	4.61
150	3.40	3.27	3.83	3.66	4.20	4.02	4.54	4.32	4.86	4.60
175	3.40	3.27	3.83	3.66	4.20	4.01	4.54	4.32	4.85	4.59
200	3.40	3.27	3.83	3.66	4.20	4.01	4.54	4.32	4.85	4.59
225	3.40	3.27	3.83	3.66	4.20	4.02	4.54	4.32	4.86	4.60
250	3.40	3.27	3.84	3.67	4.20	4.02	4.54	4.32	4.86	4.60
275	3.40	3.28	3.84	3.67	4.20	4.02	4.55	4.32	4.86	4.60
300	3.40	3.28	3.84	3.67	4.21	4.02	4.55	4.33	4.87	4.61
325	3.41	3.28	3.84	3.67	4.21	4.03	4.55	4.33	4.87	4.61
350	3.41	3.28	3.85	3.67	4.21	4.03	4.56	4.33	4.88	4.62
375	3.41	3.28	3.85	3.68	4.21	4.03	4.56	4.34	4.88	4.62
400	3.41	3.28	3.85	3.68	4.22	4.04	4.56	4.34	4.89	4.63
425	3.41	3.28	3.85	3.68	4.22	4.04	4.57	4.35	4.89	4.63
450	3.41	3.28	3.85	3.68	4.22	4.04	4.57	4.35	4.90	4.64
475	3.41	3.29	3.86	3.68	4.23	4.04	4.58	4.35	4.90	4.64
500	3.41	3.29	3.86	3.69	4.23	4.05	4.58	4.36	4.91	4.65

**Table 4, *cntd.*: Dickey-Fuller and Augmented Dickey-Fuller
cointegration tests with quarterly seasonals;**
critical values (minus sign omitted)
10% level of significance, m = 1,...,5

n	m=1		m=2		m=3		m=4		m=5	
	lower	upper	lower	upper	lower	upper	lower	upper	lower	upper
15	3.22	3.12	3.89	3.76	4.58	4.43	5.26	5.07	5.93	5.72
20	3.17	3.07	3.75	3.62	4.32	4.17	4.89	4.69	5.43	5.21
25	3.14	3.04	3.68	3.55	4.19	4.03	4.69	4.49	5.16	4.94
30	3.12	3.02	3.63	3.51	4.10	3.95	4.56	4.37	4.99	4.78
40	3.11	3.01	3.58	3.46	4.01	3.86	4.43	4.24	4.81	4.59
50	3.10	3.00	3.56	3.43	3.96	3.81	4.36	4.16	4.71	4.50
75	3.09	2.99	3.53	3.40	3.91	3.76	4.28	4.08	4.60	4.39
100	3.09	2.99	3.52	3.39	3.89	3.74	4.25	4.05	4.56	4.35
125	3.09	2.99	3.52	3.39	3.88	3.73	4.23	4.04	4.55	4.33
150	3.09	2.99	3.52	3.39	3.88	3.73	4.23	4.04	4.54	4.32
175	3.09	2.99	3.52	3.39	3.88	3.73	4.23	4.04	4.54	4.32
200	3.09	2.99	3.52	3.39	3.88	3.73	4.23	4.04	4.54	4.32
225	3.09	2.99	3.52	3.39	3.89	3.73	4.23	4.04	4.54	4.33
250	3.09	2.99	3.52	3.39	3.89	3.74	4.24	4.04	4.55	4.33
275	3.09	2.99	3.52	3.39	3.89	3.74	4.24	4.05	4.55	4.33
300	3.09	2.99	3.52	3.39	3.89	3.74	4.24	4.05	4.55	4.34
325	3.10	3.00	3.52	3.40	3.90	3.74	4.24	4.05	4.56	4.34
350	3.10	3.00	3.53	3.40	3.90	3.75	4.25	4.06	4.56	4.35
375	3.10	3.00	3.53	3.40	3.90	3.75	4.25	4.06	4.57	4.35
400	3.10	3.00	3.53	3.40	3.91	3.75	4.25	4.06	4.57	4.36
425	3.10	3.00	3.53	3.40	3.91	3.76	4.26	4.07	4.58	4.36
450	3.10	3.00	3.53	3.40	3.91	3.76	4.26	4.07	4.58	4.36
475	3.10	3.00	3.53	3.40	3.91	3.76	4.26	4.07	4.58	4.37
500	3.10	3.00	3.53	3.41	3.92	3.76	4.27	4.07	4.59	4.37

Table 5: Dickey-Hasza-Fuller integration tests
critical values (minus sign omitted)
Key: nc no constant in test equation; c constant in test equation
1% level of significance

n	nc monthly		c monthly		n	nc quarterly		c quarterly	
	lower	upper	lower	upper		lower	upper	lower	upper
100	2.53	2.37	2.57	2.38	25	2.74	2.62	2.85	2.72
150	2.54	2.37	2.55	2.37	30	2.70	2.58	2.81	2.68
200	2.54	2.38	2.54	2.35	40	2.66	2.54	2.75	2.61
300	2.55	2.38	2.52	2.34	50	2.64	2.52	2.71	2.57
400	2.55	2.39	2.51	2.33	75	2.61	2.50	2.65	2.51
500	2.55	2.39	2.50	2.32	100	2.60	2.49	2.61	2.48
600	2.56	2.39	2.50	2.31	125	2.60	2.48	2.58	2.45
800	2.56	2.39	2.49	2.30	150	2.60	2.48	2.57	2.43
1000	2.56	2.40	2.48	2.29	200	2.60	2.48	2.54	2.41
1200	2.56	2.40	2.47	2.29	250	2.60	2.49	2.52	2.39
1400	2.56	2.40	2.47	2.28	300	2.60	2.49	2.51	2.37
1600	2.56	2.40	2.47	2.28	500	2.61	2.50	2.47	2.34

2.5% level of significance

n	nc monthly		c monthly		n	nc quarterly		c quarterly	
	lower	upper	lower	upper		lower	upper	lower	upper
100	2.15	2.02	2.22	2.05	25	2.30	2.21	2.39	2.29
150	2.16	2.03	2.19	2.02	30	2.28	2.19	2.36	2.26
200	2.17	2.04	2.17	2.00	40	2.26	2.17	2.31	2.21
300	2.17	2.04	2.15	1.98	50	2.25	2.16	2.28	2.18
400	2.17	2.04	2.14	1.97	75	2.23	2.14	2.23	2.13
500	2.17	2.04	2.13	1.96	100	2.23	2.14	2.20	2.10
600	2.17	2.04	2.12	1.95	125	2.23	2.14	2.18	2.08
800	2.17	2.04	2.10	1.94	150	2.23	2.14	2.17	2.06
1000	2.17	2.04	2.10	1.93	200	2.23	2.14	2.14	2.04
1200	2.17	2.04	2.10	1.93	250	2.23	2.14	2.13	2.03
1400	2.17	2.04	2.09	1.92	300	2.23	2.14	2.12	2.01
1600	2.17	2.04	2.09	1.92	500	2.24	2.15	2.09	1.99

Table 5, *cntd.*: Dickey-Hasza-Fuller integration tests
critical values (minus sign omitted)
Key: nc no constant in test equation; c constant in test equation
5% level of significance

n	nc monthly		c monthly			n	nc quarterly		c quarterly	
	lower	upper	lower	upper			lower	upper	lower	upper
100	1.80	1.70	1.87	1.76		25	1.94	1.87	2.02	1.93
150	1.82	1.72	1.85	1.73		30	1.93	1.86	1.99	1.91
200	1.83	1.73	1.83	1.71		40	1.93	1.85	1.96	1.88
300	1.84	1.74	1.81	1.69		50	1.92	1.85	1.94	1.86
400	1.85	1.75	1.79	1.68		75	1.92	1.84	1.90	1.82
500	1.85	1.75	1.78	1.67		100	1.92	1.84	1.87	1.79
600	1.85	1.75	1.76	1.66		125	1.92	1.84	1.85	1.77
800	1.85	1.75	1.76	1.65		150	1.92	1.84	1.84	1.76
1000	1.85	1.75	1.76	1.64		200	1.92	1.85	1.82	1.74
1200	1.85	1.75	1.75	1.63		250	1.92	1.85	1.80	1.72
1400	1.85	1.75	1.74	1.63		300	1.92	1.85	1.79	1.71
1600	1.85	1.75	1.74	1.62		500	1.93	1.85	1.76	1.68

10% level of significance

n	nc monthly		c monthly			n	nc quarterly		c quarterly	
	lower	upper	lower	upper			lower	upper	lower	upper
100	2.15	2.02	2.22	2.05		25	2.30	2.21	2.39	2.29
150	2.16	2.03	2.19	2.02		30	2.28	2.19	2.36	2.26
200	2.17	2.04	2.17	2.00		40	2.26	2.17	2.31	2.21
300	2.17	2.04	2.15	1.98		50	2.25	2.16	2.28	2.18
400	2.17	2.04	2.14	1.97		75	2.23	2.14	2.23	2.13
500	2.17	2.04	2.13	1.96		100	2.23	2.14	2.20	2.10
600	2.17	2.04	2.12	1.95		125	2.23	2.14	2.18	2.08
800	2.17	2.04	2.10	1.94		150	2.23	2.14	2.17	2.06
1000	2.17	2.04	2.10	1.93		200	2.23	2.14	2.14	2.04
1200	2.17	2.04	2.10	1.93		250	2.23	2.14	2.13	2.03
1400	2.17	2.04	2.09	1.92		300	2.23	2.14	2.12	2.01
1600	2.17	2.04	2.09	1.92		500	2.24	2.15	2.09	2.99

Table 6: Perron 'additive outlier' integration test
critical values (minus sign omitted)
α % level of significance

$\lambda = 0.1$

n	α = 0.01		α = 0.025		α = 0.05		α = 0.10	
	lower	upper	lower	upper	lower	upper	lower	upper
20	4.19	4.00	3.72	3.55	3.31	3.19	2.90	2.79
25	4.09	3.91	3.65	3.48	3.28	3.15	2.89	2.77
30	4.03	3.84	3.61	3.44	3.25	3.12	2.87	2.76
40	3.96	3.77	3.56	3.39	3.22	3.09	2.86	2.75
50	3.91	3.73	3.53	3.36	3.20	3.08	2.85	2.74
75	3.86	3.67	3.49	3.32	3.18	3.05	2.84	2.73
100	3.83	3.65	3.48	3.31	3.16	3.04	2.83	2.72
125	3.82	3.63	3.46	3.29	3.16	3.03	2.83	2.72
150	3.81	3.62	3.46	3.29	3.15	3.02	2.83	2.72
200	3.79	3.61	3.45	3.28	3.14	3.02	2.82	2.71
300	3.78	3.60	3.44	3.27	3.13	3.01	2.82	2.71
500	3.78	3.59	3.43	3.26	3.13	3.00	2.81	2.70

$\lambda = 0.2$

n	α = 0.01		α = 0.025		α = 0.05		α = 0.10	
	lower	upper	lower	upper	lower	upper	lower	upper
20	4.45	4.34	3.94	3.85	3.56	3.48	3.13	3.07
25	4.32	4.21	3.85	3.76	3.49	3.42	3.09	3.03
30	4.23	4.12	3.79	3.71	3.45	3.37	3.06	3.01
40	4.13	4.02	3.73	3.64	3.39	3.32	3.03	2.97
50	4.07	3.96	3.68	3.60	3.36	3.29	3.01	2.95
75	4.00	3.88	3.63	3.54	3.32	3.25	2.98	2.93
100	3.96	3.85	3.60	3.51	3.30	3.22	2.96	2.91
125	3.94	3.83	3.58	3.50	3.29	3.21	2.95	2.90
150	3.92	3.81	3.57	3.49	3.28	3.20	2.95	2.89
200	3.91	3.79	3.56	3.47	3.27	3.19	2.94	2.89
300	3.89	3.78	3.54	3.46	3.26	3.18	2.93	2.88
500	3.88	3.77	3.53	3.44	3.25	3.17	2.92	2.87

Table 6, *cntd.*: Perron 'additive outlier' integration test
critical values (minus sign omitted)
α % level of significance

λ = 0.3

n	α = 0.01 lower	α = 0.01 upper	α = 0.025 lower	α = 0.025 upper	α = 0.05 lower	α = 0.05 upper	α = 0.10 lower	α = 0.10 upper
20	4.58	4.44	4.08	3.98	3.69	3.60	3.28	3.21
25	4.45	4.31	3.98	3.89	3.62	3.53	3.22	3.15
30	4.36	4.22	3.92	3.83	3.57	3.48	3.19	3.11
40	4.25	4.12	3.85	3.75	3.51	3.42	3.14	3.07
50	4.19	4.05	3.80	3.70	3.47	3.39	3.12	3.04
75	4.11	3.97	3.73	3.64	3.43	3.34	3.09	3.01
100	4.06	3.92	3.70	3.60	3.40	3.31	3.07	3.00
125	4.04	3.90	3.68	3.58	3.39	3.30	3.06	2.99
150	4.02	3.88	3.66	3.56	3.38	3.29	3.05	2.98
200	3.99	3.86	3.64	3.54	3.36	3.28	3.05	2.97
300	3.97	3.83	3.62	3.52	3.35	3.26	3.04	2.97
500	3.95	3.81	3.60	3.50	3.34	3.25	3.04	2.96

λ = 0.4

n	α = 0.01 lower	α = 0.01 upper	α = 0.025 lower	α = 0.025 upper	α = 0.05 lower	α = 0.05 upper	α = 0.10 lower	α = 0.10 upper
20	4.68	4.53	4.17	4.06	3.76	3.68	3.34	3.28
25	4.52	4.37	4.06	3.95	3.68	3.60	3.28	3.22
30	4.42	4.27	3.99	3.87	3.62	3.55	3.25	3.18
40	4.30	4.15	3.90	3.79	3.56	3.48	3.20	3.14
50	4.23	4.08	3.85	3.74	3.52	3.44	3.17	3.11
75	4.14	3.99	3.78	3.67	3.47	3.39	3.13	3.07
100	4.10	3.95	3.75	3.63	3.44	3.37	3.12	3.06
125	4.07	3.92	3.73	3.61	3.43	3.35	3.10	3.04
150	4.06	3.90	3.71	3.60	3.42	3.34	3.10	3.04
200	4.04	3.88	3.70	3.58	3.41	3.33	3.09	3.03
300	4.02	3.87	3.68	3.56	3.39	3.31	3.08	3.02
500	4.01	3.85	3.66	3.55	3.38	3.30	3.07	3.01

Table 6, *cntd.*: Perron 'additive outlier' integration test
critical values (minus sign omitted)
α % level of significance

λ = 0.5

n	α = 0.01		α = 0.025		α = 0.05		α = 0.10	
	lower	upper	lower	upper	lower	upper	lower	upper
20	4.68	4.58	4.17	4.10	3.78	3.73	3.37	3.31
25	4.52	4.41	4.05	3.98	3.69	3.64	3.30	3.25
30	4.42	4.31	3.97	3.90	3.63	3.58	3.26	3.21
40	4.29	4.19	3.88	3.81	3.56	3.51	3.21	3.16
50	4.22	4.12	3.83	3.76	3.52	3.47	3.19	3.13
75	4.13	4.02	3.76	3.69	3.47	3.42	3.15	3.10
100	4.08	3.98	3.73	3.66	3.44	3.39	3.13	3.08
125	4.06	3.95	3.71	3.64	3.43	3.38	3.12	3.07
150	4.04	3.94	3.70	3.63	3.42	3.37	3.11	3.06
200	4.02	3.92	3.68	3.61	3.40	3.35	3.10	3.05
300	4.00	3.90	3.67	3.60	3.39	3.34	3.09	3.04
500	3.99	3.89	3.66	3.59	3.38	3.33	3.09	3.04

**Table 7: *HEGY* seasonal integration test; without intercept
critical values (minus sign omitted for π_i , $i = 1, 2$)**

1% level of significance (99% fractile for F)

	π_1		π_2		F	
n	lower	upper	lower	upper	lower	upper
25	2.58	2.46	2.59	2.44	6.28	6.54
30	2.59	2.47	2.60	2.45	5.91	6.17
40	2.60	2.48	2.61	2.46	5.49	5.75
50	2.61	2.49	2.62	2.47	5.26	5.52
75	2.61	2.49	2.62	2.48	4.97	5.23
100	2.62	2.50	2.63	2.48	4.85	5.11
125	2.62	2.50	2.63	2.49	4.78	5.04
150	2.62	2.50	2.63	2.49	4.74	5.00
200	2.62	2.50	2.64	2.49	4.70	4.96
300	2.62	2.50	2.64	2.49	4.68	4.95
500	2.62	2.50	2.64	2.49	4.70	4.96

2.5% level of significance (97.5% fractile for F)

	π_1		π_2		F	
n	lower	upper	lower	upper	lower	upper
25	2.16	2.08	2.17	2.07	4.72	4.96
30	2.18	2.11	2.19	2.09	4.50	4.74
40	2.21	2.13	2.22	2.12	4.25	4.49
50	2.22	2.15	2.23	2.13	4.10	4.35
75	2.24	2.17	2.25	2.15	3.93	4.17
100	2.25	2.17	2.26	2.16	3.86	4.10
125	2.25	2.18	2.26	2.17	3.82	4.06
150	2.26	2.18	2.26	2.17	3.79	4.04
200	2.26	2.18	2.27	2.17	3.77	4.01
300	2.26	2.18	2.27	2.17	3.76	4.00
500	2.26	2.18	2.27	2.17	3.77	4.01

Table 7, *cntd.*: *HEGY* seasonal integration test; without intercept
critical values (minus sign omitted for π_i, $i = 1, 2$)

5% level of significance (95% fractile for F)

n	π_1		π_2		F	
	lower	upper	lower	upper	lower	upper
25	1.87	1.79	1.85	1.78	3.71	3.89
30	1.89	1.81	1.88	1.80	3.56	3.74
40	1.91	1.83	1.91	1.83	3.39	3.56
50	1.93	1.85	1.93	1.85	3.29	3.47
75	1.95	1.87	1.95	1.87	3.17	3.35
100	1.96	1.88	1.96	1.88	3.12	3.30
125	1.96	1.88	1.96	1.89	3.10	3.28
150	1.97	1.89	1.97	1.89	3.08	3.26
200	1.97	1.89	1.97	1.89	3.07	3.25
300	1.98	1.90	1.97	1.90	3.07	3.24
500	1.98	1.90	1.97	1.90	3.08	3.25

10% level of significance (90% fractile for F)

n	π_1		π_2		F	
	lower	upper	lower	upper	lower	upper
25	1.53	1.47	1.51	1.45	2.77	2.90
30	1.55	1.49	1.54	1.48	2.68	2.81
40	1.57	1.51	1.57	1.51	2.57	2.70
50	1.59	1.53	1.59	1.53	2.51	2.64
75	1.61	1.55	1.61	1.55	2.44	2.57
100	1.62	1.56	1.62	1.56	2.41	2.54
125	1.62	1.56	1.63	1.57	2.39	2.52
150	1.63	1.57	1.63	1.57	2.38	2.52
200	1.63	1.57	1.63	1.57	2.38	2.51
300	1.64	1.58	1.64	1.58	2.37	2.50
500	1.64	1.58	1.64	1.58	2.38	2.51

Table 8: *HEGY* **seasonal integration test; with intercept**
critical values (minus sign omitted for π_i , $i = 1, 2$)

1% level of significance (99% fractile for *F*)

n	π_1 lower	upper	π_2 lower	upper	*F* lower	upper
25	3.62	3.48	2.58	2.44	6.40	6.74
30	3.60	3.45	2.59	2.45	5.98	6.32
40	3.57	3.43	2.60	2.46	5.50	5.83
50	3.55	3.41	2.60	2.46	5.23	5.57
75	3.53	3.39	2.61	2.47	4.92	5.25
100	3.52	3.38	2.62	2.48	4.78	5.12
125	3.52	3.37	2.62	2.48	4.72	5.05
150	3.52	3.37	2.63	2.49	4.68	5.02
200	3.51	3.37	2.63	2.49	4.65	4.98
300	3.51	3.36	2.63	2.49	4.64	4.98
500	3.51	3.36	2.64	2.50	4.68	5.01

2.5% level of significance (97.5% fractile for *F*)

n	π_1 lower	upper	π_2 lower	upper	*F* lower	upper
25	3.20	3.10	2.16	2.07	4.81	5.12
30	3.19	3.09	2.18	2.09	4.55	4.87
40	3.18	3.08	2.21	2.12	4.25	4.57
50	3.18	3.08	2.22	2.13	4.09	4.40
75	3.18	3.07	2.24	2.15	3.89	4.21
100	3.18	3.07	2.25	2.16	3.81	4.12
125	3.18	3.07	2.25	2.17	3.77	4.08
150	3.18	3.07	2.26	2.17	3.75	4.06
200	3.18	3.07	2.26	2.17	3.73	4.04
300	3.18	3.07	2.27	2.18	3.72	4.03
500	3.18	3.08	2.27	2.18	3.74	4.05

Table 8, *cntd.*: *HEGY* seasonal integration test; with intercept
critical values (minus sign omitted for π_i , $i = 1, 2$)

5% level of significance (95% fractile for F)

n	π_1		π_2		F	
	lower	upper	lower	upper	lower	upper
25	2.85	2.77	1.84	1.76	3.79	4.00
30	2.86	2.78	1.87	1.79	3.61	3.82
40	2.87	2.79	1.90	1.82	3.40	3.61
50	2.87	2.80	1.92	1.84	3.29	3.49
75	2.88	2.81	1.95	1.87	3.16	3.36
100	2.89	2.81	1.96	1.88	3.10	3.31
125	2.89	2.81	1.96	1.88	3.07	3.28
150	2.89	2.82	1.97	1.89	3.06	3.26
200	2.90	2.82	1.97	1.89	3.05	3.25
300	2.90	2.82	1.97	1.89	3.05	3.25
500	2.90	2.83	1.97	1.89	3.07	3.27

10% level of significance (90% fractile for F)

n	π_1		π_2		F	
	lower	upper	lower	upper	lower	upper
25	2.48	2.43	1.50	1.44	2.82	2.97
30	2.50	2.45	1.53	1.47	2.71	2.86
40	2.53	2.47	1.56	1.51	2.58	2.73
50	2.55	2.49	1.58	1.53	2.51	2.66
75	2.56	2.51	1.61	1.55	2.43	2.58
100	2.57	2.52	1.62	1.56	2.40	2.54
125	2.58	2.52	1.62	1.57	2.38	2.52
150	2.58	2.53	1.63	1.57	2.37	2.52
200	2.58	2.53	1.63	1.58	2.36	2.51
300	2.59	2.53	1.63	1.58	2.37	2.51
500	2.59	2.53	1.64	1.58	2.38	2.52

Table 9: *HEGY* seasonal integration test; with seasonals
critical values (minus sign omitted for π_i, $i = 1, 2$)

1% level of significance (99% fractile for F)

n	π_1		π_2		F	
	lower	upper	lower	upper	lower	upper
25	3.59	3.42	3.59	3.42	15.9	17.1
30	3.56	3.40	3.56	3.39	14.1	15.3
40	3.53	3.37	3.53	3.36	12.0	13.2
50	3.52	3.35	3.52	3.35	10.9	12.1
75	3.50	3.34	3.50	3.33	9.54	10.8
100	3.50	3.34	3.50	3.33	8.99	10.2
125	3.50	3.34	3.50	3.33	8.71	9.96
150	3.50	3.34	3.50	3.33	8.56	9.81
200	3.51	3.34	3.50	3.33	8.44	9.68
300	3.52	3.35	3.51	3.34	8.43	9.68
500	3.53	3.37	3.52	3.35	8.60	9.84

2.5% level of significance (97.5% fractile for F)

n	π_1		π_2		F	
	lower	upper	lower	upper	lower	upper
25	3.10	2.99	3.11	2.99	12.6	13.6
30	3.11	3.00	3.11	3.00	11.3	12.3
40	3.12	3.01	3.13	3.01	9.83	10.9
50	3.13	3.02	3.13	3.02	9.02	10.0
75	3.14	3.03	3.14	3.03	8.06	9.08
100	3.15	3.04	3.15	3.04	7.67	8.69
125	3.15	3.04	3.15	3.04	7.47	8.49
150	3.16	3.05	3.16	3.05	7.37	8.39
200	3.17	3.06	3.16	3.05	7.28	8.30
300	3.17	3.07	3.17	3.06	7.28	8.30
500	3.18	3.08	3.17	3.06	7.41	8.43

Table 9, *cntd.*: *HEGY* seasonal integration test; with seasonals
critical values (minus sign omitted for π_i , $i = 1, 2$)

5% level of significance (95% fractile for F)

	π_1		π_2		F	
n	lower	upper	lower	upper	lower	upper
25	2.76	2.67	2.76	2.67	10.4	11.1
30	2.78	2.69	2.78	2.69	9.46	10.1
40	2.81	2.72	2.81	2.72	8.37	9.03
50	2.82	2.73	2.83	2.74	7.77	8.44
75	2.85	2.76	2.86	2.76	7.07	7.73
100	2.86	2.77	2.87	2.78	6.77	7.44
125	2.87	2.78	2.88	2.78	6.62	7.29
150	2.88	2.79	2.88	2.79	6.54	7.21
200	2.88	2.80	2.89	2.80	6.47	7.14
300	2.90	2.81	2.89	2.80	6.46	7.13
500	2.91	2.82	2.90	2.81	6.55	7.21

10% level of significance (90% fractile for F)

	π_1		π_2		F	
n	lower	upper	lower	upper	lower	upper
25	2.38	2.32	2.39	2.32	8.27	8.71
30	2.42	2.36	2.43	2.36	7.63	8.06
40	2.47	2.41	2.48	2.41	6.88	7.32
50	2.50	2.44	2.51	2.43	6.47	6.90
75	2.53	2.47	2.54	2.47	5.98	6.41
100	2.55	2.49	2.56	2.49	5.77	6.20
125	2.56	2.50	2.57	2.50	5.66	6.10
150	2.57	2.51	2.58	2.50	5.60	6.04
200	2.57	2.51	2.58	2.51	5.55	5.98
300	2.58	2.52	2.59	2.52	5.53	5.96
500	2.59	2.53	2.60	2.52	5.57	6.01

References

Adams, F.G. and L.R. Klein (1991), 'Performance of quarterly econometric models of the United States: a new round of comparisons', in L.R. Klein (ed.), *Comparative Performance of U.S. Econometric Models*, Oxford University Press, Oxford.

Ahumada, H.A. (1985), 'An encompassing test of two models of the balance of trade for Argentina', *Oxford Bulletin of Economics and Statistics* **47**, pp. 51-70.

Aldrich, J. (1989), 'Autonomy', *Oxford Economic Papers* **41**, pp. 15-34, reprinted in N. de Marchi and C. Gilbert (eds) (1989), *History and Methodology of Econometrics*, Oxford University Press, Oxford.

Allen, R.G.D. (1966), *Mathematical Economics*, 2nd edition, Macmillan, London.

Alogoskoufis, G. and R. Smith (1995), 'On error correction models: specification, estimation, interpretation', in: L. Oxley, D.A.R. George, C.J. Roberts and S. Sayer (eds), *Surveys in Econometrics*, Basil Blackwell, Oxford.

Amemiya, T. (1985), *Advanced Econometrics*, Basil Blackwell, Oxford.

Baba, Y., D.F. Hendry and R.M. Starr (1992), 'The demand for M1 in the U.S.A., 1960-1988', *Review of Economic Studies* **59**, pp. 25-61.

Bancroft, T.A. (1944), 'On biases in estimation due to the use of preliminary tests of significance', *Annals of Mathematical Statistics* **15**, pp. 190-204.

Banerjee, A., J. Dolado, J.W. Galbraight and D.F. Hendry (1993), *Co-integration, Error Correction and the Econometric Analysis of Non-stationary data*, Oxford University Press., Oxford.

Banerjee, A., J.J. Dolado, D.F. Hendry and G.W. Smith (1986), 'Exploring equilibrium relationships in econometrics through static models: some Monte Carlo evidence', *Oxford Bulletin of Economics and Statistics* **48**, pp. 253-277.

Bernanke, B.S. (1986), 'Alternative explanations for the money-income correlation', in Brunner, K. and A. Meltzer (eds) , *Carnegie-Rochester Conference Series on Public Policy*, Volume 25, North-Holland, Amsterdam.

Berndt, E.R. and N.E. Savin (1977), 'Conflict among criteria for testing hypotheses in the multivariate regression model', *Econometrica* **45**, pp. 1263-1278.

Blanchard, O.J. and M.W. Watson (1986), 'Are business cycles all alike?', in R.J. Gordon (ed.), *The American Business Cycle: Continuity and Change*, University of Chicago Press, Chicago.

Blanchard, O.J. and D. Quah (1989), 'The dynamic effects of aggregate demand and supply disturbances', *American Economic Review* **79**, pp. 655-673.

Blangiewicz, M. and W.W. Charemza (1990), 'Cointegration in small samples: empirical percentiles, drifting moments and customized testing', *Oxford Bulletin of Economics and Statistics* **52**, pp. 303-315.

Bodkin, R.G., L.R. Klein and K. Marwah (eds) (1991), *A History of Macroeconometric Model Building*, Edward Elgar, Aldershot.

Bollerslev, T. and S. Hylleberg (1985), 'A note on the relation between consumers' expenditure and income in the UK', *Oxford Bulletin of Economics and Statistics* **47**, pp. 153-170.

Branson, W.H. and A.K. Klevorick (1969), 'Money illusion and the aggregate consumption function', *American Economic Review* **59**, pp. 832-849.

Brown, R.L. , J. Durbin and J.M. Evans (1975), 'Techniques for testing the constancy of regression relationships over time', *Journal of the Royal Statistical Society, Series B* **37** , pp. 149-163.

Buse, A. (1982), 'The likelihood ratio, Wald, and Lagrange multiplier tests: an expository note', *The American Statistician* **36**, pp. 153-157.

Campbell, J.Y. and N.S. Mankiw (1990), 'Permanent income, current income and consumption', *Journal of Business and Economic Statistics* **8**, pp. 269-279.

Campbell, J.Y. and N.S. Mankiw (1991), 'The response of consumption to income: a cross-country investigation', *European Economic Review* **35**, pp. 723-767.

Campbell, J.Y. and P. Perron (1991), 'Pitfalls and opportunities: what macroeconomists should know about unit roots', *NBER Macroeconomics Annual*, Cambridge, Mass., MIT Press.

Caudill, S.B. (1988), 'The necessity of mining data', *Atlantic Economic Review* **26**, pp. 11-18.

Charemza, W.W. (1988), 'A note on definitions of invariance and exogeneity', Discussion Paper No. 96, Department of Economics, University of Leicester.

Charemza, W.W. (1989), 'Disequilibrium modelling of consumption in the centrally planned economy', in C.M. Davis and W.W. Charemza (eds),

Models of Disequilibrium and Shortage in Centrally Planned Economies, Chapman and Hall, London.

Charemza, W.W. (1990a), 'Large econometric models of an East European economy: a critique of the methodology', *Economic Modelling* **8**, pp. 45-61.

Charemza, W.W. (1990b), 'Parallel markets, excess demand and virtual prices', *European Economic Review* **34**, pp. 331-339.

Charemza, W.W. (1991), 'Alternative paths to macroeconomic stability in Czechoslovakia', *The European Economy*, Special edition No 2, pp. 41-56.

Charemza, W.W. and S. Ghatak (1990), 'Demand for money in a dual-currency, quantity-constrained economy: Hungary and Poland, 1956-1985', *The Economic Journal* **100**, pp. 1159-1172.

Charemza, W.W. and J. Király (1990), 'Plans and exogeneity: the genetic-teleological dispute revisited', *Oxford Economic Papers* **42**, pp. 562-573.

Charemza W.W. and J. Király (1991), 'A simple test for non-random parameter variation', Department of Economics, University of Leicester (mimeo).

Chatfield, C. (1995), 'Model uncertainty, data mining and statistical inference', *Journal of the Royal Statistical Society, Series A*, pp. 419-466.

Chong, Y.Y. and D.F. Hendry (1986), 'Econometric evaluation of linear macro-economic models', *Review of Economic Studies* **53**, pp. 671-690.

Christ, C.F. (1966), *Econometric Models and Methods*, J. Wiley & Sons, Inc., New York.

Christ, C.F. (1975), 'Judging the performance of econometric models of the U.S. economy', *International Economic Review* **16**, pp. 54-74.

Christious, L.J., M. Eichenbaum and D. Marshall (1991), 'The permanent income hypothesis revisited', *Econometrica* **59**, pp. 397-423.

Clements, M.P. and D.F. Hendry (1991), 'On the invalidity of mean square error forecast comparisons in economics', Institute of Economics and Statistics and Nuffield College, Oxford University, Oxford (mimeo).

Cooley, T.F. and S.F. LeRoy (1985), 'Atheoretical macroeconomics', *Journal of Monetary Economics* **16**, pp. 283-308.

Cooper, R.L. (1972), 'The predictive performance of quarterly econometric models of the United States', in B.G. Hickman (ed.), *Econometric Models of Cyclical Behavior*, Columbia University Press, New York.

Cox, D.R. (1961), 'Tests of separate families of hypotheses', *Proceedings of the Fourth Berkeley Symposium on Mathematical Statistics and Probability*, Volume 1, University of California Press, Berkeley.

Cryer, J.D. (1986), *Time Series Analysis*, Duxbury Press, Boston.

Cuthbertson, K. (1985), *The Supply and Demand for Money*, Basil Blackwell, Oxford.

Cuthbertson, K., S.G. Hall and M.P. Taylor (1992), *Applied Econometric Techniques*, Philip Allan, New York.

Cuthbertson, K. and M.P. Taylor (1988), 'Alternative scale variables in the U.S. demand function for narrow money; some non-nested tests', *Cyprus Journal of Economics* 1, pp. 102-110.

Darnell, A.C. (1986), 'Some observations on autoregressive distributed lag modelling', Working Paper No. 78, Department of Economics, University of Durham.

Darnell, A.C. (1988), '"General to specific" modelling: a methodological perspective', Working Paper No. 90, Department of Economics, University of Durham.

Darnell, A.C. and J.L. Evans (1990), *The Limits of Econometrics*, Edward Elgar, Aldershot.

David, F.N. and N.L. Johnson (1954), 'Statistical treatment of censored data: part 1, fundamental formulae', *Biometrika* 41, pp. 228-240.

Davidson, J.H., D.H. Hendry, F. Srba and S. Yeo (1978), 'Econometric modelling of the aggregate time-series relationship between consumers' expenditure and income in the United Kingdom', *The Economic Journal* 88, pp. 661-692.

Davidson, R. and J.G. MacKinnon (1981), 'Several tests for model specification in the presence of alternative hypotheses', *Econometrica* 49, pp. 781-793.

Davidson, R. and J.G. MacKinnon (1982), 'Some non-nested hypothesis tests and the relations among them', *Review of Economic Studies* 44, pp. 551-565.

Davidson, R. and J.G. MacKinnon (1985), 'The interpretation of test statistics', *Canadian Journal of Economics* 18, pp. 38-57.

Deadman, D. and S. Ghatak (1981), 'On the stability of the demand for money in India', *Indian Economic Journal* 29, pp. 41-54.

Deadman, D. and S. Ghatak (1989), 'Money, prices and stabilisation policies in some developing countries', *Applied Economics* 21, pp. 853-865.

Deaton, A.S. (1977), 'Involuntary saving through unanticipated inflation', *American Economic Review* **67**, pp. 899-910.

Denton, F.T. (1985), 'Data mining as an industry', *Review of Economics and Statistics* **67**, pp. 124-127.

Desai, M. (1976), *Applied Econometrics*, Philip Allan, Oxford.

Desai, M. (1981), *Testing Monetarism*, Frances Pinter, London.

Dharmapala, D. and M. McAleer (1996), 'Econometric methodology and the philosophy of science', *Journal of Statistical Planning and Inference* **49**, 9-37.

Dhrymes, P.J. (1970a), *Econometrics: Statistical Foundations and Applications*, Harper and Row, New York.

Dhrymes, P.J. (1970b), 'On the game of maximizing $\bar{R}^2$', *Australian Economic Papers* **9**, pp. 177-185.

Dhrymes, P.J. (1978), *Introductory Econometrics*, Springer Verlag, New York.

Dickey, D.A. and W.A. Fuller (1979), 'Distributions of the estimators for autoregressive time series with a unit root', *Journal of the American Statistical Association* **74**, pp. 427-431.

Dickey, D.A. and W.A. Fuller (1981), 'Likelihood ratio statistics for autoregressive time series with a unit root', *Econometrica* **49**, pp. 1057-1072.

Dickey, D.A., D.P. Hasza and W.A. Fuller (1984), 'Testing for unit roots in seasonal time series', *Journal of the American Statistical Association* **79**, pp. 355-367.

Dickey, D.A. and S.S. Pantula (1987), 'Determining the order of differencing in autoregressive processes', *Journal of Business and Statistics* **5**, pp. 455-461.

Doan, T., R.B. Litterman and C.A. Sims (1984), 'Forecasting and conditional projection using realistic prior distributions', *Econometric Reviews* **3**, pp. 1-100.

Dolado, J.J., T. Jenkinson and S. Sosvilla-Rivero (1990), 'Cointegration and unit roots: a survey', *Journal of Economic Surveys* **4**, pp. 249-276.

Doornik, J.A. and D.F. Hendry (1994), *Pc-Give Professional 8.0: An Interactive Econometric Modelling System*, International Thomson Publishing, London.

Duesenberry, J.S., G. Fromm, L.R. Klein and E. Kuh (eds) (1965), *The Brookings Quarterly Econometric Model of the United States*, North-Holland, Amsterdam.

Durbin, J. (1970), 'Testing for serial correlation in least squares regression when some of the regressors are lagged dependent variables', *Econometrica* **38**, pp. 410-421.

Durbin, P.T. (1988), *Dictionary of Concepts in the Philosophy of Science*, Greenwood Press, New York.

Eichenbaum, M. (1985), 'Vector autoregressions for causal inference: comment', in K. Brunner and A.M. Meltzer (eds), *Carnegie-Rochester Conference Series on Public Policy* Volume 22, North-Holland, Amsterdam.

Elliot, G., T.J. Rothenberg and J.H. Stock (1996), 'Efficient tests for an autoregressive unit root', *Econometrica* **64**, pp. 813-836.

Enders, W. (1995), *Applied Econometric Time Series*, J. Wiley, New York.

Engle, R.F. (1984), 'Wald, likelihood ratio and Lagrange multiplier tests in econometrics', in Z. Griliches and M.D. Intriligator (eds), *Handbook of Econometrics*, Volume 2, North-Holland, Amsterdam.

Engle, R.F. and C.W.J. Granger (1987), 'Co-integration and error correction: representation, estimation and testing', *Econometrica* **55**, pp. 251-276.

Engle, R.F. and C.W.J. Granger (eds) (1991), *Long Run Economic Relations: Readings in Cointegration*, Oxford University Press, Oxford.

Engle, R.F., C.W.J. Granger and J.J. Hallman (1989), 'Merging short- and long-run forecasts: an application of seasonal cointegration to monthly electricity sales forecasting', *Journal of Econometrics* **40**, pp. 45-62.

Engle, R.F. and D.F. Hendry (1993), 'Testing superexogeneity and invariance in regression models', *Journal of Econometrics* **56**, pp. 119-139.

Engle, R.F., D.F. Hendry and J.-F. Richard (1983), 'Exogeneity', *Econometrica* **51**, pp. 277-304.

Engle, R.F. and B.S. Yoo (1987), 'Forecasting and testing in cointegrated systems', *Journal of Econometrics* **35**, pp. 143-159.

Epstein, R.J. (1987), *A History of Econometrics*, North Holland, Amsterdam.

Ericsson, N.R. (1983), 'Asymptotic properties of instrumental variables statistics for testing non-nested hypotheses', *Review of Economic Studies* **50**, pp. 251-276.

Ericsson, N.R. (1989), 'Mean square error and forecast encompassing', Discussion Paper, International Finance Division, Board of Governors of the Federal Reserve System.

Ericsson, N.R. and J.S. Irons (eds) (1994), *Testing Exogeneity*, Oxford University Press, Oxford.

Ericsson, N.R. and J.S. Irons (1995), 'The Lucas critique in paractice: theory without measurement', in: K.D. Hoover (ed.)., *Macroeconometrics: developments tensions and prospects*, Kluwer, Boston.

Fair, R.C. (1988), 'VAR models as structural approximations', Working Paper No. 2495, National Bureau of Economic Research, Cambridge, Massachusetts.

Farebrother, R.W. (1980), 'The Durbin-Watson test for serial correlation when there is no intercept in the regression', *Econometrica* **48**, pp. 1553-1563.

Farrell, M.J. (1959), 'The new theories of the consumption function', *The Economic Journal* **69**, pp. 678-696.

Favero, C. (1989), 'The Lucas critique, feedback and feedforward mechanisms and the consumption function: an empirical study', Discussion Paper No. 73, Institute of Economics and Statistics, University of Oxford.

Ferber, R. (1962), 'Research on household behavior', *The American Economic Review* **52**, pp. 19-63.

Fisher, D. and A. Serletis (1989), 'Velocity and the growth of money in the United States, 1970-1985', *Journal of Macroeconomics* **11**, pp. 323-332.

Fisher, G.R. and M. McAleer (1981), 'Alternative procedures and associated tests of significance for non-nested hypotheses', *Journal of Econometrics* **16**, pp. 103-119.

Flavin, M.A. (1981), 'The adjustment of consumption to changing expectations about future income', *Journal of Political Economy* **89**, pp. 974-1009.

Fosu, A.K. and M.S. Huq (1988), 'Price inflation and wage inflation: a cause-effect relationship?', *Economics Letters* **27**, pp. 35-40.

Freund, J.E. and R.E. Walpole (1987), *Mathematical Statistics*, 4th edition, Prentice Hall International, London.

Friedman, M. (1957), *A Theory of the Consumption Function*, Princeton University Press, Princeton.

Frisch, R. (1936), 'Note on the term "econometrics"', *Econometrica* **4**, p. 95.

Fuller, W.A. (1976), *Introduction to Statistical Time Series*, J. Wiley & Sons, Inc., New York.

Gapinski, J.H. (1982), *Macroeconomic Theory: Statics, Dynamics and Policy*, McGraw-Hill, London.

Geweke, J. (1984), 'Inference and causality in economic time series models', in Z. Griliches and M.D. Intriligator (eds), *Handbook of Econometrics* Volume 2, North Holland, Amsterdam.

Geweke, J., R. Meese and W. Dent (1983), 'Comparing alternative tests of causality in temporal systems', *Journal of Econometrics* **21**, pp. 161-194.

Ghatak, S. and W.W. Charemza (1989), 'Financial dualism and virtual interest rate: the case of India', Discussion Paper No. 118, Department of Economics, University of Leicester.

Gilbert, C.L. (1986), 'Professor Hendry's econometric methodology', *Oxford Bulletin of Economics and Statistics* **48**, pp. 283-307, reprinted in C.W.J. Granger (ed.) (1990), *Modelling Economic Series: Readings in Econometric Methodology*, Oxford University Press, Oxford.

Gilbert, C.L. (1989), 'LSE and the British approach to time series econometrics', *Oxford Economic Papers* **41**, pp. 108-128, reprinted in N. de Marchi and C. Gilbert (eds) (1989), *History and Methodology of Econometrics*, Oxford University Press, Oxford.

Godfrey, L.G. (1984), 'On the use of misspecification checks and tests of non-nested hypotheses in empirical econometrics', *Supplement to Economic Journal Conference Papers* **94**, pp. 69-81.

Godfrey, L.G. (1989), *Misspecification Tests in Econometrics - Lagrange Multiplier Principle and Other Approaches*, Cambridge University Press, Cambridge.

Godfrey, L.G. and M.H. Pesaran (1983), 'Tests of non-nested regression models: small sample adjustments and Monte Carlo evidence', *Journal of Econometrics* **21**, pp. 133-154.

Goldberger, A.S. (1964), *Econometric Theory*, J. Wiley & Sons, Inc., New York.

Goldberger, A.S. (1991), *'A Course in Econometrics'*, Harvard University Press, Cambridge, Massachusetts.

Granger, C.W.J. (1969), 'Investigating causal relations by econometric models and cross-spectral methods', *Econometrica* **37**, pp. 24-36.

Granger, C.W.J. (1988), 'Some recent developments in a concept of causality', *Journal of Econometrics* **39**, pp. 199-211.

Granger, C.W.J. (ed.) (1990), *Modelling Economic Series: Readings in Econometric Methodology*, Oxford University Press, Oxford.

Granger, C.W.J. and P. Newbold (1974), 'Spurious regressions in econometrics', *Journal of Econometrics* **35**, pp. 143-159.

Granger, C.W.J. and P. Newbold (1986), *Forecasting Economic Time Series*, 2nd edition, Academic Press, Inc., Orlando, Florida.

Greenberg, E. and C.E. Webster, Jr. (1983), *Advanced Econometrics: a Bridge to the Literature*, J. Wiley & Sons, Inc., New York.

Gregory, A.W. and M.R. Veall (1986), 'Wald tests of common factor restrictions', *Economics Letters* **22**, pp. 203-208.

Guilkey, D.K. and M.K. Salemi (1982), 'Small sample properties of three tests for Granger-causal ordering in a bivariate stochastic system', *Review of Economics and Statistics* **64**, pp. 668-680.

Guilkey, D.K. and P. Schmidt (1989), 'Extended tabulations for Dickey-Fuller tests', *Economics Letters* **31**, pp. 355-357.

Haavelmo, T. (1944), 'The probability approach in econometrics', Supplement to *Econometrica* **12**, pp. 1-118.

Hall, R.E. (1978), 'Stochastic implications of the life cycle - permanent income hypothesis: theory and evidence', *Journal of Political Economy* **86**, pp. 971-987.

Hall, S.G. (1989), 'Maximum likelihood estimation of cointegration vectors: an example of the Johansen procedure', *Oxford Bulletin of Economics and Statistics* **51**, pp. 213-219.

Hall, S.G. and S.S.B. Henry (1988), *Macroeconomic modelling*, North-Holland, Amsterdam.

Hamilton, J.D. (1994), *Time Series Analysis*, Princeton University Press, Princeton.

Hargreaves, C.P. (1994), *Nonstationary Time Series and Cointegration*, Oxford University Press, Oxford.

Harvey, A.C. (1989), *Forecasting, Structural Time Series Models and the Kalman Filter*, Cambridge University Press, Cambridge.

Harvey, A.C. (1990), *The Econometric Analysis of Time Series*, 2nd edition, Philip Allan, Hemel Hempstead.

Hatanaka, M. (1996), *Time-series-based Econometrics: Unit Roots and Cointegration*, Oxford University Press, Oxford.

Hendry, D.F. (1974), 'Stochastic specification in an aggregate demand model of the United Kingdom', *Econometrica* **42**, pp. 559-578.

Hendry, D.F. (1979), 'Predictive failure and econometric modelling in macroeconomics. The transactions demand for money', in P. Ormerod (ed.), *Modelling the Economy*, Heinemann, London.

Hendry, D.F. (1980), 'Econometrics - alchemy or science?', *Economica* **47**, pp. 387-406.

Hendry, D.F. (1983), 'Econometric modelling: the "consumption function" in retrospect', *Scottish Journal of Political Economy* **30**, pp. 193-220.

Hendry, D.F. (1987), 'Econometric methodology: a personal perspective', in T.F. Bewley (ed.), *Advances in Econometrics: Fifth World Congress*, Volume 2, Cambridge University Press, Cambridge.

Hendry, D.F. (1988a), 'Encompassing', *National Institute Economic Review* No. 125, pp. 88-92.

Hendry, D.F. (1988b), 'The encompassing implications of feedback versus feedforward mechanisms in econometrics', *Oxford Economic Papers* **40**, pp. 132-149.

Hendry, D.F. (1989), *PC-GIVE: An Interactive Econometric Modelling System*, Institute of Economics and Statistics, University of Oxford, Oxford.

Hendry, D.F. (1993), *Econometrics: Alchemy or Science?*, Basil Blackwell, Oxford.

Hendry, D.F. (1995), *Dynamic Econometrics*, Oxford University Press, Oxford.

Hendry, D.F. and N.R. Ericsson (1991), 'An econometric analysis of U.K. money demand in "Monetary trends in the United States and the United Kingdom" by Milton Friedman and Anna J.Schwartz', *American Economic Review* **81**, pp. 8-38.

Hendry, D.F. and G.E. Mizon (1978), 'Serial correlation as a convenient simplification, not a nuisance: a comment on a study of the demand for money by the Bank of England', *The Economic Journal* **88**, pp. 549-563.

Hendry, D.F. and G.E. Mizon (1990), 'Evaluating dynamic econometric models by encompassing by the VAR', Nuffield College, Oxford (mimeo).

Hendry, D.F. and M.S. Morgan (1995), *The Foundations of Econometric Analysis*, Cambridge University Press, Cambridge.

Hendry, D.F., J.H. Muellbauer and A. Murphy (1990), 'The econometrics of DHSY', in J.D. Hey and O. Winch (eds), *A Century of Economics: 100*

Years of the Royal Economic Society and the Economic Journal, Basil Blackwell, Oxford.

Hendry, D.F., A.R. Pagan and J.D. Sargan (1984), 'Dynamic specification', in Z. Griliches and M.D. Intriligator (eds), *Handbook of Econometrics*, Volume 2, North Holland, Amsterdam.

Hendry, D.F. and J.-F. Richard (1982), 'On the formulation of empirical models in dynamic econometrics', *Journal of Econometrics* **20**, pp. 3-33.

Hendry, D.F. and J.-F. Richard (1983), 'The econometric analysis of economic time series', *International Statistical Review* **51**, pp. 111-163.

Hendry, D.F. and T. von Ungern-Sternberg (1980), 'Liquidity and inflation effects on consumers' expenditure', in A.S. Deaton (ed.), *Essays in the Theory and Measurement of Consumers' Behaviour*, Cambridge University Press, Cambridge.

Holden, D.R. and P.G. McGregor (1989), 'The deflation of nominal magnitudes in the consumption function: a note', Discussion Paper No. 89/6, Department of Economics, University of Strathclyde, Glasgow.

Holden, D. and R. Perman (1994), 'Unit roots and cointegration for the economist', in B.B. Rao (ed.), *Cointegration for the Applied Economist*, Macmillan Press, Basingstoke.

Holtz-Eakin, D., W. Newey and H.S. Rosen (1988), 'Estimating vector autoregressions with panel data', *Econometrica* **56**, pp. 1371-1395.

Houthakker, H.S. and L.D. Taylor (1966, 1970), *Consumer Demand in the United States*, 1st and 2nd editions, Harvard University Press, Harvard.

Hsiao, C. (1979), 'Causality tests in econometrics', *Journal of Economic Dynamics and Control* **1**, pp. 321-346.

Hsiao, C. (1981), 'Autoregressive modelling and money-income causality detection', *Journal of Monetary Economics* **7**, pp. 85-106.

Hylleberg, S. (1992), *Modelling Seasonality*, Oxford University Press, Oxford.

Hylleberg, S. (1995), 'Tests for seasonal unit roots - general to specific or specific to general?', *Journal of Econometrics* **69**, pp. 5-25.

Hylleberg, S., R.F. Engle, C.W.J. Granger and B.S. Yoo (1990), 'Seasonal integration and cointegration', *Journal of Econometrics* **44**, pp. 215-238.

Hylleberg, S. and G.E. Mizon (1989), 'Cointegration and error correction mechanisms', *The Economic Journal (Supplement)* **99**, pp. 113-125.

Jacobs, R.L., E.E. Leamer and M.P. Ward (1979), 'Difficulties with testing for causation', *Economic Inquiry* 17, pp. 401-413.

Johansen, S. (1988), 'Statistical analysis of cointegration vectors', *Journal of Economic Dynamics and Control* 12, pp. 231-254.

Johansen, S. (1989), *Likelihood Based Inferences on Cointegration. Theory and Applications*, Cento Interuniversitario di Econometria (CIDE), Bologna.

Johansen, S. (1995), *Likelihood Based Inference in Cointegrated Vector Autoregressive Models*, Oxford University Press, Oxford.

Johansen, S. and K. Juselius (1990), 'Maximum likelihood estimation and inference on cointegration - with applications to the demand for money', *Oxford Bulletin of Economics and Statistics* 52, pp. 169-210.

Johnston, J. (1984), *Econometric Methods*, 3rd edition, McGraw-Hill, New York.

Judge, G.G., W.E. Griffiths, R.C. Hill, H. Lütkepohl and T.-C. Lee (1985), *The Theory and Practice of Econometrics*, 2nd edition, J. Wiley & Sons, Inc., New York.

Karni, E. and B.K. Shapiro (1980), 'Tales of horror from ivory towers', *Journal of Political Economy* 88, pp. 210-212.

Kendall, M. and J.K. Ord (1990), *Time Series*, 3rd edition, Edward Arnold, London.

Kennedy, P. (1990), *A Guide to Econometrics*, 2nd edition, Martin Robertson, Oxford.

Keuzenkamp, H.A. and M. McAleer (1995), 'Simplicity, scientific inference and econometric modelling', *The Economic Journal* 105, pp. 1-21.

Keynes, J.M. (1936), *The General Theory of Employment, Interest, and Money*, Macmillan, London.

Kiviet, J.F. (1986), 'On the rigour of some misspecification tests for modelling dynamic relationships', *Review of Economic Studies* 53, pp. 241-261.

Klein, L.R. (1950), *Economic Fluctuations in the United States, 1921-1941*, J. Wiley & Sons, Inc., New York.

Klein, L.R. (1971a), *An Essay on the Theory of Economic Prediction*, Markham Publishing Company, Chicago.

Klein, L.R. (1971b), 'Whither econometrics?', *Journal of the American Statistical Association* 66, pp. 415-421.

Klein, L.R. and A.S. Goldberger (1955), *An Econometric Model of the United States, 1929-1952*, North-Holland, Amsterdam.

Kmenta, J. (1986), *Elements of Econometrics*, 2nd edition, Macmillan, New York.

Koerts, J. and A.P.J. Abrahamse (1969), *On the Theory and Application of the General Linear Model*, Rotterdam University Press, Rotterdam.

Kramer, W., W. Ploberger and R. Alt (1988), 'Testing for structural change in dynamic models', *Econometrica* **56**, pp. 1355-1369.

Kunst, R.M (1989), 'Cointegration in macroeconomic systems: seasonality and explosive roots', Research Memorandum No. 255, Institute for Advanced Studies, Vienna.

Kunst, R.M. (1990), 'Seasonal cointegration in macroeconomic systems: case studies for small and large European countries', Research Memorandum No. 271, Institute for Advanced Studies, Vienna.

Kwiatkowski, D., P.C.B. Phillips, P. Schmidt and Y. Shin (1992), 'Testing the null hypothesis of stationarity against the alternative of a unit root: how sure we are that economic time series have a unit root?', *Journal of Econometrics* **54**, pp. 159-178.

Lafontaine, F. and K.J. White (1986), 'Obtaining any Wald statistic you want', *Economics Letters* **21**, pp. 35-40.

Leamer, E.E. (1978), *Specification Searches*, J. Wiley & Sons, Inc., New York.

Leamer, E.E. (1983a), 'Let's take the con out of econometrics', *American Economic Review* **23**, pp. 31-43, reprinted in C.W.J. Granger (ed.) (1990), *Modelling Economic Series: Readings in Econometric Methodology*, Oxford University Press, Oxford.

Leamer, E.E. (1983b), 'Model Choice and Specification Analysis', in Z. Griliches. and M.D. Intriligator (eds), *Handbook of Econometrics*, Volume 1, North-Holland, Amsterdam.

Leamer, E.E. (1985), 'Vector autoregressions for causal inference?', in K. Brunner and A. Meltzer (eds), *Carnegie-Rochester Conference Series on Public Policy* Volume 22, North-Holland, Amsterdam.

Levačić, R. and A. Rebmann (1982), *Macro-Economics: An Introduction to Keynesian-Neoclassical Controversies*, 2nd edition, Macmillan, London.

Litterman, R.B. (1986), 'Forecasting with Bayesian vector autoregressions: five years of experience', *Journal of Business and Economic Statistics* **4**, pp. 25-38.

Liu, T.C. (1960), 'Underidentification, structural estimation, and forecasting', *Econometrica* **28**, pp. 855-865.

Lovell, M.C. (1983), 'Data mining', *Review of Economics and Statistics* **65**, pp. 1-12.

Lubrano, M. and V. Marimotou (1988), 'Bayesian specification searches', Document de Travail No. 8803, GREQE, Marseille.

Lubrano, M., R.S. Pierse and J.-F. Richard (1986), 'Stability of a U.K. demand equation: a Bayesian approach to testing exogeneity', *Review of Economic Studies* **53**, pp. 603-634.

Lucas, R.E. (1976), 'Economic policy evaluation: a critique', in K. Brunner and A.M. Meltzer (eds), *The Phillips Curve and Labor Markets*, *Carnegie-Rochester Conference Series on Public Policy*, Volume 1, North-Holland, Amsterdam.

Lütkepohl, H. (1991), *Introduction to Multiple Time Series Analysis*, Springer-Verlag, Berlin.

MacKinnon, J.G. (1983), 'Model specification tests against non-nested alternatives', *Econometric Reviews* **2** , pp. 85-110.

MacKinnon, J.G. (1991), 'Critical values for cointegration tests', in R.F. Engle and C.W.J. Granger (eds), *Long-run Economic Relationships*, Oxford University Press, Oxford.

Maddala, G.S. (ed.) (1981), 'Model selection', *Journal of Econometrics*, **16**, (special issue).

Maddala, G.S. (1988), *Introduction to Econometrics*, Macmillan, London.

Malinvaud, E. (1981), 'Econometrics faced with the needs of macroeconomic policy', *Econometrica* **49**, pp. 1363-1375.

Markovitz, H.M. and G.L. Xu (1994), 'Data mining corrections', *Journal of Portfolio Management* **21**, pp. 60-69.

McAleer, M. and M.R. Veall (1995), 'Data mining and the con in econometrics - the US demand for money revisited', *Mathematics and Computers in Simulation* **39**, pp. 329-333.

McAleer, M. and M.H. Pesaran (1986), 'Statistical inference in non-nested econometric models', *Applied Mathematics and Computation* **20**, pp. 271-311.

McCarthy, M.D. (1972), *The Wharton Quarterly Econometric Forecasting Model Mark III*, Wharton School of Finance and Commerce, Philadelphia.

McNees, S.K. (1979), 'The accuracy of macroeconomic models and forecasts of the U.S. economy', in P. Ormerod (ed.), *Economic Modelling*, Heinemann, London.

McNees, S.K. (1986), 'Forecasting accuracy of alternative techniques: a comparison of US macroeconomic forecasts', *Journal of Business and Economic Statistics* 4, pp. 5-15.

Miller, S.M. (1988), 'Are savings and investment co-integrated?', *Economics Letters* 27, pp. 31-34.

Mills, T.C. (1990), *Time series techniques for economists*, Cambridge University Press, Cambridge.

Mizon, G.E. (1984), 'The encompassing approach in econometrics', in D.F. Hendry and K.F. Wallis (eds), *Econometrics and Quantitative Economics*, Basil Blackwell, Oxford.

Mizon, G.E. and J.-F. Richard (1986), 'The encompassing principle and its application to testing non-nested hypothesis', *Econometrica* 54, pp. 657-678.

Monfort, A. and R. Rabemanjara (1990), 'From a VAR model to a structural model, with an application to the wage-price spiral', *Journal of Applied Econometrics* 5, pp. 203-227.

Morgan, M.S. (1990), *The History of Econometric Ideas*, Cambridge University Press, Cambridge.

Murray, M.P. (1994), 'A drunk and her dog: an illustration of cointegration and error correction', *American Statistician* 48, pp. 37-9.

Muscatelli, V.A. (1989), 'A comparison of the "rational expectations" and "general-to-specific" approaches to modelling the demand for M1', *Oxford Bulletin of Economics and Statistics* 51, pp. 353-375.

Muscatelli, V.A. and S. Hurn (1995), 'Econometric modelling using cointegrated time series', in: L. Oxley, D.A.R. George, C.J. Roberts and S. Sayer (eds), *Surveys in Econometrics*, Basil Blackwell, Oxford.

Muscatelli, V. and L. Papi (1988), 'Cointegration and "general to specific": an application to the demand for money in Italy', Discussion Paper No. 8804, Department of Political Economy, University of Glasgow.

Naylor, T.H., T.G. Seales and D.W. Wichern (1972), 'Box-Jenkins methods: an alternative to econometric models', *International Statistical Review* 40, pp. 123-137.

Nelson, C.R. and N. Kang (1981), 'Spurious periodicity in inappropriately detrended time series', *Econometrica* 49, pp. 741-751.

Nelson, C.R. and C.I. Plosser (1982), 'Trends and random walks in macroeconomic time series: some evidence and implications', *Journal of Monetary Economics* 10, pp. 139-162.

Nerlove, M. (1965), 'A tabular survey of macro-econometric models', *International Economic Review* 7, pp. 127-175.

Newbold, P. and N. Davies (1978), 'Error miss-specification and spurious regressions', *International Economic Review* 19, pp. 513-519.

Osborn, D.R., A.P.L. Chui, J.P. Smith and C.R. Birchenhall (1988), 'Seasonality and the order of integration for consumption', *Oxford Bulletin of Economics and Statistics* 50, pp. 361-377.

Osterwald-Lenum, M. (1992), 'A note with quantiles of the asymptotic distribution of the maximum likelihood cointegration rank test statistics', *Oxford Bulletin of Economics and Statistics* 54, pp. 461-472.

Pagan, A.R. (1987), 'Three econometric methodologies: a critical appraisal', *Journal of Economic Surveys* 1, pp. 3-24, reprinted in C.W.J. Granger (ed.) (1990), *Modelling Economic Series: Readings in Econometric Methodology*, Oxford University Press, Oxford.

Park, J.Y. and P.C.B. Phillips (1988), 'Statistical inference in regressions with integrated processes: Part I', *Econometric Theory* 4, pp. 468-498.

Park, J.Y. and P.C.B. Phillips (1989), 'Statistical inference in regressions with integrated processes: Part II', *Econometric Theory* 5, pp. 95-131.

Patterson, K.D. (1986), 'The stability of some annual consumption functions', *Oxford Economic Papers*, 38, pp. 1-30.

Perron, P. (1989), 'The great crash, the oil price shock and the unit root hypothesis', *Econometrica* 57, pp. 1361-1401.

Perron, P. (1990), 'Testing for a unit root in a time series with a changing mean', *Journal of Business and Economic Statistics* 8, pp. 153-162.

Perron, P. and T.J. Vogelsang (1992), 'Testing for a unit root in a time series with a changing mean: corrections and extensions', *Journal of Business and Economic Statistics* 10, pp. 467-470.

Pesaran, M.H. (1974), 'On the general problem of model selection', *Review of Economic Studies* 41, pp. 153-171

Pesaran, M.H. and A.S. Deaton (1978), 'Testing non-nested nonlinear regression models', *Econometrica* 46, pp. 677-694.

Pesaran, M.H. and R. Smith (1990), 'A unified approach to estimation and orthogonality tests in linear single equation econometric models', *Journal of Econometrics* 44, pp. 41-66.

Pesaran, M.H., R.P. Smith and J.S. Yeo (1985), 'Testing for structural stability and predictive failure: a review', *Manchester School* **53**, pp. 280-295.

Phillips, P.C.B. (1986), 'Understanding spurious regressions in econometrics', *Journal of Econometrics* **33**, pp. 311-340.

Phillips, P.C.B. (1988a), 'Reflections on econometric methodology', *The Economic Record*, **64**, pp. 344-359.

Phillips, P.C.B. (1988b), 'Regression theory for near-integrated time series', *Econometrica* **56**, pp. 1021-1043.

Phillips, P.C.B. and M. Loretan, (1991) 'Estimating long-run economic equilibria', *Review of Economic Studies* **5**, pp. 407-436.

Phillips, P.C.B. and S. Ouliaris (1990), 'Asymptotic properties of residual based tests for cointegration', *Econometrica* **58**, pp. 165-193.

Pindyck, R.S. and D.L. Rubinfeld (1991), *Econometric Models and Economic Forecasts*, 3rd edition, McGraw-Hill, New York.

Pokorny, M. (1987), *An Introduction to Econometrics*, Basil Blackwell, Oxford.

Portes, R. and D. Winter (1978), 'The demand for money and for consumption goods in centrally planned economies', *Review of Economics and Statistics* **60**, pp. 8-18.

Portes, R. and D. Winter (1980), 'Disequilibrium estimates for consumption goods markets in centrally planned economies', *Review of Economic Studies* **47**, pp. 137159.

Pratt, J.W. and R. Schlaifer (1984) 'On the nature and discovery of structure', *Journal of the American Statistical Association* **79**, pp. 9-21.

Quah, D. and S.P. Vahey (1996), 'Measuring core inflation', *Economic Journal* **105**, pp. 1130-1144.

Quandt, R.E. (1974), 'A comparison of methods for testing non-nested hypotheses', *Review of Economics and Statistics* **56**, pp. 92-99.

Rao, B.B. (ed.) (1994), *Cointegration for the Applied Economist*, Macmillan Press Ltd., Basingstoke.

Runckle, D.E. (1987), 'Vector autoregressions and reality', *Journal of Business and Economic Statistics* **5**, pp. 437-442 (also comments pp. 443-454).

Said, S.E. and D.A. Dickey (1984), 'Testing for unit roots in autoregressive moving average models of unknown order', *Biometrika* **71**, pp. 599-607.

Sargan, J.D. and A. Bhargava (1983), 'Testing residuals from least squares regression for being generated by the Gaussian random walk', *Econometrica* **51**, pp. 153-174.

Sargent, T.J. (1976), 'A classical macroeconomic model for the United States', *Journal of Political Economy* **84**, pp. 207-238.

Shannon, R. and M.S. Wallace (1985-86), 'Wages and inflation: an investigation into causality', *Journal of Post Keynesian Economics* **8**, pp. 182-191.

Sims, C.A. (1972), 'Money income and causality', *American Economic Review* **62**, pp. 540-552.

Sims, C.A. (1980), 'Macroeconomics and reality', *Econometrica* **48**, pp. 1-48.

Sims, C.A. (1982), 'Policy analysis with econometric models', *Brookings Papers on Economic Activity* **1**, pp. 107-152.

Singh, B. and B.S. Sahni (1984), 'Causality between public expenditure and national income', *Review of Economics and Statistics* **66**, pp. 630-644.

Smith, R.J. and A.M.R. Taylor (1995), 'Additional critical values and asymptotic representations for seasonal unit root tests', DAE Working Paper (amalgamated series) No. 9529, University of Cambridge.

Spanos, A. (1986), *Statistical Foundations of Econometric Modelling*, Cambridge University Press, Cambridge.

Spanos, A. (1988), 'Towards a unifying methodological framework for econometric modelling', *Economic Notes* No.1, pp. 1-28, reprinted in C.W.J. Granger (ed.) (1990), *Modelling Economic Series*, Oxford University Press, Oxford.

Spanos, A. (1989), 'Early empirical findings on the consumption function, stylized facts or fiction: a retrospective view', *Oxford Economic Papers* **41**, pp. 150-169, reprinted in N. de Marchi and C. Gilbert (eds) (1989), *History and Methodology of Econometrics*, Oxford University Press, Oxford.

Spohn, W. (1984), 'Probabilistic causality: from Hume via Suppes to Granger', in M.C. Galavotti and G. Gambetta (eds), *Causalita e modelli probabilistica*, Clueb Editrica, Bologna.

Steel, M.F.J. (1987), 'Testing for exogeneity: an application to consumption behaviour', *European Economic Review* **31**, pp. 1443-1463.

Steel, M.F.J. (1989), 'Weak exogeneity in misspecified sequential models', Discussion Paper No. 8942, CentER, Tilburg University.

Steel, M.F.J. and J.-F. Richard (1989), 'Bayesian multivariate exogeneity analysis; an application to a UK money demand equation', Discussion Paper No. 8929, CentER, Tilburg University.

Stewart, M.B. and K.F. Wallis (1981), *Introductory Econometrics*, 2nd edition, Basil Blackwell, Oxford.

Stock, J.H. and M.W. Watson (1988), 'Testing for common trends', *Journal of the American Statistical Association* **83**, pp. 1097-1107.

Stock, J.H. and M.W. Watson (1989), 'Interpreting the evidence on money-income causality', *Journal of Econometrics* **40**, pp. 161-181.

Swamy, S. (1968), 'A dynamic personal savings function and its long-run implications', *Review of Economics and Statistics* **50**, pp. 111-116.

Taylor, L.D. and H.S. Houthakker (1990), 'Co-integration and habit formation: a reformulation of the dynamics of the Houthakker-Taylor models', Paper presented at the 6th World Congress of the Econometric Society, Barcelona.

Taylor, M.P. (1988), 'An empirical examination of long-run purchasing power parity using cointegration techniques', *Applied Economics* **20**, pp. 1369-1381.

Theil, H. (1971), *Principles of Econometrics*, North-Holland, Amsterdam.

Thomas, J.J. (1989), 'The early econometric history of the consumption function', *Oxford Economic Papers* **41**, pp. 131-149, reprinted in N. de Marchi and C. Gilbert (eds), *History and Methodology of Econometrics*, Oxford University Press, Oxford.

Tinbergen, J. (1951), *Econometrics*, George Allen & Unwin Ltd., London.

Tinbergen, J. (1959), *Selected Papers*, edited by L.H. Klaassen, L.M. Koyck and J.H. Witteveen, North-Holland, Amsterdam.

Tintner, G. (1952), *Econometrics*, J. Wiley & Sons, Inc., New York.

Todd, R.M. (1990), 'Improving economic forecasting with Bayesian vector autoregression', in C.W.J. Granger (ed.), *Modelling Economic Series: Readings in Econometric Methodology*, Oxford University Press, Oxford.

Urbain, J.-P. (1991), 'On weak exogeneity in error correction models', Research Paper No. 9103, C.R.E.D.E.L., University of Liège.

Vandaele, W. (1983), *Applied Time Series and Box-Jenkins Models*, Academic Press, Orlando.

Wallace, T.D. (1977), 'Pretest estimation in regression: a survey', *American Journal of Agriculture Economics* **95**, pp. 431-443.

Wallace, T.D. and V.G. Ashar (1972), 'Sequential methods in model construction', *Review of Economics and Statistics* **54**, pp. 172-178.

Wallis, K.F. (1974), 'Seasonal adjustment and relations between variables', *Journal of the American Statistical Association* **69**, pp. 18-31.

Wallis, K.F. (1989), 'Macroeconomic forecasting: a survey', *Economic Journal* **99**, pp. 28-61.

West, K.D. (1988), 'Asymptotic normality, when regressors have a unit root', *Econometrica* **56**, pp. 1397-1417.

White, H. (1980), 'A heteroscedasticity-consistent covariance matrix estimator and a direct test for heteroscedasticity', *Econometrica* **48**, pp. 817-838.

Wickens, M.R. and T.S. Breusch (1988), 'Dynamic specification, the long-run and the estimation of transformed regression models', *The Economic Journal* **98** (Supplement), pp. 189-205.

Williams, D., C.A.E. Goodhart and D.H Gowland (1976), 'Money, income and causality: the UK experience', *American Economic Review* **66**, pp. 417- 23.

Wold, H. (1954), 'Causality and econometrics', *Econometrica* **22**, pp. 162-177.

Worswick, G.D.N. (1972), 'Is progress in economic science possible?', *The Economic Journal* **82**, pp. 73-86.

Wu, D.-M. (1983), 'Tests of causality, predeterminedness and exogeneity', *International Economic Review* **24**, pp. 547-558.

Wynn, R.F. and K. Holden. (1974), *An Introduction to Applied Econometric Analysis*, Macmillan, London.

Zellner, A. (1979), 'Causality and econometrics', in K. Brunner and A. Meltzer (eds), *Carnegie-Rochester Conference Series on Public Policy*, Volume 10, North-Holland, Amsterdam.

Author Index

Subject Index